TERRORISM AND POLITICAL VIOLENCE

EDITED BY

CAROLINE KENNEDY-PIPE, GORDON CLUBB & SIMON MABON

FOREWORD BY ALEX P. SCHMID

TERRORISM AND POLITICAL VIOLENCE

SAGE

Los Angeles | London | New Delhi
Singapore | Washington DC

Los Angeles | London | New Delhi
Singapore | Washington DC

SAGE Publications Ltd
1 Oliver's Yard
55 City Road
London EC1Y 1SP

SAGE Publications Inc.
2455 Teller Road
Thousand Oaks, California 91320

SAGE Publications India Pvt Ltd
B 1/I 1 Mohan Cooperative Industrial Area
Mathura Road
New Delhi 110 044

SAGE Publications Asia-Pacific Pte Ltd
3 Church Street
#10-04 Samsung Hub
Singapore 049483

Editor: Natalie Aguilera
Assistant editor: James Piper
Production editor: Shikha Jain
Copyeditor: Sunrise Setting Limited
Indexer: Avril Ehrlich
Marketing manager: Sally Ransom
Cover design: Francis Kenney
Typeset by: C&M Digitals (P) Ltd, Chennai, India
Printed and bound by CPI Group (UK) Ltd,
Croydon, CR0 4YY [for Antony Rowe]

Library of Congress Control Number: 2014945947

British Library Cataloguing in Publication data

A catalogue record for this book is available from
the British Library

ISBN 978-1-4462-7280-0
ISBN 978-1-4462-7281-7 (pbk)

MIX
Paper from
responsible sources
FSC® C013604

At SAGE we take sustainability seriously. Most of our products are printed in the UK using FSC papers and boards.
When we print overseas we ensure sustainable papers are used as measured by the Egmont grading system.
We undertake an annual audit to monitor our sustainability.

CONTENTS

NOTES ON EDITORS AND CONTRIBUTORS

THE EDITORS

Gordon Clubb is a lecturer in international security at the University of Leeds and is Director of the Terrorism and Political Violence Association. Recently, he has written on the disengagement and de-radicalization of Fatah and the Irish Republican Army.

Caroline Kennedy-Pipe is a professor of war studies at the University of Hull. She is the university lead on maritime and security issues. She has published extensively on these issues and has been quoted in *The Guardian* as being 'one of the UK's leading experts in war'.

Simon Mabon is a lecturer in international relations at the University of Lancaster. He is the author of *Saudi Arabia and Iran: Soft Power Rivalry in the Middle East* (I.B. Tauris, 2013), *Hizballah: From Islamic Resistance to Government* (Praeger, 2014, with Gordon Clubb and James Worrall) and *British Foreign Policy* (Routledge, 2015, with Mark Garnett). He is Director of the Richardson Institute and a research associate with the Foreign Policy Centre.

THE CONTRIBUTORS

Gilberto Algar-Faria is a politics PhD candidate within the School of Sociology, Politics and International Studies at the University of Bristol and a research associate at the Foreign Policy Centre.

Pola Zafra-Davis is an EH Carr and international postgraduate research scholar in conflict and security/international relations theory at Aberystwyth University. She holds a BA (Hons) in european social and political studies at University College London and an MSc in international relations (research) from the London School of Economics and Political Science.

Lee Jarvis is a senior lecturer in international security at the University of East Anglia. Recent books include *Times of Terror: Discourse, Temporality and the War on Terror* (Palgrave, 2009), *Terrorism: A Critical Introduction* (Palgrave, 2011, with Richard Jackson, Jeroen Gunning and Marie Breen Smyth), *Cyberterrorism:*

Understanding, Assessment and Response (Springer, 2014, with Stuart Macdonald and Tom Chen) and *Counter-Radicalisation: Critical Perspectives* (Routledge, 2015, with Christopher Baker-Beall and Charlotte Heath-Kelly).

Stuart Macdonald is an associate professor in law at Swansea University. He has written a number of articles on counterterrorism legislation and policy, which have been published in leading journals in the UK, USA and Australia, and is co-editor (with Lee Jarvis and Tom Chen) of *Cyberterrorism: Understanding, Assessment and Response* (Springer, 2014).

Marie Breen-Smyth is a professor of international politics at the University of Surrey. She has written and researched political violence, including its impact on civilian populations, and is one of the initiators of a critical approach to terrorism studies. Her interests in international intervention include processes of militarization and demilitarization, transnational justice, armed conflict and children.

Samantha Cooke is a PhD research candidate and teaching assistant in the School of Politics, University of Surrey. Her research currently focuses on women's marital rights in the Middle East.

James Lutz is a professor of political science at Indiana University – Purdue University Fort Wayne. He has published a number of books, articles, and chapters on various aspects of terrorism, often in collaboration with Brenda J Lutz.

Michael Stohl is a professor of communication and Director of the Orfalea Center for Global and International Studies at the University of California, Santa Barbara. He is the author or co-author of more than a hundred scholarly journal articles and book chapters, and the author, editor or co-editor of 15 books which focus on political violence, terrorism and human rights.

Nina Musgrave is a PhD candidate in the Department of War Studies at King's College, London. Her research focuses on Hamas and political violence in the Middle East.

Nicole Ives-Allison is a teaching fellow (temporary) with the Handa Centre for Study of Terrorism and Political Violence (CSTPV) at the University of St Andrews. Her research interests include political violence in Northern Ireland, the social organisation of violent groups and the politics of American street-gang violence.

Cristina Archetti is an associate professor in politics and media at the University of Salford, UK. She is the author of *Understanding Terrorism in the Age of Global Media: A Communication Approach* (2012, Palgrave). Her research interests cover the intersection between security, politics and strategic communication. She serves on the editorial board of the journal *Critical Studies on Terrorism* and has been teaching the master's-level course Terrorism and the Media since 2008.

William Braniff is the Executive Director of the National Consortium for the Study of Terrorism and Responses to Terrorism (START). He previously served as Director of Practitioner Education for West Point's Combating Terrorism Center, in the nuclear counterterrorism field with the Department of Energy, and as an officer in the United States Army.

Assaf Moghadam is an associate professor and Director of the MA program in Government at the Lauder School of Government at the Interdisciplinary Center Herzliya (IDC). He is also Director for Academic Affairs at the International Institute for Counter-Terrorism at IDC, and a Fellow at the Combating Terrorism Center at West Point.

Dov Waxman is a professor of political science, international affairs and Israel studies at Northeastern University and Co-director of its Middle East Center. His research focuses on Israeli foreign and security policy and the Israeli–Palestinian conflict. He is the author of *The Pursuit of Peace and the Crisis of Israeli Identity: Defending/ Defining the Nation* (Palgrave Macmillan, 2006) and *Israel's Palestinians: The Conflict Within* (Cambridge University Press, 2011, with Ilan Peleg).

Sarah Marsden is a lecturer at the Handa Centre for the Study of Terrorism and Political Violence (CSTPV). Her research interests revolve around conceptualizing and explaining the development, evolution and, in particular, the decline of terrorism and collective violence. Her work explores how political and cultural opportunity structures interact with the historical and organizational features of oppositional groups to produce particular outcomes.

Sophie A. Whiting is a lecturer in politics. Her research interests lie in the areas of Northern Irish politics, media discourse and conflict resolution, with particular focus on contemporary security and government responses to `spoiler' violence during peace processes and the role of gender in post-conflict reconstruction. Most recently Sophie is author of `Spoiling the Peace? The threat of dissident republicans to peace in Northern Ireland', to be published by Manchester University Press in early 2015.

Paul Gill is a lecturer in security and crime science at University College, London. His research examines terrorism: its causes, patterns and the actors that perpetrate terrorist attacks. His currently published research demonstrates the heterogeneous profiles of terrorists, their developmental pathways into terrorism, the behaviours that precede and underpin a terrorist attack, how terrorists fit into a wider structure and how particular group influences act to condition individuals to engage in violence.

Noemie Bouhana is a lecturer in security and crime science at the Jill Dando Institute, University College London. She is interested in the systemic and ecological processes involved in the emergence of radicalizing settings, and the role that these settings, in turn, play in individuals developing a terrorist propensity.

John Morrison is a senior lecturer in criminology and criminal justice at the University of East London. His research interests are Northern Irish terrorism, dissident Irish republican terrorism, political-organizational theories of terrorism, splits in terrorist organizations, the psychology of terrorism, international terrorism and counterterrorism strategies.

Michael Boyle is an associate professor of political science at La Salle University in Philadelphia. His most recent book is *Violence after War: Explaining Instability in Post-Conflict States* (Johns Hopkins University Press, 2014).

Terry Hathaway completed his PhD on corporate power and US oil dependence in September 2013 at the University of Leeds and has since held temporary posts at the Universities of Leeds, Salford and, currently, Sheffield.

Adam Dolnik is PhD and professor of terrorism studies at the University of Wollongong in Australia, and a former professor of counterterrorism at the George C. Marshall Center for European Security Studies in Germany. In the past, Dolnik has also served as Chief Trainer at the International Centre for Political Violence and Terrorism Research (ICPVTR) in Singapore, and as a researcher at the Weapons of Mass Destruction Terrorism Research Project at the Monterey Institute of International Studies in California and at the United Nations Terrorism Prevention Branch in Vienna. Dolnik has delivered lectures and training courses on terrorism and hostage negotiation for various governmental and nongovernmental organizations and agencies in over 50 countries, and regularly conducts field research in challenging environments (i.e. North Caucasus, Afghanistan, Pakistan, Uganda, Sudan, Southern Philippines, DRC, Colombia, etc.) Dolnik's books include *Understanding Terrorist Innovation: Technologies, Tactics, and Global Trends* (Routledge, 2007) *Negotiating Hostage Crises with the New Terrorists* (Praeger Security International, 2007), *Terrorism Field Research: A Guide* (Routledge, 2013), *Negotiating the Siege of Lal Masjid* (Oxford University Press, forthcoming 2015), as well as over 50 reports and articles on terrorism related issues. He is also a trained hostage negotiator with practical experience in overseas kidnap management.

FOREWORD
ALEX P. SCHMID

At the *Horizon Scanning 21st Century Insecurities* conference in London, 2013, I spoke of the need to broaden our approach to terrorism and look at it in a wider context. For example, the micro-level focus on individuals in order to explain radicalization has deflected attention from factors on the meso-level such as the role of radicalized constituencies and, on the macro-level, the role of government. If a reporter described a tennis match only in terms of what happens on one side of the court we would rightfully be dissatisfied. Yet that has too often been the situation when it comes to the study of terrorism: one side is covered and not the other, nor the interaction between terrorists and state actors. In my keynote address I also pleaded for the firmer incorporation of terrorism studies into the study of armed conflicts as well as social-movement studies because terrorism thrives on conflict and is often the work of fringe groups of larger social movements. I also emphasized that terrorism is not the same as political violence but a sub-category of the latter and in some contexts the peacetime equivalent of war crimes.

Looking at the contents of this volume, I am pleased to see that the authors of *Terrorism and Political Violence* have taken up some of these suggestions and put terrorism in a broader context. There has been some criticism about the quality of terrorism studies but, having surveyed the literature for three decades, I have seen considerable improvements in the years since 9/11. Yet more needs to be done: cooperation between different academic disciplines needs to be improved, and collaboration with the intelligence community needs to be sought, since working with open-source data is often not enough and fieldwork is sometimes too dangerous.

As academic research progresses in various directions, it is of great importance that students of terrorism and political violence become aware of emerging issues and debates. University students – whether they are studying on an undergraduate or postgraduate course – will appreciate that this book seeks to involve them in the conceptual and methodological challenges with which researchers are confronted. The chapter authors critically but constructively analyse key issues, as well as governmental efforts to combat terrorism. By building on the strengths of the UK's network of terrorism researchers – one of ten national networks under the flag of the Terrorism Research Initiative (TRI) – *Terrorism and Political Violence* provides the reader with a solid basis for both coursework and research.

ACKNOWLEDGEMENTS

During the course of the 18 months that it has taken to write this book we have interacted with a large number of people operating in and around the study of terrorism and political violence. A great deal of this took place at the Terrorism and Political Violence Association's *Horizon Scanning 21st Century Insecurities* conference in London in the summer of 2013. The conference was attended by numerous individuals from different professions and backgrounds, all with a shared interest in gaining a better understanding of terrorism and political violence in the twenty-first century. The insights gained from the conference were invaluable when compiling this volume. The conference stressed the need to put terrorism and political violence within a broader context and to draw upon expertise from a wide range of subjects. We have also drawn contributions from the UK, the US, Germany and Israel. This interaction of backgrounds and nationalities provides the reader with the depth of analysis necessary to understand contemporary terrorism and political violence. It is stronger for being able to do so.

This book would not have been possible without the hard work of a great many people. Collectively, we would like to thank three groups of people. Firstly, and most importantly, we wish to thank all of the authors for contributing to the volume. We thank you for your work, your patience and your understanding as we negotiated the tricky terrain of editing. Secondly, we would like to thank our team of researchers in TAPVA, who have been an invaluable source of help, energy and enthusiasm. Our thanks go to Bansri Buddhdev, Ruth Anne Coxon, Hannah Croft, Beth Gooding, Stuart Halliwell, Adam Leake, Hannah Martin, Jonathan Martin, Rebecca Shapiro, Alice Shipsey and Irina Sukhoparova. Lastly, we would like to thank our publishers, SAGE, in particular Natalie Aguilera and James Piper, for their support and encouragement throughout the process.

INTRODUCTION

Certain events are said to possess epoch-making characteristics, defining eras and setting political and cultural agendas. Perhaps the most recent of these events occurred on 11 September 2001 with the attacks on the World Trade Center and Pentagon. The response to these attacks included wars in Afghanistan and Iraq, human-rights abuses and rendition, along with thousands of deaths across the world.

The impact of the 9/11 attacks has pervaded all facets of contemporary life. Election results have been affected by terrorism (in the USA, Spain and Australia); three major wars have been started in response to terrorist attacks (Afghanistan in 2001, Iraq in 2003 and Lebanon in 2006); businesses have responded to changing threats; and popular culture has reflected the fight against terrorism (*Homeland*, *24* and *Spooks*). When we travel on airplanes the rigorous security checks are a consequence of the 9/11 attacks and those attempts that followed.[1] The rise of CCTV coverage in major cities is also, in part, a consequence of the visibility and tactics of terrorist attacks.

Yet despite the severity of the response to 9/11, the threat posed by terrorism is not new. Instead, acts of terrorism have occurred since the end of the nineteenth century, when the first war on terror was launched. In addition, the number of terror attacks in recent years has been small when compared to the discussion surrounding it, or indeed the number of deaths on the UK's roads. Furthermore, the number of individuals involved in terrorist activity remains an incredibly small percentage of the population, although the number of people aware of the actions of these individuals appears to be much larger.

Despite the prominence of terrorism in the zeitgeist, policymakers, security officials and those engaged in the study of terrorism and political violence face serious challenges when understanding, analysing, explaining and responding to acts of terrorism. These challenges are furthered by the thought that even the use of the term terrorism is problematic, meaning that the very definitions of acts of terrorism and political violence shape one's understanding of and responses to them.

This book seeks to address many of the issues arising during the study of terrorism and political violence. To do this it is split into four parts. Part 1, *Approaching the Study of Terrorism and Political Violence*, introduces key issues when embarking on the study of terrorism and political violence, providing a contextual overview. The second part, *Understanding Terrorism*, explores the inner workings of terrorist groups, looking at the relationship between society and groups that use violence, along with how the message behind the use of terrorism is communicated. The third section, *How Terrorism Ends*, explores negotiations, internal dissent, de-radicalization and military ends. The fourth and final section offers advice to those studying terrorism and political violence, providing guidance for writing coherently and conducting fieldwork in the discipline.

This book should not be the end of your journey in exploring these areas; rather, we hope that it will serve as a guide across the difficult terrain of terrorism and political violence.

Note

1   One example was that of 'shoe bomber' Richard Reid, who attempted to detonate explosives he had smuggled into his shoes while on a flight from Paris to Miami.

PART 1
APPROACHING THE STUDY OF TERRORISM AND POLITICAL VIOLENCE

This first part provides guidance for approaching the study of terrorism and political violence. It locates terrorism within the study of international relations (IR) and security studies and introduces several key philosophical issues that underpin the study of terrorism and political violence. Chapter 1 sets up many of the debates in this section with regard to the challenges in defining and theorizing terrorism. After placing terrorism in a broader context, Chapter 2 considers terrorism from a philosophical perspective, asking whether the use of terrorism can be considered ethical. Moving from the theoretical level, Chapter 3 offers a historical overview of terrorism, exploring how terrorism campaigns have evolved in terms of ideology, tactics and organizational structure. Following a discussion of whether today is the era of the New Terrorism, Chapter 4 addresses cyberterrorism. In this chapter the challenges of defining terrorism more broadly are made clear, and the authors demonstrate how a constructivist approach can be applied to overcome this challenge. Part 1 concludes with three essays that focus on theoretical debates on terrorism. Essay 1 takes a critical-theory approach to terrorism, placing it in a broader context, and applies this to a case study on violence, victims and children in warfare; Essay 2 challenges this critical-theory approach to terrorism; and Essay 3 explores the issue of state terrorism without taking an overt critical or non-critical perspective.

1

LOCATING TERRORISM STUDIES

SIMON MABON

Introduction

The attacks of 9/11 returned terrorism to the zeitgeist, resulting in increasing demands for explanations of contemporary acts of terrorism and political violence. In the aftermath of the attacks academics and policymakers alike sought a greater understanding of why and how individuals resort to violence. This understanding guided the immediate response to the attacks and influences future counterterrorism policy. Despite the importance of this task, scholars and politicians engaged in the process face serious challenges of an ontological and epistemological nature. These problems impact upon the types of questions that we need to ask when studying terrorism and political violence and will be introduced later in this chapter.

The changing nature of international politics after the end of the Cold War and the 9/11 attacks posed new challenges to efforts to define and explain contemporary terrorism. In an effort to understand and explain these changing security threats many scholars have drawn upon work conducted in neighbouring disciplines. Given this, it is important to be familiar with these discussions. As such, this chapter begins by locating terrorism studies within the broader cannon of work in international relations (IR), strategic studies and security studies. Following this, the chapter will unpack the problem of defining terrorism and introduce you to key problems and debates that exist within terrorism studies, before exploring the importance of identity in the discipline. Many of these problems and debates will be discussed in greater detail in later chapters, but they come up throughout the textbook. As such, students should familiarize themselves with the questions that this chapter poses.

At the end of this chapter you should be able to:

- Locate terrorism studies within the broader politics, international relations and security studies literatures
- Identify problems with defining terrorism

- Understand the emergence of Critical Terrorism Studies
- Understand the importance of identity in Terrorism and Political Violence

Locating terrorism studies

Before embarking on a discussion of terrorism and political violence it is imperative to locate this body of work within the wider political field. Scholars and students of terrorism studies and political violence are operating within the umbrella discipline of political science. Under this umbrella discipline are numerous sub-disciplines, many of which themselves have sub-disciplines. Terrorism and political violence falls within the discipline of security studies, which is itself a sub-discipline of IR.

IR seeks to explain the 'interaction of actors, operating at state, sub-state and trans-state levels' (Mabon, 2013: 8). Fred Halliday, a prominent IR scholar, argued that 'the task of social science, IR included, is [...] namely to explain, in as persuasive a manner as possible, what has occurred and to identify what constitute significant contemporary trends' (Halliday, 2005: 6). These trends occur across different levels of analysis: at the international level, where interactions occur between inter-governmental organizations and states; at the state level; and at the sub-state level. While IR scholars have historically focussed upon the interaction between states, the emergence of new actors within the international environment has shifted the focus away from the state and opened up new areas for analysis. This has also resulted in a broadening of focus within the sub-disciplines of IR.

Within IR, sub-disciplines focus upon different areas, ranging from exploring the foreign-policy-making process, through international political economy, international organizations, peace studies and strategic studies, to security studies, which is of paramount importance for this volume. Strategic studies and security studies have predominantly been concerned with identifying threats to a state, yet, in light of a changing international environment, the threats faced have changed. Historically, these threats have been taken to be external to a state; but by purely focussing on external threats many contemporary security threats are missed out of the analysis. Scholars such as Barry Buzan (1991), along with Ole Waever and Jaap de Wilde (1998), have sought to broaden the security agenda so that a greater number of potential threats are open to analysis. By broadening the security agenda to reflect the changing international security environment, we are now able to examine threats to human security, economic security and environmental security.

One of the main areas of analysis within security studies is the phenomenon of terrorism, with terrorism studies, along with the study of political violence, concerned with understanding the relations, dynamics and reasons for the emergence of violent actions. Yet despite the location of terrorism studies within the security studies canon, many scholars have approached the study of terrorism from different disciplines, ranging from anthropology to law and psychology.

The main criticism of conventional terrorism research is that it is driven by 'state-centric, problem-solving approaches that by and large accept the state's definition of the terrorism problem, and that stemming from this, research on issues pertaining to Terrorism and Political Violence should possess policy relevance.[1] As a consequence, research into 'terrorism' needs a more critical engagement with the problem' (Gunning, 2007: 236). This echoes much of the criticism of security studies broadly, prior to the broadening of the security agenda by Buzan and Waever (Buzan et al., 1998). However, recent moves within the literature exploring terrorism and political violence have approached the subject matter in a different way (see Jackson, et al., 2009). The emergence of critical terrorism studies has shifted the focus of analysis, offering a new research agenda for scholars of terrorism.

As Jeroen Gunning suggests, there are several reasons why the emergence of a critical turn in terrorism studies is necessary. Firstly, it is important to move beyond the dominance of state-centric approaches. Indeed, to be critical one must 'explicitly challenge state-centric, problem-solving perspectives and call into question existing definitions, assumptions, and power structures' (Gunning, 2007: 237). The importance of the emergence of critical terrorism studies is especially important when considering some of the problems in defining terrorism, as discussed below.

It is important, at this stage, to make the distinction between terrorism and insurgency, with both falling under the banner of political violence. Insurgency is a political movement, for which terrorism is a tactic that can be, but does not necessarily have to be, used. Indeed, there are cases where insurgent groups use terrorism as a tactic (see al-Qaeda in Iraq, for example), but politically violent groups need not necessarily use fear as a tactic. Rather, insurgent groups can use guerrilla warfare as a strategy which does not target civilians. While we have located terrorism within the wider canon of security-studies literature, it is now important to unpack exactly what we mean by the term terrorism.

Definitional problems: terrorism and the 'Holy Grail'

Terrorism as a term, despite its presence in contemporary vernacular, appears to be without a universally agreed definition. As Alex Schmid suggests, 'terrorism' is perhaps the most important word in the vocabulary of contemporary life (Schmid, 2004: 376), yet it remains an essentially contested concept (Gallie, 1956). The idea of an essentially contested concept emerges when groups of people disagree about 'the proper use of concepts [...] When we examine the different uses of these terms and the characteristic arguments in which they figure we soon see that there is no one clearly definable general use of any of them which can be set up as the correct or standard use' (Gallie, 1956: 168).

One immediate consequence of the idea that terrorism is a contested concept is the suggestion that one man's terrorist is another man's freedom fighter. This ethical problem is discussed in greater detail in Chapter 2, by Gilberto Algar-Faria. What can be agreed, however, is that the term terrorism is a pejorative label for a particular type of political violence. At this point it is pertinent to unpack what is understood by 'violence'. In order to explore the emergence of violence it is important to know what it is that we are looking for. While this may seem obvious, many different definitions of violence also exist – often contained within the definition of terrorism.

In his influential work within the field of peace studies Johan Galtung explores understandings of violence. He identifies a narrow concept of violence, 'according to which violence is somatic incapacitation, or deprivation of health, alone (with killing as the extreme form), at the hands of an actor who intends this to be the consequence' (Galtung, 1969: 168). From this it is clear that there must be a subject and an object of the violence, with the subject intentionally instigating an act of violence upon the object. In the article Galtung offers a much broader understanding of violence to include structural and cultural violence, which has a clear impact on an individual's ability to flourish as a human. While this understanding of violence may offer explanations for the emergence of terrorism and political violence, this typically manifests itself in the narrower understanding of violence. However, several questions emerge:

- Is it possible to talk about the subject–object distinction clearly?
- Do acts of violence always have a clear subject?
- Do acts of violence always have a particular object in mind when they are committed?
- Is there always an intention to commit somatic incapacitation, or deprivation of health?

Many of these questions emerge when considering acts of cyberterrorism, as discussed by Lee Jarvis and Stuart MacDonald in Chapter 4, where acts which may appear to be cyberterrorism have no direct object, or indeed somatic incapacitation. As such, it is important to think critically about how we understand violence, for this shapes our understanding of terrorism.

Returning to the definition of terrorism, as Bruce Hoffman suggests, 'It is a word with intrinsically negative connotations that is generally applied to one's enemies and opponents, or to those with whom one disagrees and would otherwise prefer to ignore' (Hoffman, 1998: 31). However, the lack of a universal definition and the pejorative nature of the term can be problematic when it is used. Indeed, as Walter Laqueur suggests, the term terrorism is 'dangerous ground for simplificateurs and generalisateurs' (Laqueur, 1987: 9).

The search for a universally applicable definition of terrorism has been compared by scholars such as Geoffrey Levitt, Omar Malik and Nicholas Perry to the quest for the Holy Grail, with 'eager souls set[ting] out, full of purpose, energy and self-confidence, to succeed where so many others have failed' (Levitt, 1986: 97). As Nicholas Perry correctly states, unlike the Grail quest, many scholars have located a definition of terrorism, but if this is the case then perhaps we have different terrorisms rather than one terrorism.

But why is searching for a universal definition of terrorism important? In asking this question we must also ask several other questions that are analytically linked to it. Who is to identify what acts should be considered acts of terrorism? Should an act of terrorism be viewed as an independent act of violence, or should it be located as an act within a conflict, guerrilla war, or even just as a crime?

There are several reasons why possessing a definition of terrorism is important. The main reason why a definition is important is that it helps us to identify instances of terrorism. It also aids our understanding of why terrorism occurs and helps us identify its root causes. This discussion of root causes is undertaken by Nina Musgrave in Chapter 5. Possessing a definition of terrorism also helps to identify an appropriate response to terrorism.

But, surely, we are all able to identify terrorism when we see it? We all know what terrorism looks like, and so, much like Justice Stewart on obscenity, 'I'll know it when I see it' (Perry, 2004: 250), we know what terrorism is when we see it. But when we try to define it we are struck by the number of factors and complexities that we must take into account in our definition. These complexities are evident in the numerous disciplines in which scholars are researching terrorism.[2] Those who are researching terrorism do so from numerous angles and perhaps would not necessarily consider themselves to be terrorism scholars. Indeed, scholars studying terrorism may be doing so by exploring numerous other issues including typologies of violence, area studies, the role of religion in violence, law or anthropology.

As a consequence of this varied research base, different perspectives and definitions will emerge, complicating the search for a universally applicable definition. It is important to note that there is no intrinsic essence in the term terrorism and, thus, what we understand by the term is entirely constructed. In addition, one must also consider who the people are who have to respond to acts of terrorism on the ground. At first glance it includes members of the emergency services, but when one takes a closer look the list grows longer to include:

- policymakers
- the security services
- doctors
- academics
- nurses
- lawyers
- local councils
- small business owners
- large business owners
- students
- society as a whole?

This last point is especially evident when considering the requests for all to 'be vigilant' and report 'suspicious packages' to the police. Given that terrorism impacts all facets of society, it is important to question who should be responsible for defining what constitutes terrorism. One's first instinct would perhaps be to say that the responsibility belongs to governments or members of the judiciary, but both sets of people approach this discussion with their own agendas and biases. As it is typically governments and policymakers who are responsible for defining what constitutes terrorism (politically and legally), the emergence of critical terrorism studies is incredibly important.

While then it is increasingly difficult to agree on a definition and, moreover, on who should be doing the defining, there are key characteristics that are typically held to be key elements of terrorism:

1. The demonstrative use of violence against human beings
2. The (conditional) threat of (more) violence
3. The deliberate production of terror/fear in a target group
4. The targeting of civilians, non-combatants and innocents
5. The purpose of intimidation, coercion and/or propaganda
6. The fact that it is a method, tactic or strategy of conflict waging
7. The importance of communicating the act(s) of violence to larger audiences
8. The illegal, criminal and immoral nature of the act(s) of violence
9. The predominantly political character of the act
10. Its use as a tool of psychological warfare to mobilize or immobilize sectors of the public

(Schmid, 2004: 404)

Within this list are numerous terms that are subjective and thus open to interpretation. Take the definition of particular individuals as civilians, non-combatants and innocents as an example of this. Terrorism's subjectivity is present in how it is interpreted, constructed and defined, which has serious consequences for countering terrorism.

Alex Schmid found 109 different definitions of terrorism between 1936 and 1980; yet in the aftermath of the 9/11 attacks and the increased attention on terrorism studies (from policymakers and academics alike) this number is bound to have increased. Within Schmid's study only three elements (violence/force, political, and fear/terror) appeared in at least half of the definitions (Perry, 2004: 250). As a consequence of this difficulty, there are several questions that arise when attempting to define terrorism:

1. Should the term terrorism be applied to governments and states in the same way as it is applied to non-state groups?
2. Should we differentiate between terrorism and the right of a people to self-determination, resistance, and to combat occupation?
3. Should the activities of national armed forces, while on official duty and in armed combat, be included?
4. Should the use of nuclear, chemical, or biological weapons by states be included, given that their use is 'terrifying'?

The first two of these clauses appear to be the key impediments to arriving at a universal definition.[3] Indeed, we must remember that in creating a universal definition of terrorists, it is necessary to negotiate at the international level with other state actors. It is sometimes the case that these actors have been involved in acts of terrorism (under one definition or another), or perhaps have sponsored groups who have embarked on terrorist campaigns. If this is the case, and given our earlier assertion that terrorism is a pejorative term, then arriving at a conclusion that is broad enough to catch all acts of terrorism, but not so broad as to include acts that certain actors do not wish to be included, appears problematic.

Further complicating our problem is the idea that the term has been misused by the numerous media outlets reporting on acts of violence that may or may not have been acts of terrorism, an issue explored in greater detail by Cristina Archetti in Chapter 7. The loose use of the term has only clouded general understandings of what terrorism is, which casts doubt on whether one can fall back on our earlier idea that we'll recognize it when we see it.

Bearing the above problems in mind, we can begin to realize why terrorism is such a difficult term to define. Schmid suggests that there are four main reasons underpinning this difficulty:

1. Because terrorism is a 'contested concept' and political, legal, social science and popular notions of it are often diverging
2. Because the definition question is linked to (de-)legitimization and criminalization
3. Because there are many types of 'terrorism', with different forms and manifestations
4. Because the term has undergone changes of meaning in over 200 years of its existence

(Schmid, 2004: 395)

This first point is especially pertinent and is reflected in the emergence and development of critical terrorism studies as discussed in the previous section. It is worth restating the importance of subjectivity here, which is reflected in the construction of threats, given interpretations of a situation that are grounded in particular sociopolitical and historical contexts. This idea of construction is important when considering definitions of terrorism and will be discussed at greater length in Chapter 4.

As we shall discuss, terrorism became common vernacular in the late nineteenth century with the outbreak of anarchist terrorism. This differs greatly from our understanding of terrorism today, and, as such, having a 'catch-all' definition of terrorism appears somewhat problematic, especially if it has to include all previous acts of terrorism, each with their own context.

Yet, despite these problems, the search for a definition of terrorism remains incredibly important. Boaz Ganor suggests that there are eight key reasons why having an internationally recognized understanding of terrorism is important:

1. Developing an effective international strategy requires agreement on what it is we are dealing with; in other words, we need a definition of terrorism.
2. International mobilization against terrorism [...] cannot lead to operational results as long as the participants cannot agree on a definition.
3. Without a definition, it is impossible to formulate or enforce international agreements against terrorism.
4. Although many countries have signed bilateral and multilateral agreements concerning a variety of crimes, extradition for political offences is often explicitly excluded, and the background of terrorism is always political.
5. The definition of terrorism will be the basis and the operational tool for expanding the international community's ability to combat terrorism.
6. It will enable legislation and specific punishments against those, involved in, perpetrating, or supporting terrorism, and will allow the formulation of a codex of laws and international conventions against terrorism, terrorist organizations, states sponsoring terrorism, and economic firms trading with them.

7.   At the same time, the definition of terrorism will hamper the attempts of terrorist organizations to obtain public legitimacy, and will erode support among these segments of the population willing to assist them (as opposed to guerrilla activities).

8.   Finally, the operational use of the definition of terrorism could motivate terrorist organizations, due to moral and utilitarian considerations, to shift from terrorist activities to alternate courses (such as guerrilla warfare) in order to attain their aims, thus reducing the scope of international terrorism.

Ganor, (2002: 287–304)

The above discussion has provided a brief overview of a broad literature within terrorism studies, highlighting some of the key issues that one should be aware of when thinking about, confronting and using the term terrorism.

The evolution of terrorism

When studying the evolution of terrorism and political violence, David Rapoport's work on the waves of terrorism provides a useful conceptual overview (2002; 2004). As noted in the previous section, the first instance of terrorism occurred in the late nineteenth century, yet acts of terrorism became increasingly common from the turn of the twentieth century onwards.

In his analysis Rapoport suggests that there have been four waves of terrorism, which suggests that acts of terrorism should not be viewed as a new phenomenon. Instead, he argues that incidences of terrorism should be traced back to the turn of the twentieth century and the first wave of terrorism, or the Anarchist Wave. For Rapoport the length of a wave is typically 40 to 45 years (apart from the New Left Wave), reflecting a human life pattern, where 'dreams that inspire fathers lose their attractiveness for the sons' (Rapoport, 2004: 2).

In the 1880s an initial Anarchist Wave of terrorism appeared and then continued for some 40 years. Following this, the Anti-colonial Wave began in the 1920s, and by the 1960s had largely disappeared. The late 1960s witnessed the birth of the New Left Wave, which dissipated largely in the 90s leaving a few groups still active in Sri Lanka, Spain, France, Peru, and Colombia. The fourth, or Religious Wave, began in 1979, and, according to Rapoport's theory, it still has 20 to 25 years to run (Rapoport, 2004).

These waves were triggered by revolution, taken to be the restructuring of authority, often driven by the desire for self-determination. It is possible to identify the key events that led to the emergence of a new wave; these are summarized in Table 1.1.

While there are some shortcomings with Rapoport's analysis, such as his failure to account for state terrorism and the idea that waves are homogenous, his view offers a way of tracking the evolution of terrorism and is discussed in greater detail in Chapter 3 by Pola Zafra-Davis.

Table 1.1   The Waves of Terrorism

Wave	Event
Anarchist	Vera Zasulich wounding a police officer who had abused prisoners. Zasulich surrendered her weapon and proclaimed she was a terrorist not a killer.
Anti-colonial	The Treaty of Versailles broke up the empires of losing powers according to the principles of self-determination. Where this was not possible, mandates were used. However, this questioned the legitimacy of the victors' empires.
New Left	The Vietnam War, where the successes of asymmetric warfare offered hope to those ambivalent towards the existing system.
Religious	The Iranian Revolution, which gave traction to the idea that one's religious beliefs had greater power than political ideology.

The post-Cold War context

As noted earlier in this chapter, the changing nature of international politics after the Cold War required a shift in the focus of IR. The end of the Cold War ushered in an era of increased globalization and with it the perceived growth of capitalism, secularization and democratization. This opening up of space allowed new actors to emerge, at different levels of analysis, both state and non-state. The rise of the non-state actor poses serious problems for state security and counterterrorism specifically (for our line of inquiry these are actors not affiliated to states, with the ability to influence change, located within or across state boundaries). These actors often operate across state borders, which is problematic when considering that state counterterrorism policies are typically limited to operating within their own borders. While this era allowed many to flourish, it also increased the risk posed by groups using violence as a tactic, as terrorist groups were able to take advantage of new opportunities, namely information technology, to exploit cross-border regimes, and to gather resources (Cronin, 2002/3).

The shift in focus in IR also necessitated a shift in focus for scholars of terrorism and political violence. In light of these changing international dynamics, coupled with the increased lethality of violence (Cronin, 2002/3: 42), many scholars sought to explain why certain groups resorted to violence. Post-9/11 many were seduced by the work of Samuel Huntington, particularly his idea of a clash of civilizations. Huntington's *Clash of Civilizations* thesis first appeared in the *Foreign Affairs* journal in 1991, in the immediate aftermath of the end of the Cold War, but gained international attention in public discussion of terrorism after 9/11 (Neumayer and Plumper, 2009: 712).

Huntington suggested that conflict in the post-Cold War world would not be driven by ideology, as the Cold War was, or by the decline of the nation state; rather, he suggested that scholars missed a key factor – culture. On the first page of his article Huntington states the following:

It is my hypothesis that the fundamental source of conflict in this new world will not be primarily ideological or primarily economic. The great divisions among humankind and the dominating source of conflict will be cultural. Nation states will remain the most powerful actors in world affairs, but the principal conflicts of global politics will occur between nations and groups of different civilizations. The clash of civilizations will dominate global politics. The fault lines between civilizations will be the battle lines of the future. (Huntington, 1993: 1)

Huntington argued that with the end of the ideologically driven Cold War, conflict would occur between 'seven or eight' major civilizations of the world. For Huntington these civilizations are: Western; Latin American; Sub-Saharan African; Orthodox; Islamic; Sinic; Hindu; Buddhist; and Japanese. Huntington suggested that the most serious violence will occur at 'fault lines' between civilizations, with the examples of the Balkans, Chechnya, Kashmir, Sri Lanka and Tibet used to support this argument.[4] For those seduced by Huntington's argument it is the conflict between 'the West' and 'Islam' that can explain the rise of groups such as al-Qaeda, and thus much of the terrorism and political violence of the twenty-first century.

While Huntington's thesis has serious flaws, as discussed below, its legacy in the post-9/11 world remains incredibly powerful. Its influence on policymakers in the West is reflected in some of the reviews of his book. Henry Kissinger, a secretary of state for US Presidents Richard Nixon and Gerald Ford, suggested that it was one of 'the most important books to have emerged since the end of the Cold War'. Zbigniew Brzezinski, a national security adviser to President Jimmy Carter between 1977 and 1981, referred to Huntington's work as an 'intellectual tour de force: bold, imaginative, and provocative. A seminal work that will revolutionize our understanding of international affairs'.

While for some this may seem like a compelling argument, Huntington's thesis is riddled with severe errors. Initially, it appears that Huntington is essentializing civilizations, paying little attention to what occurs within these blocs. As Edward Said argues, 'The personification of enormous entities called "the West" and "Islam" is recklessly affirmed, as if hugely complicated matters like identity and culture existed in a cartoonlike world where Popeye and Bluto bash each other mercilessly, with one always more virtuous pugilist getting the upper hand over his adversary' (Said, 2001). Said is not the only scholar to offer a damning retort to Huntington. Ken Booth, the 'father' of the critical security studies turn, is also highly critical of Huntington, referring to this text as 'the worst book on international politics I have read for a long time' (Booth, 2008: 1). Despite the flaws in Huntington's thesis, the importance of identity remains integral in our quest to understand the emergence of groups who use violence as a tactic. Yet it is important to move below this 'civilizational' level of analysis to focus upon the importance of identities at societal, community and individual levels. It is at these levels where differences between identities exist and friction between these different identities can emerge.

Differences exist between people from Yorkshire and Lancashire, between Christians and Muslims, between Catholics and Protestants, or between segments that cross-cut these identities. Indeed, it is pertinent to note here that individuals are often in possession of more than one identity, commonly referred to as hybrid identities, which take into account the numerous ways in which individuals define themselves. However, differences do not necessarily result in violence, or indeed even in friction. Yet when an identity appears threatened by a more dominant identity or ideology then the scope for violence increases. Cronin articulates how, for some, 'Westernization, secularization, democratization, consumerism, and the growth of market capitalism represents an onslaught to less privileged people in conservative cultures repelled by the fundamental changes that these forces are bringing – or angered by the distortions and uneven distributions of benefits that result' (2002/3: 46). The impact of this is discussed in more detail in Chapter 3.

As such, in understanding the move to violence it is important to look at the context within which this violence takes place. This often requires the analysis of the identity mix within a particular location, be it a city, county, or state. These issues are covered in Chapter 5, by Nina Musgrave, and also in Chapter 6, by Nicole Ives-Allison.

Conclusion

To fully understand the dynamics of terrorism and political violence it is important to be aware of the complex web of factors that have shaped the nature of the action. This book attempts to provide you with the theoretical and conceptual tools that will allow you to do that. Before beginning your journey through the book, this chapter has introduced you to some of the key debates when studying terrorism and political violence. It is important to remember where terrorism studies is located within academic discussions, namely within security studies and, more broadly, IR. In order to proceed with the study of terrorism one must be aware of the debates highlighted earlier and think critically about definitions of terrorism. Ask yourself the following questions:

- Who is providing this definition of terrorism?
- Why are they defining it in this way?
- How is violence being defined?
- Does it exclude certain acts that could also be understood as terrorism?
- If so, why?

While many of the debates and questions raised may appear daunting, the remainder of this book will unpack these issues in greater detail, offering perspectives on terrorism and political violence from numerous different contexts, reflecting Alex Schmid's wish for co-operation between different academic disciplines within the study of terrorism.

STUDY BOX CHAPTER 1

Key reading

Buzan, B., Waever, O. and de Wilde, J. (1998) *Security: A New Framework for Analysis* (Boulder, CO: Lynne Rienner Publishers).

Ganor, B. (2002) 'Defining Terrorism: Is One Man's Terrorist Another Man's Freedom Fighter?', *Police Practice and Research: An International Journal*, 3(4): 287–304.

Jackson, R., Smyth, M. B. and Gunning, J. (Eds.) (2009) *Critical Terrorism Studies: A New Research Agenda* (London: Routledge).

Levitt, G. (1986) 'Is Terrorism Worth Defining?', *Ohio Northern University Law Review*, 13: 97–115.

Schmid, A. (2004) 'Terrorism – The Definitional Problem', *Case Western Reserve Journal of International Law*, 36: 2.

Study questions

1   How do you define acts of terrorism?

2   Is it possible (and desirable) to agree upon a universal definition of terrorism?

3   Why is the emergence of critical terrorism studies important?

Notes

1   Policy relevance suggests that the research conducted by scholars operating within a particular area should be useful for those engaged in the policymaking process. This is also reflected in the academy, where scholars are striving for their work to make an impact. If this is the case then the research agendas of academics appear skewed towards this policy relevancy.

2   Individuals studying terrorism can be found within the following departments: politics, philosophy, religious studies, law, human geography, sociology, anthropology, computer science, and business management.

3   The cases of Palestine and Kashmir highlight this.

4   The Balkan conflict was driven by the interaction of different religious groups.

References

Booth, K. (2008) 'Huntington's Homespun Grandeur', *The Political Quarterly*, 68(4): 425–428

Buzan, B. (1991) *People, States' and Fear: An Agenda for International Security Studies in the Post-Cold War Era.* (Harlow: Pearson)

Buzan, B., Waever, O. and de Wilde, J. (1998) *Security: A New Framework for Analysis.* (Boulder: Lynne Rienner Pub.)

Cronin, A. K. (2002/3) 'Behind the Curve: Globalization and International Terrorism', *International Security*, 27(3): 30–58.

Gallie, W. B. (1956) 'Essentially Contested Concepts', *Proceedings of the Aristotelian Society*, New Series, 56 (1955–1956): 167–198.

Galtung, J. (1969) 'Violence, Peace and Peace Research', *Journal of Peace Research*, 6(3): 167–91.

Ganor, B. (2002) 'Defining Terrorism: Is One Man's Terrorist another Man's Freedom Fighter?', *Police Practice and Research: An International Journal*, 3(4): 287–304.

Gunning, J. (2007) 'Babies and Bathwaters: Reflecting on the Pitfalls of Critical Terrorism Studies', *European Political Science*, 6(3): 236–243.

Halliday, F. (2005) *The Middle East in International Relations*. (Cambridge: Cambridge University Press)

Hoffman, B. (1998) *Inside Terrorism*. (Columbia: Columbia University Press)

Huntington, S. P. (1993) 'The Clash of Civilizations', *Foreign Affairs*, Summer, pp. 22–49.

Jackson, R., Smyth, M. B., and Gunning, J. (eds) (2009) *Critical Terrorism Studies: A New Research Agenda*. (London: Routledge)

Laqueur, W. (1987) *The Age of Terrorism*. (Boston, Massa: Little, Brown and Company)

Levitt, G. (1986) 'Is Terrorism Worth Defining', *Ohio NU Law Review*, 13: 99–116.

Mabon, S. (2013) *Saudi Arabia and Iran: Soft Power Rivalry in the Middle East*. (London: I.B. Tauris)

Neumayer, E. and Plumper, T. (2009) 'International Terrorism and the Clash of Civilizations', *British Journal of Political Science*, 39(4): 711–734.

Perry, N. J. (2004) 'The Numerous Federal Legal Definitions of Terrorism: The Problem of Too Many Grails', *30 J. Legis. 249*, 249–250

Rapoport, D. C. (2002) 'The Four Waves of Rebel Terror and September 11', *Anthropoetics*, 8(1): 42–43.

Rapoport, D. C. (2004) 'The Four Waves of Modern Terrorism. In A. K. Cronin and J. M. Ludes (eds.) *Attacking Terrorism: Elements of a Grand Strategy*. (Washington: Georgetown University Press, pp. 46–73).

Said, E. (2001) 'The Clash of Ignorance', *The Nation*, available at: http://www.thenation.com/article/clash-ignorance (accessed on 1 June, 2014).

Schmid, A. (2004) 'Terrorism – The Definitional Problem', *Case Western Reserve Journal of International Law*, 36(2): 375–420.

2

TERRORISM AND ETHICS
GILBERTO ALGAR-FARIA

Introduction

It may seem odd to talk about the ethics of terrorism when it is so often assumed to be an inherently unethical or underhand form of violence. However, most of us are well acquainted with various permutations of the phrase 'One person's terrorist is another person's freedom fighter'.[1] Despite the lethargy experienced by most people on reading the phrase once more, it raises an important point: terrorists and freedom fighters are both engaging in political violence; which of these labels is applied to them depends on how they are perceived by the audience awarding them that label, the former generally being an inherently amoral character and the latter a morally righteous one. The idea of speaking of just terrorism in the same way as some speak of just war seems bizarre (Nathanson, 2012: 79). But could there be such a thing as just terrorism, if we take away the value judgment and call it political violence, for example? Could fighting for freedom be just? It certainly sounds a lot more ethical than fighting for the sake of causing terror.

When referring to violence of any type we speak of it with constant reference to ethics. Terrorism and political violence[2] are no different; arguments for or against the employment of this type of violence are couched in concepts of morality. This is because violence is only considered to be acceptable if it is deemed to be legitimate. Stephen Nathanson has argued that out of a selection of traditional theories[3] none categorically condemns terrorism (Nathanson, 2012: 80–92). However, in practice there is an ambiguity when it comes to who exactly defines the legitimacy of a violent act. Legitimacy is a notion that is often polluted by other concepts and assumptions. In particular, James Caporaso notes: 'Our collective understanding of legitimacy seriously overstates the importance of notions of political support, informed by modern theories of public opinion' (Caporaso, 2000: 8–9). In the case of terrorism and political violence a group will generally receive support from a certain demographic of a population because those supporters see the violent actors' means and ends as appropriate and therefore justified. Moreover, a terrorist group must also face charges of illegitimacy in both its means and its ends by the entity it opposes, generally taken to be (although not always) one or other nation-state. At times this chapter will refer to morality and ethics interchangeably; while there are differences between the two, for the purposes of this chapter we will be talking about ethics and ethical issues throughout.

This chapter's purpose is firstly to provide the reader with a wide-ranging overview of the current knowledge on the ethics of terrorism and political violence, grounded in the context of Western philosophy, before moving on to critically analyse the more problematic of these claims, in so doing highlighting key questions on the topic. It is important from the outset for the reader to be aware that by engaging with ethical arguments about terrorism and political violence we are engaging with a critical strand of literature. That is, the material covered in this chapter may lead you to raise questions over the validity of mainstream arguments about the morality of terrorism. However, do be aware as you read through this chapter that the contrasting moral positions that we explore are all contrasting subjective judgments. With this in mind, by the end of this chapter you will understand:

- The basics about the ethics of political violence
- What ethics are used for and by whom
- How ethics affect our perceptions of violence in the context of terrorism; and
- Why ethics can be incorrectly used and the problems with claims made about the ethics of terrorism and political violence.

The ethics of terrorism and political violence: a paradox in terms?

Can terrorism and political violence be ethical? You may have a gut-reaction answer to this question; political violence is, after all, a contentious topic that surrounds us in our everyday lives. The phrase 9/11 is ingrained into most people's minds as representing a series of coordinated terrorist attacks against the USA on 11 September 2001, killing almost 3,000 civilians. Similarly, 7/7 represents to many the London transport bombings of 7 July 2005. There are other cases, too, that are prominent in one's mind when asked to think of terrorism, and one would most probably find it difficult to call those attacks in any way ethical. Yet, as Nathanson suggests, most people find conventional warfare in some ways morally just, even though a large proportion of them over the last two centuries have involved the deliberate targeting of civilians (Nathanson, 2012: 79). Can terrorism and political violence therefore ever be justified? Perhaps or perhaps not; terrorism is an emotive phrase that attaches inherently immoral connotations to political violence. But regardless of what it is called, there is something ethically questionable, at least, wherever violence is chosen as a method of political contestation. That is the reason why we are now embarking on a brief overview of ethics pertaining to terrorism and political violence, as well as the morality of the responses to them.

Kantian ethics

To engage with Kantian ethics is important because it may offer a grounding for those who believe that certain actions such as terrorist attacks are *prima facie* wrong, regardless of the effects those attacks might have. For Immanuel Kant and his followers the key issue determining whether an action could be morally justified has nothing to do with the consequences brought about by that action but rather with Kant's categorical imperative. In short, political violence is judged under Kantian ethics according to 'a rule that demands the value of rational agents [i.e. humans] be respected' (Corlett, 2003: 55). Kant's categorical imperative – to him, the most supreme moral principle – is often paraphrased into various forms, but in full was once stated as follows:

> Now I say: a human being and generally every rational being *exists* as an end in itself, *not merely as a means* for the discretionary use for this or that will, but must in all its actions, whether directed towards itself or also to other rational beings, always be considered *at the same time as an end*. (Kant, 2012 [1785]: 40, emphasis in original)

TEXTBOX 1   THE CATEGORICAL IMPERATIVE

For Kant, there were two types of imperatives, as explained by Christine Korsgaard:

> Imperatives may be either *hypothetical* or *categorical*. A *hypothetical imperative* tells you that if you will something, you ought also to will something else: for example, if you will to be healthy, then you ought to exercise. That is an imperative of skill, telling you how to achieve some particular end. Kant believes that there are also hypothetical imperatives of prudence, suggesting what we must do given that we all will to be happy. A *categorical imperative*, by contrast, simply tells us what we ought to do, not on condition that we will something else, but unconditionally. (Korsgaard, 2012: xviii–xix, emphasis added)

Remember, the interest here is not in consequences, but rather in intentions. This is problematic for political violence. Given that we are focusing only on intentions and not at all on consequences, an attack on a human being in order to fulfil a cause, no matter how great that cause may be, cannot be ethically sound under Kant's categorical imperative. However, like all forms of ethics (as we will find out), Kantian ethics do not necessarily absolutely condemn all acts of terrorism and political violence.

Kant's absolutist stance can and has been critiqued in the context of arguments about the ethics of political violence, for example by Thomas Hill, who rejects Kant's absolute opposition to revolution, producing instead what he refers to as 'a reasonable Kantian perspective for thinking about the problem' (Hill, 1997: 136), but also highlighting potential flexibility in Kant's assumptions. Hill argues, in short, that even within a Kantian reading of ethics certain acts of violence – those targeting very specific individuals or properties, as a last resort, in order to bring about a more peaceful state of affairs, for example – are less unethical than others, such as those using indiscriminate violence as a general strategy from the start in order to bring down a governing structure (Hill, 1997: 137–40). Hill insists that this view can be considered to be quite different from a consequentialist perspective (Hill, 1997: 139–40), although whether you find this modified Kantian framework to be persuasive is up to you. Kantian ethics can be quite rigid to a degree and they are not the only type of ethical framework available. We have seen that, fundamentally, Kantian ethics are about the intentions of the rational being. However, an alternative viewpoint – utilitarianism – provides quite the contrary view: that consequences of an action are the most important thing to consider when judging its ethics.

Utilitarianism

Utilitarian ethics were developed primarily by Jeremy Bentham (2007 [1789]) and, later, John Stuart Mill (2001 [1863]). Under utilitarian ethics an action may be justified if the benefits (the ends) outweigh the costs (the means to reach those benefits or ends). Utilitarianism houses a level of flexibility, therefore, that can allow acts of terrorism and political violence to be carried out without moral condemnation. Because its interest is in the consequences of an action and whether the goodness of those consequences outweighs the badness of the means required to attain them, utilitarian morality appears to permit, and in some instances even require, terrorist attacks on civilians (Nathanson, 2012: 88–9). This seems relatively simple as an equation, but actually it is quite complex due to its flexibility. As Paul Butler notes, terrorism 'is efficient when its benefits outweigh its costs', but while the costs are tangible (lives lost on both sides, retaliatory violence from the target country, public backlash within the perpetrators' own country, and so on), the benefits are difficult to measure because they are highly subjective (Butler, 2002: 5–6). Someone sanctioning or committing an act of terrorism may be interested in all different sorts of benefits that may or may not make sense to others; for example, monetary gain, a fortunate situation in the afterlife, the freedom of their people, and so on.

Just as Kantian ethics can be manipulated to allow a justification for political violence, so can utilitarianism be deployed against such activities. For example, in the case of counterterrorism techniques – by distancing the utilitarian argument from a specific situation, and instead applying it to the overall system of practices, arrangements, laws, personnel, equipment and institutions required to be in place at all times in order for torture of terrorist suspects to be carried out – Jean Arrigo finds that, in fact, the cost of carrying out these activities would far outweigh the potential benefits (Arrigo, 2004: 561–3). The application of Kantian and utilitarian ethics to counterterrorism will be explored later in the discussion of the ticking-bomb scenario, but first we will apply these theories to terrorism and political violence.

The ethics of terrorism as war

Terrorism and political violence are now arguably integral to most modern wars, which can feature at least three types of combat: conventional warfare, (counter) insurgency and (counter) terrorism (Hashim, 2013: 32). It is therefore worth briefly encountering the ethics of warfare itself. An essential part of any war, from the war maker's perspective, is the idea that the war they are waging is just, i.e. ethical. Military leaders and terrorist leaders alike may be called immoral by the opposing side, but their motivations and objectives will inevitably be couched in moral terms to their own supporters.

The just-war tradition can be broken down into two main elements. The first is known in Latin as *jus ad bellum* (the justice of the decision to wage war) and typically includes 'just cause, right authority, right intention, proportionality, reasonable hope of success, and last resort' (Snauwaert, 2004: 127). The second element, *jus in bello*, refers to the actual ethical conduct of the warfare, which is governed by international humanitarian law. This is all well when a war is fought between two states, but increasingly wars are fought between states and non-state entities (take, for example, the most recent war in Afghanistan, which has been fought by a coalition of states against, broadly, 'the Taliban', 'al-Qaeda', 'insurgents' and 'terrorists').

Terrorist organisations and states alike can be accused of resorting to violent means where they are not absolutely necessary. Perhaps the most common excuse for acts of terrorism is that they have been employed as a last resort to address a grievance neglected by the opposing party (Hughes-Wilson, 2004: 356) once all non-violent means of negotiation have been exhausted. However, as Michael Walzer notes, it is in fact exceptionally difficult to reach a 'last resort' situation in reality. He notes: 'one must indeed try everything... and not just once... Politics is an art of repetition' (Walzer, 2004: 53). The contention here is over whether it is even possible to qualify and then reach a situation of 'last resort' in the first place.

It can be argued that concepts such as 'last resort' are too loose: surely the 'last resort' for those with a *deontologist* outlook is measured very differently to the 'last resort' from a utilitarian point of view, for instance. The deontologist approach adopts Kant's categorical imperative. In the context of terrorism and political violence, violence against a rational being is judged to be morally wrong and therefore cannot ever be justifiable. Contrast this with utilitarianism, under which relatively costly means can be justified if they are outweighed by the ends. The *jus ad bellum* principles have, consequentially, been compared to 'a checklist of items to be ticked off, with some items as broad and vague as any warmaker could wish' (Wills, 2004). One could look, for example, to the case of the London 7/7 bombings in 2005, which were soon followed by a statement by Ayman al-Zawahiri (at the time al-Qaeda's second-in-command) justifying the attacks as a last-ditch response to UK and US interventions in the Middle East (Kelsay, 2007: 156–7). This might have been the type of thing concerning Walzer when he commented that '[f]irst oppression is made into an excuse for terrorism, and then terrorism is made into an excuse for oppression' (Walzer, 2006: 62). However, whatever the case may be in this regard, terrorism comes up against a major issue in just-war theory when the other half of the theory, *jus in bello*, is applied.

No matter how just or unjust the cause of a warring party may be considered to be, the rules of conduct within war apply equally to all. A major element of *jus in bello* is the prohibition of all intentional attacks on civilians. Nathanson discusses this issue with reference to collateral damage and the principle of 'double effect':

> The principle of double effect emphasizes the moral importance of the difference between acts that *intentionally* cause deaths and injuries and acts that cause these harms *unintentionally*. According to double effect, actions that would be wrong if the harms are intended may be right if the harms are not intended ... Applying these ideas to war, the principle of double effect tells us that fighting a war may be morally permissible as long as innocent people are not killed or injured intentionally. Attacks that kill civilians may be permissible if they are directed at military targets. What is crucial is that the attackers have no intention to harm the civilians. (Nathanson, 2012: 96, emphasis in original)

Double effect, therefore, allows some degree of latitude for terrorism and political violence; such methods might be considered legitimate so long as civilian casualties are not actually an intended outcome of terrorist attacks. Nathanson employs a hypothetical alternative version of the events of 9/11 where al-Qaeda specified that the primary objective of the attacks was to destroy the Twin Towers; that they did not intend to cause civilian casualties;[4] and that, although they were aware of the likely possibility that many innocents would die, they believed that the gains for their cause resulting from the attack would 'offset the evils of the collateral damage'. Through this framing, he suggests, just-war theory would actually permit such terrorist attacks to take place legally (Nathanson, 2012: 101–3). Nathanson's argument at this point leads on to proportionality, which, like right intention, is subjective and may be defined very differently by different actors. This is because, as Andrew Fiala explains, proportionality is a just-war principle favoured by utilitarians, given that under the principle of proportionality 'the benefit of war is supposed to outweigh the harms caused' (Fiala, 2010: 114). As we have discussed, the weight attached to these benefits will depend largely on the views of the beholder. Terrorism, therefore, is difficult to frame in terms of ethics. However, counterterrorism is also an issue that encounters serious ethical questions.

Can counterterrorism be ethical?

We will now consider some more arguments and concepts in order to unpack issues with torture and other methods in the inventory of counterterrorism. Haig Khatchadourian makes a useful distinction here between act-utilitarianism and rule-utilitarianism. He notes that the former school of thought will argue that 'assassination is justified wherever the assassination's bad consequences are outweighed by its good consequences', while the latter is more interested in 'whether a state or societal *policy* or *practice* of assassination of terrorist suspects would have greater benefits than bad consequences for the particular country or society (or even for human society in general)' (Khatchadourian, 2005: 182–3, emphasis in original). At this point it is important to ask yourself: which is the most important of the two abovementioned utilitarian views, if either is acceptable at all? Additionally, which of these schools of thought do you think, for example, the USA subscribes to most closely? The counterargument to these utilitarian standpoints would be that the creation of a principle of assassination or torture as an acceptable policy option is instantly unacceptable.[5] These viewpoints have significant relevance to today's policies. We will return to issues surrounding the assassination (sometimes referred to as targeted killing) of actual or suspected terrorists in due course, but first we will consider interrogation as a form of counterterrorism.

When dealing with the ethics of interrogation and torture as part of a counter-terrorism strategy one is commonly faced with two juxtaposed views. The first position is broadly that of utilitarianism, the various elements of which have been discussed above. The second of the two positions that might be adopted (that violence can never be justifiable) is termed the deontological perspective which, as aforementioned, follows from an assumption that violence against rational beings is always morally wrong and unjustifiable. This argument between deontologists and utilitarians is often framed in the context of what is known as the ticking-bomb scenario. The dilemma is established roughly as follows:

- You are a security officer responsible for the security of a specific city within a country.
- There is a bomb on a timer ticking away somewhere in the city that you are responsible for.
- If the device goes off it will almost certainly kill at least 100,000 people.
- There is absolutely no way of stopping this device from detonating without the coordinates and the codes required in order to locate and deactivate it.
- You have in your custody an individual who, according to credible intelligence reports, has the information you require, but they are refusing to speak when questioned.
- The timer is now running out and you have very little time in which to find out these vital details.
- You have been briefed by your superior that you may use any means necessary against this individual in order to extract from them the information required to save the lives of at least 100,000 people.
- You are the only person in the world who has the interrogation skills required to make this individual talk.
- You will not personally or professionally suffer any repercussions whatsoever regardless of what you choose to do, including if you decide to walk away.

The question then falls to you: how far should you go in order to extract the information from this person? The true deontologist would instantly say that they would walk away from this situation without hesitation owing to the categorical imperative of never treating a rational being as a means to an end (i.e. an object that can be manipulated in order to attain information). The utilitarian, however, would refute this.

In response to Kantian ethics some utilitarians will cite pragmatism. Their argument would be that *some* level of violence against the detained person would be justifiable if there was a chance that as a result the detainee *could* give up information that *could* save the lives of the 100,000 people at risk from the bomb blast. Rather than making a *prima facie* value judgment, utilitarians make a calculation. In this scenario the utilitarian may weigh up the definite suffering of one individual versus the potential suffering and deaths of 100,000 people and make the judgment that this violence against one person is better than the potential alternative. But not all utilitarians will agree with this view; this argument can be completely reversed, even under a utilitarian framework (recall, for example, Arrigo's aforementioned argument about the costs of maintaining the overall system of torture) (Arrigo, 2004: 561–3).

Thankfully, it is highly unlikely that the ticking-bomb scenario would ever exist in real life. However, interrogation of various types does happen. Indeed, David Luban has rightly noted that the prevalence of the false idea that such a scenario actually existed led the US government to create and follow a liberal ideology of torture (Luban, 2005: 1461). While the question the scenario raises pertains specifically to the ethics of torturing an individual who might be a terrorist, it is useful as a thinking exercise and it should have helped you to decide whether you have a broadly Kantian or utilitarian approach towards this sort of situation. With this in mind it is now time to look at the USA's counterterrorism strategy in some more detail.

As part of its wider counterterrorism strategy the USA has made use of both targeted killings and forms of 'enhanced interrogation'. The latter covers a variety of relatively harsh interrogation techniques used by the USA, criticised by some as constituting torture (Bassiouni, 2006: 389–90). The topic of torture has been murky; Jack Goldsmith, who was at one time the George W. Bush administration's legal adviser to the Department of Defense, later noted that he was at times uncertain about the legal standing of these techniques (Goldsmith, 2009: 158). Under the Third Geneva Convention of 1949 the coercive interrogation of prisoners of war is strictly prohibited. In order to avoid this the Bush administration simply reclassified detainees in Guantánamo Bay and other detention facilities as 'enemy combatants', as opposed to prisoners of war, affording them none of the protections enjoyed by soldiers and civilians captured in war (Allhoff, 2009: 268). Whatever the case may be, the justifications for the USA's counterterrorism techniques continue to be contested. Fritz Allhoff makes an interesting observation challenging rule-utilitarianism in this regard, arguing:

> If deterrence was all that mattered, then we could accomplish the same effect by creating a myth that criminals are tortured without actually torturing any of them. The results would be the same and nobody would have to endure the hardship. (Allhoff, 2009: 111)

Allhoff's point encourages us to question what exactly the point of torture is. If the objective is truly to deter others from participating in terrorism, and this can be achieved through non-violent means, can it be ethical to actually interrogate or torture individuals? More subtly, however, in referring to 'criminals' Allhoff raises another point: why should terrorists be dealt with by military rather than civil means?

The 'war on terrorism'

Unlike the USA's other 'wars' against concepts – crime, drugs and poverty, for example – the war on terror continues to involve war and other military action taken against those suspected of terrorism, alongside law enforcement (Roth, 2004: 2). The emotive nature of 9/11 led to numerous justifications employing ethical arguments for war, the targeting of terrorist suspects, and so on. Soon after the 9/11 attacks (in some cases within the same month) ethics were treated as an afterthought, if anything as a justification for decisions already made:

> ... having identified [those directly responsible for funding and directing the activities of the now-deceased hijackers] to a moral certainty (a standard far short of what would be required by legal criteria of proof, it should be noted), there is no moral objection to targeting them... Indeed, one of the benefits of framing these operations as 'war' rather (sic) than 'law enforcement' is that it does not require the ideal outcome to be the apprehension and trial of the perpetrators. Instead, it countenances their direct elimination by military means if possible. (Cook, 2001)

As time passed, however, legal justifications were increasingly drawn on, often to imply that the USA's response to 9/11 was ethical. Among other incredibly complex measures employed to justify the detention, extraordinary rendition, interrogation and torture of terrorist suspects (Kennedy-Pipe, 2008: 414), the Bush administration found that as this practice was supposedly in line with American law it must be consistent with international law (Sands, 2005: 146). This was made possible by a belief that the USA's principles are exceptional; that is, the USA sees itself as 'not only different in kind from other countries but superior in its morality and institutions' (Sands, 2005: 146). This in turn meant that the types of ethics discussed earlier in this chapter were not so much discarded but superseded by strategic necessity and emergency. Thus, the arguments in favour of military responses to 9/11 were to do with the necessity of protecting the USA, with ethics relegated to a secondary position.

The 2002 National Security Strategy of the United States of America (NSS) (White House, 2002) was, as far as can be judged, written almost entirely with 9/11 in mind, justified by utilitarian ethics. The document also lays down the foundations for something that characterised post-9/11 foreign policy: the doctrine of pre-emption. However, Luban highlights that this was less like pre-emption in the traditional sense, where a threat is imminent and the use of force in self-defence is justified, and more like prevention, where the threat is much more distant (Luban, 2004: 212–13). In other words, the USA argued that the *potential* result of *not* pre-empting a genuine threat would be so dire that the risk could not be tolerated (Kennedy-Pipe, 2008: 415). Specifically, as argued by then US Vice President Dick

Cheney, if there was a 1 per cent likelihood of attack it should be treated as if its likelihood were 100 per cent.[6] Therefore, the NSS made the *intent* and *capabilities* of others into potential justifications for counterterrorist methods against those defined as terrorists, thereby favouring a utilitarian approach to ethics. As noted by Gerard Huiskamp, the problem with this is that those people who are detained, in many cases indefinitely, have never actually committed the crime for which they are being held (Huiskamp, 2004: 399). Preventative imprisonment is one thing, but preventative killing of suspects is quite another. The latter issue is one that has had to be confronted as US foreign policy increasingly prefers drones[7] as a new method of counterterrorist warfare in the twenty-first century.

Law and war: the case of drone usage

Drones have been used extensively since 9/11 to observe and execute suspected terrorists, taking the concept of targeted killings to a new remote extreme where the individuals controlling the drones (i.e. doing the killing) are often located hundreds if not thousands of miles away from the actual machines they are piloting. Notably, these drones have been used by the USA to carry out killings in a number of countries with which it is not actually at war. They do not require Congressional authorisation, and many strikes are carried out by drones belonging to the USA's Central Intelligence Agency, which means even less oversight (Singer, 2011: 400). According to the Bureau of Investigative Journalism, between 2002 and 30 November 2013 over 500 US drone strikes occurred in Pakistan, Yemen and Somalia (although some of these cases are unconfirmed). While deaths resulting from these strikes are inherently difficult to establish, the lower estimates number the dead at over 3,000, some of which are reported to have been civilians (Serle and Ross, 2013). This issue speaks to the heart of the ethical concern with counterterrorism tactics.

As will be apparent by this point, terrorism and counterterrorism (and the ethical issues related to them) are today more complicated than ever before. The Geneva Conventions, which outline certain fundamental precepts about what is and is not legal (and ethical) in warfare, and which all parties to a conflict are supposed to obey, came into being when the world looked strategically very different and inter-state warfare was perceived to be the main threat to peace and stability. This was because, like most mechanisms of their type, the Conventions were backward-looking, designed to prevent past mistakes (atrocities occurring during World War II) from occurring again. However, the Conventions were never designed to address the possibilities opened-up by political violence, counterterrorism and asymmetric warfare. The result of this has been the evolution of increasingly malleable ethical and legal norms with regards to terrorism and counterterrorism, with the former generally being looked down upon and the latter being occasionally criticised but for the most part accepted as a necessity within Western societies. With this in mind it is time to consider the drone debate.

The debate on drones tends to be polarised and zero-sum. Such a debate occurred in a 2013 issue of *Foreign Affairs*. The pro-drone position, as we will call it, by Daniel Byman, prioritises US security above all other arguments. After briefly acknowledging that some criticisms of drones 'are valid; others less so', he argues that:

> In the end, drone strikes remain a necessary instrument of counterterrorism. The United States simply cannot tolerate terrorist safe havens in remote parts of Pakistan and elsewhere, and drones offer a comparatively low-risk way of targeting these areas while minimizing collateral damage. (Byman, 2013: 32)

While conceding that 'Washington must continue to improve its drone policy', Byman only thinks this necessary so that 'tyrannical regimes will have a harder time pointing to the U.S. drone programme to justify attacks against political opponents' (Byman, 2013: 32–3). The article, in fact, makes no mention of ethics and morals, and the only association of a 'right' is of the USA's 'limited right to conduct drone strikes against U.S. citizens' (Byman, 2013: 41). Byman's position was disputed in an anti-drone response article by Audrey Cronin. Cronin mentions morals, first noting that drones assist al-Qaeda 'to frame Americans as immoral bullies who care even less about ordinary people than al Qaeda does' (Cronin, 2013: 46) and then arguing that morals need to feature more prominently in the drone strategy:

> Drone strikes must be legally justified, transparent, and rare. Washington needs to better establish and follow a publicly explained legal and moral framework for the use of drones, making sure that they are part of a long-term political strategy that undermines the enemies of the United States. With the boundaries for drone strikes in Pakistan, Somalia, and Yemen still unclear, the United States risks encouraging competitors such as China, Iran, and Russia to label their own enemies as terrorists and go after them across borders. (Cronin, 2013: 54)

Both articles, therefore, note some level of responsibility for the USA to behave as an example to other actors. While Byman believes that the USA should be accurate when conducting drone strikes so as not to give political ammunition to its opponents, Cronin is concerned with the possibility that the USA's competitors will take up similarly indefinite forms of warfare across borders. Neither of these authors, however, addresses the ethical implications of breaching another state's sovereignty.

Although sovereignty is often omitted from the ethical debate, it is in fact important to consider, especially in the case of drone warfare. Drones diminish the importance of the sovereignty principle (Brunstetter and Braun, 2011: 356). After all, states still have a *moral* obligation to keep their citizens safe from harm, and, correspondingly, it is expected that states will respect one another's right to sovereignty; yet in drone warfare this principle is often ignored. Article 51 of the UN Charter establishes that states may attack one another in self-defence,[8] but drone warfare sometimes occurs without war actually being declared at all (Brunstetter and Braun, 2011: 344–5). The implication of this is that killing occurs outside of warfare, which in turn raises serious questions about respect for sovereignty and the morality of killing people in such a way.

What of the actual damage done by drones to their targets? The principle of last resort is important here. One ethical concern related to drone strikes is that the targeted killing of people who may or may not actually be terrorists becomes the default tactic as opposed to the last resort (Brunstetter and Braun, 2011: 346). This issue is compounded by concerns over collateral damage. Cronin notes that an advantage of the drone programme over al-Qaeda's terrorist attacks is that the former has, under the presidency of Barack Obama, avoided civilian casualties 86 per cent of the time, whereas the latter specifically targets civilians (Cronin, 2013: 47). This is a fair point: bearing in mind our earlier discussion of collateral damage, it is ethically more dubious to specifically target civilians than it is to avoid them. However, Cronin later concedes that 'because the targets of [drone] strikes are so loosely defined, it seems inevitable that they will kill some civilians' (Cronin, 2013: 47). The law aside, how much more ethical are 'inevitable' civilian casualties resulting from drone strikes than terrorist attacks targeting civilians? In both cases, although the primary tactical aim differs (in the former case usually to kill terrorist suspects; in the latter case generally to kill civilians and therefore terrify others through spectacle), the actual result is that civilians *will* be killed. To this accusation Byman's response would be one of cold utilitarianism:

> Admittedly, drones have killed innocents. But the real debate is over how many and whether alternative approaches are any better… even the most unfavorable estimates of drone casualties reveal that the ratio of civilian to militant deaths… is lower than it would be for other forms of strikes. (Byman, 2013: 37)

The ethical justification for drone strikes, therefore, is simply that they kill fewer civilians in the process of accomplishing a military objective (often a secret one) than other methods. Byman further notes that, in actuality, when conducting a drone strike the US government often does not recognise civilian casualties because it 'assumes that all military-age males in the blast area of a drone strike are combatants' (Byman, 2013: 36). In this way, counterterrorist policy does not necessarily have to confront the issue of collateral damage, as 'military' status is attributed broadly to people who happen to be in the area of an attack. This is ethically problematic: if the number of civilian casualties is low due to the way in which they are framed then collateral damage is effectively being (re)defined for strategic expediency. As you can probably gather, ethics are becoming more difficult to define in this context where the lines between combatant and non-combatant are increasingly blurred. According to Daniel Brunstetter and Megan Braun, critics argue that drone strikes constitute targeted assassinations and are therefore illegal under international law, whereas proponents will argue that such attacks are a more proportional response to terrorism (Brunstetter and Braun, 2011: 343). Perhaps, then, we are seeing a range of responses to terrorism that are as difficult to judge through a moral lens as the acts of terrorism themselves.

Conclusion: which ethics and for whom?

The ethics of terrorism and political violence are becoming increasingly difficult to map. In particular, new and complex forms of counterterrorism raise the question of whether either side in any war on terrorism can or will ever conduct ethical operations. In the most recent evolution of this debate, ethics seem to be being used as a tool by which arguments against certain tactics can be justified. However, they do not appear to be addressed seriously by the other side. Those promoting various forms of violence will argue that there is strategically too much to lose to start thinking about ethical concerns, or they will employ a utilitarian view of ethics, justifying their actions by portraying them as the more humane of various methods or as the most efficient or only way of choosing their politico-strategic goals.

Of course, and here is the paradox, or loophole, if you will: different actors will define the value of various goals very differently from one another. A terrorist organisation may perceive the killing of 1,000 civilians in a foreign country acceptable if there is a chance that it will lead to the withdrawal of that country's troops from the terrorist organisation's home territory. The foreign country, of course, will perceive this as completely disproportionate and insane, given that it does not believe in the same ends or even see a causal link between civilian deaths and the withdrawal of its troops. The Kantian view outlined at the beginning of this chapter does not fare well in this argument, which is more about how many civilian deaths (what means) are acceptable for any specific end, rather than whether or not the sacrifice of human life is acceptable in the first place. Those who adopt the latter position are likely to be accused of being idealists who may well have brilliant ideas but whose claims could not possibly work in the cold world of *realpolitik*.

STUDY BOX CHAPTER 2

Key reading

Arendt, H. (1970) *On Violence* (Orlando: Harcourt).

Byman, D. (2013) 'Why Drones Work: The Case for Washington's Weapon of Choice', *Foreign Affairs*, 92: 32–43.

Cronin, A. K. (2013) 'Why Drones Fail: When Tactics Drive Strategy', *Foreign Affairs*, 92: 44–54.

Miller, S. (2009) *Terrorism and Counter-Terrorism: Ethics and Liberal Democracy* (Malden: Blackwell Publishing).

Nathanson, S. (2012) *Terrorism and the Ethics of War* (Cambridge: Cambridge University Press).

Study questions

1   Bearing in mind the concept of collateral damage, is it ethical for a terrorist to attack a civilian establishment? What about a military one?

2   Ultimately, do the ends of counterterrorism justify the means? If so, why?

3   Can terrorism ever be just? What about resistance movements that represent a legitimate grievance employing violence amongst other tools to achieve their aspirations? Justify your answer.

Notes

1   This phrase, repeated many times since, was originally penned by Gerald Seymour in *Harry's Game* (Seymour, 1999: 91): 'The Red Cross man from Switzerland, in his little white suit, even with a big bright cross on his hat so [gunmen] woudn't throw a grenade at him from the rooftop, had come to visit [Harry's] unit once. He'd said to the colonel something like, "One man's terrorist is another man's freedom fighter." The colonel hadn't liked that.'

2   In order to keep this chapter concise, we will be referring to terrorism and political violence as being effectively one and the same, although, in fact, terrorism is a kind of political violence (Schmid and Jongman, 2005: 58–9).

3   Nathanson selects for discussion political realism, commonsense morality, Michael Walzer's rights-based theory, and utilitarianism.

4   In reality, of course, al-Qaeda showed no remorse whatsoever for civilian deaths and, indeed, it seemed that the attacks were calibrated in order to cause the maximum number of civilian casualties at the same time as creating a spectacle.

5   This argument is often made with reference to torture; see, for example, Luban (2005: 1425–61) and Opotow (2007: 457–61).

6   For more on this see Suskind (2007).

7   Drones are known technically as Unmanned Aerial Vehicles (UAVs).

8   See United Nations (n.d.). Bear in mind, however, that the principle of the 'responsibility to protect' dictates that under certain conditions states forfeit their right to sovereignty and, therefore, can still be intervened in by another state which does not have to be acting in self-defence; see International Commission on Intervention and State Sovereignty (2001).

References

Allhoff, F. (2009), 'The War on Terror and the Ethics of Exceptionalism', *Journal of Military Ethics*, 8(4): 265–88.

Arrigo, J.M. (2004), 'A Utilitarian Argument Against Torture Interrogation of Terrorists', *Science and Engineering Ethics*, 10(3): 543–72.

Bassiouni, M.C. (2006), 'The Institutionalization of Torture under the Bush Administration', *Case Western Reserve Journal of International Law*, 37(1): 389–425.

Bentham, J. (2007 [1789]), *An Introduction to the Principles of Morals and Legislation* (Mineola: Dover).

Brunstetter, D. and M. Braun (2011), 'The Implications of Drones on the Just War Tradition', *Ethics & International Affairs*, 25(3): 337–58.

Butler, P. (2002), 'Foreword: Terrorism and Utilitarianism: Lessons from, and for, Criminal Law', *Journal of Criminal Law and Criminology*, 93(1): 1–22.

Byman, D. (2013), 'Why Drones Work: The Case for Washington's Weapon of Choice', *Foreign Affairs*, 92: 32–43.

Caporaso, J.A. (2000), 'Changes in the Westphalian Order: Territory, Public Authority, and Sovereignty', *International Studies Review*, 2(2): 1–28.

Cook, M.L. (2001), 'Ethical Issues in Counterterrorism Warfare', *Markkula Center for Applied Ethics*, September [accessed 26 December 2013], available from: http://www.scu.edu/ethics/publications/ethicalperspectives/cook.html.

Corlett, J.A. (2003), *Terrorism: A Philosophical Analysis* (Norwell: Kluwer Academic Publishers).

Cronin, A.K. (2013), 'Why Drones Fail: When Tactics Drive Strategy', *Foreign Affairs*, 92: 44–54.

Fiala, A. (2010), *Public War, Private Conscience: The Ethics of Political Violence* (London: Continuum International Publishing Group).

Goldsmith, J. (2009), *The Terror Presidency* (New York: Norton).

Hashim, A.S. (2013), *When Counterinsurgency Wins: Sri Lanka's Defeat of the Tamil Tigers* (Philadelphia: University of Pennsylvania Press).

Hill, T.E. (1997), 'A Kantian Perspective on Political Violence', *Journal of Ethics*, 1(2): 105–40.

Hughes-Wilson, J. (2004), *Military Intelligence Blunders and Cover-ups* (London: Robinson).

Huiskamp, G. (2004), 'Minority Report on the Bush Doctrine', *New Political Science*, 26(3): 389–415.

International Commission on Intervention and State Sovereignty (ICISS) (2001), *The Responsibility to Protect* (Ottawa: International Development Research Centre).

Kant, I. (2012 [1785]), *Fundamental Principles of the Metaphysics of Morals* (Mineola: Dover Publications).

Kelsay, J. (2007), *Arguing the Just War in Islam* (London: Harvard University Press).

Kennedy-Pipe, C. (2008), 'American Foreign Policy after 9/11', in M. Cox and D. Stokes (eds), *US Foreign Policy* (Oxford: Oxford University Press): 401–19.

Khatchadourian, H. (2005), 'Counter-Terrorism: Torture and Assassination', in G. Meggle (ed.), *Ethics of Terrorism & Counter-Terrorism* (Piscataway: Transaction Books): 177–96.

Kielsgard, M.D. (2012), 'National Self-defence in the Age of Terrorism: Immediacy and State Attribution', in A. Masferrer (ed.), *Post-9/11 and the State of Permanent Legal Emergency: Security and Human Rights in Countering Terrorism* (London: Springer): 315–44.

Korsgaard, C.M. (2012), 'Introduction', in: M. Gregor and J. Timmermann (eds.), *Kant: Groundwork of the Metaphysics of Morals* (Cambridge: Cambridge University Press): ix–xxxvi.

Luban, D. (2004), 'Preventive War', *Philosophy & Public Affairs*, 32(3): 207–48.

Luban, D. (2005), 'Liberalism, Torture, and the Ticking Bomb', *Virginia Law Review*, 91: 1425–61.

Mill, J.S. (2001 [1863]), *Utilitarianism* (Indianapolis: Hackett).

Nathanson, S. (2012), *Terrorism and the Ethics of War* (Cambridge: Cambridge University Press).

Opotow, S. (2007), 'Moral Exclusion and Torture: The Ticking-Bomb Scenario and the Slippery Ethical Slope', *Peace and Conflict: Journal of Peace Psychology*, 13(4): 457–61.

Roth, K. (2004), 'The Law of War in the War on Terror: Washington's Abuse of "Enemy Combatants"', *Foreign Affairs*, 83: 2–7.

Sands, P. (2005), *Lawless World: America and the Making and Breaking of Global Rules* (London: Allen Lane).

Schmid, A.P. and Jongman, A.J. (2005), *Political Terrorism: A New Guide to Actors, Authors, Concepts, Data Bases, Theories, and Literature* (New Brunswick: Transaction).

Serle, R. and A.K. Ross (2013), 'November 2013 Update: US covert actions in Pakistan, Yemen and Somalia', *The Bureau of Investigative Journalism*, 3 December 2013 [accessed 26 December 2013], available from: http://www.thebureauinvestigates.com/2013/12/03/november-2013-update-us-covert-actions-in-pakistan-yemen-and-somalia/

Seymour, G. (1999), *Harry's Game* (London: Corgi).

Singer, P.W. (2011), 'A World of Killer Apps', *Nature*, 477: 399–401.

Snauwaert, D.T. (2004), 'The Bush Doctrine and Just War Theory', *Online Journal of Peace and Conflict Resolution*, 6(1): 121–35.

Suskind, R. (2007), *The One Percent Doctrine: Deep Inside America's Pursuit of Its Enemies Since 9/11* (New York: Simon & Schuster Paperbacks).

United Nations (n.d.), 'Charter of the United Nations: Chapter VII: Action with Respect to Threats to the Peace, Breaches of the Peace and Acts of Aggression' [accessed 26 December 2013], available from: http://www.un.org/en/documents/charter/chapter7.shtml

Walzer, M. (2004), *Arguing About War* (New Haven: Yale University Press).

Walzer, M. (2006), *Just and Unjust Wars* (New York: Basic Books).

White House (2002), *The National Security Strategy of the United States of America* (Washington, D.C.: The White House).

Wills, G. (2004), 'What is a Just War?', *New York Review of Books*, 51(18).

Yoo, J. (2006), *War by Other Means: An Insider's Account of the War on Terror* (New York: Atlantic Monthly Press).

3

A HISTORY OF TERRORISM: IDEOLOGY, TACTICS AND ORGANIZATION

POLA ZAFRA-DAVIS

Introduction

Since the events of 9/11 there has been increasing public attention paid to the connectivity of terrorists across borders, where movements such as jihadism and al-Qaeda have been presented as a new, mysterious, and global threat. What is absent from these news snippets is the reality that forms of terrorism have been a force since the Middle Ages, with the Ismailis and Nizari religious sects struggling against Saladin's Empire, and during the French Revolution, where the term was coined. More recently, before there was a network of jihadists there were networks of anarchists, nationalists, and Marxists using terrorist tactics in almost every region of the world (Tucker, 2001). Despite these early instances of terror, terrorism continues to be interpreted by scholars as a modern phenomenon.

This chapter provides a historical background to terrorism, exploring how international campaigns of terrorism have transformed in terms of ideology, tactics, and organizational structure. The first section outlines Rapoport's theory of Waves of Terrorism, which provides an historical overview of terrorism campaigns and how these have evolved in terms of their features, such as ideology and tactics. The second section explores the New Terrorism debate, which emphasizes a greater distinction between terrorism campaigns from the 1990s onwards, epitomized by al-Qaeda, and terrorism campaigns that preceded it. The chapter outlines the critiques of the New Terrorism debate, showing where there is greater continuity between types of terrorism, as illustrated by the Waves of Terrorism theory. From this chapter students will gain valuable insight into the history of terrorism and the different types of campaign. Crucially, the chapter outlines the cyclical and interconnected nature of terrorism that underpins the contributions in the rest of the book.

TEXTBOX 2   TERRORISM IN HISTORY

One of the first terror groups that we have written reports of are the Zealots in first-century Palestine. Flavius Josephus wrote about the group in *Antiquities of the Jews*, published in 93–4 C.E., denoting them as *sicarii*, or an old variation of the Latin word for 'dagger men' (Chaliland and Blin, 2007). Their political cause was the Jewish rebellion against Rome, which started when the Romans instituted a census throughout the empire, humiliating Jewish inhabitants who resented their apparent submission to a foreign power. The Zealots launched their first attack against Roman imperial authorities in the sixth century. This was the pinnacle of Jewish fervor in the fight for self-determination after Herod the Great passed away, and was characterized by spontaneous eruptions of insurrections throughout Palestine. The Zealots were one of four philosophical sects in Judea, and their character was both religious and political; their religious aims could not be separated from their political aims. They imposed a degree of rigor in political practice and wanted independence from Rome. Their armed struggle included guerrilla warfare, such as urban fighting, as well as psychological tactics to keep the populace on their side.

The Assassins (otherwise known as the Ismailis) were also a pre-modern terror organization, claiming to represent Islam. They were based in what is now present-day Syria and Iran. The Assassins' first instance of an attack was in 1092, with the assassination of Nizam al-Mulk, a dignitary who wrote the basic handbook for political leaders of the Iranian, Ottoman and Mongol empires. One of their later targets was the Crusaders. The Assassins were active from the eleventh to the thirteenth century. Earlier uses of terror as politics can be found in the state-sponsored terrorism of the Mongols within their own empire, or 'terrorism as war' as experienced in the Thirty Years War (Chaliland and Blin, 2007). The first instance of the use of the word terrorism was during the Reign of Terror, following the French Revolution, in 1793. One of the twelve leaders of the new state, Maximillian Robespierre, justified the execution of enemies of the revolution, hailing France's transition from a monarchy to a liberal democracy:

'Subdue by terror the enemies of liberty, and you will be right, as founders of the Republic.' In 1798 the Academie Francaise defined terrorism for the first time as a 'system or rule of terror'. Essentially these acts of political violence advocated the use of violence to help usher in a better system. (Robespierre, 1794)

Waves of terrorism, ideology and the organization of terrorism

Defining a wave of terrorism

In the early 2000s Rapoport identified four distinct waves of terrorism in his historical analysis of the phenomenon (Rapoport, 2002). Waves are cycles of activity situated in different time periods and have both expansion and contraction phases. For David Rapoport these are linked to the lifeline of most terrorist organizations. Waves are abstract and a way to structure, classify, and group different terrorist events and organizations around distinct, separable ideologies. A defining feature of a wave is that it is international in character. Similar activities would occur in several countries in a specific time period, all with a predominating 'energy' that shapes the groups' characteristics and relationships with each other (Rapoport, 2004). Some groups can last longer than the wave, known as stragglers, although they may experience a decline or need to adapt to the newly emerging wave; for example, the Palestine Liberation Organization outlasted the decline of the Anti-colonial Wave and began to use the Islamist discourse of the Religious Wave to maintain support.

Each wave has special characteristics that shape their era-specific organizations differently. Waves can be distinguished and tracked through changes in four themes: socio-cultural change, tactics, ideology, and the organizational structure of groups. Looking at different types of terrorism in waves enables scholars to track the general ideological trends inside terrorism of the past 130 years (Transnational Terrorism, Security and the Rule of Law, 2002). The waves that Rapoport has identified include: the Anarchist Wave that started in the 1880s and lasted until the 1920s; the Anti-colonial Wave of the 1920s–60s; the New Left Wave, which faded in the 1990s; and the Religious Wave from the 1970s onward (Rasler and Thompson, 2009). Waves can coincide and overlap and be located in different regions. Furthermore, waves can gain their energy by inspiring groups to copy each other within a wave – for example, the IRA copied much of the anti-colonial language used by other groups in the Nationalist Wave – and there can be connections between waves. The first wave was dependent on two critical factors. The first was a transformation in communication and transportation. The second was doctrine and culture. Both were necessary to create wave-defining tactics. Each wave perpetuates factors that lead to successive waves. The brevity of each wave seems to suggest that waves have their own momentum and lose steam once disillusionment sets in amongst followers and fails to inspire the next generation to continue the struggle.

Doctrines create a strategy of terror that successors try to improve upon. Rapoport has noted that the anarchist doctrine, Nechayev's (1869) *The Revolutionary Catechism*, could be compared to Osama bin Laden's (1998) training manual, *Military Studies in the Jihad against the Tyrants*. Both works sought to become more efficient by learning from the experiences of their allies and enemies. Each wave has produced works on the 'science' of terrorism. Generally, the overwhelming doctrine in each wave is driven by a unique conception of revolution. Revolutionaries were used to create a sense not only of legitimacy but also of national self-determination or rule by the people, which can be traced back to the French Revolution. Revolution in other instances can mean the destruction of an authority in eliminating all forms of inequality. This was seen in the first and third waves, while fourth-wave groups gather their legitimacy from sacred religious texts. The following sections will outline Rapoport's four waves of terrorism further.

The Anarchist Wave

Anarchist groups in the first wave of terrorism included the Armenian Hunchaks and the Serbian Black Hand. Notable acts of terror by anarchist groups between 1881 and 1921 included the high-profile assassinations of Russian Czar Alexander in 1881, the French president in 1884, the king of Italy in 1900, US President McKinley in 1901, and the 1914 assassination of the Archduke of Austria–Hungary and heir to the throne, partly sparking World War I.

There were two substantial socio-cultural changes that led to the emergence of the Anarchist Wave of terrorism. The Russian Emancipation Reform of 1861 was the socio-cultural change which emboldened citizens to commit the first modern tactic of terrorism: public assassinations. Unlike later waves forming around international events, the catalyzing event was a domestic political situation. The reforms created mass dissatisfaction and exposed the vulnerability of the Russian state. The systematic execution of prominent officials by Russian anarchist groups began. The second socio-cultural change was technology, which enabled people to communicate more quickly and to broader audiences. While the concept of 'revolution' was endemic in violent political acts before the first wave (i.e. the French Revolution and its Reign of Terror), how revolution reached the minds of the people had changed. The transformation in communication came with the advent of the telegraph, mass newspapers, and railroads. The development of dynamite and the revolver helped to privatize the means of violence. Political events, which are used to form and justify doctrines, can occur in one country and more readily be known in others. This could also be interpreted as a process of globalization. Like-minded individuals from separate countries can meet and exchange ideas or be influenced by one another. When one of these individuals is mobile the newly formed idea/doctrine can hold an audience beyond the ideas' origins, and this is called diffusion. Transport also created mass emigrations and diaspora communities. Those in the communities who held revolutionary ideals, grievances, or ideology now had a greater geographic reach. These extracted communities would soon become important in the politics of both their homeland and their new adopted country.

The predominant ideology or doctrine during the first wave was the anarchist doctrine. Anarchists saw societal conventions as stifling and society filled with 'huge reservoirs of latent ambivalence and hostility'. Anarchists believed these conventions were historical creations, and that acts currently judged as immoral would be seen as the liberation of humanity by later generations. Terror was the quickest and most effective means to destroy conventions so that their children could achieve this liberation in heroic efforts through a tactic known as 'propaganda of the deed'. The society anarchists referred to did not mean a global society. Rather, it was the society the anarchist-thinker occupied at the time. During the first wave, while the resources and means were arguably globalized, the grievances remained local.

Anarchist revolutionaries in the early nineteenth century, like Mikhail Bakunin, were able to spread their ideals through pamphlets and leaflets during their travels. However, as much as globalization, communication and technology enabled the spread of ideas, the first modern terrorist groups such as Narodnaya Volya still saw these 'traditional revolutionaries' as obsolete. Rapoport claims that the first

Anarchist Wave of terrorism was started by the Russian group *Narodnaya Volya*, or 'The People's Will'. Their move towards terror stemmed from a dissatisfaction that pamphlets, books, and meetings were no longer effective in reaching their political goals. Repeated acts of terror became the way in which they could polarize society, which they saw as necessary for revolution. The main tactic employed by anarchist groups was the assassination of authority figures. During the 1890s a 'Golden Age of Assassinations' took place. Prime ministers, monarchs, and presidents were killed by assassins who crossed international borders (Rapoport, 2004: 52). Terror could be considered a subversive way to use violence where violence had been regulated (war and punishment/crime). Russian rebels, by the nature of their shocking acts, explicitly referred to themselves as terrorists rather than guerrillas. This was because the term terrorism had not been constructed as a pejorative term at this point. Their targets were intentionally political in order to provoke a change in public attitudes. Supporters were mobilized through a hope for change by exploiting unexpected public-event crises in the process (as in the 1861 reform, discussed above).

During this first wave of terrorism the organizational structure of global terrorism was very loose and in its infancy. Because of the globalizing socio-cultural changes mentioned above, terror tactics spread. Russian rebels travelled and trained other groups of political dissidents, even where these groups had a different ideology from their own. The structure of terror groups influenced by Russian rebels can be subdivided into two categories: those committed to the tactic versus those committed to the cause. The former includes political groups that were reliant on assassinations and bank robberies. These groups, while trained by Russian rebels, did not hold the same anarchist doctrine which characterized the majority of the groups in this wave. Such groups were found in the Balkans as dissatisfaction spread over the new boundaries after the collapse of the Ottoman Empire. The latter group, which was devoted to the cause, stemmed from Russian anarchists who fled to the West and reconvened with Russian diaspora communities and other anti-Czarist elements. The influence was felt as far as India. To highlight the internationalization of terror, the Terrorist Brigade of 1905 had its headquarters in Switzerland, launched attacks from Finland, and offered financing from the Japanese to be laundered through US millionaires. Contrast this with previous pre-modern terror groups, such as the Zealots, who stayed within their own religious traditions and locality.

The Anti-colonial (Nationalist) Wave

The end of the Anarchist Wave came after World War I. The period between the two wars encouraged both reform and revolution. These were realized among the dominant governing bodies in states, outside the strategy and tactics of anarchist groups. Hence, the incentives for anarchist terrorism decreased. The second wave of global terror, the Anti-colonial (or Nationalist) Wave, was sparked by the Versailles Treaty in 1919 at the end of World War I. The Versailles Treaty also provided for the constitution of the League of Nations, which would execute the terms of a series of decolonizations. Essentially, this new wave was a reaction to empires being broken up and territories becoming 'mandates', soon to be independent.

Generally, the post-World War I treaties had the losing side dissolve imperial (such as Austria–Hungary) and colonial structures, with all colonial territories given self-determination under temporary mandates. This was not the case for the victors, who were able to retain their colonial holdings and empires until they decided to dissolve them twenty years later.

Yet self-determination as an ideal still existed in the remaining imperial holdings of the victors. Thus the socio-cultural change following Versailles was the delegitimization of empire. The victors of the treaty ran into their own problems of legitimacy inside colonial territories. Rebels of the second wave of terrorism found supporters and causes in territories where withdrawal was more problematic. These groups fed on the conflicting aspirations of the imperial power and its inhabitants. Wars sprung up during this Anti-colonial Wave, mostly in UK or French territories in the developing world. In the UK case, wars sprung up in the Malay Republic, Ireland, Palestine, and Kenya while France experienced terrorist-driven wars in Algeria and Indochina. The anti-colonial movements of the 1920s overlapped with and inspired a number of nationalist organizations that emerged in this period and in the 1960s, such as ETA, the Provisional IRA, and the Palestine Liberation Organization.

Tactics during this time were predominantly hit-and-run guerrilla-like actions against troops and beyond the rules of war, with concealed weapons and no identifying insignia. In contrast to the Anarchist Wave, the Anti-colonial Wave thought the assassination of senior figures counterproductive. The practice of robbing banks became less prevalent, as groups started to receive more funding from diaspora communities. The targets in the second wave were the police, or the government's 'eyes and ears', knowing that military units would replace them. The military replacements were proven to be too clumsy to cope with guerrilla tactics. As the term terrorist, associated with the Anarchist Wave, began to be understood pejoratively, the Anti-colonial Wave began to describe themselves as freedom fighters.

The prevailing ideology in the Anti-colonial Wave was nationalism and self-determination, which became the main political cause. The principle of self-determination is the right, under international law, for nations to seek equality of rights, opportunities and international political status through sovereignty without external interference. Sovereignty is both the power to have independent authority over a geographic area, and equality under law of other sovereign bodies. Terrorist groups in the second wave supported the idea of 'nations' to identify themselves and become self-governing territories. The problem in many cases was that these territories were already inside defined states. Nationalism, as an ideology, proclaims that an individual's loyalty to their nation surpasses all other individual and group loyalties. This carries over to the ideological belief in the second wave that all nations have the right to form a state. Terrorism was the vehicle to realize these state aspirations of nations/ethnicities. These nations/ethnicities felt they were being oppressed and sought self-determination as a solution. To such nationalist groups in the second wave, the anti-colonial struggle was seen as more outwardly legitimate than the anarchist struggle. Consequently, groups of the second wave attempted to gain the support of the UN, the successor to the League of Nations, which had the principle of self-determination in its founding articles.

The organizational structure of anti-colonial groups was more localized and self-contained than in the previous wave. The groups were not reliant on a single locus point from which to receive training, as Russian rebels had been the locus point in the past. They also used four international assets derived from the first wave in different and progressive ways. The four international assets were international ideals of revolution, diaspora communities, foreign states with kindred populations, and third-party states. Despite a commitment to an international ethos of revolution, heroes of second-wave groups were overwhelmingly national heroes. The rationale was that the strengthening of ties with foreign terrorists would lessen the effectiveness of the other international assets. Diaspora communities were able to use leverage to persuade their home countries to take their side in conflicts. One example was the Irish-American community influencing the US government to support an independent Irish state. During the Algerian uprisings against France, Arab states gave their support to the Algerian Liberation Front, including providing sanctuary. Second-wave groups also exploited a new fifth international asset: international organizations. The organization of choice was the League of Nations and its successor, the UN. Both were responsible for mandates and the decolonization process, with its state members almost always being colonial powers. Second-wave groups presented themselves as freedom fighters to these organizations. The anti-colonial sentiment in the League of Nations and the UN gave second-wave groups opportunities, focus, and a structure of rules to exploit. The Anti-colonial Wave ended with the achievement of independence, specifically in the 1960s when the old European powers began to officially end the colonial system. However, some campaigns in the Anti-colonial Wave ended with unsatisfactory compromises which would lead to new campaigns emerging; for example, the IRA's campaign in the 1920s may have led to an independent Ireland, but the north, with a Catholic minority, would still remain a part of the UK.

The New Left Wave

The New Left Wave – the third wave – was spurred by the psychological repercussions of the Vietnam War. The success of the VietCong against the US military rekindled hopes about the vulnerability of the West. The primitive weapons used by the VietCong triumphed over the US's modern technology. This demonstrated that a contemporary system of highly developed states, dominating and intervening in the developing world, was vulnerable. Groups sprung up in the developed world and included the West German Red Army Faction (RAF), Italian Red Brigades, American Weather Underground, Japanese Red Army and the French Action directe. The third wave of terrorism mixed aspects of the first wave's blending of nationalism and radicalism with the second wave's emphasis on self-determination. Although the first wave's nationalist groups failed, this was blended with ethnic concerns during the New Left Wave, expanding its appeal beyond mere radicalism. The second wave's anti-colonial groups failed to root in the New Left

Wave, despite the durability of nationalist groups. This was because the importance of self-determination during the second wave obscured radicalism and nationalism – and France, Spain and the UK did not consider themselves colonial powers. This non-colonial recognition took away the feelings of ambivalence necessary for nationalism to be successful. The socio-political environment of the New Left Wave was the triumph of counter-status-quo systems in international politics. This emboldened radical ethnic-nationalist groups on the home front of developed countries.

Tactics such as hostage taking were carried out by small guerrilla groups inflicting damage on smaller targets. The hostage crisis became a third-wave characteristic. Kidnappings occurred in seventy-three countries, most of them in Spain, Italy, and Latin America. Hostages gained political leverage for their captors. But as companies began to insure their higher executives, hostage-taking also became a lucrative business. Kidnappers found that when money and not politics was the issue it was easier to leverage the hostage negotiation on their terms. The New Left also went back to the previously abandoned practice of assassinating prominent figures. The IRA targeted and killed the UK ambassador to Ireland in 1976 and Lord Mountbatten in 1979. The Palestinian Black September assassinated the Jordanian prime minister in 1971 and attempted to assassinate King Hussein in 1974. The difference between these and first-wave assassinations was their motivations. While in the first wave the target was selected primarily because of their public office, the New Left Wave assassinations acted as 'punishments', or retaliatory strikes. The attempt to assassinate Margaret Thatcher in 1984 was motivated by her 'responsibility' for the death of nine IRA hunger strikers, who did not wish to be treated as ordinary criminals. The assassination of Jordan's Prime Minister in 1971 by the Palestinian Black September was retaliation for pushing the PLO out of their country in battle (Rapoport, 2004).

Third-wave groups saw themselves as vanguards for the masses in the third world. They were also embroiled in proxy wars alongside the USSR, financing many militant groups that emerged from the third world, particularly Latin America. The tactics moved from the countryside into the city where the tactics would be more noticeable. The pivotal pamphlet produced in Latin America was the *The Minimanual of the Urban Guerrilla* by Carlos Marighella (1969). Radicalization became paired with nationalism, such as in the IRA and the Basque Country and Freedom (ETA). This was similar to the first wave when the anarchists allied themselves to national aspirations in India, Armenia, and Macedonia. The notion was that self-determination has a broader appeal than radical aspirations.

The end of the New Left Wave occurred with the high price of negotiating conflicting demands. These demands were split between international elements, or allied foreign groups, and the domestic supporters they represented. This resulted in the neglect of the latter. The PLO was especially conflicted since it had internal divisions about how to reclaim Palestinian territories. The PLO was established in Jordan in May 1964 following the Arab League Cairo Summit, proclaiming the creation of an organization that would represent the Palestinian people. Structurally, it is a confederated structure of political groups with foreign allegiences, such as the

Popular Front for the Liberation of Palestine–General Command and Syria, the Democratic Front for the Liberation of Palestine and Jordan, the Popular Front for the Liberation of Palestine, Fatah in Lebanon, etc. (Katzman, 2002). Outside interests complicated matters further with the entanglement of Arab states. Such was the cost of being part of proxy wars between the USA and Arab states during the 1950s through the 1970s. The New Left Wave began to ebb in the 1980s when revolutionary terrorists were defeated in several countries. This started with Israel's invasion of Lebanon in 1982 and increased as counterterrorist cooperation evolved between states, particularly through the UN. The wave ended around the time of the Soviet Union's collapse.

TEXTBOX 3   EUSKADI TA ASKATASUNA (ETA): 'BASQUE COUNTRY AND FREEDOM'

Year formed: 1958

ETA was created by university students who began meeting in 1952 to discuss Basque politics and promote the use of Euskera (the Basque language). The publication of the underground journal *Ekin* ('to do', also the group's initial name) increased support for the group before recruitment of students from Deusto University in Vizcaya began. Their first assembly was held in 1962 in Bayonne (France), where activist cells were established alongside a declaration of principles. They are the only remaining terrorist organization in Western Europe that emerged in the wave of political violence of the late 1960/70s. Their first assassination killed police chief Melitón Manzanas in 1968.

Aim

ETA's nationalist ideology centres on achieving a separate, independent nation state for the Basque people. The Basque country spans the border of northern Spain and southern France and is inhabited by 2.1 million people who have practiced their own language and culture since before the sixteenth century (exact origins are unknown).

Ideological framework

By 1960 ETA had agreed to pursue an ideology of armed struggle for Basque independence as well as a largely socialist agenda that would empower the working class. They initially aimed to avoid civilian casualties, targeting government officials, but are estimated to have killed approximately 800 people in over 1,500 attacks. 1973 saw the organization's most emblematic attack: the assassination of Admiral Luis Carrero Blanco on 20 December.

(Continued)

(Continued)

Despite renewed support from the Basque people, the attack contributed to the direct split within the organization a year later into ETAm (militar) and ETApm (político-militar), the latter disbanding in 1982. Batasuna (originally Herri Batasuna) was the unofficial political wing of ETA (banned by the Spanish Supreme Court in 2003) and is currently listed as a terrorist organization by the European Union.

To some extent they have been successful in their objectives, though under the fascist Franco regime Basque nationalism was heavily suppressed. Since 1979 the democratic government has offered greater autonomy to Basque provinces.

Organizational structure and tactics

ETA is strongly hierarchical, operating through a three-tiered structure: *top*: executive committee (ten people, based in France); *centre*: operational committee (approximately four to six members, based in Spain); *base*: commandos/cells (approximately three to five members) working in isolation from the larger groups.

Two types of membership exist within the organization – legales and ilegales. Those that physically carry out attacks receive a salary from ETA.

Other roles include those involved in the communication network, and those that provide administrative support: transport, false papers, and shelter. These actors are known to involve civilian Basques.

ETA pursue both extortionist tactics (for example, bombing public areas, though this is not their primary technique) similar to those used by other terrorist organizations such as the IRA, and violence to demand negotiations with the Spanish government, with the final intention of gaining full independence. Some academic interpretations refer to a method adopted by ETA dubbed 'action-repression-action' spiral theory (no longer exercised). In accordance with the theory ETA would provoke the Spanish government into repressive acts in response to their terrorist attacks. For every police reaction ETA would commit an even more provocative act, encouraging the government to act with greater force. The eventual escalation of violence would see the public rise in rebellion. It never came to significant fruition during the years it was practiced.

The Religious Wave

Rapoport's fourth wave is called the Religious Wave. At the heart of the wave is a radicalized version of Islam with Islamist groups conducting the majority of attacks. This wave is also characterized by the aim of mass casualties. Much of the attention of the Religious Wave has focused on Islam; however, the emphasis should be placed on religious elements in general as terrorism is multi-confessional. Although some may refer to the wave as Jihadi, there are also Christian groups that operate in this wave as well. During the 1990s there was a tenuous link between Christian Identity and the Oklahoma City bombing of 1995. This is linked to the rise of racist interpretations of the Bible during the American 'Christian Identity' movement, where armed rural communes isolated themselves inside the USA to await an end-times racial war. Another religious-based group, Aum Shinrikyo, combined Christian, Buddhist, and Hindu elements. The group launched nerve-gas attacks on the Tokyo subway in 1995, which killed 12 and injured 3,000, causing a mass panic about bioterrorism. While religion had featured in previous waves of terrorism, what distinguishes groups in the fourth wave from previous groups with a religious element was that religion overlapped with ethnicity and the end political goal was the creation of secular states.

However, the Religious Wave would be typified by Islamist terrorism, as it was Islamist groups conducting the most internationally high-profile and deadly attacks, later inspiring other religious-based groups (Rapoport, 2004). The spark that created the Jihadi or Islamist elements of the Religious Wave centered around three events. The events were the Iranian Revolution in 1979, the period of Islamic revivalism following the new Islamic century, and the unsuccessful Soviet invasion of Afghanistan. The Iranian Revolution showed that religion had more political appeal than the earlier New Left ethos, since the Iranian Marxists only mustered meager support for the Shah, the Western-backed Iranian ruler (Rapoport, 2004: 62). As unexpected as the Iranian Revolution was, many Muslims believed that the year marked a new Islamic century owing to the disintegration of the secular state. There was hope that a redeemer would come who would usher in the new century. Around this time Sunni terrorism erupted in Egypt, Tunisia, Morocco, Algeria, the Philippines, and Indonesia. The failed Soviet invasion of Afghanistan gave more hope to terrorist groups that they had a chance of success against superpowers and what they saw as corrupt Muslim rulers.

The most deadly tactical innovation associated with the Religious Wave has been the suicide bomb. However, this tactic did not necessarily entail a religious motivation, since the secular Tamil Tigers of Sri Lanka soon adopted this tactic after seeing its success in strikes in Lebanon. To enhance political leverage at home Palestinian Islamist groups also began using suicide bombers, and the tactic was later adopted by the PLO.

There are two aspects to Islamist groups in the Religious Wave. Some Islamist groups tend to fuse nationalism or state identities, such as Hamas or Hezbollah, with their goals being limited to Islamicizing the country they operate within and fighting against the Israeli occupation. A subset of Islamist groups are the jihadists. Ideologically, the main political aim for most jihadist terrorist groups is the creation of a single state under Sharia law. Most al-Qaeda recruits come from the Sunni world, with most volunteers hailing from Egypt, Saudi Arabia, and Algeria. Previously, recruits were drawn from a single national base, like the PLO training other organizations. However, al-Qaeda predominantly recruits individuals through social networks. This signals a change in recruitment styles, which may be linked to the advent of the internet and cyberspace in which jihadist messages are received by geographically dispersed individuals. The practical aim was American withdrawal from the Middle East. US troops in the 1990s were driven out of Lebanon and Somalia by Islamist groups, which gave confidence to jihadists. There were also attacks on military posts in Yemen and Saudi Arabia, and the destruction of the USS Cole in 2000. Al-Qaeda was responsible for the 9/11 attacks, the first major attack on the US mainland, resulting in almost 3,000 deaths and prompting US President Bush to announce the war on terror.

The announcement of the war on terror led the USA and its allies to invade Afghanistan and Iraq, coinciding with an upsurge in terrorist attacks by jihadist groups throughout the 2000s. A decline in jihadist attacks, their localization in certain countries, and their initial marginalization during the Arab Spring suggested that the Religious Wave was declining. However, the eruption of conflicts in countries such as Syria, where jihadists have sought to carve out a central role, suggests that the decline of waves of terrorism is not necessarily inevitable.

While Rapoport's Waves of Terrorism theory has been a useful means by which to frame the historical development of terrorism, there have been a number of critiques or debates which have either emerged from Waves of Terrorism or overlapped in terms of content. One such debate is Old Terrorism versus New Terrorism, whose proponents argue that the Religious Wave of terrorism is so different from the other waves that it requires new ways of analyzing it and new ways of countering it. Those who challenge the notion of New Terrorism often build on Rapoport's theory to show the continuity over the decades between terrorism campaigns in terms of tactics, ideology, and organizational structure. The next section outlines the New Terrorism argument.

New Terrorism

Within the context of terrorism in general, the current political and media discourse emphasizes that mid-1990s religious terrorism was a new form of terrorism emerging after the end of the Cold War. The proponents of the New Terrorism perspective argued that the terrorism of the 1990s was uniquely different from terrorism in the past in terms of ideology, tactics, and organizational structure.

A new era

The term New Terrorism has been popular since the late 1990s and reached its peak following the 11 September 2001 attacks on the US World Trade Center and the Pentagon. The start of New Terrorism is unclear. Thomas Copeland proposes that the inaugural events of New Terrorism were the 1993 World Trade Center bombings and the 1995 Sarin gas attack on the Tokyo subway (Copeland, 2001). One school of thought was that the characteristics of New Terrorism, and thus New Terrorism's start, were the product of the end of the Cold War. Stephen Sloan states that the end of the Cold War and the demise of communist governments worldwide unmasked dormant ethnic and religious conflicts (cited in Copeland, 2001). The disappearance of Marxism as a viable political ideology changed the once-secular-ideological motivations of many leftist groups.

The end of the two-power system ended the practice of superpowers using regional surrogates as proxies for their political aims and thus one form of state-sponsored terrorism. The end of the Cold War signaled the emergence of regional powers, such as Iran. These new powers had different political motivations due to their location in the world/regional power system, and thus for their use of terrorism as a diplomatic tool, either by financing groups that held (often ethnic) grievances against their opponents or by providing safe havens. Sponsors changed, not only in the type of state that financed terror, but also in the type of financier to non-state actors. The decline in the legitimacy, power, and authority of the nation-state in developing countries has led violent non-state actors to step in to fill the void left by the breakdown in central authority. These new non-state financiers often include drug traffickers, such as the case of Tamil Tigers operating in Western Europe and the USA, Shining Path's connections with Peruvian drug traffickers, and FARC and M19's alliance with Colombian drug cartels.

Globalization is identified as another contributing factor to New Terrorism. While there are many facets that cannot be explored here, globalization is generally seen as the increasing international integration of economic and political institutions, culture and ideas (Holm and Sorenson, 1995). The perception that globalization was a force to assert US and Western dominance, coupled with the erosion of the nation-state, may be seen as creating grievances that led to the emergence of New Terrorism, which sought to cultivate a global counter-movement. While terrorist groups (e.g. the PLO) in the past have been as 'global' as New Terrorist groups like al-Qaeda, one supposed feature of globalization is how greater interconnectedness can lead to self-radicalization. A technological innovation associated with this period of globalization, the internet, has facilitated changes in the organizational structure of terrorist groups and their recruitment. The chapter below explores the main aspects that lead scholars to claim that there is a New Terrorism, emergent from either changes in the international system and/or processes of globalization.

New ideologies and tactics

Advocates of the New Terrorism thesis identify the Old Terrorism as being tied ideologically to left-wing and ethno-nationalist sentiments, particularly revolutionary Marxism and nationalism. It was also commonly believed that old-style terrorism had limited and more well-defined political aims. This leads to one of Old Terrorism's tendencies to use carefully calibrated violence or specific targeting (Stern, 1999). Some of the limited tactics of Old Terrorism included airline hijackings, assassinations, and kidnappings, as well as the targeting of symbolic political targets. Benjamin and Simon (2002) have stated that groups would be reluctant to use excessive force that could cause mass casualties. Reasons for the relatively limited use of violence include fear that the use of excessive force would both deny the groups a place at the political bargaining table with a targeted state and alienate potential supporters. The Old Terror groups also relied on the changed attitudes of an audience to attract converts to their worldview and achieve their goals (Roy et al., 2000).

This is contrasted with the New Terrorism, which, ideologically, is seen to be other-worldly insofar as its claims to legitimacy and goals are often based on religion and spirituality. The New Terrorism thesis also emphasizes the emergence of right-wing terrorism and single-issue groups like ecologists or animal-rights groups (Hoffman, 2013). Unlike targeted, 'rational', and secular political killings that were manifest in Old Terrorism, New Terrorism is presented as something unique in its religious motivations and willingness to partake in indiscriminate mass-casualty killings, such as suicide bombings, because of being freed of the need to possess legitimacy from a community. Therefore, a key argument of the New Terrorism perspective is that it is more lethal than terrorism in the past because of its ideological differences. Connected to the emphasis on mass-casualty killings, proponents of the New Terrorism also highlight the increased incentive to acquire and use chemical, biological, nuclear, and radiological weapons (CBNRWs) or weapons of mass destruction (WMDs). Therefore, the New Terrorism proponents argue that the difference in ideology has led groups to engage in mass-casualty attacks on the basis of achieving broader goals.

However, while it is recognized that a terrorist attack with nuclear weapons is possible, Martin argues that the probability is low, and that inflating New Terrorism's access to WMDs can be at the detriment of policies aimed at countering more likely threats (Martin, 2010). Furthermore, while groups associated with New Terrorism, such as al-Qaeda, may be different from the 1980s leftist groups, Spencer argues that many groups in the past, such as the Ulster Volunteer Force, have also been influenced by religion (Spencer, 2010). Ideologically, Islamist groups can also be traced back to the early twentieth century, and the argument that the New Terrorism ideologies lead to excessive violence is disputed. Firstly, suicide bombings have also been used by nationalist groups such as the Tamil Tigers from 1983 onwards, and the Provisional IRA used proxy suicide bombers. Secondly, there are numerous examples of high-casualty terrorism attacks in the so-called Old Terrorism (e.g. the Lockerbie bombing), and the supposed increase in casualties could also be attributed to improvements in technology and the tightening of security that has encouraged attacks on softer targets (Spencer, 2010). Nevertheless, it is contested whether New Terrorism causes more fatalities than terrorism in the 1970s and 1980s, with conflicts in Iraq and Syria – motivated by many reasons not associated with the New Terrorism – playing a contributing factor to any spike in fatalities.

Organizational structure: from hierarchy to networks

In terms of training, organization, and finance, what distinguishes Old Terrorism during most of the twentieth century – according to the Old versus New Terrorism argument – was the level of professionalism, organizational discipline, and a comparably advanced organization, like a state, to finance terrorism activities. The profile of many terrorists in this period was not poor or uneducated, leading experts to believe that 'terrorism was largely a bourgeois endeavor'. This socio-economic educated status was true for Russian anarchists of the late nineteenth century as well as German Marxists of the Baader-Meinhof gang of the 1970s, and the 1990s

Japanese terror cult Aum Shinrikyo (Crenshaw, 2009). Old Terrorists, owing to the emphasis on the actual group or ideology rather than the individual, saw their political cause as a lifelong calling. The typical terrorist from the old school would thus be, by and large, professionally trained and constantly involved in conspiracies and the planning of future attacks (Crenshaw, 2009).

It was believed that the high level of training and planning involved in targeted and measured attacks that were a hallmark of Old Terrorism was executed via well-defined control and command structures. These were inspired by revolutionary theory or ideology and are described as hierarchical and cellular structures (*The New York Times*, 2000). Hierarchical organizations feature a vertical chain of command, control and responsibility. This well-defined vertical chain enables the close monitoring of data and information flows through the appropriate channels corresponding to each link on the chain. Vertical hierarchies enable greater coordination and specialization of functions in subordinate cells such as support, intelligence, and operations (US Army Training and Doctrine Command, 2007).

Proponents of the New Terrorism thesis emphasize that the New Terrorists have deviated from a hierarchical structure to a more flexibly networked organization, with autonomous units that can function without directions from above. The motivation of tasks and attacks are self-inspired rather than directed, as networks are informal communities of individuals that share common values and beliefs. New Terror groups are also composed of part-timers, sometimes with high technological and operational competence thanks to the information-technology revolution. This allows New Terrorists to operate without state sponsorship if necessary.

The problem of the application of network analysis in terrorism studies is the assumption that networks are 'deadlier' forms of organization – or that a networked form is a new characteristic for terror groups and that understanding a network is dependent on the parallel forward march of technology and new world politics. As autonomous units, members can sense and respond independently to any new counter-terror situation, thus increasing adaptability. However, the networked structure does have its pitfalls. Autonomous units diminish control and coordination, making it difficult to accomplish complex tasks. It also increases the likelihood of ill-judged actions undermining the entire network (Tucker, 2001). When added to a multitude of funding, outreach, and training sources, and control over the number, the increasing multitude of communication types taking place over the network leads to diminished control over communications. Networks thus increase the chances of discovery and entry opportunities into cells from external enemies that can exploit the diversified communication channels. The assumed leaderless nature of networks and their cells are also seen as adaptation to a terrorist organization under duress. Leaderless resistance becomes necessary as a response to increasingly effective counterterror measures against the 'patriots' or professionals that used to occupy the seats of hierarchies (Tucker, 2001).

However, a network is not the sole means of organization, nor does it have to stand alone, and this is one of the main criticisms against the argument that New Terrorism is defined by new forms of organization. Most networks can and are overlaid on traditional hierarchical command structures, while the most highly structured terrorist groups are described as being networked with concentric circles of supporters and sympathizers (Tucker, 2001). Anarchist terrorism was conducted by similarly loose networks across Europe, and groups such as the PLO and the Provisional IRA have consisted of a mix of hierarchical and network structures (Spencer, 2010). Finally, it may be that networks themselves are not new but that the analysis of networks is, and the use of this framework can provide valuable insights into terrorist activity over a broad range of cases.

More recently the New Terrorism debate has tended to fade away in its significance, with some of its proponents even conceding that there is greater overlap between the epochs, as demonstrated by the Waves of Terrorism theory. However, Waves of Terrorism has been critiqued for being too vague in explaining what drives waves – usually describing it as 'energy' – and its broad sweeps have led to claims that it is interesting rather than useful in explaining terrorism. Furthermore, it tends to homogenize ideologies, thus either underplaying the nuances in groups which may pay lip-service to being in alliance with one another (when in reality there is little real connection), or underplaying groups that are mixes of waves, both religious and nationalist, for example. Nevertheless, empirical data tends to suggest there is some accuracy in Waves of Terrorism as a theory, especially in explaining how ideas spread (Nacos, 2009) or how terrorism declines through a fall in support between generations (Sageman, 2010).

Conclusion

This chapter has provided a broad historical overview of terrorism internationally over the centuries, demonstrating how terrorism has transformed in terms of ideology, tactics, and organizational structure. It outlined the New Terrorism debate, which contends that terrorism from the 1990s onwards, symbolized by al-Qaeda, has exhibited substantial differences from previous forms of terrorism. While there are a number of perspectives, the emphasis on the newness of terrorism can be contrasted with those who propose a degree of continuity in terrorism throughout the last century (and perhaps even beyond). Waves of Terrorism theory provides another perspective which, to an extent, breaks down the Old–New distinction, demonstrating that old and new overlap at the same time, and that old aspects can be reinvigorated.

STUDY BOX CHAPTER 3

Key reading

Chaliland, E. and Blin, A. (2007) 'Zealots and Assassins'. In E. Chaliland and A. Blin (Eds.) (2007) *The History of Terrorism: From Antiquity to al Qaeda* (Los Angeles: University of California Press), pp. 55–78.

Copeland, T. (2001) 'Is the "New Terrorism" Really New? An Analysis of the New Paradigm for Terrorism'. *Journal of Conflict Studies*, 21(2).

Crenshaw, M. (2009) 'The Debate over "New" vs. "Old" Terrorism'. In
I. A. Karawan, W. McCormack and S.E. Reynolds (Eds.) *Values and Violence*
(Netherlands: Springer), pp. 117–36.

Hoffman, B. (2013) *Inside Terrorism* (New York: Columbia University Press).

Rapoport, D. C. (2004) 'The Four Waves of Modern Terrorism'. In A. K. Cronin and
J. M. Ludes (eds.) *Attacking Terrorism: Elements of a Grand Strategy.* (Washington,
DC: Georgetown University Press), pp. 46–73.

Study questions

1   To what extent is religiously inspired terrorism different from other forms of
terrorism?

2   Has globalization caused or enabled terrorism?

3   What are the advantages and disadvantages that a network structure poses to
counterterrorism?

References

Académie Française. (1838). *Dictionnaire de l'Académie française* (Vol. 1). Paris: Adphlphe
Wahlen.

Ahmed, E., Elgazzar, A.S. and Hegazi, A.S. (2005). 'On Complex Adaptive Systems and
Terrorism'. *Physics Letters A*, 337(1–2), pp. 127–9.

Al-Rodhan, N. and Stoudmann, G. (2006). 'Definitions of Globalization: A Comprehensive
Overview and Proposed Definition'. Program on the Geopolitical Implications of
Globalization and Transnational Security. Geneva Center for Security Policy.

Andersen, P. B., Emmeche, C. et al. (2000). Downward causation, Aarhus University Press
Aarhus, Denmark.

Benjamin, D. and Simon, S. (2002). *The Age of Sacred Terror.* New York: Random House Inc.

Bergesen, A. J., and Lizardo, O. (2004). International Terrorism and the World-System.
Sociological Theory, 22(1), 38–52.

Blomberg B. and Rosendorff, P. (2009). 'A Gravity Model of Globalization, Democracy and
Transnational Terrorism.

Brecher, J., and Smith, B. (2000). *Globalization from below: The power of solidarity.* South
End Press.

Chaliland, E. and Blin, A. (2007). Zealots and Assassins. In Chaliland, E. and Blin, A.
(Eds.) *The History of Terrorism: From Antiquity to al Qaeda..* Los Angeles: University of
California Press, pp. 55–78.

Cobban, H. (1981). *The Palestinian Liberation Organisation: People, Power and Politics,*
Cambridge University Press, Cambridge, p. 140.

Copeland, T. (2001). Is the 'New Terrorism' Really New? An Analysis of the New Paradigm
for Terrorism. *Journal of Conflict Studies, 21*(2).

Corelli, R. (1986). The Menacing Face of New Terrorism', Macleans (99), April.

Crenshaw, M. (2007). The Debate over "New" vs. "Old" Terrorism, Annual Meeting of the
American Political Science Association, Chicago, Illinois, 30 August – 2 September: 28.

Crenshaw, M. (2009). The Debate over 'New' vs. 'Old' Terrorism. In Karawan, I.A.,
McCormack, W. and Reynolds, S.E. (Eds.) *Values and Violence: Intangible Aspects of
Terrorism.* The Netherlands: Springer, pp. 117–36.

Cronin, A.K. (2002/3). 'Behind the Curve: Globalization and International Terrorism', *International Security*, 27(3): 30–58.

Edwards, S. (1993). 'Openness, trade liberalization and economic growth in developing countries', *Journal of Economic Literature*, 31: 1358–93.

Enders, W. and Sandler, T. (1993). 'The Effectiveness of Antiterrorism Policies: A Vector-autoregression-intervention analysis.' *American Political Science Review*. 87: 829–44.

Eubank, W. and Weinberg, L. (1994). 'Does Democracy encourage Terrorism?', *Terrorism and Political Violence*, 6: 417–43.

Frankel, J. and Romer,D. (1999). 'Does trade cause growth?' *American Economic Review*, 89: 379–99.

Giddens, A. (1990). *The Consequences of Modernity*. Cambridge Polity Press. Pg.64.

Gladwell, M. (2002). *The Tipping Point: How Little Things Can Make A Big Difference*. New York: Little Brown and Co.

Gupta, D. K. (2010). 'Accounting For the Waves of International Terrorism.' Perspectives on Terrorism 2(11).

Harrow, M. (2008). 'Inside a wave of terrorism: The dynamic relation between terrorism and the factors leading to terrorism.' *Journal of Global Change and Governance*, 1(3): 1–18.

Heath, C. and D. Heath (2007). *Made to Stick: Why Some Ideas Survive and Others Die*. New York: Random House.

Heath-Kelly, C. (2013). *Politics of violence: militancy, international politics, killing in the name*. Abingdon: Abingdon: Routledge.

Hoffman, B. (1999). Terrorism trends and prospects. *Countering the new terrorism*, 7, 13.

Hoffman, B. (2001). 'Change and Continuity in Terrorism', *Studies in Conflict and Terrorism*, 24:426.

Hoffman, B. (2013). *Inside Terrorism*. New York: Columbia University Press.

Holm, H. and Sorenson, G. (1995). *Whose World Order? Uneven Globalization and the End of the Cold War*. Boulder, CO: Westview Press.

International Monetary Fund (1997). 'World Economic Outlook, A Survey by the Staff of the International Monetary Fund', Meeting the Challenges of Globalization in the Advanced Economies', in the World Economic and Financial Surveys

Jackson, R., Smyth, M. B. and Gunning, J. (Eds.). (2009). *Critical terrorism studies: a new research agenda*. Abingdon: Routledge.

Johnston, A. (2001). 'Disparities in wealth are seen as fuel for terrorism'. *International Herald Tribune*, December 19.

Kaplan, J. (2007). 'The Fifth Wave: The New Tribalism?.' *Terrorism and Political Violence* 19(4): 545–70.

Karagiannis, E. (2005). 'Political Islam and social movement theory: the case of Hizb ut-Tahrir in Kyrgyzstan.' *Religion, State and Society*, 33 (2): 137–50.

Katzman, K. (2002). *The PLO and its Factions*. CRS Report for Congress. Accessed on April 20, 2014: http://www.au.af.mil/au/awc/awcgate/crs/rs21235.pdf

Kellner, D. (2007). Globalization, terrorism, and democracy: 9/11 and its aftermath. In *Frontiers of Globalization Research* (pp. 243–68). Springer US.

bin Laden, O. (1998). *Military Studies in the Jihad against the Tyrants*. Accessed on October 14, 2014: http://www.justice.gov/sites/default/files/ag/legacy/2002/10/08/manualpart1_1.pdf

Lee, R. and Perl, R. (2002). 'Terrorism, the Future and Foreign Policy', issue brief for congress, Congressional Research Service.

Li, Q. and Schaub, D.(2004). 'Economic Globalization and Transnational Terrorism: A Pooled Time-Series Analysis', *The Journal of Conflict Resolution*, 48(2): 230–58.

Livingstone, N.C. (1982). *War Against Terrorism*. Lexington Books, New York.

Lizardo, O. A. and A. J. Bergesen (2003). "Types of Terrorism by World System Location." *Humboldt Journal of Social Relations*, 27(2): 162–192.

Marighella, C. (1969). *The MiniManual of the Urban Guerrilla*. Accessed on October 14, 2014: http://www.marxists.org/archive/marighella-carlos/1969/06/minimanual-urban-guerrilla/

Martin, G. (2010). *Understanding Terrorism: Challenges, Perspectives and Issues* (3rd edn.). London: Sage Publications.

Mueller, J. (2006). *Overblown : How Politicians and the Terrorism Industry Inflate National Security Threats, And Why We Believe Them*. New York : Free Press.

Mockaitis, T. R. (2007). *The 'new' terrorism: myths and reality*. Greenwood Publishing Group. pp. 37–8.

Nechayev, S. (1869). *The Revolutionary Catechism*. Accessed on October 14, 2014: http://www.worldfuturefund.org/wffmaster/Reading/Communism/Sergei Nechayev.htm

The New York Times (2000). The New Face of Terrorism, January 4.

Olson, M. (1968). *The Logic of Collective Action*. Cambridge, Mass: Harvard University Press.

Pillar, P.R. (2001). Terrorism and US Foreign Policy. Brookings Institute. Washington DC. p. 47.

Ranstorp, M. (1994). 'Hizbullah's Command Leadership: Its Structures, Decision-Making and Relationship with Iranian Clergy and Institutions,' *Terrorism and Political Violence*, 6(3): 304.

Rapoport, D.C. (2002). The Four Waves of Rebel Terror and September 11. *Anthropoetics* 8(1): 42–3.

Rapoport, D.C. (2004). The Four Waves of Modern Terrorism. In A.K. Cronin and J.M. Ludes (Eds.) *Attacking Terrorism: Elements of a Grand Strategy*. Washington, DC: Georgetown University Press. pp. 46–73.

Rasler, K. and Thompson, W.R. (2009). Looking for Waves of Terrorism 1. *Terrorism and Political Violence*, 21(1): 28–41.

Robespierre, M. (1794). *Virtue and Terror*. Accessed on October 14, 2014: http://courses.washington.edu/hsteu302/Robespierre speech.htm

Rodrik, D. (1992). The Limits of Trade Policy Reform in Developing Countries. *Journal of Economic Perspective*, 6:87–105.

Rodrik, D. (2001), 'Trading in Illusions'. *Foreign Policy*, 123: 55–62.

Roy, O., Hoffman, R., Paz, B., Simon, S. and Benjamin, D. (2000). America and the New Terrorism: An Exchange. *Survival*, 42(2): 156–72.

Sageman, M. (2010). Ripples in the Waves: Fantasies and Fashions. In Rosenfeld, J.E. (Ed.) *Terrorism, Identity and Legitimacy: The Four Waves Theory and Political Violence*. New York: Routledge, pp. 87–93.

Simon, S. and Benjamin, D. (2000). America and the New Terrorism. *Survival*, 42(1): 70.

Spencer, A. (2006). Questioning the Concept of 'New Terrorism'. *Peace Conflict and Development*, 8: 1–33.

Spencer, A. (2010). The New Terrorism of al Qaeda is Not So New. In Gottlieb, S. (Ed.) *Debating Terrorism and Counterterrorism*. Washington, DC: CQ Press, pp. 4–15.

Spulak, R.G. and Turnley, J.G. (2005). 'Theoretical Perspectives of Terrorist Enemies as Networks', JSOU Report 05-3, Joint Special Operations University.

Stiglitz, J. and Squire, L. (1998). 'International development: Is it possible?' *Foreign Policy*, 110: 138–51.

Stern, J. (1999). *The Ultimate Terrorist*. Cambridge, MA: Harvard University Press.

Straits Times (2002). 'Cash Moves a Sign that Al Qaeda is Regrouping'. *Straits Times*. March 18 2002.

Transnational Terrorism, Security and the Rule of Law (2002). Concepts of Terrorism: Analysis of the Rise, Decline, Trends and Risks. Accessed on April 10, 2014: http://www.transnationalterrorism.eu/publications.php

Tucker, D. (2001). What's New about New Terrorism and How Dangerous Is It? *Terrorism and Political Violence, 13*(3): 1–14.

US Army Training and Doctrine Command, TRADOC G. 2. (2007). *Handbook No.1 Terrorism in the Twenty-First Century. TRADOC Intelligence and Support Activity-Threats.* Fort Leavenworth, Kansas.

Weimann, G. (2006). Terror on the Internet: The New Arena, The New Challenges. Washington. The United States Institute for Peace Press.

Weimann, G. (2011). 'Cyber Fatwas and Terrorism.' *Studies in Conflict and Terrorism,* 34(10): 765–81.

Weiner, R.G. (2001). 'The Financing of International Terrorism,' *Terrorism and Violence Crime.*

4

CYBERTERRORISM: WHAT IS IT AND WHAT THREAT DOES IT POSE?

LEE JARVIS AND STUART MACDONALD

Introduction

The meaning of 'terrorism' is notoriously challenging to pin down, as the preceding chapters ably demonstrate. Although the reasons for this are many, one particularly important factor is the term's capacity to 'travel' to new types of activities, organisations, behaviours and environments (Weinberg et al. 2004: 779). Agro-terrorism, bio-terrorism, eco-terrorism, narco-terrorism, suicide terrorism, WMD terrorism and so on: are all neologisms made possible by the ease with which new prefixes can be attached to this most powerful – and most politically useful – of words. And yet – and importantly – as the term terrorism becomes applied to an ever increasing list of activities it becomes ever more difficult to pin down with precision what, if anything, terrorism actually is. What, in other words, do such disparate behaviours as hijack-ings, beheadings and suicide bombings have in common, and how might we separate these from other types of human activity such as war, crime or political protest?

In this chapter we focus our attention on one of terrorism's better-known offspring: cyberterrorism. Familiar to any follower of contemporary popular culture – think *GoldenEye, NetForce, Die Hard 4.0* or *Skyfall* (Conway, 2007) – and to any consumer of the news media, cyberterrorism has achieved considerable social and cultural prom-inence since the term was first coined in the 1980s (Collin, 1997). Government departments, internet-security corporations and academic authors all speak regularly on this seemingly new threat, and yet, as outlined below, there is remarkably little agreement on any of the major questions that we might expect to ask of it. Not least amongst these are: what is cyberterrorism and how significant a threat does it pose?

Unfortunately, this chapter cannot promise a definitive answer to such ques-tions! What it can do, however, is offer an overview of the state of current debate on these big issues. To this end we begin our discussion with a section exploring some of the most important definitional questions that surround cyberterrorism, before turning to the risk that it presents to different social and political actors:

governments, corporations, ordinary citizens and so forth. Debate in both of these areas, we argue, is characterised by the recycling of definitional, conceptual and political controversies that have long engulfed discussions of terrorism more widely. At the same time, however, the social and strategic environment upon which we are focused – cyberspace – throws up additional issues and confusions, not least because of how ill understood it is within terrorism research (Weimann 2005). To demonstrate, our discussion draws on contemporary academic literature in this area, as well as on findings from a global survey of researchers working on this issue that we conducted with colleagues of ours associated with *The Cyberterrorism Project* (Macdonald et al., 2013). This survey received a total of 118 responses from researchers working across 24 different countries in six different continents. These researchers, importantly, come to the topic of cyberterrorism from a range of disciplinary backgrounds including international relations, political science, law, engineering, computer science and psychology.

What is cyberterrorism?

The coining of the term cyberterrorism in the 1980s was not coincidental, as the term spoke to the growing importance of computers and the internet across many areas of social, political and economic life. It also resonated with the then widespread view that the post-Cold War world would be characterised by radically 'new' security threats of a sort not witnessed before (Jarvis et al., 2014b). Yet, despite this comparatively brief existence, the meaning of cyberterrorism remains dogged by considerable contestation. There are two reasons for this in particular which we discuss in this section. The first is the issue of denotative breadth. While some writers understand the term cyberterrorism quite broadly, others prefer a far narrower and – in their view – more precise construction. The second issue is a relational one. This, simply, is the question: how is cyberterrorism similar to, and different from, other forms of terrorism? Should we approach cyberterrorism as a sub-species of terrorism more broadly – in other words, the application of something old (terrorism) to something new (computers)? Or should we approach cyberterrorism as a distinctive phenomenon with its own characteristics?

Before turning to these issues in more detail it is worth briefly reflecting on the preliminary question of whether there is even any value at all in defining cyberterrorism. This was a question we asked in our survey in an attempt to establish whether a specific definition of cyberterrorism is viewed by researchers as necessary for both policymakers and the research community. On a scale of 1 to 5 – where 1 was 'not at all' and 5 was 'essential' – the majority view was that a specific definition of this term is, indeed, necessary (see Table 4.1). More than half (56 per cent) of our respondents entered a score of either 4 or 5 in respect of researchers. This rose to almost two-thirds (66 per cent) in respect of policymakers. Various reasons were offered for why a specific and satisfactory definition of cyberterrorism is important. Some of these were focused on the process of conducting research, including setting the parameters of a project, helping to communicate findings to others and ensuring consistency across different projects (such as databases of terrorist events). Other answers focused on the implementation of policy and legislation. Those that discussed these issues argued that a specific definition of cyberterrorism was necessary in order to help identify the boundaries between different criminal offences, to distinguish terrorism from 'ordinary' crime and to facilitate cooperation across international boundaries and different systems of law and policing.

Whilst the majority of respondents to our survey argued that a specific definition of cyberterrorism was necessary, this was not a view shared by all researchers. Roughly one-fifth doubted the necessity of such a definition, entering a score of either 1 or 2 out of 5 in answer to the above question (17 per cent in respect of policymakers, 23 per cent in respect of researchers). Some of these respondents argued that it would be premature, artificial and potentially counterproductive to attempt to define cyberterrorism now, not least because the cyber realm is still relatively young, rapidly developing and, arguably, not yet adequately understood by researchers working in this area. Others questioned the necessity of definitions in this context in general. One of these did so by highlighting the constructivist argument that cyberterrorism only exists to the extent that we – as citizens, policymakers, researchers – believe in its existence and continue to act as if this is the case (see also Jackson et al., 2011). In their words: 'Security practice does not require definition of threat. It is performative – it constructs its own threats and its reasons for being. Cyberterrorism, or "terrorism", performs an oppositional construct that doesn't require specific definition.'

Table 4.1 How important is a specific definition of cyberterrorism? (Macdonald et al., 2013)

| | Not at all | | | | Essential |
	1	2	3	4	5
For policymakers	6%	11%	17%	35%	31%
For researchers	6%	17%	21%	32%	24%

Broad and narrow conceptions of cyberterrorism

Broad conceptions of cyberterrorism encompass a wide spectrum of ways in which terrorist groups might employ and engage with the internet. These range from cyber attacks perpetrated through computer technologies and networks, through to a host of seemingly more mundane activities. Such activities include: intra-group communication – for example, with the use of email or 'dead drop' communications (which involve saving draft emails for others to read, thereby minimising the possibility of detection); preparation and planning for future attacks – for example, via internet search engines and online maps; propaganda – including the dissemination of audio-visual materials such as speeches or videos; training – for example, through the circulation and accessing of instructions relating to weapon construction and deployment; and fundraising in order to generate resources through overt or surreptitious means (Brunst, 2010; Talihärm, 2010). Those who advocate a broad understanding of cyberterrorism to encompass these and other activities warn that a focus on 'pure cyberterrorism' has the potential to obscure the diversity of ways in which the internet has penetrated all aspects of 'the terrorism matrix' (Gordon and Ford, 2002: 638). As Gordon and Ford (2002: 637) point out, 'computers and, in particular, the Internet, played a key role in the execution of the September 11th attacks'; hence a far narrower, more specific, understanding of cyberterrorism 'poses a significant barrier to our ability to protect ourselves' (2002: 641) from the intersection of cyber technologies and terrorist violence.

Several respondents to our own survey of researchers approached cyberterrorism in broad terms that were similar to these. In response to one question – 'In your view, does cyberterrorism constitute a significant threat? If so, against whom or what is the threat focused?' – a number of possible threat scenarios were given to us which extended far beyond the conduct of attacks on people, property, critical infrastructures or essential services. Several referred to cyberterrorists threatening national security by obtaining sensitive intelligence and classified information. Others pointed to the risk of terrorists committing cybercrime, including obtaining individuals' bank details and accessing financial and other information from both public- and private-sector institutions. One respondent understood cyberterrorism as sufficiently comprehensive to include online harassment, while another warned of cyberattacks being perpetrated to influence elections (Jarvis et al., 2014a). The important point is that these were all provided to us as examples of cyberterrorism itself, not as examples of acts related or preparatory to cyberterrorism.

Broad understandings of cyberterrorism were also evident in responses we received to a follow-up question: 'With reference to your previous responses, do you consider that a cyberterrorism attack has ever taken place?' Those respondents who answered yes offered a total of 15 specific examples as well as a number of more general ones (Jarvis et al., 2014a). The 15 specific examples not only included instances in which cyber technologies have been weaponised – such as in Stuxnet (Farwell and Rohozinski, 2011) or the cyberattacks on Estonia and Georgia in 2007 and 2008. They also included the campaigns of WikiLeaks and Anonymous, and the use of social-networking sites to send threatening messages and pictures during the Assam riots of 2012. More general or hypothetical examples included the theft of monies to fund terrorist organisations, the preparation of terrorist attacks, calls for home-grown terrorism, and cyber espionage.

Understandings of cyberterrorism that are sufficiently wide to incorporate all of the above events and activities may be subject to challenge for a number of reasons, many of which were mentioned by the researchers we surveyed. First is the argument that the most prominent cyberattacks to date, such as Stuxnet, and those upon Estonia and Georgia, do not qualify as terrorist (and, therefore, as examples of cyberterrorism) because they were – or are widely believed to have been – carried out by state actors. In this view, these events might be better understood as examples of cyber warfare, with the distinction between cyberterrorism and cyber war seen by some as an important one in order not to lose precision in our terminology. A second argument is that the known cyberattacks to date have lacked at least some of the following features which are necessary for an attack to qualify as terrorist: violence against people or property, creation of fear in a wider audience (or an intention to create such fear) and a political or ideological motive. Third, it is possible also to argue that a distinction must be drawn between, on the one hand, cyberterrorism and, on the other hand, cybercrime committed for terrorist purposes – such as to raise funds. In this view, while terrorists might commit cybercrime in order to facilitate their activities, this does not render the criminal activity terrorist. And, fourth, we might also suggest that protest activities including 'hacktivism' should be distinguished from cyberterrorism, although some of the experts we surveyed argued that the activities of groups such as Anonymous render this distinction more problematic.

Narrow understandings of cyberterrorism were far more common in responses to our survey than their more expansive counterparts. This was particularly evident in the responses to two questions we asked. First, we asked respondents to select 'important elements of cyberterrorism' from a list of ten items. The three most common responses were: a political or ideological motive (selected by 87 per cent of our respondents); digital means or target (77 per cent); and fear as an outcome (70 per cent). These findings are consistent with the reasons outlined in the previous paragraph for why many cyber activities may not be viewed as cyberterrorism. Second, we also provided respondents to our survey with a total of eight distinct scenarios, each comprising a different combination of either physical or digital preparation, means and target for an attack. Respondents were asked to decide which scenarios would constitute acts of cyberterrorism – the options being yes, no or potentially. Two findings emerged (Jarvis and Macdonald, 2014) from this question. First, digital preparatory activities were generally regarded as insufficient for an attack to qualify as cyberterrorism. In response to a scenario which involved digital preparation but physical means and physical target, 61 per cent said that such an attack would not constitute cyberterrorism, with only 20 per cent arguing that it would. In other words, an argument that 9/11 could be classed as cyberterrorism because the internet was used for planning and in order to purchase airplane tickets beforehand appears to be a minority one. Second, the means and target of an attack were of far greater significance to our respondents than its preparation. Of these, digital means was regarded as the most important. For example, 38 per cent suggested that an attack which involved digital means but physical preparation and target – for example targeting an air-traffic-control system with a computer virus – was cyberterrorism but 18 per cent said that it was not. In contrast, 33 per cent said that an attack which involved a digital target but physical means and preparation – for example, blowing up a computer server – was cyberterrorism but 32 per cent said that this was not.

Narrower understandings of cyberterrorism such as these are also far more prevalent in the academic literature on this topic. Perhaps the best-known definition of cyberterrorism is the one offered by Dorothy Denning in her testimony before the US House of Representatives in 2000, which offers a precise and succinct understanding of this term:

> Cyberterrorism is the convergence of terrorism and cyberspace. It is generally understood to mean unlawful attacks and threats of attack against computers, networks, and the information stored therein when done to intimidate or coerce a government or its people in furtherance of political or social objectives. Further, to qualify as cyberterrorism, an attack should result in violence against persons or property, or at least cause enough harm to generate fear. Attacks that lead to death or bodily injury, explosions, plane crashes, water contamination, or severe economic loss would be examples. Serious attacks against critical infrastructures could be acts of cyberterrorism, depending on their impact. Attacks that disrupt nonessential services or that are mainly a costly nuisance would not. (Denning, 2000)

Two features of Denning's definition are worth highlighting. First, it is clear from this paragraph and from passages later in her testimony that Denning's definition only applies where computers are present as both the *means* of an attack and its *target*. In this view, using a bomb to blow up a computer server would not constitute an example of cyberterrorism, whereas remotely interfering with air-traffic-control systems in order to cause two passenger aircraft to collide might. Second, an attack only qualifies as cyberterrorism under Denning's definition if it possesses all the features normally associated with traditional terrorist attacks. In this respect, the attacker must have had a political or social objective and an intention to intimidate or coerce a government or its people, and the attack must have resulted in violence against people or property or severe economic loss.

Other commentators also advance definitions of cyberterrorism with similar restrictions. For example, Weimann's definition of cyberterrorism as 'the use of computer network tools to harm or shut down critical national infrastructures (such as energy, transportation, government operations)' combines an insistence on computers as the means of attack with a requirement of 'real-world' – or offline – consequences (Weimann, 2005: 130). Conway's understanding of cyberterrorism also includes a requirement that offline damage is caused (Conway, 2002). In contrast to Gordon and Ford, she draws a distinction between cyberterrorism and terrorists' use of computers, and warns that, although online terrorist activities are prevalent, they have 'been largely ignored ... in favour of the more headline-grabbing "cyberterrorism"' (Conway, 2007).

The relationship between cyberterrorism and other forms of terrorism

A second important area of disagreement on this question of definition concerns the relationship between cyberterrorism and other forms of terrorist violence. There are at least four different approaches to this relationship that can be identified (Jarvis and Macdonald, 2014). The first of these regards cyberterrorism as an unlikely or purely hypothetical counterpart to the reality of other, more conventional, types of terrorism. For example, Conway (2014) identifies four reasons why no act of cyberterrorism (as she defines the term) has ever occurred or is likely to occur in the near future. These are: first, that terrorists lack the technical capability required for this type of attack and are unlikely to outsource this work to others who do possess this knowledge because this would create new risks including possible infiltration; second, that cyberattacks are unlikely to produce the sort of easily captured, spectacular (live, moving) images that are associated with contemporary forms of terrorism; third, the possibility that an attack may be apprehended or simply portrayed as an accident, thereby removing its communicative value for its perpetrator; and, fourth, the sheer costs that would be involved in the successful conduct of a cyberterrorist attack, especially in relation to more conventional types of terrorism (to which we return below). Lewis makes a similar argument, noting that:

> Explosions are dramatic, strike fear into the hearts of opponents and do lasting damage. Cyber attacks would not have the same dramatic and political effect that terrorists seek. A cyber attack, which might not even be noticed by its victims, or attributed to routine delays or outages, will not be their preferred weapon. (Lewis, 2002: 8)

Even though, on this view, cyberterrorism is little more than a remote possibility, commentators such as Conway have nonetheless engaged in definitional questions. The rationale for this is to divert attention away from cyberterrorism and towards other ways in which terrorists use the internet and other forms of terrorism which are regarded as posing a greater threat.

A second approach is similar to the first in that it again emphasises the importance of terrorist uses of the internet other than cyberattacks. Unlike the previous view, however, it embraces a broader definition of cyberterrorism and treats it not only as a reality but one that is qualitatively distinct from other forms of terrorism. These qualitative differences mean that cyberterrorism is regarded here as entailing its own definition. Holt, for example, has argued that the term 'must encapsulate a greater range of behaviour than physical terror due to the dichotomous nature of cyberspace as a vehicle for communications as well as a medium for attacks' (Holt, 2012: 341). Referring to a definition offered by Foltz (2004), Holt argues that an attack may qualify as cyberterrorist even if it does not cause physical harm and the attacker lacks any intention to generate fear – as long as the attack was intended either to interfere with the political, social or economic functioning of a group, organisation or country, or to induce either physical violence or the unjust use of power. This difference, he argues, recognises the way in which terrorists may use the internet to disseminate information in order to incite violence and harm.

The responses to our own survey on this issue (detailed above) revealed that many of our respondents also regard cyberterrorism as something which is qualitatively distinct from terrorism in its traditional forms. Strikingly, fewer than half of all our respondents (47 per cent) identified violence against people or property as an important element of cyberterrorism. This stands in stark contrast to the findings of Schmid and Jongman's earlier review of definitions of terrorism. Their study identified 'violence, force' as the most prevalent of word categories, appearing in 83.5 per cent of the definitions discussed (Schmid and Jongman, 2008).

A third approach to this issue is to reject any qualitative differences between cyberterrorism and other forms of terrorism, and simply to view the former as a particular subset or type of the latter. In this approach, an attack only qualifies as cyberterrorism if all of the components of a definition of terrorism are also satisfied, irrespective of how the cyber technologies are being used (for examples see Pollitt, 1998; Stohl, 2006). In particular, an attack only qualifies as cyberterrorism if it results in violence against people or property. Or, as Collin succinctly puts it, cyberterrorism is 'hacking with a body count' (quoted in Ballard et al., 2002: 992). From the responses to question five of our survey it seems that this is a common view: 47 per cent identified violence against people or property as an important element of cyberterrorism. So, in this approach, if an extremist group interfered with an air-traffic-control system and caused two passenger aircraft to collide in midair this would constitute cyberterrorism. But if the same group were to interfere with a nation's stock exchange via digital technologies in order simply to cause severe economic damage, this would not.

The fourth approach is an amalgam of the second and third approaches: it simultaneously regards cyberterrorism both as a subset of terrorism in general and as qualitatively distinct from other forms of terrorism. It is this approach that is employed in the UK's Terrorism Act 2000. According to section one of the Act, an attack qualifies as terrorist if: (1) it was carried out with an intention to influence the government or an international governmental organisation, or intimidate the public or a section of the public; (2) the purpose was to advance a political, religious, racial or ideological cause; and (3) the attack falls within one of the five actions listed in subsection (2). Paragraphs (a) to (d) of subsection (2) focus on acts which endanger life, cause serious violence or serious property damage, or create a serious risk to public health and safety. Paragraph (e), on the other hand, applies whether or not human life or property was endangered. It encompasses acts which are designed seriously to interfere with or seriously to disrupt an electronic system. The stock-exchange example in the previous paragraph would therefore be regarded as an act of terrorism under UK law. Cyberattacks on internet service providers and controls of national power and water could also potentially qualify as cyberterrorism (Home Office, 2007). This leads us to the second half of this chapter, which examines the significance of the cyberterrorism threat and possible responses.

Assessing and responding to the cyberterrorism threat

As the above section has shown, understandings of cyberterrorism differ markedly. There are narrow and broad conceptions of this phenomenon, and we can differentiate between those who see cyberterrorism as little more than 'terrorism plus computers' and those who see it as something more distinctive in its own right. Unsurprisingly, different conceptions of cyberterrorism lend themselves to different assessments of the threat that it poses. Where cyberterrorism is understood in broad terms – to include, for instance, terrorist communication via email – risk assessments of its occurrence are likely to be high. Where cyberterrorism is understood in more constrained terms – delimited to cyberattacks for terrorist purposes, for instance – this higher threshold frequently translates into reduced fears. In this section we focus on the latter (narrow) understanding of cyberterrorism, and contrast three different positions on the threat that it poses (Jarvis et al., 2014a). These are, first, the 'concerned' position which sees cyberterrorism as a significant security threat; second, the arguments of the 'sceptics' for whom cyberterrorism poses little, if any, credible threat; and, third, the constructivist stance which departs from the assumptions that underpin cost/benefit responses to this question. The chapter's conclusion explores the importance of these competing assessments for the equally thorny issue of how to respond to cyberterrorism.

Reasons for concern

The earliest discussions of cyberterrorism in the 1980s and 1990s tended to be accompanied by graver threat assessments than more contemporary ones, at least within academic discussion of this issue. While there does exist a significant industry of cyber-security companies and policymakers who potentially benefit – financially or politically – from worst-case scenarios, researchers have tended to be more circumspect in their assessments of the threat posed by cyberterrorism. At the same time, however, there are several prominent concerns that recur within debate in this area, relating primarily to the means and opportunities available to would-be cyberterrorists. These issues, for some, increase the risk of cyberterrorism by raising the likelihood or impact of an attack (Weimann, 2005: 137).

Beginning with means, it is possible to argue that cyberterrorism bears fewer financial and other costs than alternative types of attack that might be considered. Whereas the purchase, preparation and testing of explosive devices produces risks of detection, injury and even death, the basic tools needed for cyberterrorism are either readily available, commercial, off-the-shelf technologies (such as modems and laptop computers), or purchasable via the internet. As Wilson (2014) notes, there exists a legal market for relatively affordable 'zero-day exploits' that exploit as yet unknown or unexploited technological vulnerabilities. In this sense, even ill-resourced organisations – or individuals – may have the materials and access required to commit attacks in this domain.

Second, in terms of opportunity, there are a number of reasons that cyberattacks might prove attractive to terrorist groups. These include the scope for anonymity that cyberspace offers to those with sufficient technological competence; the potential that cyberattacks have to impact upon a wide range of possible targets; and the ability to conduct attacks at a distance from the target itself (Furnell and Warren, 1999; Weimann, 2005). In the survey of researchers that we carried out, 58 per cent of respondents argued that cyberterrorism does indeed constitute a significant security threat. The potential target most commonly identified amongst these was states and their governments, although a number also pointed to other possible targets including financial institutions, intelligence agencies, emergency services, ordinary civilians and private-sector corporations (see Jarvis et al., 2014a: 75).

Interestingly, when we asked whether a cyberterrorist attack has ever taken place 49 per cent answered yes and 49 per cent no.

Reasons for scepticism

A first major reason for scepticism regarding the threat posed by cyberterrorism may be found in analyses of the costs that it poses in relation to other forms of attack (Rathmell, 1999). Although estimations of costs are often challenging and imprecise, it is possible to contrast the (financial) expense of more traditional, offline forms of terrorism with the relatively more prohibitive costs of cyberattacks. Beginning with the former, even a major, coordinated attack such as the 1998 bombing of the US embassies in Kenya and Tanzania cost no more than $10,000, according to the CIA (cited in Hoffman, 2006: 134); 9/11 itself cost less than $500,000, according to the 9/11 Commission (Hoffman, 2006), while Conway (2014) notes that the average cost of constructing a car bomb in Afghanistan in 2006 was $1675. The cost of the 1995 Oklahoma City bombing which resulted in the death of 168 people was less than $5000. In contrast to these relatively low figures, Giacomello (2004: 397) estimates the cost of a cyberattack on a hydroelectric dam at $1.2–1.3 million, including logistical and personnel costs, and estimates the total cost of an attack against an air-traffic-control system at $2.5–3 million, or five to six times that of the 9/11 attacks. If terrorism is always a 'choice among alternatives' (McCormick, 2003: 474), then so too are the instruments of its conduct; analysed thus cyber weapons appear a relatively unattractive option.

Second, beyond the perceived costs of cyberterrorism is the issue of its potential benefits. Many of those who are most sceptical of worst-case scenarios around cyberterrorism are so because of the limited utility they see cyberattacks possessing for terrorist groups. For some, such as Conway (2014), terrorism (and consequently cyberterrorism) have an important communicative or performative dimension. That is, the purpose of terrorism is to impact upon – and, specifically, to cause fear within – an external audience not directly or immediately affected by an attack. Seen in this way, the benefits of cyberterrorism are limited because there is no guarantee that they would generate the publicity sought by their protagonists. As Conway (2014) argues, a cyberattack might go unnoticed even by its initial target, be mistakenly identified as an accident rather than a deliberate, malicious attack, or might even be hidden by governments or corporations seeking to downplay vulnerabilities to citizens and shareholders.

A third reason for scepticism relates to the difficulties that would be faced by a terrorist organisation seeking to perpetrate a cyberattack. Thus, irrespective of motivation, there are important questions to be asked in relation to the extent to which critical infrastructures are actually vulnerable to penetration (Dunn Cavelty, 2008: 20), and of the technical competence of would-be terrorists seeking to attack via the internet. As Weimann (2005: 143) notes, 'Many computer security experts do not believe that it is possible to use the Internet to inflict death on a large scale.' This is, not least, because of considerable investment in cyber security by governments, corporations and other potential targets, as well as due to the development of techniques such as 'air-gapping' in which nuclear weapons and other military systems are deliberately not connected to the internet (Weimann, 2005). While these mechanisms might not guarantee security from cyberterrorism, they do add a sceptical counterbalance to the more concerned perspectives considered above.

It is noteworthy that in our survey only 20 per cent of researchers stated that cyberterrorism does not constitute a significant security threat. In addition to the arguments just outlined that terrorist organisations lack the capability and motivation to perpetrate cyberattacks, these researchers also offered one additional reason: the absence of any meaningful precedents (Jarvis et al., 2014a: 76).

The constructivist critique

The above discussion has focused on competing views of the cost/benefit analyses that would-be (cyber)terrorists might make when considering potential attack scenarios. These assessments of vulnerabilities, motivations and the financial and other complexities of cyber attacks all fit broadly into a rationalist framework for exploring the threat that cyberterrorism poses. In other words, they imply that (cyber)terrorists are instrumental, utility-maximising actors who weigh up the value of different strategies for achieving their desired ends. It is, however, possible to explore this issue of threat from a different, broadly constructivist, angle in order to reframe this question from 'What threat does cyberterrorism pose?' to 'How is cyberterrorism constructed or framed as a security threat?' Asking this question involves moving away from estimates of costs and benefits and looking instead at how political and other actors frame cyberterrorism and the threat that it poses in their language or performances.

Myriam Dunn Cavelty (2008) has provided an important analysis of how cyberterrorism is discursively framed. In it she demonstrates that cyberterrorism is constructed as a subset of broader cyber-security concerns, although the boundaries between these are often imprecise and unclear. She notes that the constructions of this threat are particularly powerful because they marry fear of the arbitrariness associated with terrorism to distrust of computer technologies. As she elaborates:

> Terrorism is feared, and is meant to be feared, because it is perceived as being random, incomprehensible, and uncontrollable. Technology, including information technology, is feared because it is seen as complex, abstract, and arcane in its impact on individuals. Because computers do things that used to be done by humans, there is a notion of technology being out of control, a recurring theme in political and philosophical thought (Winner, 1977) that is even strengthened by the increase in connectivity that the information revolution brings. They are ultimately seen as a threat to society's core values, especially national security, and to the economic and social well-being of a nation. Therefore, they are inevitably presented as a national security issue. (Dunn Cavelty, 2008; 29)

In a more recent study Dunn Cavelty (2013) contextualises this threat construction vis-à-vis others. In so doing she argues that representations of the risk posed by cyberterrorism have gained increasing currency after 9/11, evolving out of earlier constructions of the risk posed by hackers. Cyberterrorism, in turn, however, is now being replaced by fears of 'highly professional state-sponsored cyber-mercenaries, able to develop highly effective cyber-weapons. Such conceptions are supported by reports from anti-virus companies, which describe the main threat as one from increasingly organized professionals' (Dunn Cavelty, 2013: 112). In a related study Bendrath et al. (2007) employ securitisation theory (a variant of 'thin' or conventional constructivism within the security-studies literature) to investigate the emphasis on the threat posed by cyberterrorism – rather than state actors or criminal organisations using the internet – within Bill Clinton's administration. This cyberterrorism discourse was driven, in part, they argue, by the experience of two major offline attacks which lifted the threat of terrorism up the security agenda: the World Trade Center attack of 1993 and the Oklahoma City bombing of 1995. In their view, within US political discourse, 'Cyberterrorism is still on the agenda, but with a considerably lower priority than during the Clinton administration and in the months immediately following 9/11. Cyberterrorism is still considered more of a *potential* than an *immediate* threat' (Bendrath et al., 2007: 77, original emphasis).

Conclusion: how to respond?

As we have seen, there is precious little agreement over what cyberterrorism is, and – in part as a consequence of this – over the threat that it poses to governments, citizens or others. While vulnerabilities in, and contemporary dependences on, critical infrastructure of various sorts causes considerable concern to some, others argue that the technical challenges and financial costs of cyberattacks render them far less appealing than comparatively more accessible alternatives. There are considerable differences, too, in estimations of the likely motivations of terrorist groups contemplating the weaponisation of cyberspace or technologies. Finally, we considered the constructivist critique of these rationalist models, and its emphasis on exploring *how* cyberterrorism is produced as a potential or imminent security threat within political discourse, popular culture, the news media and beyond.

To conclude this chapter we turn now to the issue of how the threat of cyberterrorism might best be addressed. As we saw above, those most concerned about the cyberterrorism threat were so for reasons of means, motive and opportunity. In this sense, adjusting the ratio of costs to benefits in any of these areas is likely to have a positive impact in reducing the likelihood or consequences of cyberterrorism. Potential responses will follow specific conceptualisations of this threat – and its connection to other cybersecurity issues – but, as Dunn Cavelty (2013: 115–16) notes, these responses might include technological developments such as firewalls, political frameworks (such as multilateral agreements or norms), law enforcement tools, and measures aimed at critical-infrastructure protection or enhancing societal resilience to this and related security threats. In our own survey twelve types of countermeasure were identified by researchers working in this field. One of these – target hardening – dominated our responses with 38 per cent of the researchers who answered this question mentioning it. Some of these responses were framed quite generally, including 'technical security' or 'enhanced IT security'. Other experts, however, gave more specific suggestions, pointing to the importance of fire-walls, closed secure networks and encrypted data.

Those more sceptical of this threat will emphasise the importance of other security threats vis-à-vis cyberterrorism. These will include offline threats, such as more traditional types of terrorism, as well as other cyber-security issues such as terrorist uses of the internet for activities other than attacks. Those more optimis-tic about the resistance of critical infrastructures to attack might, for example, appeal for a more measured approach to threat assessment that might include 'a much more detailed assessment of redundancy, normal rates of failure and response, the degree to which critical functions are accessible from public net-works and the level of human control, monitoring and intervention in critical operations' (Lewis, 2002: 10). As Lewis (2002) argues, while vulnerabilities to cyberterrorism might exist, these are far more limited than often assumed, and potentially dwarfed by the threat posed by other (far more adequately resourced) states in this strategic environment.

From a constructivist standpoint the crucial task is not necessarily to respond to the risk of cyberterrorism in the real world via measures such as those identified above. Instead, the emphasis shifts to deconstructing and challenging construc-tions of this phenomenon and the threat that it poses. This might involve, among other things, critiquing efforts to exaggerate the likelihood of cyberterrorism occurring or the consequences of such an eventuality; or, more simply, demon-strating the implicit assumptions and contestable claims upon which such constructions of threat rest. Constructivist analysis would also, importantly, pull attention to the political and other consequences of discourses around cyber-terrorism. These might include the commitment of valuable, finite resources to counter this threat that could otherwise be used in other areas of security policy, or public policy more broadly. Nine per cent of the researchers we surveyed argued that refusing to exaggerate the threat posed by cyberterrorism constituted the most effective countermeasure against this threat. Moreover, when asked what *the* most pressing issue in the field of cyberterrorism was for policymakers and researchers, avoiding exaggerated claims of its threat was identified by 13 per cent and 14 per cent of our respondents respectively. Doing so, however, might be less straightforward than we might hope, for as Weimann points out:

> Combating cyberterrorism has become not only a highly politicized issue but also an economically rewarding one. An entire industry has emerged to grapple with the threat of cyberterrorism: think tanks have launched elaborate projects and issued alarming white papers on the subject, experts have testified to cyberterrorism's dangers before Congress, and private companies have hastily deployed security consultants and software designed to protect public and private targets. Following the 9/11 attacks, the federal government requested $4.5 billion for infrastructure security, and the FBI now boasts more than one thousand 'cyber investigators'. (Weimann, 2009: 3)

STUDY BOX CHAPTER 4

Key readings

Conway, M. (2014) 'Reality Check: Assessing the (Un)Likelihood of Cyberterrorism'. In T. Chen, L. Jarvis and S. Macdonald (Eds.) *Cyberterrorism: Understanding, Assessment, and Response* (New York, NY: Springer), pp. 103–121.

Gordon, S. and Ford, R. (2002) 'Cyberterrorism?' *Computers and Security* 21: 636–47.

Jarvis, L., Macdonald, S. and Nouri, L. (2014) 'The Cyberterrorism Threat: Findings from a Survey of Researchers', *Studies in Conflict and Terrorism* 37(1): 68–90.

Weimann, G. (2009) 'Cyberterrorism: How Real is the Threat?', *United States Institute of Peace Special Report* 119.

Study questions

1   In your opinion, what is cyberterrorism?

2   What threat does cyberterrorism pose, and to whom?

3   How do states respond to cyberterrorism and what issues do they face in doing this?

References

Ballard, J. D., Hornik, J. G. and McKenzie, D. (2002) 'Technological Facilitation of Terrorism: Definitional, Legal and Policy Issues' *American Behavioral Scientist* 45: 989–1016.

Bendrath, R., Eriksson, J. and Giacomello, G. (2007) 'From "Cyberterrorism" to "Cyberwar", Back and Forth', in J. Eriksson and G. Giacomello (eds.) *International Relations and Security in the Digital Age*. Abingdon: Routledge: 57–82.

Brunst, P. W. (2010) 'Terrorism and the Internet: New Threats Posed by Cyberterrorism and Terrorist Use of the Internet', in M. Wade and A. Maljevic (eds.) *A War on Terror? The European Stance on a New Threat, Changing Laws and Human Rights Implications*. New York, NY: Springer: 51–78.

Collin, B. (1997) 'The Future of Cyberterrorism' *Crime and Justice International* 13: 15–18.

Conway, M. (2002) 'Reality Bytes: Cyberterrorism and Terrorist "Use" of the Internet' *First Monday* 7 available at http://dx.doi.org/10.5210/fm.v7i11.1001 (last accessed 20 December 2013).

Conway, M. (2007) 'Cyberterrorism: Hype and Reality', in L. Armistead (ed.) *Information Warfare: Separating Hype from Reality*. Washington, USA: Potomac: 73–93.

Conway, M. (2014) 'Reality Check: Assessing the (Un)Likelihood of Cyberterrorism', in T. Chen, L. Jarvis, and S. Macdonald (eds.) *Cyberterrorism: Understanding, Assessment, Response*. New York, NY: Springer: 103–121.

Denning, D. (2000) 'Cyberterrorism: Testimony Before the Special Oversight Panel on Terrorism, Committee on Armed Services, U.S. House of Representatives' available at www.stealth-iss.com/documents/pdf/CYBERTERRORISM.pdf (last accessed 20 December 2013).

Dunn Cavelty, M. (2008) 'Cyber-terror – Looming Threat or Phantom Menace? The Framing of the US Cyber-threat Debate' *Journal of Information Technology and Politics* 4(1): 19–36.

Dunn Cavelty, M. (2013) 'From Cyber-bombs to Political Fallout: Threat Representations with an Impact in the Cyber-Security Discourse' *International Studies Review* 15(1): 105–22.

Farwell, J. P. and Rohozinski, R. (2011) 'Stuxnet and the Future of Cyber War' *Survival* 53: 23–40.

Foltz, C. B. (2004) 'Cyberterrorism, Computer Crime, and Reality' *Information Management and Computer Security* 12: 154–66.

Furnell, S. M. and Warren, M. J. (1999) 'Computer Hacking and Cyber Terrorism: The Real Threats in the New Millennium?' *Computers and Security* 18: 28–34.

Giacomello, G. (2004) 'Bangs for the Buck: A Cost–Benefit Analysis of Cyberterrorism' *Studies in Conflict and Terrorism* 27 (5): 387–408.

Gordon, S. and Ford, R. (2002) 'Cyberterrorism?' *Computers and Security* 21: 636–47.

Hoffman, B. (2006) *Inside Terrorism* (Revised and Expanded Edition). New York, NY: Columbia University Press.

Holt, T. J. (2012) 'Exploring the Intersections of Technology, Crime, and Terror' *Terrorism and Political Violence* 24: 337–54.

Home Office (2007) *The Definition of Terrorism: A Report by Lord Carlile of Berriew Q.C. Independent Reviewer of Terrorism Legislation* Cm 7052.

Jackson, R., Jarvis, L., Gunning, J. and Breen Smyth, M. (2011) *Terrorism: A Critical Introduction*. Basingstoke: Palgrave.

Jarvis, L. and Macdonald, S. (2014) 'What is Cyberterrorism? Findings from a Survey of Researchers' *Terrorism and Political Violence*. DOI: 10.1080/09546553.2013.847827.

Jarvis, L., Macdonald, S. and Nouri, L. (2014a) 'The Cyberterrorism Threat: Findings from a Survey of Researchers' *Studies in Conflict and Terrorism* 37(1): 68–90.

Jarvis, L., Nouri, L. and Whiting, A. (2014b) 'Understanding, Locating and Constructing Cyberterrorism', in T. Chen, L. Jarvis and S. Macdonald (eds.) *Cyberterrorism: Understanding, Assessment, and Response*. New York, NY: Springer: 25–41.

Lewis, J. A. (2002) *Assessing the Risks of Cyber Terrorism, Cyber War and Other Cyber Threats* (Centre for Strategic and International Studies), available at http://www.mafhoum.com/press4/128T41.pdf (last accessed 20 December 2013).

Macdonald, S., Jarvis, L., Chen, T. and Lavis, S. (2013) *Cyberterrorism: A Survey of Researchers*. Cyberterrorism Research Report (No. 1), Swansea University, available via www.cyberterrorism-project.org (last accessed 20 December 2013).

McCormick, G. (2003) 'Terrorist Decision Making' *Annual Review of Political Science* 6(1): 473–507.

Pollitt, M. M. (1998) 'Cyberterrorism: Fact or Fancy'? *Computer Fraud and Security* 2: 8–10.

Rathmell, A. (1999) 'Cyber-terrorism: The Shape of Future Conflict?' *Journal of Financial Crime* 6: 277–83.

Schmid, A. P. and Jongman, A. J. (2008) *Political Terrorism: A New Guide to Actors, Authors, Concepts, Data Bases, Theories, and Literature* (updated edn.). New Brunswick, NJ: Transaction.

Stohl, M. (2006) 'Cyber Terrorism: A Clear and Present Danger, the Sum of All Fears, Breaking Point or Patriot Games?' *Crime, Law and Social Change* 46: 223–38.

Talihärm, A. (2010) 'Cyberterrorism: In Theory or in Practice?' *Defense Against Terrorism Review* 3: 59–74.

Weimann, G. (2005) 'Cyberterrorism: The Sum of all Fears?' *Studies in Conflict and Terrorism* 28: 129–49.

Weimann, G. (2009) 'Cyberterrorism: How Real is the Threat?' *United States Institute of Peace Special Report* 119.

Weinberg, L., Pedahzur, A. and Hirsch-Hoefler, S. (2004) 'The Challenges of Conceptualizing Terrorism' *Terrorism and Political Violence* 16(4): 777–94.

Wilson (2014) 'Cyber Threats to Critical Information Infrastructure', in T. Chen, L. Jarvis and S. Macdonald (eds.) *Cyberterrorism: Understanding, Assessment and Response*. New York, NY: Springer.

Essay 1

A CRITICAL APPROACH: VIOLENCE, 'VICTIMS' AND 'INNOCENTS'

MARIE BREEN-SMYTH AND SAMANTHA COOKE

... On behalf of those who are suffering now I make this protest against the deception which is being practised on them; also I believe that I may help to destroy the callous complacence with which the majority of those at home regard the continuance of agonies which they do not share, and which they have not sufficient imagination to realize. (Siegfried Sassoon, July 1917)

Introduction

These lines, written by Siegfried Sassoon, far from home in the trenches of World War I, accuse observers of war and political violence of 'callous complacence' about suffering in war, and of lacking the imagination to realise the depth of the suffering. War and political violence does not affect all equally, even those who experience it at close quarters. Some individuals suffer more than others, some lose their lives, their limbs, their sanity, whilst others emerge comparatively unscathed. Certain categories of individual are more vulnerable, the most vulnerable sections of any population being usually the weakest and poorest: women, older people, disabled people, those with insufficient resources to relocate out of danger, and children. In the case of children and other vulnerable groups whose ability to describe their situation is limited, is there 'sufficient imagination to realise' the impact of war?

We look to research, to war reporting, to personal contact and the accounts of victims and survivors to gain some sense of the suffering inflicted by war. Yet attention is not always focused on the most vulnerable, or those who have suffered most. In societies where political violence is rife and killings are commonplace, often only recent horrors, multiple killings and killings that are out of the ordinary qualify as worthy of attention. Other horrors recede into oblivion having failed to attain the threshold above which they are noted, remarkable. Many human-rights transgressions, killings and other physical and epistemic violence in political battlefields are taken for granted, forgotten, unnarrated. Seremetakis (1996) points out that it is the narration of the public account that defines the unnarrated, silenced stories:

> This cultural construction of the 'public' and the sayable in turn creates zones of privatized, inadmissible memory and experience that operate as spaces of social amnesia and anaesthesia. (Seremetakis, 1996: 19)

In the competition for public attention the most heroic, the most 'attractive', the most tragic, the most affirming of particular political narratives or hegemonies are most likely to be heard. Tragedies, spectacular or 'sensational' events are 'sensational' because they occur alongside and are differentiated from the mundane. Juxtaposing the remarkable and tragic alongside the everyday and mundane allows them to define one another (Seremetakis, 1996: 19). In the case of accounts from victims and child soldiers the accounts must be historically contextualised since only then can the political work that they do be understood.

Violence and meaning

Richard Slotkin, writing about America, the meaning of violence and the American frontier, points out:

> What is distinctively 'American' is not necessarily the amount or kind of violence that characterizes our history, but the mythic significance we have assigned to the kinds of violence we have actually experienced, the forms of symbolic violence we imagine or invent, and the political uses to which we put that symbolism. (Slotkin, 1992: 13)

Slotkin was describing how accounts of the American frontier are deployed in the justification of expansionist violence, yet his observation applies more broadly to the fluidity and historical specificity with which violence is understood. And it is within this fluidity and contextual specificity that victims in general and child soldiers in particular are represented. For example, in the America of the nineteenth century, child soldiering was common during the Revolutionary War (Hull, 1998; Keesee, 2001).

Yet in 2008 the US Congress had adopted the Child Soldiers Prevention Act, thus equipping the US government to pressure military allies to end child soldiering by withholding US military training and assistance. The US has waived these sanctions more frequently than not, failing to provide many governments with incentives to take child soldiering seriously (Becker, 2013). However, in October 2013 the US government announced that it would withhold military assistance from the Central African Republic, the Democratic Republic of Congo, Somalia, and Rwanda because of their use of child soldiers.

In 2011 UNICEF (2011) estimated that there were approximately 300,000 soldiers in various locations around the world under the age of 18. The greatest overall numbers of child soldiers are to be found in the global south. It is estimated that child soldiers are fighting in at least 14 countries around the world, with both boys and girls forced into combat, exploited for their labour and subjected to multiple forms of violence (Human Rights Watch, 2012). The UN Secretary-General reports annually to the Security Council on children being used in armed conflict, and he is required to list all armed groups – both state and non-state – that recruit children under the age of 18. In 2012, 55 state and non-state armed groups operating across three continents were listed, of whom 32 had been listed annually for at least five years and were 'persistent perpetrators'. Seven of these were state armies (the Roméo Dallaire Child Soldiers Initiative, 2013).

Political violence inflicts harm on all sections of the population: civilians, combatants, state forces; even journalists, visitors and those living outside the contested territory. Often little is known about the scale of those permanently disabled, either physically or emotionally, by conflict; but the effects of political violence are typically concentrated in certain geographical locations. It is these communities, already blighted by violence, that also suffer the highest levels of socio-economic deprivation.

Smyth et al. (1994) and later Hayes and Campbell (2005) found that the emotional impact of bereavement due to political violence does not necessarily diminish over time; indeed, psychological symptoms may appear for the first time many years later. Psychological injuries may include phobias, anxiety-related conditions, agoraphobia, depression and sleep disturbance. Alcohol and drug misuse, including misuse of prescribed medication, are often misguided attempts to cope with psychological sequelae. Until levels of violence diminish, many of these problems and issues will remain unacknowledged and unaddressed.

The attribution of the term victim to these casualties of war and political violence is not straightforward. In South Africa a determination of who could be considered a victim was made as part of the Truth and Reconciliation Commission's (TRC) deliberations and entitled those thus recognised to reparations. Yet there are those who consider themselves victims yet who failed to meet the TRC's criteria. A survey of the population of Northern Ireland (Bloomfield, 1998) some seven years into the peace process found that 12 per cent of the sample saw themselves as victims of the conflict and that those who considered themselves victims were older, less likely to be in professional/managerial occupations, had lower levels of psychological well-being and were less likely to live in areas of low violence.

The legitimacy of claims to victim status is determined contextually within a wider culture of victimhood. Victims are often represented stereotypically as passive, suffering, powerless, helpless, dependent, bereft, absolved from responsibility, needy, innocent and morally entitled to support and help (Smyth, 2000; 2001; 2003). The status of victimhood thus affords certain dispensations and political advantages to the individual victim and the victimised community. A victim deserves sympathy, support and outside help from others to overthrow the victimiser. Any aggressive or violent act by the victim can be justified as self-defence, thereby excusing or legitimising violence by or on behalf of victims. Armed factions in the conflict, particularly those who have killed and injured others, might wish to lay claim to victim status for their constituency, since without such a status their violence becomes perceived as morally indefensible and thus politically damaging to them.

A political culture in which victimhood is routinely deployed as a way of escaping guilt, shame or responsibility, and in which there are competing claims to victimhood, may constitute a 'war by other means'. Such cultures legitimise violence, are unlikely to support the taking of political responsibility or shared decision-making, and are prone to returns to direct violence. Thus, how victimhood is conceptualised and managed has wide-ranging implications, not merely for those considered victims but for the wider society and prospects for peace.

There is a wide range of definitions of victims and varieties of official practices in terms of endorsement of victim status. A very broad conceptualisation of victimhood was contained in Northern Ireland's Bloomfield Report which found

> some substance in the argument that no-one living in Northern Ireland
> through this most unhappy period will have escaped some degree of damage.
> (Bloomfield, 1998)

However, broad, universal definitions of victims do not help to target humanitarian resources towards victims, and they tend to mask the way in which damage and loss have been concentrated in particular sub-populations. Nevertheless, it provides an antidote to proposals to include only 'innocent' victims – however defined – that bedevilled victims' politics, for example in Northern Ireland, where welfare provision for victims was interpreted as the *quid pro quo* for prisoner early releases in the peace process. The use of 'innocent' or 'real' as qualifications for victimhood can be seen as a process of disidentification (De Swaan, 1997), demarcating the population of victims along lines that correspond to divisions in the broader society.

In public discourses about political violence, victims often acquire a status as 'moral beacons' (Thomas, 1999). Victims may be seen as role models, living examples of some higher state – some feat of stoicism – that others should aspire to. Victims' accounts of suffering often inspire awe at the resilience of the human spirit, and those who forgive without hesitation and are conciliatory in their political attitudes are often held up as models of moral superiority. The response of the victim can become a moral benchmark by which the public can gauge their own entitlement to anger and desire for revenge or retaliation. Victims' disposition in relation to the allocation of blame or to the quest for revenge is influential and sets a standard for the reactions of others less affected by the violence. It is this function, this power of victims, which politicians strive to appropriate into their political repertoire. By association with victims politicians bring unassailable moral authority to their cause. The collectivisation of emotions arising out of victimisation of a group or nationality is a powerful impetus which binds the individual to the group. It is a formidable political force. This collective emotion in social movements has been described by Patočka (1996) as the 'solidarity of the shaken' following the collective experience of catastrophic events such as war.

The public role of victims is also socially and politically significant. Yet the outcome of victimisation by political violence may not be moral improvement but rather compunction to retaliate and hate. Suffering *per se* is not sufficient moral qualification. To qualify as a 'moral beacon' in Thomas' (1999) terminology the victim's identity and role must be congruent with the dominant political values. The suffering must be recognised as 'undeserved' according to those values, and the victim must belong to a group that is not stigmatised. Contests about the legitimacy of victim status are common, and efforts to exclude others from the category of victim are often based on antagonism related to the conflict itself. If 'war is merely a continuation of politics', as Clausewitz opined, then contests over the definition of victimhood compose a 'war by other means'.

This representation of victims conceals the true complexity of the diversity of identities, histories and affiliations of those doing harm and being harmed by political conflict. The definition of victimhood and the role of victims are a set of political practices, where issues of inclusion and exclusion are played out in an ongoing contest in public life. Some, enthralled by recent political violence, fight to keep it black and white, right and wrong, denying that one can be both a perpetrator and a victim, that one cannot hold these roles simultaneously (Smyth, 2003). This bifurcated conceptualisation does not correspond with the complexities of roles that people often play in violent conflict. To build victims policy on unilateral claims to the moral high ground, based on rigid distinctions between the innocent and the guilty, is to support the conduct of a 'war by other means'. Only by engaging with the complex nature of victimisation and harm-doing and deconstructing the rigid black-and-white divisions associated with the conflict can such policies be built on solid foundations.

Humanitarian law and the rules of war

Although the share of civilians killed and injured in any conflict has been contested, it is clear that civilians suffer at least as much and often more than combatants in any given conflict. A significant global decline in the number of armed conflicts has meant a corresponding decline in casualty rates since the end of the Cold War. However, the increase in the number of intra-state conflicts that are internationalised where external states support one or other side of the conflict has given rise to an increase in casualty rates and the prolonging of conflicts (SIPRI, 2013). The emergence of multipolarity in international relations and this pattern of proxy warfare have implications not only for the international order but also for conflict management and prevention and compliance with international humanitarian law and the rules of war.

The laws of armed conflict (or international humanitarian law) are legislative attempts to mitigate the worst excesses of war. They attempt, *inter alia*, to regulate the forms of weaponry and define the legitimacy of targets. The 1949 Geneva Conventions and the 1977 Additional Protocols set out specific rules aimed at protecting civilians. A central concern is to minimise the harm caused to civilians, and two specific principles, those of proportionality and distinction, specify how this is to be operationalised. In intra-state conflicts that are outside the purview of these treaties civilians are protected by international human-rights law and by domestic laws compatible with these international laws.

There are strong ethical, strategic and legal reasons for limiting civilian harm, and warring parties use evidence of attacks on civilians to discredit parties to conflict. Harm caused to women and children, attacks on hospitals and on other vulnerable groups, and the use of torture or chemical weapons are regarded as indefensible, and may be used to justify further military intervention against a party that uses such measures. In many instances, however, these principles and legal requirements are more honoured in the breach than the observance, not because of the lack of regulations and laws but owing to poor compliance, and this is particularly the case with the use of children for war and political violence.

International law and children in armed conflict

Children in situations of armed conflict are protected under international humanitarian law. However, children also join armed groups and directly engage in armed conflict as child soldiers. Nevertheless, the child soldier is represented as a victim, even though not all child soldiers are forcibly recruited. The Cape Town Principles (1997) define a child soldier as:

> ... any person under 18 years of age who is part of any kind of regular armed force or armed group in any capacity, including but not limited to cooks, porters, messengers and anyone accompanying such groups, other than family members. The definition includes girls recruited for sexual purposes and for forced marriage. It does not, therefore, only refer to a child who is carrying or has carried arms. (UNICEF, 1997)

Some children volunteer, whilst others are press-ganged and some kidnapped. It has been argued that the concept of voluntary recruitment of children is meaningless since those children who volunteer are usually doing so out of a desperate attempt to survive. The appeals of regular meals, shelter, medical attention and a soldier's wage can also incentivise children to join. Some children are offered to armed groups by poverty-stricken parents, and wages may be paid to their families, whilst some girls are encouraged to become soldiers if they have poor marriage prospects (UNICEF Special Concerns UN). A child may be motivated to join an armed group through witnessing the humiliation of family members or the oppression of their community on the basis of ethnicity, religion or other differences and the desire to defend or avenge their community. Other children may be drawn to take what they see as a heroic stand and may find the notion of martyrdom appealing (McIntyre, 2003). Children may either perform direct military roles or support roles such as cooks, porters, messengers and spies, and some may be used sexually.

The case of the child soldier clearly demonstrates the complexities of victim politics. Is the child soldier a victim, a perpetrator or both? On the one hand, childhood confers on an individual a degree of moral dispensation, whereby a child cannot be held culpable for his or her actions before a certain age. Even where the child has not been abducted by an armed group but has volunteered to join, such volition does not have legal probity below a certain age. On the other hand, children who are members of armed groups inflict injury and death on others, some on members of their own family and community, albeit under duress.

Concern and understanding of the plight of child soldiers rely on several legal and social conceptualisations: the definition of child and the concept of childhood.

The child and childhood

First, a child is a person under a certain age: for the purposes of international protocols, such as the UN Convention on the Rights of the Child, a child is 'every human being below the age of 18 years' (Organization of African Unity, 1990) unless a different majority age is specified by law. The rights of the child have been enshrined in international human-rights law since the UN General Assembly adopted the Convention on the Rights of the Child on 20 November 1989, which came into force in September 1990. Numerous subsequent resolutions – 1261 (1999), 1314 (2000), 1379 (2001), 1460 (2003), 1539 (2004), 1612 (2005), 1882 (2009) and 1998 (2011) – by the UN Security Council (UNSC) form part of a continuing project to progress the protection of children.

Childhood on the other hand is, according to Aries (1979), a social institution which emerged in the west during the eighteenth century amongst the bourgeoisie. Prior to the eighteenth century the concept of childhood applied only to children below the age of five. Those over the age of five were not socially separate from adults and were often economically active in factories and mines. Childhood, then, is associated with the development of schooling as moral instruction outside the home and involves the social segregation of children from the world of adults.

By the end of the nineteenth century the concern about children's moral development and changing patterns of work and family life led to new conceptualisations of the responsibility of parents, and the importance of privacy, morality and domesticity in child development (Bowlby, 1953). The introduction of workplace regulation, with the Factory Acts in the 1840s, began a broader process of constructing the notion of citizenship, a concept that included children. Eventually, the legal enshrinement of children's rights to education and welfare gave rise to the state's legal right to intervene in the family to protect the child from parents and to ensure that the child has access to education. The conditionality of parental rights over children was further institutionalised in the UK and elsewhere by a series of Children's Acts and their equivalents. More recent educational attitudes have conceptualised children as innocent and in need of adult protection.

Being chronologically young has not always been associated with childhood as we currently understand it, nor is childhood a universal or timeless phenomenon. Childhood is a comparatively recent idea, a socially constructed phenomenon that acts as a deep structure, regulating and reproducing the language, expectations and content of relationships between adults and children. In the west and increasingly elsewhere childhood is manifest by, for example, the legal protection of children from economic, sexual and other forms of exploitation; legal limits on the age of marriage and criminal responsibility; compulsory schooling; tolerance of ignorance and mistakes on the part of children; and formalising the duty to care of all adults, not only the child's parents. The concept of childhood marshals adult recognition of the special needs and vulnerabilities of children and the attendant adult moral and legal duties towards them.

Kingsolver's fictional account of a childhood in the Congo captures something of the societal specificity and conditional nature of childhood for the white narrator and her Congolese playmate:

> It struck me what a wide world of difference there was between our sort of games – 'Mother May I?' and 'Hide and Seek' – and his: 'Find Food,' 'Recognise Poisonwood,' 'Build a House.' And he was a boy no older than eight or nine. He had a younger sister who carried the family's baby everywhere she went and hacked weeds with her mother in the manioc field. I could see the whole idea and business of Childhood was nothing guaranteed. It seemed to me, in fact, like something more or less invented by white people and stuck onto the front end of grown-up life like a frill on a dress. (Kingsolver, 1999: 114)

The disappearance of childhood

Postman (1982) argues that childhood is disappearing in Western society because of increased divorce rates, absent fathers, women working outside the home, the 'discovery' of childhood sexual abuse and so on. According to Postman (1982), there are three preconditions for childhood – literacy, education and shame – and that these disappeared during Europe's descent into what is called the dark ages, hence childhood too disappeared. War and political violence can have a similar effect on literacy and education, thus jeopardising childhood.

During armed conflict childhood as a state of being for children is under threat and may disappear altogether. In Postman's analysis this is due to alterations in societal shame, particularly under conditions of armed conflict and political violence. Norbert Elias (1994) holds that a personal internalised sense of shame is central to the practice of self-regulation which at the individual level ultimately composes a societal 'civilising process'. This process, according to Elias, is the main societal mechanism for the deterrence of violence and killing. Ideologies that support war or the commission of acts of political violence neutralise such shame. Acts of violence are (re)interpreted as honourable and the fulfilment of a duty to fight. Just-war theory, used to qualify military intervention and cultures of warrior honour, are mechanisms that overwhelm Elias's self-regulating and civilising shame. They are (highly gendered) cultures that create ideological conditions permissive of violence. In the absence of shame the 'normal' rules of childhood are dissipated; children may see, know and do things that in peacetime should not be seen, known or done by children. Children can experience brutality, injury, death and threat at first hand, either as victims or witnesses, or as perpetrators. Often childhood disappears.

The child soldier: the legal context

Until the year 2000 there was no universal outright ban on child soldiers under international law. Whilst customary international law in the form of Additional Protocol I (1977) of the Geneva Conventions and the Convention on the Right of the Child (1989) – ratified by 192 states – both prohibited states and non-state actors from recruiting soldiers below the age of 15, children volunteering to fight in conflict were not covered by legal prohibition. The African Charter on the Rights and Welfare of the Child of 1990 was the only regional treaty that specified that persons under the age of 18 should take no direct part in hostilities and that states should refrain from recruiting any child. The Rome Statute of the International Criminal Court of 1998 established a permanent court to try war crimes, crimes against humanity and genocide. This statute defined 'conscripting or enlisting children under the age of fifteen years into armed forces or groups or using them to participate actively in hostilities' as a war crime. By March 2012 seven people from the Democratic Republic of Congo and Uganda had been charged with recruiting and using child soldiers. Subsequently, the Worst Forms of Child Labour Convention in 1999, ratified by over 170 countries, prohibited the forced or compulsory recruitment of children under the age of 18 for use in armed conflict and defined it as one of the worst forms of child labour. It was only in 2000 that Optional Protocol 1379 to the Convention on the Rights of the Child on the Involvement of Children in Armed Conflict, ratified by 144 countries, set 18 as the minimum age for direct participation in hostilities, for recruitment into armed groups and for compulsory recruitment by governments. Significant progress in protecting the rights of the child was made when the first list was submitted to the UN Security Council in 2003, naming parties known to use children as combatants in conflict (UNICEF, 2003: 9). These provisions were later augmented by Resolution 1882, which prohibited the killing and injuring of children, and Resolution 1998, which prohibited attacks on schools and hospitals (UNICEF, 2003: 9).

UN Resolution 1379 was seen to have made pioneering contributions towards identifying groups that recruit and use children in armed conflict at an international level. Rather than basing the list on identified groups, the report provides analysis by country, showing why some groups are to be monitored by the UNSC and the Office of the Special Representative of the Secretary-General for Children and Armed Conflicts (OSRGS/CAC) and others are not (Coalition to Stop the Use of Child Soldiers 2002). It is because of these ground-breaking provisions that 1379 can be seen as one of the most significant resolutions adopted and this will be examined further.

Irrespective of international law and protocols, young children may be found in government armies and, more commonly, in armed rebel groups. Human Rights Watch report that child soldiers are fighting in at least 14 countries: Afghanistan, Burma, Central African Republic, Chad, Colombia, Democratic Republic of Congo (DRC), India, Iraq, Philippines, Somalia, South Sudan, Sudan, Thailand and Yemen (Human Rights Watch, 2012). Farrell and Schmitt (2011) add Burundi and Uganda to this list and point out that the use of more than 10,000 child soldiers in Sierra Leone led the UN to establish a special tribunal to prosecute the use of child soldiers. In Sierra Leone 80 per cent of rebel soldiers were between the age of 7 and 14.

In Columbia in 1998, 15,000 soldiers in the national armed forces were between the ages of 15 and 17 (International Bureau for Children's Rights, 2002). Nor is recruitment limited to economically underdeveloped contexts; it also occurs in industrialised countries. In Europe the UK has the lowest minimum age for recruitment into the armed forces – 16 years old, with recruitment in schools beginning at 14. The UK also has the highest recruitment of under-18-year-olds into its armed forces (Forces Watch, 2011). Between March 1998 and March 1999, 36 per cent of the total annual recruits in the UK were under 18 (Amman Conference Report, 2001).

The effects of child soldiering

Child soldiers may suffer psychological trauma, and Amnesty International believes that recruitment ultimately jeopardises the mental and physical integrity of anyone below the age of 18, in addition to violating their human rights. Child combatants can also be exposed to violence as witnesses, victims and perpetrators, and this can lead to injury, disability or death. Disabilities acquired through exposure to political violence may also make it difficult for the combatants to do other work once the fighting is over.

Indeed, some, such as Pinto (International Bureau for Children's Rights, 2002: 1), have argued that participation in combat roles may actually be necessary and sensible for children's survival.

> *Children will participate. It is the healthiest thing for them to do, especially in stressful situations. Participation can only enhance their mental and survival needs.*

Graca Machel (1996) has pointed out that children who have participated in combat may find it difficult to disengage and may find the transition to a non-violent lifestyle difficult. In a study of South African youth Straker and Moosa (1994) found that most of the group who had previously been engaged in violence as part of the mass anti-apartheid movement had learned that violence is not acceptable in civilian life. Machel's research also revealed that in 10 per cent of the respondents a general capacity for empathy had been damaged, and they admitted to being unable to control their aggression. Engagement in political violence had become so central to their identity that some young people experienced difficulty in developing new constructive social roles. Former child combatants lose the sense of power and perhaps strong bonds with their group. The end of war can be disappointing and boring in comparison to their experience of conflict, and they may resist going back to subservient or traditional roles and be angry at authority. Former child soldiers suffer from severe physical and psychological trauma and they may be returning to communities that have also been deeply affected by conflict.

Child soldiers: disarmament, demobilisation, reinsertion and reintegration (DDRR)

The preferred strategy for the rehabilitation and reintegration of child soldiers into society – either when the conflict ends or when they are out of the armed group – is known as disarmament, demobilisation, reinsertion and reintegration, or DDRR. Formal DDRR programmes are put in place following a peace agreement, but not in all cases. DDRR programmes for child soldiers are modelled on similar programmes for adult combatants. In the case of children, however, family reunification, psychological support and education, and economic opportunities are emphasised (Knight and Özerdem, 2004). The programmes are implemented in three stages. In the first phase disarmament takes place. Combatants' weapons are collected, which frequently involves the exchange of weapons for money or vocational training opportunities. The second phase is demobilisation, which requires the dismantling of military structures and chains of command. The third phase is reintegration, during which the combatants return to life as civilians.

DDR programmes are the preferred method of returning the child soldier to civilian life, but they are frequently not implemented for a range of reasons. State and non-state parties to a conflict may deny their use of child soldiers and, as a result, children may not be included in the demobilisation programme. The UNHCR and the International Save the Children Alliance found that in Mozambique only 1.5 per cent of all demobilised combatants were female, yet 40 per cent of the children found at the sites of military bases during the war were girls. DDR programmes are available only to a small percentage of children who could benefit from them.

These children frequently return to deprived communities, and their lack of education and skills further constrains their opportunities. In addition, former child soldiers can also be stigmatised by their communities, especially if they have been sexually assaulted or, in the case of girls, have borne children. For these reasons the risk of re-recruitment can be high after children are released from an armed group. It is not surprising, therefore, that when attempts at demobilising children are carried out whilst hostilities are continuing some re-recruitment occurs. The child soldier may also be put under pressure by the armed group to rejoin; they may be better fed and safer as a member of an armed group; they may be bonded to that group; or they may desire to fight for the cause. Thus, the complex situation, particularly of the older child soldier, may demonstrate both victim status and political agency.

Analysis

The heavy emphasis on age as a decisive factor in the vulnerability of the child soldier points to several problems in the discussion of child soldiering. First, chronological age rather than developmental stage is the defining factor, yet it is possible to conceive that someone over the age of 18 might be as psychologically vulnerable as someone under that age. Whilst age limits may be important for legislative purposes, they are a crude indicator of individual capacity and circumstances. Furthermore, this lack of differentiation within the under-18 age group tends to mask the difference between the young adolescent seeking to defend his or her community and the much younger child used unwittingly by armed actors. Flowing from this, the proscription of children volunteering for armed action constructs the child as without political agency in situations where, for example, their community is under attack or occupation. Yet children have political views and are capable of forming opinions and making decisions, even if these abilities and views are formed differently by younger people. In the extreme circumstances that some children find themselves in, proscribing armed action may be to frustrate their own desires and instincts for their own and their family's survival. Whilst in peacetime the involvement of children in armed action is regarded with abhorrence by most observers, there is little equivalence between war and peacetime. In the earlier discussion of childhood it was argued that certain conditions are required for childhood to exist. Yet in conditions of armed conflict these conditions may not exist and therefore childhood as a social institution becomes unsustainable.

The recruitment of children for war is not confined to theatres of violent conflict in the global south, yet it is non-state actors in these conflicts that receive a disproportionate amount of critical publicity and international opprobrium. State actors such as the UK government recruit soldiers from the age of 16 and militarise children by recruiting into cadet forces even younger than that. Indeed, the UN Committee on the Rights of the Child asked the UK in 2008 to 'reconsider its active policy of recruitment of children into the armed forces and ensure that it does not occur in a manner which specifically targets ethnic minorities and children of low-income families'. In 2009 the Joint Human Rights Committee called on the UK government to raise the minimum age to 18; they recommended that the 'UK adopt a plan of action for implementing the Optional Protocol, including these recommendations, fully in the UK, together with a clear timetable for doing so'. The UK has no such plans.

The UK is the only European country to recruit children. British Army policy is not to deploy children until the age of 18, following the deaths of three 17-year-old soldiers, John McCaig, Paul Reid and George Muncaster in Northern Ireland between 1971 and 1977. However, in 2007, in response to a parliamentary question by the Liberal Democrats, it was revealed that the British Army had sent 15 soldiers under the age of 18 – four of them female – to fight in Iraq. Defence Minister Adam Ingram told parliament that soldiers under the age of 18 had been sent to Iraq over a two-year period between June 2003 and July 2005 by mistake. Ingram blamed a shortage of soldiers, and said that most of these had been despatched only shortly before their eighteenth birthdays and those who saw combat were withdrawn after a few days (BBC, 2007).

Teenagers make up the bulk of the UK armed forces' intake. In 2006, of the new recruits to the three armed services 2,760 were 16 years old, 3,415 were 17, whilst 980 recruits were aged 23, and 160 aged 28. Under the Freedom of Information Act an increase in the scale of recruitment in schools was discovered. There were 14 army recruitment visits to Scottish schools in 2003/2004 but this rose to 153 in 2005/2006. Stephen Armstrong (2007) describes how working-class schoolchildren between the ages of 14 and 16 from poor urban communities are regularly bussed to army 'encounter days' with the Duke of Lancaster's Regiment where they do rifle drill, learn to use a climbing wall, negotiate an obstacle course and complete a one-mile run. On completion the pupils are given a certificate signed by the commander of recruitment, a glossy teen magazine called *Camouflage*, a DVD and other recruitment material. All three British armed forces' advertising depicts joining the forces as almost like a gap year. Emphasis is placed on future career prospects and leisure activities; the possibility of killing and being killed is sidestepped.

A recruiting sergeant in the Liverpool army careers office told Armstrong that half of the applicants who walk in have difficulty filling in the form, supporting research by the MoD that found that the reading age of 50 per cent of those joining the army at non-officer level is at or below that of an average 11-year-old. Some recruits fake a parent's signature, permitting them to join in order to escape a difficult home life. There are no statistics available to quantify it, but many of the recruits come from the most disadvantaged working-class families and communities.

Colonel David Allfrey, the officer with responsibility for child recruitment through the Camouflage youth-information scheme, told the *New Statesman* how the armed forces strive to maintain the interest of children who are too young to join up but are interested in doing so (Armstrong, 2007). The Camouflage strategy, which began in 2000, had 271,000 children involved with the magazine and other marketing operations.

Conclusion

At face value, the issue of child soldiers is a straightforward humanitarian issue of child protection during war and armed conflict. International law and Optional Protocols set out clear age limits for recruitment into armed groups, and those who recruit below that age are setting themselves outside the law or, at a minimum, outside the agreed norms, however aspirational. In terms of international law, child soldiers as 'children' are victims of war when recruited into both non-state and state militaries. This chapter has argued that it is difficult to sustain a universal 'one size fits all' approach to child soldiering. Whilst this may be clear in some cases, and in the younger age groups, the case can be made that some child soldiers who volunteer for either non-state or state militaries demonstrate political agency. Furthermore, the idea of the military deployment of a child offends our Western conceptualisations of childhood, yet it can be argued that the protections and exclusions that childhood affords children are often swept aside in times of war, and, for some children, to take up arms or engage in fighting may well be a route to survival in extreme circumstances. These complexities raise important questions about our understanding of childhood, the power relations between adults and young people, and young people's political agency and involvement in political processes. The existence of child poverty, even in economically developed nations, together with poor educational achievement or provision are risk factors that contribute to the recruitment of children to the militaries of non-state actors and of states such as the UK. Furthermore, the moral imperative to urge compliance has been undermined by the behaviour of states such as the UK.

The protection of children in times of war is perhaps better attempted through improving the position of children in pre-war societies by addressing issues of social inequality and justice and by ending child poverty. These measures, together with greater reluctance to resort to military responses to domestic and international political disputes, are likely to be more successful in the long run in the matter of child protection. At this point, when both state and non state armed groups continue to recruit those under the age of 18, these approaches appear to promise more by way of contributing to ending the recruitment of children for war than international legal measures such as Optional Protocols.

The solution, then, surely, is to work for an end to hostilities rather than relying on bans on child recruitment. Peace and poverty alleviation – rather than attempting to regulate war – are the best guardians of childhood.

References

Amman Conference Report (2001). www.warchild.org/links_resources/childsoldiers/childsoldiers. html (Last accessed 2 October 2014).

Aries, P. (1979) *Centuries of Childhood*. Harmondsworth: Penguin.

Armstrong, S. (2007) 'Britain's Child Army'. *New Statesman* 5 February. Available at http://www.newstatesman.com/politics/2007/02/british-army-recruitment-iraq (Last accessed 30 September 2014).

Bawa, U. (1995) 'Organised Violence in Apartheid South Africa: Children as Victims and Perpetrators' in *Children – War and Persecution*. Osnabruck: UNICEF.

Becker, J. (2013) 'Dispatches: US Pushes Some Countries to End Child Soldier Use, But Lets Others Off'. Human Rights Watch. Available at http://www.hrw.org/news/2013/09/30/dispatches-us-pushes-some-countries-end-child-soldier-use-lets-others (Last accessed 21 April 2014).

BBC (2007) 'Under-18s Were Deployed to Iraq'. 4 February. Available at http://news.bbc.co.uk/1/hi/6328771.stm (Last accessed 30 September 2014).

Bloomfield, K. (1998) *We Will Remember Them: Report of the Northern Ireland Victims Commissioner, Sir Kenneth Bloomfield*. Belfast: HMSO.

Bowlby, J. (1953) *Child Care and the Growth of Love*. Harmondsworth: Penguin.

Breen-Smyth, M. (2012) 'The needs of individuals and their families injured as a result of the Troubles in Northern Ireland'. Available at: www.wavetraumacentre.org.uk/uploads/pdf/1404222308--WAVE-Final-Report1.pdf (Last accessed 30 September 2014).

Cairns, E., Mallet, J., Lewis, C. and Wilson, R. (2003) 'Who Are the Victims? Self-assessed Victimhood and the Northern Ireland Conflict'. Report No 7; Research and Statistical Series. Belfast: Northern Ireland Office, Northern Ireland Statistics and Research Branch.

Coalition to Stop the Use of Child Soldiers (2002) *Child Soldiers: 1379 Report*. November 2002, London.

De Swaan, A. (1997) 'Widening Circles of Disidentification: On the Psycho- and Sociogenesis of the Hatred of Distant Strangers; Reflections on Rwanda'. *Theory, Culture and Society*, 14(2): 105–122.

Elias, N. (1994) *The Civilising Process*. Oxford: Blackwell.

Farrell, T. and Schmitt, O. (2011) *The Causes, Character and Conduct of Armed Conflict, and the Effects on Civilian Populations, 1990–2010*. Geneva: Division of International Protection, United Nations High Commissioner for Refugees(UNHCR). Available at http://www.refworld.org/docid/4f8c3fcc2.html (Last accessed 30 September 2014).

ForcesWatch briefing: 'The recruitment of under 18s into the UK Armed Forces'. Available at: www.parliament.uk/documents/joint-committees/humanrights/Briefing_from_Forces_Watch_age_of_recruitment.pdf (Last accessed 30 September 2014).

Hayes, P.J. and Campbell, J. (2005) *Bloody Sunday: Trauma, Pain and Politics* London: Pluto.

Hull, S.R. (1998) *Boy Soldiers of the Confederacy*. Fort Worth: Eakin.

Human Rights Watch (2012) The Red Hand Day Campaign against the Use of Child Soldiers. Available at http://www.hrw.org/sites/default/files/Resource Pack 2012_updated_0.pdf (Last accessed 15 May 2014).

International Bureau for Children's Rights (2002) *Rites of Peace: Responding to the Rights of Children in Armed Conflict: 2000–2001*. Montreal: Peacemedia.

International Relations and Security Network (n.d.) *Child Soldiers: Disarmament, Demobilization and Reintegration (DDR)* Available at: http://www.ourmediaourselves.com/archives/43pdf/williamson.pdf (Last accessed 30 September 2014).

Keesee, D. M. (2001) *Too Young to Die: Boy Soldiers of the Union Army 1861-1865.* Huntington, WV: Blue Acorn Press.

Kingsolver, B. (1999) *The Poisonwood Bible.* London: Faber and Faber.

Knight, M. and Özerdem, A. (2004) 'Guns, Camps and Cash: Disarmament, Demobilization and Reinsertion of Former Combatants in Transitions from War to Peace'. *Journal of Peace Research*, 41(4): 499–516.

Knudsen, C. (2004) 'Demobilization and Reintegration During an Ongoing Conflict'. *Cornell International Law Journal*, 37: 497–504.

Machel, G. (1996) *Impact of Armed Conflict on Children.* UN Department for Policy Co-Ordination and Sustainable Development (DPCSD).

McIntyre, A. (2003) 'Rights, Root Causes and Recruitment: The Youth Factor in Africa's Armed Conflicts'. *African Security Review*, 12(2): 91–99.

Ministry of Defence (MoD) (2004–5) *Analysis of Socio-economic and Educational Background of Non-officer Recruits,* submitted as written evidence to House of Commons Defence Committee Duty of Care, Volume II, Ev255.

Organization of African Unity (1990) *African Charter on the Rights and Welfare of the Child,* 11 July, CAB/LEG/24.9/49.

Patočka, J. (1996) *Heretical Essays in the Philosophy of History,* trans Erazim Kohák, ed. James Dodd. Chicago: Open Court.

Pinto Borrego, M.E., Ballen, A.V. and Percipiano, Y.L. (2002) 'Diagnóstico del programa de reinserción en Colombia: mecanismos para incentivar la desmovilización voluntaria individual'. Archivos de Economia. Available at: www.dnp.gov.co.portalDNP/subdireccion-de-seguridad/211.PDF (Last accessed 30 September 2014).

Postman, N. (1982) *The Disappearance of Childhood.* New York: Delacorte Press.

Rivard, L. (2010) 'Child Soldiers and Disarmament, Demobilization and Reintegration Programs: The Universalism of Children's Rights vs. Cultural Relativism Debate'. *Journal of Humanitarian Assistance.* Available at http://sites.tufts.edu/jha/archives/772 (Last accessed 30 September 2014).

The Roméo Dallaire Child Soldiers Initiative (2013) *Child Soldiers: A Handbook for Security Sector Actors.* Halifax, Canada. Available at http://reliefweb.int/report/world/child-soldiers-handbook-security-sector-actors (Last accessed 15 May 2014).

Sassoon, S. (1917) *To My Dead Officer (Who Left School for the Army in 1914).* Cambridge: R.I. Severs.

Serematakis, C. N. (1996) *The Senses Still: Perception and Memory as Material Culture in Modernity.* Chicago: University of Chicago Press.

Slotkin, R. (1992) *Gunfighter Nation: The Myth of the Frontier in Twentieth Century America.* New York: Atheneum.

Smyth, M. (2000) 'The Human Consequences of conflict: constructing "victimhood" in the context of Northern Ireland' in A. Guelke and M. Cox (eds), *A Farewell to Arms: From War to Peace in Northern Ireland.* Manchester: Manchester University Press, pp. 118–135.

Smyth, M. (2001) 'The "Discovery" and Treatment of Trauma in Northern Ireland' in Democratic Dialogue Future Policies for the Past. Belfast: Democratic Dialogue, pp. 57–64.

Smyth, M. (2003) 'Burying the Past? Victims and Community Relations in Northern Ireland Since the Cease-fires' in N. Biggar (ed.) *Burying the Past: Making Peace and Doing Justice after Civil Conflict.* Washington DC: Georgetown University Press, pp. 125–154.

Smyth, M., Hayes, P. and Hayes, E. (1994) 'Post-Traumatic Stress Disorder and the Families of the Victims of Bloody Sunday: A Preliminary Study'. Paper to the Centre for the Study of Conflict/N.I. Association for Mental Health Conference on Violence and Mental Health, Queen's University, Belfast.

Stockholm International Peace Research Institute (SIPRI) (2013) *SIPRI Yearbook*. Available at http://www.sipri.org/yearbook/2013 (Last accessed 30 September 2014).

Straker, G. and Moosa, F. (1994) 'Interacting with Trauma Survivors in Contexts of Continuing trauma' *Journal of Traumatic Stress*, 7(3): 457–465.

Thomas, L. M, (1999) 'Suffering as a Moral Beacon: Blacks and Jews' in H. Flanzbaum (ed) *The Americanization of the Holocaust*. Baltimore: Johns Hopkins, pp. 198–210.

UN Committee on the Rights of the Child (2008) *Forty-Ninth Session: Consideration of Reports Submitted by States' Parties under Article 8 of the Optional Protocol to the Convention on the Rights of the Child on the Involvement of Children in Armed Conflict*. Concluding Observations: United Kingdom of Great Britain and Northern Ireland CRC/C/OPAC/GBR/CO/117 (2008). Available at http://www2.ohchr.org/english/bodies/crc/docs/advanceversions/crc.c.opac.gbr.co.1.pdf (Last accessed 30 September 2014).

UN Children's Fund (UNICEF) (2003) *Guide to the Optional Protocol on the Involvement of Children in Armed Conflict*. Available at http://www.un.org/rights/concerns.htm (Last accessed 30 September 2014).

UNICEF *Special Concerns*. Available at http://www.un.org/rights/concerns.htm (Last accessed 30 September 2014).

UNICEF (1997) *The Cape Town Principles and Best Practices*. Available at http://www.unicef.org/french/emerg/files/Cape_Town_ Principles.pdf (Last accessed 30 September 2014).

UNICEF (2011) *Fact Sheet: Child Soldiers*. Available at http://www.unicef.org/emerg/files/childsoldiers.pdf (Last accessed 15 May 2014).

Essay 2

A CRITICAL VIEW OF CRITICAL TERRORISM STUDIES

JAMES LUTZ

Introduction

Scholars involved in the subfield of critical terrorism studies (CTS), like many others who study terrorism, discuss the issue of definition. In part, they correctly note that many (legal) definitions have been specifically formulated so that they only apply to dissident movements because they only refer to sub-state actors. It is further argued that these types of definitions and others provide criteria that are based on the needs of governments (Gunning, 2007). Of course, definitions created by states need to provide criteria that can be used in a legal system; these definitions are not designed for use by academic analysts (Lutz and Lutz, 2008). There have been additional definitions of terrorism that rely on similar criteria but which do not automatically exclude actions by governments, as noted below. In any event, it is necessary to provide a basic definition of terrorism that can be used in the discussions to follow. Despite the fact that there are hundreds of such definitions, most analysts agree on something like the following:

Terrorism involves political aims and objectives through the use of violence or the threat of violence. It is intended to generate fear in a target audience that goes beyond the immediate victims. The violence involves an identifiable organization. Finally, the violence is designed to change the balance of power among contestants. The violence is often directed against civilian or non-combatant targets (Claridge, 1996; Lutz and Lutz, 2008).

This definition does not exclude action by states. It does not even explicitly exclude actions by one state against another during 'hot' or cold wars (USA and the Soviet Union, Israel and the Arab countries, India and Pakistan). Such overt or covert conflicts between states might be, and often are, considered special cases or are considered elsewhere within the framework of the study of international relations.

Are state activities ignored?

One of the most basic complaints present in the CTS literature is the idea that the violent activities used by governments, especially against their own citizens, have largely been ignored by 'orthodox' scholars studying terrorism. Critics further argue that terrorism has been defined by governments as dissident violence from below, thus intentionally excluding state activities (Jackson, 2008; Blakely, 2007; George, 1991). The exclusion of state violence from being considered as terrorism is, in their view, a consequence that flows from viewing terrorism from the perspective of the state and has, they claim, encouraged and created an orthodoxy in dealing with terrorism (Jackson, 2007). One element of this orthodoxy is the focus only on dissident violence – in line with the interest of governments to ignore their own questionable actions (or such actions by allied governments). Further, there have been suggestions by CTS scholars that only dissident violence directed against Western interests is considered terrorism (Jackson, 2008). One consequence of this situation is, in the eyes of CTS scholars, that terrorism 'has always been a pejorative rather than analytical term' (Jackson, 2007: 246). Is this true? It can be argued that it is in the period after World War II that the term terrorism came to have a mainly negative connotation among its practitioners. Members of the Jewish Irgun, for example, called themselves terrorists in the 1930s and 40s with little concern about negative connotations associated with the term. Yet even though the terms terrorism and terrorist have come to have a pejorative connotation in today's political vocabulary this does not mean that academic analysts are incapable of dealing with the issue in an unbiased fashion.

While this basic claim, that government actions are excluded from definitions of terrorism, is overstated in some respects, the CTS argument is based on the fact that many of those who study terrorism do focus on dissident terrorism rather than state violence. The analysts who focus on dissident terrorism take what may be termed a 'homeland security study' approach to the subject. It seeks to provide answers to governments on how they can deal with threats from either domestic groups or international terrorist organizations. Of course, when looking at foreign organizations some attention will be given to supporters of the dissident groups, including, in some cases, foreign governments. There is also a tendency within this approach to look more at the tactics of terrorist groups (and how to counter them) rather than at the underlying causes that drive individuals and organizations to resort to this specific type of violence.

There is little doubt that one of the reasons for the increase in homeland security studies is that government grants and contracts are more readily available for these types of analysis, since terrorist attacks can be a major threat to the security of states and the safety of their citizens. The consequent increase in the number of studies that deal with this type of threat is a response to the needs of governments that are attempting to provide better security, even if these studies do not necessarily enhance a more basic understanding of the sources of violence – terrorist and otherwise. Governments, much to the dismay of academics everywhere, are more interested in practical research (often narrowly defined) and not very interested in the pure research that so many academics are particularly fond of. This focus on homeland security is, therefore, a rather natural government response; it does not necessarily constitute proof of any effort to eliminate or prevent any alternative analysis of violence by the state from those interested in terrorism studies, even if it does lead some researchers to focus on dissident terrorism. Moreover, the claim that a 'terrorism industry' has been established that serves the state (Burnett and Whyte, 2005; Jackson, 2007) appears to be something of an overstatement; the intent is to portray the researchers as adjuncts of the government who focus only on political violence directed against the state, and state actions are ignored.

The claim that the study of state uses of terrorism has been ignored pre-dates the emergence of the CTS perspective. One earlier search of the literature in 1987 claimed that there have been virtually no discussions of state uses of terrorism in the social science literature (Slann, 1987), a claim that the CTS perspective has widely accepted. Yet while political scientists may not have referred to the use of violence by governments as terrorism (see the next section) they actually have a long history of looking at violent state activities in domestic arenas. In the past, political scientists regularly divided forms of government into totalitarian, authoritarian, and democratic regimes. The authoritarian category has perhaps been an overly broad one as it was used to encompass everything not fitting easily in the other two categories. In discussions of totalitarian societies, however, one criterion that was inevitably applied was the use of terror as a means of social control, especially through secret police agencies (Friedrich and Brzezinski, 1965; Hagopian, 1983; Neumann, 1986). Stalinist Russia, Nazi Germany, and Mao's People's Republic of China were held up as classic examples of totalitarian systems. More recent examples would include North Korea and the regime of Saddam Hussein in Iraq, at least before he engaged in a war to 'liberate' Kuwait. Many of the authoritarian regimes in a variety of forms also relied on the explicit or implicit use of illegal or illegitimate force against dissenters. Some of the rulers, such as Idi Amin in Uganda, or Francois Duvalier in Haiti, were notorious for the level of violence perpetuated by their security forces or (para-)military units. To reiterate the basic point, violence by governments against domestic populations has hardly been ignored by political scientists in academia. The fact that it has not been analyzed under the heading terrorism does not mean that it has not been studied. It has, in fact, been studied for a long time and in some depth, in the literature on human-rights violations, for instance.

State reliance on terrorist techniques directed against its own citizens has also been considered in the 'orthodox' terrorist literature. Wilkinson in one of his early works discussed the differences between revolutionary terrorism and repressive (state) terrorism, in a period well before terrorism became a hot topic (Wilkinson, 1975). Before him Thornton noted that terrorism could begin with the state and its security forces, and not with dissidents (Thornton, 1964). More recently David Claridge provided not only a very good definition of terrorism covering both dissident and regime terrorism, but also a rather compelling argument that some governments could and did indeed engage in campaigns of terrorism (Claridge, 1996). These early references in the literature suggest that the field of terrorism studies has not ignored terrorism from above or been pre-empted by homeland security analysts or 'the establishment' in quite the way that CTS scholars claim. While a majority of those interested in the use of terrorism may not focus on state activities, it does not mean that they deny the existence of state terrorism.

Some directly state-inspired or state-supported violent activities in international politics have not been ignored by social scientists, or by governments themselves. There has been a great deal of interest in practices that would generally be considered terrorist. Security agencies such as the CIA (United States), KGB (Soviet Union), SIS (Britain), and PIDES (Portugal), and a multitude of others have been directly responsible for assassinations, bombings, and other types of unlawful behavior – some more than others. Further, they have provided support for existing violent insurgent groups in other countries. This goes back a long way in history. Bulgarian governments supported the Internal Macedonian Revolutionary Organization (IMRO) in the 1920s, the Italian OVRA aided Croatian dissidents in Yugoslavia in the 1930s, the East German Democratic Republic (DDR) supported the (West German) Red Army Faction in the 1970s, the Czech communist regime provided support for the Italian Red Brigades in the same decade, the US Reagan administration supported the Nicaraguan Contras in the 1980s, while Pakistan has provided various types of support for Islamist groups active in Kashmir and Afghanistan for decades. These and other examples are well known enough to suggest that such government activities in the international arena have not been ignored by academia. In fact, these kinds of covert operations, while different from attacks against one's own citizens, have been well studied, most frequently in the context of international relations rather than terrorism studies. This also explains in part why discussions of war by proxy have been under-represented in key terrorism journals (Gunning, 2007; Jackson, 2008).

Terrorism versus repression

A second distinction relevant to a consideration of the claims advanced by CTS scholars about certain state actions involves the essential difference between state repression and state terrorism. All countries and their governments can be considered repressive in the sense that they enforce laws with which some citizens will disagree – and ordinary criminals are, of course, concerned with repression by the police. Repression can also occur in institutional contexts where a particular group in society is disadvantaged. These inequalities can take an institutional form and even be considered structural violence (e.g. if woman are legally prohibited from voting, or from engaging in certain occupations, or are not allowed to own property). Certain religious or ethnic groups may have fewer rights or face special barriers to social mobility. If a day of worship does not fall on the traditional 'weekend', adherents can perceive themselves as suffering disadvantages. It has been suggested that such inequalities and injustices in the system have become an underlying cause of terrorism (Jackson, 2007). While all of these situations of discrimination and unequal treatment are clearly deplorable, they are not necessarily examples of terrorism. They may not constitute terrorism even in cases of governments that are truly repressive – that deny or deprive some or all of their citizens of their most basic civil rights and liberties – since there are many other forms of political violence and repression.

Distinguishing between repression and terrorism is important. Sproat made a key distinction between the two (Sproat, 1990). Repression involves state uses of violence against specific individuals who have violated the laws of the land, however unfair these laws may be. Any citizen, however, can avoid such negative actions by state authorities by obeying the laws. Individuals who are arrested for violating laws do serve as an example and a deterrent to others, but the persons who are arrested are chosen because of their individual transgressions. Terrorism by the government, on the other hand, occurs when a member of a group is selected for victimization, usually at random, to provide a negative example for others belonging to the same (sub-)group. The choice of victims does not distinguish between the innocent and the guilty. The key element is the external audience that is being targeted (Jackson, 2008). In such circumstances it is not possible for any individual to avoid negative state action by obeying the laws of the land. Such exemplary violence meant to intimidate others qualifies as terrorism and is different from mere repression. It is important to note that not all repression is terrorism, even though state terrorism in most cases probably would qualify as repression.

It is also worth noting that a resort to state terrorism or collective repression is usually a sign of state weakness on the part of government rather than a sign of strength. A strong repressive state is normally able to control its population through crackdowns on individual dissidents based on good intelligence. Even the assassination of a leading opponent involves targeting an individual for his or her specific actions. Weaker states, however, often rely on extra-judicial processes, including attacks against members of 'suspicious' groups (ethnic, religious, regional, or ideological), thereby ignoring individual guilt. When, in 1933, Hitler came to power the first attacks on Jewish citizens in Germany were carried out by the paramilitary SA rather than by the official state security forces. The actions by the paramilitary groups permitted Hitler to at least make the claim to foreign governments that the attacks were spontaneous actions by private citizens. Such actions were, however, state-tolerated (and -promoted) terrorism, as Jews were not selected on the basis of their individual behavior but at random. Later, of course, when Hitler was more firmly in power, he was quite willing and able to use the full weight of a repressive state apparatus in Germany to turn all Jews first into second-class citizens and then into targets for the 'final solution' – genocide.

This distinction between repression and terrorism is important to bear in mind when charges are made that Western countries have actively supported terrorist regimes. To some extent this claim would appear to result from confusing repression with terrorism. It loses a great deal of its salience when it is recognized that it has been repressive states that have been supported by the West, but not necessarily terrorist regimes. The distinction, of course, may not be important for the citizens who suffer in one form or another at the hands of security forces and secret police agencies. Yet for analytic purposes it is important to distinguish terrorism (a technique of intimidation and group punishment) from repression, or even from harsh repression – a technique for governing against the will of the population or sectors thereof.

Terrorism versus terror (fear)

In addition to the distinction between terrorism and repression, there is also an important difference between terrorism and fear (or terror). In many situations criminals induce fear in their victims, but the goal of that is to reduce resistance in burglaries or extortions – there is no politics involved. The use of fear for financial gain is most obvious in kidnappings for profit or with demands for protection money by organized crime groups. Similarly, governments are usually able to induce some fear in criminals because of the prospect of arrest, conviction, and punishment. At some level there is also the political objective of enhanced peace and security for citizens. Yet such fear of punishment generally occurs within the rule of law; it is not arbitrary – or at least not consistently arbitrary, certainly in democracies. If normal, everyday activities become crimes, there is fear, but the situation generally reflects one of repression rather than government terrorism. Thus, the presence of fear cannot by itself be used to define the existence of the use of terrorism by the state.

The failure to distinguish between terror and terrorism also occurs when analysts make comparisons with military actions, which normally involve governments. Most generals prefer to find a way to create overwhelming fear or terror among opposing troops. An army that panics and runs away yields an easy victory. Fear is present in these circumstances, but not terrorism. Aerial or artillery bombardment of villages or urban areas will induce fear and terror among local residents. Often the goals of such bombardments are military objectives only distantly related to the political objectives that are inevitably part of any military conflict. If the bombardment occurs on enemy territory during a war the resulting action may constitute a wartime atrocity or massacre if there was no military necessity, but it is a conceptual stretch to call this terrorism even if it creates great fear (Jackson, 2008). The same may be true in domestic military campaigns in circumstances of rebellion or civil war. Civilian areas can become targets as part of efforts to subdue rebellious regions or territories in turmoil, even though, in point of fact, such bombardments are often counterproductive from a political perspective.[1] Military commanders, however, may be more interested in limiting casualties among their own troops than in furthering their government's political objectives. Many military officers are either not interested or not trained to look at the political consequences of their combat decisions; often they hold political goals in some disdain if these interfere with military objectives. Even in circumstances where heavy casualties result, such as the devastation of large sections of the town of Hama in Syria in February 1982 (which cost up to 40,000 lives at the hands of government forces), or, more recently, relatively indiscriminate attacks by Nigerian military forces against communities in the Niger delta, this might not be best described as terrorism. Rather, such massacres could either been described as gross human-rights violations or qualify as war crimes under humanitarian law.

Everything evil is not terrorism

It needs to be recognized that not every form of violence that is evil or reprehensible, when performed by governments, constitutes terrorism. Genocide is far worse than terrorism, but genocide does not primarily seek to create fear in a target audience. In fact, governments undertaking genocide may even seek to lull victims into a false sense of security to make the killing easier. This was the case with the Armenians in the Ottoman Empire, the Jews during the Holocaust, and more recently, according to some reports, with the Tutsi in Rwanda. Similarly, harsh repression of non-violent dissent is evil, but it is usually not terrorism as long as it is not indiscriminate. Slavery is a pernicious attack on human dignity, but it is not terrorism. Institutional violence in which some citizens have fewer rights or situations where equal rights are not equally protected are to be deplored, but they are not terrorism (unless accompanied by government-tolerated vigilante violence intended to enforce the control of particular groups). It is quite legitimate and desirable to focus public and scholarly attention on these issues, but it is not appropriate to consider them to be examples of terrorism. To fault those who study other forms of terrorism than state terrorism, as CTS scholars do, is unjust since these types of situation are actually frequently analyzed in other academic (sub-)disciplines. Therefore, it cannot be said that 'orthodox' analysts 'refuse to examine cases of state terrorism' (Jackson, 2008: 26), and the term state terrorism is very broadly defined. If almost every example of government use of force to maintain law and order is labelled state terrorism then the concept of terrorism ceases to have any real meaning and simply becomes a polemic term used to apply a negative and pejorative label to a government or state that an observer dislikes.

Supporters of the CTS perspective also argue that the conventional approach to terrorism noticeably ignores the violence involved in the counterterrorism strategies of governments. They further argue that governments take advantage of the presence of dissident terrorist actions to crack down on their opponents. It has even been suggested that the recent wave of attacks by dissident groups has led governments 'to manufacture' a new concept of terrorism in order to further the interests of the elite (Burnett and Whyte, 2005). Governments in many circumstances have long greeted threats and acts of violent protest from dissidents as not-unwelcome pretexts for crackdowns on dissenters, or for other political purposes. Such manipulation of public events, however, does not necessarily qualify as terrorism even when it frequently involves manipulation and repression.

The use of dissident actions as an excuse for government repression or the excesses of counterterrorism has also been cited by CT scholars to allege that the conventional 'orthodox' terrorism perspective is flawed in another way. They often suggest that the research focus has been on government reactions, as discussing terrorism from the perspective of the terrorists is 'a taboo stance within Western scholarship' (Sederberg, 2003). While much of the conventional literature on terrorism does not directly address the viewpoint of the terrorists directly, the whole issue of the causes of terrorism (e.g. in studies on radicalization) does address the perspectives of those involved in terrorist actions. For example, arguments that repression or lack of participation leads to political violence, including acts of terrorism, clearly involves looking at events from the perspective of the dissidents (Jackson, 2007). Admittedly, since it is – at least in Western democracies – much easier to get documentary material on the perspectives of governments and their counterterrorism strategies, greater attention has been given to these. Even so, communiqués and statements by leaders of dissident groups to provide insights into their perspectives have been used for analyses of the origins and motives of dissident and insurgent groups using tactics of terrorism. Further, considerations of reform and concessions as counterterrorist strategies implicitly view events from the perspective of the terrorist groups rather than merely that of the government (Crenshaw, 2011).

In defense of the critical-terrorism-studies perspective

Notwithstanding the above comments, it is important to recognize that the CTS perspective has something valuable to offer to analysts, since it reminds everyone that many governments can and do use terrorism (in a narrowly defined sense of the term). Death squads operating with government tolerance or active support are designed to create terror in target audiences. Such para-military squads also provide the state with a shield, however thin, of plausible deniability (Campbell, 2000). When Black Americans were lynched in the American south (and elsewhere) in the years before World War II local government officials in southern states of the USA often tolerated such actions. In effect, a number of local governments supported terrorism against a minority population as a form of social control. The support was especially obvious where perpetrators of the lynchings were rarely charged. Moreover, on the rare occasions that they were even brought to trial they were generally acquitted. If a Black American was accused of a crime or of violating 'appropriate' social norms and the actual culprit could not be discovered or caught, then any Black person could be killed to serve as a message to the entire community to remind its members of their place in society (Dollard, 1978). Clearly, this type of action goes beyond repression and institutional violence and reaches the level of terrorism.

Other examples of state terrorism have been documented. In Burundi the periodic pogroms against Hutus by the Tutsi elite qualified as terrorism. The targets of the violence were not able to avoid death by individual lawful behavior. Pogroms against Jews in central and eastern Europe that occurred after the 1970s with the tacit or active consent of governments would qualify as terrorism as well. More recently the government of Sudan has unleashed Arab Janjaweed militias against its domestic opponents, first in the southern, mainly Christian part of the country and then in Darfur (which is mainly populated by African Muslims) as part of efforts to terrify dissident groups into submission. The quasi-governmental ruling groups in the Serbian portions of Bosnia and Herzegovina used terror in the 1990s as part of a very conscious policy of ethnic cleansing. Murder and rape became weapons of choice, convincing Muslims to flee the areas that Serb paramilitaries were claiming for their own. The actions of some of the supporters of President Mugabe in Zimbabwe also qualify as state terrorism. There state authorities have consistently ignored violence by the government's paramilitaries and veterans of the independence struggles when directed against members of the opposition. One circumstance that makes state terrorism so important to study is that it is much more deadly in terms of number of victims than dissident terrorism (Jackson, 2008).

Conclusion

To conclude this discussion it is worth emphasizing first that precision is always important when discussing political and social phenomena. The consent of state terrorism cannot be stretched to include all the forms of political violence and repression that non-democratic but also some democratic states perform. Nor can the term terrorism be allowed to become a negative term to apply to capitalist states only, whether democratic or not. It needs to be defined in a way that has a clear and consistent meaning for everyone. Nor should analysts who choose to focus on dissident terrorism be accused of being pawns of the state. Second, while state terrorism has not received the attention that those in favor of the CTS perspective think that it should have, it clearly has not been ignored by academics. Negative state actions and state repression have been frequently studied, sometimes in great detail. Finally, with a more balanced and limited view of how governments can and do use terrorism, it should be possible for scholars embracing the CTS perspective to contribute in a much more constructive way to the analysis of the notion of government terrorism and the techniques that such regimes use.

Note

1   Israeli reprisals against Palestinians in Gaza or the West Bank have led to fear among the Palestinian population, but the attacks have been ineffective in limiting opposition.

References

Blakely, R. (2007) 'Bringing the State Back into Terrorism Studies,' *European Political Science*, Vol. 6, No. 3.

Burnett, J. and Whyte, D. (2005) 'Embedded Expertise and the New Terrorism,' *Journal for Crime, Conflict and the Media*, Vol. 1, No. 4.

Campbell, B. D. (2000) 'Death Squads: Definition, Problems, and Historical Context,' in B. D. Campbell and A. D. Brenner (eds.), *Death Squads in Global Perspective: Murder with Deniability* (New York: St. Martin's).

Claridge, D. (1996) 'State Terrorism? Applying a Definitional Model,' *Terrorism and Political Violence*, Vol. 8, No. 3.

Crenshaw, M. (2011) *Explaining Terrorism: Causes, Processes and Consequences* (London: Routledge).

Dollard, J. (1978) 'Caste and Class in a Southern Town,' in R. Lane and J. J. Turner, Jr. (eds.), *Riot, Rout, and Tumult: Readings in American Social and Political Violence*, Contributions in American History No. 69 (Westport, CN: Greenwood Press).

Friedrich, C. and Z. K. Brzezinski (1965) *Totalitarian Dictatorship and Autocracy*, 2nd edn. (Cambridge: Harvard University Press).

George, A. (ed.) (1991) *Western State Terrorism* (Cambridge: Polity Press).

Gunning, J. (2007) 'A Case for Critical Terrorism Studies,' *Government and Opposition*, Vol. 42, No. 3.

Hagopian, M. N. (1983) *Regimes, Movements, and Ideologies*, 2nd edn. (New York: Addison-Wesley Longman).

Jackson, R. (2007) 'The Core Commitments of Critical Terrorism Studies,' *European Political Science*, Vol. 6, No. 3.

Jackson, R. (2008) 'An Argument for Terrorism,' *Perspectives on Terrorism*, Vol. 2, No. 2.

Lutz, J. M. and B. J. Lutz (2008) *Global Terrorism*, 2nd edn. (London: Routledge).

Neumann, F. L. (1986) 'Notes on the Theory of Dictatorship,' in R. Macridis and B. E. Brown (eds.), *Comparative Politics: Notes and Readings*, 3rd edn. (Homewood, IL: Dorsey Press).

Sederberg, P. C. (2003) 'Global Terrorism: Problems of Challenge and Response,' in C. W. Kegley, Jr. (ed.), *The New Global Terrorism: Characteristics, Causes, Controls* (Upper Saddle River, NJ: Prentice Hall).

Slann, M. (1987) 'The States as Terrorist,' in M. Slann and B. Schechterman (eds.), *Multidimensional Terrorism* (Boulder, CO: Lynne Reinner).

Sproat, P. A. (1990) 'Can the State be Terrorist?' *Terrorism*, Vol. 14, No. 1.

Thorton, T. P. (1964) 'Terror as a Weapon of Political Agitation,' in H. Eckstein (ed.), *Internal War* (New York: Free Press).

Wilkinson, P. (1975) *Political Terrorism* (New York: John Wiley).

Essay 3

THE GLOBAL WAR ON TERROR AND STATE TERRORISM[1]

MICHAEL STOHL

While it is often proclaimed that the events of 9/11 changed 'everything', it is important to stress that the response of the Bush administration and its impact on multiple audiences around the world have been more important than the al-Qaeda attacks in shaping the post-9/11 world. As Stohl (2008) argues, despite the etymological roots and historical employment of violence and terrorism by the state against its own citizens, scholars who consider themselves experts on 'terrorism' rarely consider the violence perpetrated by the state against its own population or those of states beyond its borders. This also results in databases for terrorism research which, in addition to their many other problems, do not include the state's use of terror and thus operationalize out the study of state terror. In the case of evaluating the Bush administration and terror the primary foci have been the numbers and possibilities of attacks by al-Qaeda and other organizations identified as part of the global war on terror, and the state of al-Qaeda as an organization and/or network. The focus of scholarly concern on the data of terrorism has been the quality of the state-department-provided data on insurgent attacks and not with the absence of reported incidents of state terror (Krueger and Laitin, 2004).

Much of the Bush administration's response to 9/11 has focused on (a) criticism of the choice to fight a global war on terrorism, (b) the concentration on military power, (c) the choices made in the prosecution of the war in Afghanistan and then (d) linking Saddam Hussein to the war on terrorism and attacking Iraq. Each of these policy critiques arose out of the choice the Bush administration made to pursue a war-fighting rather than criminal-justice approach to counterterrorism. The critiques then focus on the logic behind choosing to go to war in Iraq and how the war has been mismanaged; they often only secondarily confront the inability (or unwillingness) of the Bush administration to differentiate among terrorists and their motivations, geographic foci and targets. For its part, the administration, which came into office believing that rogue states and their sponsorship of terrorism were the key to the terrorism problem (see for example Condoleezza Rice's 2000 *Foreign Affairs* article laying out the administration's foreign policy assumptions), continues to justify its decision to attack Iraq as part of the GWOT (global war on terror). Thus, their policy choices remain consistent with their pre-9/11 beliefs on confronting terrorism.

The Bush administration's counterterrorism strategy was initiated in October 2001 with the official launching of Operation Enduring Freedom and was followed eighteen months later by the attack on Iraq in what was dubbed Operation Iraqi Freedom. As has been noted previously (Stohl and Stohl, 2007), the strategic approach for which the administration has opted, i.e. counterterrorism as war, does not recognize the difference between terrorism and other forms of violence in that it does not recognize the core communicative role that the violence of terrorism and counterterrorism plays. There has been much recognition that the choices made by the administration with respect to its willingness to challenge long-standing principles of American military and legal policy (such as the Geneva conventions and the use of torture, the CIA policy of rendition, as well as the unintended consequences of the scandal at Abu Ghraib) have all diminished the standing of the USA in the eyes of much of the world's public. US policymakers seem to have reinvented the logic of the 1950 Hoover Commission to justify policies and tactics that would 'normally' be considered outside the bounds of acceptable behavior justifications, which would certainly appeal to Dostoevsky's brooding brothers Smerdyakov and Ivan Karamazov, who concluded that 'if there is no God, all behavior is permissible'.

But what has not been examined closely is the relationship between these choices and the subsequent increase in both human-rights violations and state repression in states that the USA has recruited into its war on terror. Because scholars of terrorism have seen state violence and terrorism as outside the bounds of terrorism studies, they do not consider how the choices in the Bush administration's counterterrorism strategy enable, acquiesce to or ignore the violence of the recruited states, and this has deleterious effects not only for the populations that are repressed but also for the counterterrorism efforts of the USA.

To pursue its strategic choices the USA engaged in coalition building, creating the global coalition against terrorism and, as a key component of that coalition building, dramatically altered its arms sales and arms-sales policies, as well as significantly praising its new diplomatic partners for their assistance in the GWOT. I will argue that a direct consequence of this strategy has been an increase in state repression and state terror. In addition, the prosecution of the GWOT in this manner has had the clearly unintended consequence of further alienating the very audiences that the USA requires to support its goals if its war on terrorism is to have any chance of success in the long term. The material and diplomatic alterations in US policy and the decision calculus of states are the most important nexus to consider in government choices to engage in state terrorism. In the context of state terrorism it is important to examine the consequences of the US decision to build this coalition, in terms of not only its impact in confronting al-Qaeda and reducing the threat of terrorism to the USA, but also the impact that such a strategy and its implementation have on the conditions within the states that became members of the coalition.

Duvall and Stohl (1983) and Stohl (1984) explored the considerations that states may make in choosing to employ terror against their own citizens and in assisting other states to do so. The underlying argument was that state decision makers pursued what Weiner (1972) refers to as an 'Expectancy X Value' theory or expected-utility theory of motivation in which 'the direction and intensity of behavior is a function of the expectation that certain actions will lead to the goal, and the incentive value of the goal object'. The argument assumes that an actor behaves in accordance with a basic calculation which consists of three main elements: (1) the benefits that the actor would receive from some desired state of affairs; (2) the actor's beliefs about the probability with which the desired state of affairs would be brought about if the actor were to engage in a particular action; and (3) the actor's beliefs about the probable costs or negative consequences that it would have to bear as a result of its engaging in that action. It assumes, therefore, that the greater the relative expected utility of terrorist action for an actor as compared to other forms of governance, the greater the probability that the actor will engage in terrorist action.

When governments consider the costs of engaging in terrorist behaviors two kinds of costs can be distinguished: response costs and production costs. Response costs are costs which might be imposed by the target group and/or sympathetic or offended bystanders. The bystanders in the foreign-policy realm may include domestic and foreign audiences, while the target in international as in domestic affairs may be wider than the attacking party may have intended. When governments consider various means of governance they are also attentive to the expected responses of others. What others are likely to do in reaction affects the utility of a particular strategy. Most relevant to a consideration of terrorism are what might be called punitive or retributive costs imposed by the target group and/or sympathetic or offended bystanders. Governments are sensitive to the costs imposed by other governments for their behaviors. Foreign-government diplomatic condemnations, sanctions and trade embargoes push governments to caution or secrecy in terms of their 'unacceptable' behaviors, such as state terrorism, repression and other forms of human-rights violations.

In discussions of insurgent terrorists it is often remarked that these terrorists attempt to make themselves invulnerable. There are at least two means to this end. One is inaccessibility. Retaliators may know in general, or even in particular, who the terrorist is but be unable to locate him. The anonymity of refugee camps or urban areas, and physical mobility, provide this inaccessibility for insurgent terrorists. Insurgents seek safe havens amongst supporters or within populations (or states) which are unwilling to confront them and make the calculation to acquiesce to the presence of terrorists within their midst. One of the key elements of any counterterrorism strategy is the struggle to convince populations that the costs of offering safe haven – or simply allowing safe havens – are greater than the cost of assisting governments in eliminating such havens.

In general, we don't think of governments and governmental decision makers as inaccessible in these terms, except to the extent that they completely insulate themselves from popular contacts, and to the degree that they are immune to international pressure. They tend to rely more on the second means of invulnerability, that is, secrecy of action. State terrorism can often be expected to be covert action because in this way the government effectively reduces its vulnerability to retaliation even below its vulnerability to the (otherwise lesser) response costs expected for other means of governance. This implies that, in general, state terrorism will not have publicity of its cause as an objective; this does not suggest that the government wishes the terror to be unknown, but rather that the government does not publicize its role and relies on the communication of the threat through word of mouth and rumors. Also, it means that as public accessibility to governmental officials is greater, and/or as regime vulnerability to international pressure is greater, terrorism is more likely to be secretive or carried out by paramilitaries whose connections to the government are officially denied.

Production costs are the costs of taking the action regardless of the reactions of others. In addition to the economic cost – paying the participants, buying weapons and the like – there is the psychological cost of behaving in a manner which most individuals, under normal conditions, would characterize as unacceptable.

The psychological costs that an actor can expect from perpetrating violence on an incidental, instrumental victim involves two conjoining factors. The first factor is the extent to which human life is valued (or, conversely, the strength of internalized prohibitions against violence in general). The second is the extent to which the victim can be or has been dehumanized in the mind of the violent actor. Where moral/normative prohibitions are weak, and especially where victims can be viewed in other than human terms, the self-imposed costs of terrorist actions are apt to be low and hence the choice of terrorist actions more frequent (Duvall and Stohl, 1983: 209).

The extent to which victims and potential victims can be dehumanized is affected by two important variables (for an extended discussion of this point see the seminal piece by Herbert Kelman, 1973). The first is the perceived social distance between the government and the victim population. The second is the extent to which action is routinely and bureaucratically authorized, so that personal responsibility is perceived by all actors in the decisional chain to be lower for governments (a) in a conflict situation with those they define as 'inferior' and/or (b) with a highly bureaucratized coercive machinery. In the context of the global coalition the USA identified al-Qaeda as an organization that operated in 'more than sixty countries'. Stohl and Stohl (2007) have critiqued the administration's use of the network designation through which organizational 'links' were transformed into organizational control, and which obscured the differing organizational goals, recruitment patterns and tactical and operational coordination. States, however, were happy to request assistance or to be asked to accept assistance from the USA, which would aid them in rooting out al-Qaeda and the designated 'al-Qaeda organizational affiliate' from within their states. Al-Qaeda (and violent jihadis in general) were characterized as apocalyptic and hateful, devoid of reasonable political aims, interested only in death and destruction and thus incapable of rational thought or political bargaining. Since, from the administration's view, these terrorists and their organizations are only interested in death and destruction the obvious strategic conclusion is that they must be eliminated because they cannot be neutralized or moderated. Thus, in Kelman's terms, the identification of political opponents, minority groups and other terrorists as al-Qaeda served the function of increasing the perceived social distance between the government and the victim population for the government itself, but even more importantly perhaps for the external 'publics', in this case the US government and population (and others in the West), reducing response costs as well. Thus, all things being equal, a reduction in either or both production and response costs should increase the expected utility of the choice of state repression and/or terrorism by states.

We would therefore expect that increasing US assistance to states in the global coalition against terrorism which have identified themselves as having terrorism problems linked to al-Qaeda should show declining human-rights situations and increases in state repression and terror. Further, the communication of US approval for the actions of such states should serve to reduce support for the USA within those countries, as populations there (and elsewhere) recognize the role that US support for these repressive states plays in their ability to engage in repression and state terror. Thus, beyond those states that have received material support, states whose repressive policies have received such approval are likely to bring negative responses to the USA over time and thus reduce the USA's ability to mobilize these populations against the terrorists it seeks to confront.

These important consequences of counterterrorism policy thus far have received much less consideration than warranted by their implications and we should briefly consider why. First, many scholars continue to have difficulty with the concept of state terrorism – except as it is applied to illegitimate rulers or non-democratic regimes. Violence by legitimate states tends to be considered well within the legitimate practices of the state and hence not terrorist in nature. Sproat noted in 1991, 'As Crelinstein phrased it, "the legitimacy and power of the state tend to cloak any overt forms of (its) violence in different guises, such as arrest instead of abduction ... imprisonment instead of hostage taking, execution instead of murder," and internationally coercive diplomacy instead of blackmail.' In addition, the discussions that have taken place about violations of the Geneva conventions and the use of torture with respect to the Bush administration in general focus on either the ticking-bomb question or the issue of violations of law and the expectations of the behavior of democratic states, rather than on the repressive states who join the coalition. The behavior of other national states who are 'helping' the USA in the global war against terrorism and domestic conditions within those states have not been traditional concerns of 'realist' scholars or political commentators, who have no expectations that these states 'should' behave better. Further, both international-relations scholars and scholars of terrorism and counterterrorism have been far more concerned with hard rather than soft power (Nye, 2008) and do not think in terms of multiple global audiences in the contemporary global communication and media environment. Thus, they do not normally consider the role of public diplomacy in counterterrorism. It is time to recognize that not only is the whole world watching – it is watching the whole world.

Note

1   This essay is a reprint of an essay previously published as The Global War on Terror and State Terrorism in *Perspectives on Terrorism*, 2, June 2008, 4–10 at www.ptv.com

References

Crelinstein, R. D. 1987. 'Power and Meaning: Terrorism as a Struggle over Access to the Communication Structure,' in *Contemporary Research On Terrorism*, eds. P. Wilkinson and A. M. Stewart (Aberdeen: Aberdeen University Press): 440.

Duvall, R. D. and Stohl, M. 1983. 'Governance by Terror,' chapter six in Stohl, M. (ed.) *The Politics of Terrorism*. Second edition, Marcel Dekker: 179–219. Third Edition, Revised and Expanded, 1988: 231–71.

Kelman, H. 1973. 'Violence Without Moral Restraint: Reflections on the Dehumanization of Victims and Victimizers,' *Journal of Social Issues*, 29, 4: 26–61.

Krueger, A. and Laitin, D. 2004. 'Misunderestimating Terrorism,' *Foreign Affairs* 83, 5: 8–13.

Nye, J. 2008. 'Public Diplomacy and Soft Power,' *The ANNALS of the American Academy of Political and Social Science*, 616: 95–109.

Sproat, P. 1991. 'Can the State be Terrorist?' *Studies in Conflict and Terrorism*, 14, 1: 19–29.

Stohl, C. and Stohl, M. 2007. 'Networks of Terror: Theoretical Assumptions and Pragmatic Consequences,' *Communication Theory*, 47, 2: 93–124.

Stohl, M. 1984. 'National Interests and State Terrorism,' *Political Science*, 36, 2: 37–52.

Stohl, M. 2008. 'Old Myths, New Fantasies and the Enduring Realities of Terrorism,' *Critical Studies on Terrorism*, 1, 1: 5–16.

Weiner, B. 1972. *Theories of Motivation*. Chicago: Markham.

PART 2
UNDERSTANDING TERRORISM

Part 2 charts how terrorism campaigns emerge and operate within a broader context. Chapter 5 explores the root causes of terrorism, tracing the contexts in which terrorism emerges and examining the significance of poverty and failed states as causes of terrorism. Building on the previous chapter, Chapter 6 focuses on the supporters of terrorist groups and how these relationships can help or hinder their mobilization. The chapter also outlines the reasons why a state might support a terrorist group and how this can affect that group's behaviour. Expanding on how terrorist groups operate, Chapter 7 shows how terrorism is as much a means of communication as it is a form of political violence. It then discusses terrorism in the context of the media and the internet, providing a robust challenge against common conceptions of its role in facilitating terrorist mobilization. Part 2 concludes with three essays which look at different aspects of terrorist mobilization in a broader context. Essay 4 goes into depth on the role of improvised explosive devices (IEDs) in Iraq, placing terrorism tactics within the broader context of civil wars and insurgency. Drawing on many of the points made in Chapter 3, particularly the organizational aspects of terrorism campaigns, Essay 5 analyses the mobilization and evolution of al-Qaeda at the global level. Essay 6 continues the theme of placing terrorism within a broader context, looking at the impact of terrorism in Israel at the individual, social, political and economic levels.

PART 2

5

THE ROOT CAUSES OF TERRORISM

NINA MUSGRAVE

Introduction

A large proportion of studies on terrorism investigate what have come to be called the root causes of terrorism. In 1981, Martha Crenshaw described the study of terrorism as being 'organized around three questions: why terrorism occurs, how the process of terrorism works, and what its social and political effects are' (Crenshaw, 1981: 379). This chapter attempts to deal with the first part of this question: why terrorism occurs. The analysis of the root causes of terrorism refers to the academic investigation of the causal relationship between certain political, social, demographic and economic factors and the implementation of terrorist acts. In this investigation the factors that are generally considered encompass a wide range of issues, such as poverty, state failure, state sponsorship, social inequality and exclusion. More recently topics such as religious terrorism and the psychological aspects of terrorism have also been analysed in the general field of root causes. This chapter will address the two most frequently debated ones: poverty and failed states.

The rationale behind the root causes approach is that if certain conditions can be established as providing an environment for terrorism to emerge or grow then changing or improving these conditions will ameliorate terrorism. Writing in 1993, Jeffrey Ian Ross described the analysis of terrorism as 'descriptively rich but analytically barren' (Ross, 1993: 326) and called for deeper analysis. Ross explained that the main causes in the literature could generally be placed into one of three categories: structural, psychological and rational choice (Ross, 1993). This frame of analysis emerged from Crenshaw's 1981 work on the causes of terrorism. Here, Crenshaw advised a conceptual distinction between *preconditions*, 'factors that set the stage for terrorism over the long run, and *precipitants*, specific events that immediately precede the occurrence of terrorism' (Crenshaw, 1981: 381).

This chapter looks at poverty and failed states as preconditions, as these are two main factors that have been considered to provide fertile territory for terrorism to emerge. As this chapter will explain, the question about whether poverty contributes to terrorism has been one of the most frequently debated. Analysing and understanding the poverty debate is necessary for two reasons. Firstly, it has been one of the most frequently argued debates. Secondly, it has been linked to debates about other root causes, such as religion or lack of education. Therefore, understanding the poverty debate brings to light other contested root causes of terrorism. The failed states debate has been chosen because the examination of failed states gained increased currency in the aftermath of the 9/11 attacks, as perceived failed states such as Afghanistan were seen as supporting terrorism (Call, 2008).

As Omer Taspinar explains, the 9/11 attacks resulted in the emergence of two schools of thought about the origins of terrorism. For those with left-of-centre political leanings there was a move to understand terrorism with the assumption that socio-economic factors contributed directly to the emergence of terrorism. In this sense, addressing these supposed root causes through socio-economic development would help eradicate terrorism. There were academics in complete disagreement with this argument: 'most terrorists are neither poor nor uneducated' (Taspinar, 2009: 75). In this way Taspinar explains that terrorism was then understood only as a security threat (Taspinar, 2009).

Identifying root causes of terrorism is indeed challenging, and trying to attribute terrorism to such clearly defined categorisations can be problematic. The reality of terrorism is extremely complex and more so than the assumptions of this approach would suggest. Terrorist acts take place for reasons such as ideology, nationalism and political disenfranchisement, to name but a few. Therefore, to argue that a terrorist act can be attributed to such rigid categorisations means that subtleties and nuance can get lost along the way. As Edward Newman argues, 'root causes can never form the whole picture' (Newman, 2006: 756). Furthermore, the ongoing academic debate about the definition of terrorism leads to the argument that root causes as a field of enquiry will remain problematic as there is so much disagreement about what actually constitutes 'terrorism' (Gupta, 2005). However, as Newman argues, despite frequent academic dismissal of root causes as a level of analysis, it can actually be useful when analysed in conjunction with other precipitant factors (Newman, 2006). Here, Newman is advocating the model put forth by Crenshaw in 1981, that which distinguishes between preconditions and precipitants (Crenshaw, 1981).

In addition, and linked to the argument about the link between poverty and terrorism, there is a body of literature that more specifically argues that it is not necessarily poverty itself that causes terrorism but other social factors that frequently accompany poverty. John Horgan calls for terrorism to be understood as being affected by 'strategic and psychological factors' (Horgan, 2005: 47). Horgan argues that root causes cannot be ascertained by viewing terrorism as 'a homogenous threat deriving from some homogenous origin' and that the complexities of root causes of terrorism should also be viewed from a psychological perspective (Horgan, 2005).

Therefore, the structural factors of poverty and weak governance feed into societal grievance – and it is argued that terrorism can emerge from this type of grievance. For example, the blockade of the Gaza Strip has caused serious poverty for Palestinians living there and, while this is acknowledged as fuelling radicalism, it is also the general political grievance of Israel occupying Palestinian land that fuels radicalism. For example, in a study of Palestinian suicide bombers Nasra Hassan explained that none of them were poor or uneducated, or even depressed, but that they justified the tactic of suicide bombing in both political and Islamic terms (Hassan, 2001). Martha Crenshaw wrote in 1981 that 'the outstanding common characteristic of terrorists is their normality' (Crenshaw, 1981: 390). Scott Atran builds on this by explaining that there is a received wisdom about suicide bombers being 'crazed cowards bent on senseless destruction who thrive in poverty and ignorance' (Atran, 2003: 1534). Atran reiterates the argument that poverty and lack of education are not enabling factors when considering suicide bombing. Atran argues that suicide bombers have 'no appreciable psychopathology' and, considering this, calls for a more nuanced understanding as to why seemingly educated and stable people become suicide bombers (Atran, 2003). Jerrold M. Post makes a similar argument about terrorists in general by saying that 'policies designed to deter terrorists from their acts of terrorism should be based on an understanding of "what makes terrorists tick"' (Post, 2005: 66).

Poverty as a root cause of terrorism

William O'Neill argues that the root causes of terrorism cannot be explained by poverty alone but that 'Terrorism is thus often linked to a sense of injustice and impotence rather than sheer poverty' (O'Neill, 2002: 22). In this way people feel left out and terrorism becomes a form of 'vengeance'. Furthermore, O'Neill argues that this makes recruitment easier for terrorist leaders. Francisco Gutiérrez argues that there is a strong link between terrorism and inequality but that this is not enough to justify the argument of inequality being a root cause. Gutiérrez instead argues that while this link exists, it is 'politically mediated' and that political structures 'act as regulatory variables that decide how the people placed on the wrong side of the inequality ladder will behave' (Gutiérrez, 2002: 45).

The aftermath of the 9/11 attacks saw frequent instances of politicians and policymakers citing poverty as being a root cause of terrorism. In terms of academic enquiry, James Piazza explains that poverty is analysed through the following barometers: 'per capita income, literacy, life expectancy, more equal distribution of wealth, growth of GDP, stable prices, employment opportunities, and food security' (Piazza, 2006: 170). At a development summit in Mexico in 2002 Michael Moore, head of the World Trade Organization, addressing leaders from over 50 countries, said: 'Poverty in all its forms is the greatest single threat to peace, security, democracy, human rights and the environment' (quoted in *The New York Times*, 2002). On the first anniversary of 9/11 President George W. Bush wrote an op-ed for the *New York Times* stressing the importance of the perceived link between poverty and terrorism:

> Poverty does not transform poor people into terrorists and murderers. Yet poverty, corruption and repression are a toxic combination in many societies, leading to weak governments that are unable to enforce order or patrol their borders and are vulnerable to terrorist networks and drug cartels. (Bush, 2002)

Similarly, writing only eight days after the 9/11 attacks, then State Senator Barack Obama wrote that terrorism:

> may find expression in a particular brand of violence and may be channeled by particular demagogues or fanatics. Most often, though, it grows out of a climate of poverty and ignorance, helplessness and despair. (Quoted in Keating, 2013)

Despite academic research that has claimed to nullify the direct link between poverty and terrorism, the perception expressed by George W. Bush has survived; this sentiment is what James Piazza terms the 'rooted-in-poverty hypothesis' (Piazza, 2006). As Robert Jervis explained in the aftermath of 9/11, there was a move among the more liberal establishment in the USA to look to the root causes of terrorism as a way to fully understand why terrorist acts take place so that they could be pre-empted. Central to this was the opinion that poverty was a root cause. As Jervis explained, the thinking at the time was that, 'We must get at the root causes of terrorism: we must understand why we are hated' (Jervis, 2002: 41). The understanding of the link between poverty and terrorism has therefore survived and as recently as January 2014 US Secretary of State, John Kerry, expressed this view:

> And so we have a huge common interest in dealing with this issue of poverty, which in many cases is the root cause of terrorism or even the root cause of the disenfranchisement of millions of people on this planet. (Quoted in Bier, 2014)

The assumption is that poverty provides conditions for the emergence and growth of terrorism; that the lack of education associated with poverty means the fostering of ideological extremism; and that the hopelessness brought about by poverty is a radicalising factor.

Despite these assertions about the link between poverty and terrorism, there is ample scholarly insistence that this is not the case. To date, one of the most widely cited studies in this regard is by Alan B. Krueger and Jitka Maleckova (2003). Krueger and Maleckova include education in their analysis on the assumption that the link between poverty and education can be analysed in conjunction with terrorism. They analysed support for terrorist activities and focused on the models of Hamas in the Palestinian Territories and Hezbollah in Lebanon. By using opinion-poll data from interviews with 1357 Palestinians, Krueger and Maleckova show that higher levels of education do not show a decreased support for attacks against Israel. Furthermore, they show that support for attacks against Israel actually increased in correlation with educational achievement. For example, they explain that 'By a 68 percentage point margin those with *more than* a secondary school education support armed attacks against Israeli targets, while the margin is 46 points for those who are illiterate and 63 points for those with an elementary school education' (Krueger and Maleckova, 2003: 125). They then further explain that the unemployed are less likely to support armed attacks, concluding that 'If poverty was the wellspring of support for terrorism, one would have expected the unemployed to be more supportive of armed attacks than merchants and professionals, not less' (Krueger and Maleckova, 2003: 127).

Krueger and Maleckova's approach to the education, poverty and terrorism connection in Lebanon takes a different methodological route. In this case they analyse the biographies of 129 members of Hezbollah's military wing. They explain that the poverty rate is 28 per cent for Hezbollah militants, but 33 per cent for the Lebanese population. They also explain that Hezbollah militants are more likely to get a secondary school education than the general population.

Krueger and Maleckova's argument, then, as they explain, agrees with Berrebi's 2003 study of Palestinian terrorist acts. Within this, Krueger and Maleckova explain that once Berrebi's data about suicide bombing is extracted his results corroborate theirs. Berrebi argues that despite popular wisdom, Palestinian suicide bombers (generally members of Hamas and Palestinian Islamic Jihad) have a higher standard of education than the societal mean. When Berrebi's 2003 work was republished in 2007 he argued that 'Both higher education and standard of living appear to be *positively* associated with membership in terror organizations such as Hamas or PIJ and with becoming a suicide bomber' (Berrebi, 2007: 30). A similar argument was made about Mohammad Atta, who was one of the 9/11 hijackers. The argument was that Atta came from a wealthy Egyptian family and had received a relatively high level of education (Ajami, 2001). Furthermore, there were reports that, in fact, all the 9/11 hijackers were middle class and 'not the poor and dispossessed' (McDermott, 2011).

In this sense, these arguments are used to bolster the point that if the perpetrators of terrorist acts are not themselves poor, then this means that the link between poverty and terrorism is broken. However, as Thomas Homer-Dixon argues, 'this argument assumes that people act only in response to their direct, personal circumstances, which is absurd' (Homer-Dixon, 2001). Krueger and Laitin also admit in a 2007 study that, while their cross-country analysis shows that terrorism seems to be linked to repression rather than poverty, 'Individuals can become terrorists because of poverty in their country, even if they are themselves not impoverished' (Krueger and Laitin, 2008).

Krueger and Maleckova also conducted a cross-country analysis and concluded that, again, there is no direct link between poverty and terrorism (Krueger and Maleckova, 2003). However, despite their claims, there is one methodological flaw in their argument. While they attest to be analysing terrorism, by looking at Palestinian support for armed attacks against Israel, it could be argued that this constitutes support for terrorism rather than terrorism itself. This is something Ethan Bueno de Mesquita raises. He argues that in the pool of sympathisers there will be both high- and low-ability people but 'that does not imply that everyone is equally willing to mobilize' (Bueno de Mesquita, 2005: 5). Martha Crenshaw explained similarly in 1981: 'the motivations for terrorism vary immensely. Many individuals are potential terrorists, but few actually make that commitment' (Crenshaw, 1981: 396).

In addition to this, and as Krueger and Maleckova acknowledge, there was difficulty getting general agreement among their population as to what exactly constitutes a terrorist act. In fact, the particularities of the Palestinian–Israeli conflict make a study of Palestinian terrorism more problematic in this way. This point brings the root causes debate full circle. When it is difficult to agree on what constitutes terrorism, and to analyse an environment which does not necessarily consider armed attacks against Israel as terrorism, we see that the root causes of terrorism avenue becomes more difficult to justify.

This debate shows the complexity of the argument about whether there is a link between poverty and terrorism. In fact, Omer Taspinar calls for the term poverty to be disregarded in this instance as it 'is no longer an absolute concept in the context of globalization' (Taspinar, 2009: 78). Taspinar calls for the levels of analysis to be changed. While academic enquiry addresses the relationship between terrorism and poverty, Taspinar calls for this to be changed to an analysis of the relationship between radicalism and 'relative deprivation' (Taspinar, 2009: 78).

Interestingly, the analysis of motivations for suicide terrorism seems to have fallen into the broader debate about whether there is a causal relationship between poverty and terrorism. As mentioned above, Berrebi argues that Palestinian suicide bombers generally have an educational level above the societal mean. Krueger and Maleckova make a similar argument about suicide bombing. However, this line of argument is problematic in terms of linking suicide terrorism to poverty.

Firstly, suicide terrorism is frequently understood as a tactic of terrorism. That is to say, terrorist groups that tend to employ suicide terrorism employ it alongside other military tactics. If we look at the case of Hamas's pre-political participation, for example, it can be seen that as Hamas was employing suicide bombings it was doing so in conjunction with car bombing and rocket firing. A similar case could be made with Hezbollah, who actually inspired Hamas to start using suicide bombings. While Hezbollah was using suicide bombing it was also engaged in a guerrilla campaign in southern Lebanon. The same case could be argued for al-Qaeda or any of its affiliates. Suicide terrorism rarely exists in isolation. However, this is not to argue that suicide terrorism should not be studied in isolation but rather that linking suicide terrorism to poverty does not necessarily address whether or not poverty is a root cause of terrorism. This is for two reasons. Firstly, suicide bombers only represent a certain cohort in any terrorist group. For a terrorist group to survive it needs a general and consistent military command. In this sense, terrorist groups are generally composed of different levels of command and are frequently characterised by members with different socio-economic and educational backgrounds. Therefore, the suicide bombers themselves are not wholly representative of the groups they represent; in undertaking an act of suicide terrorism a suicide bomber is representing a possible range of socio-economic and educational backgrounds. Empirically analysing suicide terrorists, Ariel Merari concluded that suicide terrorism is a 'group rather than an individual phenomenon' (Merari, 2005: 71).

Secondly, if there is evidence that these suicide bombers have an educational level above the societal mean then this does not necessarily mean that their decision to join the terrorist group or become a suicide bomber is not about poverty. Ethan Bueno de Mesquita refutes this line of argument by explaining that there is a difference between studying 'those who are *willing to become terrorists*' to 'studying those who actually do become terrorists' (Bueno de Mesquita, 2005: 515). Bueno de Mesquita explains that the causal link between poverty and terrorism cannot be made methodologically, if only because of screening (where terrorist groups actively screen their pools of volunteers). As William O'Neill also explains, 'modern terrorist organizations require management and technological skills found in the upper and middle classes yet they also need foot-soldiers who overwhelmingly hale from the poor and down-trodden' (O'Neill, 2002). According to Bueno de Mesquita, terrorist groups choose suicide bombers according to their ability, and this addresses the question of why suicide bombers tend to be of a higher educational and socio-economic background. However, Bueno de Mesquita also contests that those from a lower socio-economic background would be more willing to mobilise. He attests that, consistent with other empirical research, instances of economic downturns correlate with higher levels of terrorism. The logic is that in these periods of economic downturns there would be an increased interest in mobilization but that terrorist groups tend to employ the 'better' or more educated candidates. Beuno de Mesquita therefore argues that, while saying there is no link between economics and terrorism would be misleading for these reasons, a model that would also incorporate ideology would be more effective as a determinant of mobilisation (Bueno de Mesquita, 2005).

In an empirical study of the rooted-in-poverty hypothesis, which extended the timeframe of previous studies into the 2000s, James Piazza studied inter-state terrorism and its link to socio-economic variables. He concluded that there is no empirical evidence to support the rooted-in-poverty thesis. However, Piazza also condoned the literature on social-cleavage theory, which partly puts forth the idea that over time the increased number of political parties in a system will create social divisions, or cleavages. According to Piazza, this 'may be a better explanatory tool' than the rooted-in-poverty thesis (Piazza, 2006).

In a 2009 edited volume Piazza engaged in a debate about the poverty–terrorism relationship with Karin von Hippel (Gottlieb, 2009). He said that the ten poorest states in the world in 2005 had experienced very little terrorism, despite their civil wars and unrest. Looking at transnational terrorist attacks from 2000 to 2006 only 2 per cent were committed by nationals of the countries involved. In agreement with Berrebi and Krueger and Maleckova, Piazza also discussed terrorists and their socio-economic and educational backgrounds, noting, like Berrebi and Krueger and Maleckova, that supporters of terrorism and terrorists themselves come from an educational and socio-economic background that is above the societal mean. This is problematic because the evidence he cites relates to suicide bombers more specifically and, as explained earlier in this chapter, suicide terrorism is only one tactic in the general strategy of terrorism. Piazza then tentatively discusses two factors that could possibly be factors in transnational terrorism: failed and failing states and human rights abuses. Piazza points to ungoverned territories as providing terrorist movements with the opportunity to operate without state control. Regarding human rights abuses, Piazza said that countries with poor human rights records tend to be more susceptible to both domestic and transnational terrorist attacks (Piazza, 2009).

Karin von Hippel argues that research to date has been 'too narrow and not current enough to rule out poverty' as a cause of terrorism (Karin von Hippel, 2009: 52). Similar to this chapter arguing that suicide bombers or terrorist militants are only one particular strand or social grouping of a terrorist group, von Hippel argues that there has been little investigation at the foot-soldier level of terrorist groups (von Hippel, 2009). She also argues that the 'enabling environments' are where terrorist groups gain their legitimacy and, in this way, groups such as al-Qaeda and Hamas have gained legitimacy by providing much-needed social services in these poor environments. Additionally, she points to the difficulty in measuring the link between poverty and terrorism and that the research is 'by no means conclusive and, if anything, reveals a mixed picture' (von Hippel, 2009: 61).

Failed states and terrorism

Following on from the debate about the link between poverty and terrorism, the notion of failed states as a root cause of terrorism has gained currency among terrorism academics. Under the assumption of the link between failed states and terrorism, in 2002 the US government first outlined its goal of strengthening weak and failing states in order to address this security challenge. Since then the notion of dealing with this assumed link has remained part of the USA's National Security Strategy (Sun Wyler, 2008). Bilgin and Morton attribute this to the USA's policy shift from focusing on rogue states, to focusing on failed states. Bilgin and Morton explain this shift as part of a preventative strategy to deal with international terrorism (Bilgin and Morton, 2004).

The term failed states is debated in academia, with calls by some to disregard it and instead refer to terms such as collapsed or imploded (von Hippel, 2002). However, the term still has currency in policymaking and the Fund for Peace annually publishes a list of failed states and categorises them using the following 12 indicators, divided between social/economic indicators and political/military indicators.

Social and economic indicators:

- Demographic pressures
- Refugees and IDPs (Internally Displaced Persons)
- Uneven economic development
- Group grievance
- Human flight and brain drain
- Poverty and economic decline

Political and military indicators:

- State legitimacy
- Public services
- Human rights and rule of law
- Security apparatus
- Factionalised elites
- External intervention

Rotberg's general description of a failed state is as follows: 'Nation-states fail because they can no longer deliver positive political goods to their people. Their governments lose legitimacy and, in the eyes and hearts of a growing plurality of its citizens, the nation-state itself becomes illegitimate' (Rotberg, 2002a: 85). Rotberg also cites failed states as being characterised by civil wars, difficulty in controlling borders and growing criminal violence. Furthermore, Rotberg attests that 'In most cases, driven by ethnic or intercommunal hostility or by regime insecurity, failed states prey on their own citizens (Rotberg, 2002a: 86). In this context, he argues that failed states are conducive to the growth of terrorism, the aforementioned conditions providing the perfect environment for terrorist groups to emerge and prosper. He therefore argues that 'understanding the dynamics of nation-state failure is central to the war against terrorism' (Rotberg, 2002a: 85).

Von Hippel, however, refutes the notion of the failed state by arguing that 'The term "failed" implies that there are standards of success to which all states aspire, which is not the case' (von Hippel, 2002: 30). Von Hippel's argument is that no state can fully control organised violence, and its existence does not necessarily denote a failed state, as states considered successful frequently exhibit the same characteristics of failed states and vice versa. She calls, therefore, for the terms collapsed or imploded to be used in order to address the complexity that is not addressed by the term failed.

Rotberg also acknowledges the difficulty with the concept of failed states, as 'States are not created equal' (Rotberg, 2002b: 131). Rotberg's conception of the failed state is linked to the specific nature of violence that states experience, but not the intensity. For example, Rotberg explains that a failed state can be identified by the way in which violence is executed. If violence is directed against the nation state to the point where the struggle for power or autonomy results in an internal war then the ramifications of this will result in 'failure for a nation-state' (Rotberg, 2002a: 86).

As explained by Rotberg in 2002, the events of 9/11 resulted in a stronger emphasis on the concept of failed states. As much as this area of enquiry was not new, the new perception of terrorism meant that it was imperative to prevent states from failing (Rotberg 2002b: 127–40). In 2002 Stephen Mallaby argued that the decline in American imperialism after World War II was partly to blame for the growth of power vacuums in failed states, and 'orderly societies now refuse to impose their own institutions on disorderly ones' (Mallaby, 2002: 2). Mallaby called this pattern an 'anti-imperialist restraint' and argued that the Muslim world was most susceptible to demographic challenges such as population growth and violent disorder. Mallaby listed Afghanistan, Pakistan, Saudi Arabia, Yemen and the Palestinian Territories as 'all Islamic societies with powerful currents of anti-Western extremism'. Due to this, Mallaby called for a new approach to nation building to offset the potential for failed states and ungoverned spaces to foster terrorism and to confront this 'growing danger' (Mallaby, 2002: 7). He also asserted that terrorism was only one of the challenges brought about by failed states. Walter Laqueur also linked population growth in the Arab world and the resulting unemployment to the potential for the growth of terrorism (Laqueur, 2007).

In 2005 Stephen Krasner and Carlos Pascual at the US Department of State also called for the recognition of the problems state failure can bring, with terrorism being but one on a list of threats. Krasner and Pascual used the example of Afghanistan as a failed state and as being the base for the September 11 attacks (Krasner and Pascual, 2005).

The idea that failed states are frequently characterised by ungoverned spaces results in the idea that these ungoverned spaces will become havens for terrorist groups to grow and prosper. The US Department of State lists areas ranging from the Middle East to Africa and South East Asia. One example is the Pakistani government's inability to control certain areas of its own territory, resulting in the Federally Administered Tribal Areas (FATA), which has become home to groups such as the Haqqani Network, the Quetta Shura and Lashkar-e-Tayyiba.

In a comprehensive explanation of the link between failed states and terrorism, Takeyh and Gvosdev explain that the increasingly globalised nature of terrorism can be likened to international business and, therefore, 'these failed states are the global terrorist network's equivalent of an international business's corporate headquarters' (Takeyh and Gvosdev, 2002: 98). Their argument is that terrorist groups actually seek out weak states in order to have freedom of movement and operation and for the following additional reasons. Terrorist groups seek to acquire control over particular areas of territory without seeking control over the whole country. This failed state will have a cohort of potential terrorist recruits and sympathisers. Precarious law enforcement in the failed state will allow the terrorist group to engage in illegal activity as a way of raising funds. Finally, the sovereign nature of this failed state will discourage any outside intervention in order to quash the terrorist activity: 'Failed states may be notoriously unable to control their own territory, but they remain loath to allow access to any other state to do the same' (Takeyh and Gvosdev, 2002:100). In a case study on state failure in Lebanon, El Khazen argues that the security vacuum created by the Syrian-backed government has facilitated the growth of militancy, with Hezbollah as an example. El Khazen argues that Lebanon's state failure has not followed the traditional model but has instead been consciously designed to benefit a range of state and non-state actors, Syria and Iran in particular (El Khazen. 2005).

Conversely, writing in 2003, Menkhaus argued that in putting together effective nation-building strategies there was a 'misdiagnosis' of the relationship between failed states and terrorism (Menkhaus, 2003). Menkhaus argued this on the basis that, while the argument that failed states can provide safe havens to terrorist groups is certainly compelling, the case of Somalia refuted this. Menkhaus argued that Somalia exhibited most of the characteristics of a failed state but yet was not exhibiting the growth of a significant terrorist threat. Von Hippel made a similar case about Somalia in 2002, arguing that states that are not experiencing full-scale wars are less attractive to terrorist groups because there is no known entity to fight against or definite groups to form allegiances with (von Hippel, 2002).

Somalia was again used as a case study by Hagmann and Hoehne in 2009 (Hagmann and Hoehne, 2009). Here, Haggman and Hoehne argue that the failed-states paradigm has not been used properly to address the problems of African statehood, and that it has been too frequently analysed using the convergence model, or the assumption that states eventually 'converge towards a model of Western liberal democracy' (Hagmann and Hoehne, 2009: 43). They explain that the varying political orders that have emerged in the Horn of Africa refute the idea that state collapse will result in anarchy.

In a 2007 empirical study Piazza analysed 19 Middle Eastern countries. In an investigation of the link between democracy in the region and the propensity for terrorism, Piazza concluded that democratic regimes were more likely to experience terrorism than autocratic regimes. This finding is also in line with the argument put forth by Enders and Sandler: 'The political and civil freedoms that define a liberal democracy provide a favorable environment for terrorists to wage their terror campaigns' (Enders and Sandler, 2006: 24). Piazza, therefore, explains that promoting democracy in the Middle East will not provide protection against terrorism; he also explains that countries in the region that experience more significant state failure are more likely to experience the growth of terrorism. Piazza says that the purpose of his findings is to refute the notion that democracy promotion will prevent terrorism, but also to encourage a systematic understanding of political regimes and state failure and to incorporate this into policy (Piazza, 2007).

In another empirical study in 2008 Piazza analysed 197 countries from 1973 to 2003 in order to investigate whether failed and failing states resulted in an increase in transnational terrorism (Piazza, 2008). It is important to distinguish between this and Piazza's 2007 study. Whereas the 2007 study focused on terrorism more generally and was specific to the Middle East, the 2008 study focused on transnational terrorism more specifically, and Piazza's conclusions generally agreed with the failed-states thesis, concluding that the data showed that 'chronic state failures are more likely to host terrorist groups that commit transnational attacks' (Piazza, 2008: 469). Furthermore, countries experiencing higher state failure 'disproportionately' contribute to transnational terrorism (Piazza, 2008: 483). However, Piazza explains that, despite this, all types of state failure can be associated with transnational terrorism. Even though states experiencing higher levels of state failure experience a disproportionate amount of transnational terrorism, there is no evidence that weak states are more likely to experience higher levels of transnational terrorism.

Menkhaus also argued that collapsed states would be unattractive to terrorist groups owing to lack of protection from counterterrorism measures. Piazza states that his empirical analysis refutes this claim: 'Countries categorized as the highest at-risk for state failure ("Alert") are on average most frequently the location of transnational terrorist attacks' and 'most frequently the source of transnational terrorist attacks abroad' (Piazza, 2008: 475). Furthermore, Piazza argues that this cohort would be two to three times more likely to experience or be the source of an attack than the next two categories in his study (Piazza, 2008: 469–88). Importantly, Piazza also stresses that the degree of state failure does not impact the statistical likelihood of promoting transnational terrorism – there is no statistical difference between states experiencing moderate state failure and states that have experienced total collapse: 'all types of state failure are found to be positively associated with transnational attacks' (Piazza, 2008: 483).

Simons and Tucker refute the link between failed states and international terrorism altogether. They argue that there is no evidence that international terrorists come from failed states. One example they cite is that only one of the eleven hijackers on 9/11 came from a failed state (Simons and Tucker, 2007). They cite two reasons for this. Firstly, the skills that international terrorists have would be in demand more locally. Secondly, they say it is unlikely an international terrorist from a failed state would have the right training in order to pass through border controls or work unnoticed in more developed societies. However, Simons and Tucker acknowledge the difference between linking international terrorists to failed states and linking failed states and international terrorism itself. They acknowledge the propensity for failed states to provide training and they explain that it is in failed states where many low-cost terrorist tactics are invented and perfected (Simons and Tucker, 2007). Furthermore, they outline the potential for this expertise to be disseminated.

Lia and Skjolberg argue that there is much empirical evidence that weak or collapsed states could facilitate the growth of terrorism. They use the examples of Lebanon and Afghanistan: Lebanon has become home to Hezbollah and other militant groups, while Afghanistan became an amenable environment for the growth of terrorism in the 1990s (Lia and Skjolberg, 2000). Plummer acknowledges the link between failed states and terrorism but argues that the relationship is more complex than frequently acknowledged. In his empirical study, using the case studies of Ivory Coast and Somalia, Plummer contends that rather than looking at states that have failed, and taking this as a point of analysis, the actual process of state failure needs to be analysed (Plummer, 2012).

Bilgin and Morton also argue that practitioners tend to analyse the symptoms of state failure (with terrorism being one of them) rather than looking at the conditions that contribute to the process of state failure (Bilgin and Morton, 2004). They argue that these conditions are almost never investigated and that the approach to fostering state success has focused on pushing states towards political control and stability, an approach which has its roots in the Cold War. Bilgin and Morton specifically argue that the prevention of international terrorism calls for both an understanding of state building in the medium to long term and the understanding and investigation of the root causes of state failure themselves (Bilgin and Morton, 2004).

Patrick argues that, despite the preponderance of claims and policy decisions about the link between failed states and terrorism, there is little empirical evidence that supports this (Patrick, 2006). Patrick argues that policymakers have not adequately distinguished between weak and failing states and have attributed a 'blanket connection' between failing states and the threat of terrorism (Patrick, 2006). Patrick does acknowledge that there is no agreed definition of weak and failing states and that, even if there was, not all weak or failing states would have the same characteristics. Patrick makes three important observations. Firstly, he says that not all weak and failing states experience terrorism and that other dynamics such as culture, ideology and religion also shape the growth of terrorism.

For Patrick, the argument of weak governance alone is not enough to explain a definitive link to terrorism. Secondly, Patrick explains that a lot of terrorism that emerges in weak and failing states is not transnational terrorism, despite claims by policymakers to the contrary. Patrick asserts that these states frequently experience more localised terrorism. Thirdly, terrorist groups are more attracted to weak states than they are to completely collapsed states as the weakness of governance in these states allows the terrorist group to manoeuvre at will but with the provision of much needed technological and infrastructural support (Patrick, 2006).

Conclusion

This chapter has highlighted the main debates surrounding two of the most commonly cited root causes of terrorism: poverty and failed states. With both supposed root causes it can be seen that there is considerable disagreement within each debate. Within the poverty debate there is disagreement about whether analysing individual terrorists' socio-economic backgrounds can in itself answer the question of a link between poverty and terrorism. There is also disagreement about analysing the socio-economic status of one particular cohort of a terrorist group, such as suicide bombers. However, it can also be seen that the issue of poverty does continue to resonate in policy circles. In the failed-states debate there is an initial question over the legitimacy of the notion of a failed state. Discussions then centre on how these failed-states provide conditions that foster terrorism – factors such as lack of law enforcement and ungoverned spaces. There are also discussions over the attractiveness of a failed state for potential terrorists, and there is considerable doubt that failed states can realistically produce the type of person with the required attributes to carry out a successful terrorist act. To conclude, then, while appreciating the popularity of these two root causes of terrorism – poverty and failed-states – it is also necessary to appreciate the debates within them.

STUDY BOX CHAPTER 5

Key reading

M. Crenshaw (1981) 'The Causes of Terrorism', *Comparative Politics*, 13:4, 379–399.

Gupta, D. K. (2005) 'Exploring Roots of Terrorism'. In T. Bjørgo (Ed.), *Root Causes of Terrorism* (Abingdon: Routledge), pp. 16–32.

Krueger, A. B. and Maleckova, J. (2003) 'Education, Poverty and Terrorism: Is There a Causal Connection?', *Journal of Economic Perspectives*, 17(4): 119–144.

Piazza, A. (2008) 'Incubators of Terror: Do Failed and Failing States Promote Transnational Terrorism?', *International Studies Quarterly*, 52(3): 469–488.

(Continued)

(Continued)

Ross, J. I. (1993) 'Structural Causes of Oppositional Political Terrorism: Towards a Causal Model', *Journal of Peace Research*, 30(3): 317–329.

von Hippel, K. (2009) 'Yes: Poverty Is an Important Cause'. In S. Gottlieb (Ed.), *Debating Terrorism and Counterterrorism* (Washington DC: CQ Press), pp. 51–66.

Study questions

1   What does it mean to cause terrorism? How do cities as a cause of terrorism differ from poverty as a cause of terrorism?

2   To what extent does democracy cause terrorism?

3   Does relative deprivation, rather than absolute poverty, explain the causes of terrorism?

References

Ajami, Faoud, 'Nowhere Man', *The New York Times*, 7 October 2001.

Atran, Scott, 'Genesis of Suicide Terrorism', *Science*, vol.299, 2003, pp.1534–9.

Berrebi, Claude, 'Evidence about the Link between Education, Poverty and Terrorism among Palestinians', *Peace Economics, Peace Science and Public Policy*, vol.13, no.1, 2007, pp.1–36.

Bjorgo, T. (ed.), *Root Causes of Terrorism: Myths, Reality and Ways Forward*, London and New York: Routledge, 2005.

Bier, Jeryl, 'Kerry: "Root Cause of Terrorism" Is Poverty', *The Weekly Standard*, 15 January 2014.

Bilgin, Pinar and David Morton, 'From "Rogue" to "Failed" States? The Fallacy of Short-termism', *Politics*, vol.24, no.3, 2004, pp.169–80.

Bueno de Mesquita, Ethan, 'The Quality of Terror', *American Journal of Political Science*, vol.49, no.3, 2005, pp.515–30.

Bush, George W., 'Securing Freedom's Triumph', *The New York Times*, 11 September 2002.

Call, Charles T., 'The Fallacy of the 'Failed State'', *Third World Quarterly*, vol.29, no.8, 2008, pp.1491–1507.

Crenshaw, Martha, 'The Causes of Terrorism', *Comparative Politics*, vol.13, no.4, 1981, pp.379–99.

El Khazen, F., 'Patterns of State Failure: The Case of Lebanon'. In T. Bjorgo (ed.), *Root Causes of Terrorism: Myths, Reality and Ways Forward*, London and New York: Routledge, 2005, pp.178–188.

Enders, Walter and Todd Sandler, *The Political Economy of Terrorism*, New York: Cambridge University Press, 2006.

Gottlieb, Stuart (ed.), *Debating Terrorism and Counterterrorism*, Washington DC: CQ Press, 2009.

Gupta, Dipak K., 'Exploring Roots of Terrorism'. In T. Bjorgo (ed.), *Root Causes of Terrorism: Myths, Reality and Ways Forward*, London and New York: Routledge, 2005, pp.16–32.

Gutiérrez, F., 'Terrorism and Inequality'. In C. Lee (ed.), *Responding to Terrorism: What Role for the United Nations?*, International Peace Academy (Meeting notes), 25–26 October 2002, pp.45–48.

Hagmann, Tobias and Markus V. Hoehne, 'Failures of the State Failure Debate: Evidence from the Somali Territories', *Journal of International Development*, vol.21, no.1, 2009, pp.42–57.

Hassan, Nasra, 'An Arsenal of Believers', *The New Yorker*, 19 November 2001.

Homer-Dixon, Thomas, 'Why Root Causes Are Important', *Toronto Globe and Mail*, 26 September 2001.

Horgan, J., 'The Social and Psychological Characteristics of Terrorism and Terrorists'. In T. Bjorgo (ed.), *Root Causes of Terrorism: Myths, Reality and Ways Forward*, London and New York: Routledge, 2005, pp.44–53.

Jervis, Robert, 'An Interim Assessment of September 11: What Has Changed and What Has Not?', *Political Science Quarterly*, vol.117, no.1, 2002, pp.37–54.

Keating, Joshua, 'Was State Senator Obama Right that Poverty Causes Terrorism?', *Slate*, 11 September 2013.

Krasner, Stephen D. and Carlos Pascual, 'Addressing State Failure', *Foreign Affairs*, vol.84, 2005, pp.153–63.

Krueger, Alan B. and David D. Laitin, 'Kto Kogo? A Cross-country Study of the Origins and Targets of Terrorism', *Terrorism, Economic Development and Political Openness*, 2008, pp.148–73.

Krueger, Alan B. and Jitka Maleckova, 'Education, Poverty and Terrorism: Is there a Causal Connection?', *Journal of Economic Perspectives*, vol.17, no.4, 2003, pp.119–44.

Laqueur, Walter, *No End to War: Terrorism in the Twenty-First Century*, New York and London: Continuum, 2007.

Lia, Brynjar and Katja Skjolberg, 'Why Terrorism Occurs – A Survey of Theories and Hypotheses on the Causes of Terrorism', Norwegian Defence Research Establishment, 30 May 2000.

Mallaby, Sebastian, 'The Reluctant Imperialist: Terrorism, Failed States, and the Case for American Empire', *Foreign Affairs*, vol.81, no.2, 2002, pp.2–7.

McDermott, Terry, 'Mohammed Atta and the Egypt Revolution', *The Daily Beast*, 14 February 2011.

Menkhaus, Ken, 'Quasi-States, Nation-Building, and Terrorist Safe Havens', *Journal of Conflict Studies*, vol.23, no.2, 2003.

Merari, A., 'Social, organizational and psychological factors in suicide terrorism'. In T. Bjorgo (ed.), *Root Causes of Terrorism: Myths, Reality and Ways Forward*, London and New York: Routledge, 2005.

Newman, Edward, 'Exploring the "Root Causes" of Terrorism', *Studies in Conflict and Terrorism*, vol.29, no.8, 2006, pp.749–72.

O'Neill, William, 'Responding to Terrorism: What Role for the United Nations?', *International Peace Academy*, 25–26 October 2002.

Patrick, Stewart, 'Weak States and Global Threats: Fact or Fiction?', *The Washington Quarterly*, vol.29, no.2, 2006, pp.27–53.

Piazza, James, 'Rooted in Poverty? Terrorism, Poor Economic Development and Social Cleavages', *Terrorism and Political Violence*, vol.18, no.1, 2006, pp.159–77.

Piazza, James A., 'Draining the Swamp: Democracy Promotion, State Failure, and Terrorism in 19 Middle Eastern Countries', *Studies in Conflict and Terrorism*, vol.30, no.6, 2007, pp.521–39.

Piazza, James A., 'Incubators of Terror: Do Failed and Failing State Promote Transnational Terrorism?', *International Studies Quarterly*, vol.52, no.3, 2008, pp.469–88.

Piazza, James, A., 'Does Poverty Serve as a Root Cause of Terrorism'. In Gottlieb, Stuart (ed.), *Debating Terrorism and Counterterrorism*, Washington DC: CQ Press, 2009, pp.37–50.

Plummer, Chelli, 'Failed States and Connections to Terrorist Activity', *International Criminal Justice Review*, vol.22, no.4, 2012, pp.416–49.

Post, Jerrold M., 'The Socio-cultural Underpinnings of Terrorist Psychology: "When Hatred is bred in the bone"'. In T. Bjorgo (ed.), *Root Causes of Terrorism: Myths, Reality and Ways Forward,* London and New York: Routledge, 2005, pp.54–69.

Ross, Jeffrey Ian, 'Structural Causes of Oppositional Political Terrorism: Towards a Causal Model', *Journal of Peace Research,* vol.30, no.3, 1993, pp.317–29.

Rotberg, Robert I., 'The New Nature of Nation-State Failure', *The Washington Quarterly,* vol.25, no.3, 2002a, pp.83–96.

Rotberg, Robert I., 'Failed States in a World of Terror', *Foreign Affairs,* vol.81, no.4, 2002b, pp.127–40.

Simons, Anna and David Tucker, 'The Misleading Problem of Failed States: A "Socio-geography" of Terrorism in the Post-9/11 Era', *Third World Quarterly,* vol.28, no.2, 2007, pp.387–410.

Sun Wyler, Liana, 'Weak and Failing States: Evolving Security Threats and U.S. Policy', *CRS Report for Congress,* 28 August 2008.

Takeyh, Ray and Nikolas K. Gvosdev, 'Do Terrorist Networks Need a Home?', *The Washington Quarterly,* vol.25, no.3, 2002, pp.97–108.

Taspinar, Omer, 'Fighting Radicalism, Not "Terrorism": Root Causes of an International Actor Redefined', *SAIS Review,* vol.XXIX, no.2, 2009, pp.75–86.

von Hippel, Karin, 'The Roots of Terrorism: Probing the Myths', *The Political Quarterly,* vol.73, s.1, 2002, pp.25–39.

von Hippel, Karin, 'Does Poverty Serve as a Root Cause of Terrorism?'. In Gottlieb, Stuart (ed.), *Debating Terrorism and Counterterrorism,* Washington DC: CQ Press, 2009, pp.51–66.

6

SUPPORTING TERRORISM

NICOLE IVES-ALLISON

There is a widely held assumption that terrorists and insurgents need popular support in order to operate, survive and succeed. Under this view, it follows that disrupting this support can be an effective approach to combating these individuals and groups (Paul, 2009). As stated by Lutz and Lutz, '[t]errorist organizations do not exist in a vacuum. They need to have some sources of support in order to survive for more than a brief period' (Lutz and Lutz, 2011: 82). As unimaginable as it may be that a prolonged terrorist campaign could be waged entirely self-sufficiently, technological advances indicates that it may be more possible now than ever before for a terrorist group to launch a relatively sophisticated attack without outside help. Technological change, globalisation and the changing strategies of terrorist groups and responses to them have raised a number of questions around the relationship between support and terrorist activity. Three of the most basic, and most important, questions to emerge include: (1) What exactly does it mean when it is said someone (or some group) 'supports' terrorism? (2) What specific needs does external support help terrorist groups meet? (3) Who supports terrorism and why? Using these three questions as a guide, this chapter explores the nature and role of support for terrorist groups, particularly as it relates to the effectiveness of counterterrorism efforts.

An understanding of the support systems and structures surrounding terrorist groups can help give us insight as to why some groups become 'household names' around the world while other groups disappear quickly without any notice. Gaining popular support can be a fundamental goal for terrorist groups and it can play a substantial role in determining their success. For example, groups who tend to be larger and have a greater support network tend to last longer and tend to be more successful in achieving their objectives, either partially or fully (Jones and Libicki, 2008). For those states who are engaged in counterterrorism operations, understanding the sources, level and forms of external support can help reveal important information about how to go about countering a terrorist group (Wellman, 2013: 5). Indeed, for some, such as Frank Foley, the stemming of support is part of the very definition of a defining component of counterterrorism operations. He argues, '[c]ounterterrorist operations can be understood as the surveillance, investigation, disruption and arrest of terrorists *and their supporters*' [emphasis added] (Foley,

2013: 244). Terrorist groups know that they are engaged in an asymmetric conflict and have adapted accordingly in order to make the most out of their relative size and flexibility. However, cutting a group off from its support network can limit the flow of resources (and ideas) inwards, disrupting the organisation. Depending on the extent of internal disruption caused by these efforts, a group may collapse on its own. Alternatively, disruption can weaken a terrorist group to the point that it becomes vulnerable to external pressure, with counterterrorism efforts significantly limiting the threat a group poses, if not bringing about its ultimate end (Byman, 2005; Cole, 2003; Cronin, 2006; Jones and Libicki, 2008).

Yet despite how important support mobilisation is for terrorist groups, and reducing support is for counterterrorism operations (Cohen, 2012), the very definition of support is subject to debate. Firstly, while there has been extensive discussion on the importance of support for large insurgent groups, there has been far less research conducted on the role of support in terrorist groups which tend to be smaller, therefore challenging existing conceptualisations of support. Secondly, there exists a divide in the literature between those who approach the issue of support from an operational perspective and those who see it as a matter of expressed attitudes (Paul, 2009). Using the concepts of active and passive support, it will be illustrated that the conflict between these two approaches can be resolved by adding greater conceptual clarity (Byman, 2005; Cohen, 2012). This will be followed by a survey of the main forms of support, including financing, material resources, sanctuary and intelligence. From here it is possible to move into a discussion of the sources of support for terrorist groups. We will then study the different roles played by supporters in society and state sponsors. This section will also illustrate that the reasons why sections of society support terrorist groups are rather different from those underpinning state sponsorship.

Defining 'support'

In order to even begin to discuss support in any great detail it is first necessary to determine what exactly is meant by the term's use. In spite of the rapid growth of terrorism-studies literature post-9/11, there is still relatively little work dealing with support directly in any meaningful way (Stampnitzky, 2013). Generally speaking, support can be divided into: (a) sympathy (or attitudinal support), involving beliefs and verbal expressions of support, and (b) material or behavioural support, which can involve providing a terrorist group with information, food, finance or the supporter's own time and involvement. A crucial problem in defining support is the relationship between sympathy/attitudinal support and material/behavioural support. Most studies explore how sympathy leads to the provision of material support (Byman, 2006), yet there are others that explore how changes in attitudes and sympathy can transform the attitudes of terrorists (Malthaner, 2011).

On the one hand, there exists a strong body of literature that has defined support as the expression of sympathy (or attitudinal support) for: (1) the cause or objectives a terrorist group claims to represent or pursue; (2) the use of violence in the pursuit of the cause/objectives; and/or (3) the terrorist group itself (Hayes and

McAllister, 2001; Paul, 2009). Those who look at support from this perspective are often concerned with its quantitative measurement and analysis (Bloom, 2004; Fair and Shepherd, 2006; Hayes and McAllister, 2001; 2005; Hewitt, 1990; Khashan, 2003; La Free and Morris, 2012). They speak of 'levels' of public support or of a terrorist group 'gaining'/'losing' support. However, these quantitative measurements seek to capture emotional expression, for what is really counted is whether (and the degree to which) the individual in question shares the political concerns of the terrorist group or sympathises with those individuals engaged in it (Vincent, 2005). As will be explored in our discussion of public support, understanding the emotional connection between a terrorist group and its supporters is essential in planning counterterrorism efforts (especially if it is in this relationship that a group stakes its claim to legitimacy) (Malthaner, 2011). However, sympathy alone is not capable of keeping terrorist groups afloat, even if they do factor into its continued capacity to act. This is a distinction that has already been recognised in some of the literature, setting a precedent for relabelling supportive expressions of individual or group attitudes as sympathy (Freytag et al., 2011; Mascini, 2006; Waugh, 1983).

On the other hand sits a body of literature that takes an operational approach to defining support, connecting it to the resourcing of terrorist groups. When Paul distinguishes between sympathy and support he defines the latter as, 'actual material support or other direct or indirect aid or abetment', roughly corresponding to Khalil's (albeit narrower) definition of behavioural support as 'a set of actions that provide direct benefits to one of these groups' (Khalil, 2012: 221; Paul, 2009: 115). Since it is easier to stop the flow of resources into a terrorist group than it is to eliminate expressions of sympathy, this is how support has generally been conceptualised in a legal context as well, at both the national and international levels (Aust, 2010: 265; Aziz, 2003; Gardella, 2004: 427–9). There are a number of advantages to further developing this conception of support and advocating for its general use.

Firstly, while sympathy may often underpin the provision of material support, it is not always necessary, and the relationship between attitude and behaviour is still not entirely clear (Paul, 2010; Gerges, 2005). In some cases material support can be extracted by a terrorist and insurgent group without any sympathy from the public (Khalil, 2012). Furthermore, a group's sympathisers will always outnumber those they can count on to help provide material support to the group, which in turn will outnumber the group's formal membership (German, 2007: 103; White, 2012: 73–4). This is to be expected given that in most cases involvement in aiding or abetting a terrorist group carries much greater risks than a simple declaration of support, especially when one considers the wording of anti-terrorism legislation. Prosecuting a thought is a much murkier proposition than prosecuting an action (Normand and Zaidi, 2008: 266). Thus, exclusive reliance on a measure of attitudes, while in many ways useful, provides an incomplete picture of a terrorist group's immediate strength or capability.

Secondly, it is possible to expand an operationally focused definition of support to be sufficiently inclusive, especially if the term sympathy can be used to refer to those attitudes not translating into action. In other words, sympathy for a terrorist group may lead to deliberate inaction, enabling them to conduct operations. This can be explained by turning to Byman's conception of support, as laid out in *Deadly Connections: States that Sponsor Terrorism*, which remains the most extensive exploration of the topic to date. Here Byman conceives of support as being either active or passive (or both). Cohen argues that active sponsorship or support can be defined as 'the intentional transfer of resources such as money, arms, and logistics, or the provision of territorial sanctuary to the terrorist group by the regime or state. It can also involve assistance with organization, training and operations, ideological direction, and diplomatic support or recognition' (Cohen, 2012: 254; Byman, 2005). Byman argues that a 'regime can be said to be guilty of passive support if it *knowingly allows* a terrorist group to raise money, enjoy a sanctuary, recruit or otherwise flourish without interference, but does not directly aid the group itself' (Byman, 2006: 118). He goes on to argue that passive sponsorship or support is defined by the following characteristics: (1) the actor does not provide assistance him/her/themselves, but is aware of and actively allows others to provide such aid; and (2) the actor has the capacity to stop the flow of aid, but has not developed this capacity by choice (Byman, 2006). Taken together, active and passive support include both overt and covert activities, going beyond Paul's direct or indirect 'aid and abetment' encompassing all support activities whether based in action or conscious inaction.

In this light, support can be defined as the wilful provision of those resources, material and non-material, which allow a terrorist group to sustain or grow their operations; or deliberate non-cooperation with lawful efforts to counter and obstruct the activities of the group. Sympathy thus comes to be defined as the expression of a personal or group affection for a terrorist group, the goals it claims to pursue, and/or the violent means taken in pursuit of these goals, regardless of whether affection translates into action. With these definitions in our analytical tool belt, it becomes possible to move on to a discussion of the different ways in which terrorist groups are supported, who provides this support and the difference this makes to the persistence of terrorism.

Forms of support

Unlike the issue of definition, there is much greater coherence in the literature over what forms support can take, despite discrepancies on some terms. Taking both the commonalities and the slight discrepancies of the existing descriptions of support types into account, the following four categories of support can be proposed: (1) financing; (2) material resources; (3) sanctuary; and (4) intelligence.

Financing

The first of these categories, financing, refers to the provision of monetary support to a terrorist group. Like any major project or organisation, terrorist groups require financial resources to be able to operate. From paying for the travel of operatives for reconnaissance missions to purchasing weaponry that cannot be obtained through other support channels, the financing available to a group has a significant impact on the scale of operations and the types of targets that can be selected. Those groups better at raising funds, either internally or externally, can train greater numbers of operatives to a higher standard, acquire more advanced weaponry and increase their capacity to engage in social and charitable projects (helping to strengthen ties with their communities at a grassroots level) (Koh, 2006: 12–15). Though the costs of some attacks, such as the 7/7 bombings in London, have been minimal when considered in relation to impact, organisations that see a future for themselves beyond a single attack (unless they have tremendous personal wealth), will at some point need outside funding in order to remain viable (Baumert, 2008: 102). Terrorist financing is explored extensively elsewhere in this volume and by other scholars (Costigan and Gold, 2007; Giraldo and Trinkunas, 2007; Koh, 2006).

However, before moving on, it is worth at least briefly mentioning the two related concepts of *zakat* and *hawala*, which have played an important role in the financing of Islamist groups engaged in political violence. *Zakat* refers to the Islamic religious obligation to donate at least 2.5 per cent of the wealth one accumulates over the course of a year to charity. As one of the five pillars of faith in Islam, it is taken quite seriously both at an individual and collective level (Koh, 2006: 21–2; Croissant and Barlow, 2007: 210). While it is a fundamentally benevolent practice that has done a tremendous amount of good for centuries, over the past several decades some terrorist groups have appropriated funds earmarked for charitable purposes (often without the donors' knowledge or consent). In some cases terrorist groups have established a 'front' charity, while others are more open about the purposes to which donations will be put, arguing that because jihad is also a religious obligation, funds are still contributing to the greater good (Burr and Collins, 2006; Chugani, 2008). *Hawala*, translated as 'transfer', can be described as, 'an informal Islamic banking network that links brokers around the world who advance funds to depositors on a handshake and, sometimes, a password' (Combs, 2009: 98). Though in the immediate wake of 9/11 a number of policymakers and scholars were quick to identify *hawala* as a source of terrorist financing, it has just as strongly been argued that its use is not nearly as extensive as has been purported (Combs, 2009: 98; de Goede, 2003; Passas, 2007: 29–30).

Material resources

While financing can have a significant impact on the organisational capacity of a terrorist group, material resources are needed to turn ideas into action. Material resources can be defined as all of the goods a terrorist group will consume over the course of its planning and operations, ranging from the food provided to new recruits at a training camp, all the way to sophisticated weaponry such as rocket-propelled grenades (RPGs) or (less likely) weaponised CBRN materials (chemical, biological, radiological, nuclear) (Combs, 2009: 273–93; Hoffman, 2006: 268–71). States, individuals and sub-state entities are involved in the provision of material resources to terrorist groups. The Provisional Irish Republican Army (IRA), for example, used an assortment of support channels to acquire the weaponry needed to sustain its 30-year campaign of political violence. During the early part of its life, the Provisional IRA depended heavily on weapons sourced through the large Irish-American community in the USA (also a lucrative source of financial support), even though the American government was itself strongly opposed to its use of terrorism (English, 2004: 117). Irish emigrants played an important role in establishing the gunrunning network that plied the group with guns and ammunition (English, 2004: 115). In 1973 and in the late 1980s arms also started flowing into the organisation from Libya, with Colonel Gaddafi's regime becoming a key source of external support (Byman, 2005: 60; English, 2004: 249–50; Moloney, 2007: 3–34).

Sanctuary

According to Byman, sanctuary can be roughly defined as a safe space in which a terrorist group is able to 'plot, recruit, proselytize, contact supporters around the world, raise money and – perhaps most important – enjoy a respite from the enemy regime's counterterrorism effort that enables operatives to escape from the constant stress that characterizes life underground' (Byman, 2005: 65). Sanctuary spaces are also known as safe havens. Though there is debate over how large an area must be to qualify as sanctuary, there is no question surrounding the importance of sanctuary to the long-term success of terrorist groups (Byman, 2005: 65; McAlister and Schmid, 2011: 210; Paul, 2009: 118).

Over the course of its history al-Qaeda's ability to find sanctuary in a number of states has contributed greatly to its growth as an organisation. Though al-Qaeda was born in Afghanistan in the late 1980s, in 1992 it moved its base of operations to Sudan after the country's ruling party, the National Islamic Front, in alliance with President General Omar Hassan al-Bashir, openly declared solidarity with the international Muslim community, especially those who found themselves oppressed (van Linschoten et al., 2012: 127; Sageman, 2004: 39). Given the hard currency that someone like Osama bin Laden was able to bring into an economically disastrous Sudan, it appeared to have the potential to be a mutually beneficial arrangement. However, with the Sudanese government facing intensifying international pressure and the impact of bin Laden's business activities on the local economy unclear, al-Qaeda was asked to leave (Hellmich, 2011: 40; van Linschoten et al., 2012: 128). The group returned to Afghanistan, then in the midst of an ongoing civil war, where it built a strategic alliance with the Taliban who had loose control over large parts of the country but themselves faced considerable resource constraints (Hellmich, 2011: 45–6). Enjoying sanctuary in the Afghan hinterland, al-Qaeda was able to increase its international profile with a string of attacks on high-profile US targets, including the USS Cole, embassies in Kenya and Tanzania and, ultimately, the World Trade Center and Pentagon in New York City and Washington respectively. With the launch of the war on terror and the US invasion of Afghanistan which deposed the Taliban regime al-Qaeda was again forced to move. While there was some scattering, a sizeable percentage of al-Qaeda's leadership, including Osama bin Laden, headed just over the border to Pakistan

(Hellmich, 2011: 21; van Linschoten et al., 2012: 242). The Pakistani government has been outspoken in its opposition to al-Qaeda, and has, at least publicly, proclaimed its support for the US-led war on terror; but the extent to which it is capable of controlling what happens in the far reaches of the state is questionable.

Intelligence

Finally, the importance of intelligence should not be underestimated. As a conceptual category it covers both the knowledge resources of a terrorist group as well as those of the state authorities or other opposing parties. Intelligence differs from the other three resource categories in that its provision can be considered as important as its denial (Kalyvas, 2006: 12, 104–5, 173). Provision, meaning to provide or give, would include such activities as informing a terrorist group of a planned ambush by the authorities or offering detailed directions/local mapping of a given area to assist in the planning of an attack. More controversially, there is a case to be made for also including knowledge-transfer activities under this category. James JF Forest argues that there are two key types of knowledge-transfer in the terrorist world: motivational knowledge-transfer (ideological) and operational knowledge-transfer (skills-based) (Forest, 2006: 12). Motivational knowledge-transfer would encompass ideological direction, highlighted as a resource need by Cohen. Meanwhile, operational knowledge-transfer would include logistics, organisation (taken to mean organisational skills) and training/operational assistance, highlighted as important needs by Cohen and Byman (Byman, 2006; Cohen, 2012: 254). Though knowledge-transfer may stretch a traditional defence-focused definition of intelligence, when one looks at the broader concept of organisational intelligence the role played by these activities is clearer. Mary Ann Glynn, in her work at the intersection of sociology and management theory, offers the following definition: 'Organizational intelligence is an organization's capability to process, interpret, encode, manipulate, and access information in a purposeful, goal-directed manner, so it can increase its adaptive potential in the environment in which it operates' (Glynn, 1996: 1088).

As alluded to earlier, the denial of intelligence also plays an important role in the success of terrorist groups and the specific attacks for which they are responsible. Denial is a form of passive support. It occurs when someone (or a group) refuses to provide information to assist authorities in their lawful counterterrorism efforts upon request, or where this information is not volunteered although the person has the capacity to do so. In denying the authorities this intelligence, the activities of the terrorist group are allowed to remain undetected. There are numerous cultural, social and purely practical reasons why someone (or a group) may engage in the denial of information, and while sympathy for the terrorist group or its cause may often play a role, it just as easily may not (Khalil, 2012: 225).

Who supports terrorism?

Hinted at throughout this chapter, there are two main channels through which terrorist groups receive support. The first is the group's constituent public and its allies, their support most commonly labelled 'public support'. Those who provide support in this capacity do so as non-state actors. Given that the law is often clear-cut when it comes to supporting terrorist groups, those who provide support generally knowingly do so in defiance of state counterterrorism efforts. Though in some cases state officials (individual civil servants and members of the armed forces) may support terrorist groups, where their actions are not officially sanctioned this still constitutes public support. The second common channel of support is state support, also known more specifically as state sponsorship. Sean K Anderson and Stephen Sloan, in their *Historical Dictionary of Terrorism*, provide a particularly robust definition of state sponsorship, writing:

> State sponsorship of terrorism is defined as the support by a nation-state government of terrorist agents, including non-nationals, whether individuals or groups. Such support is counted as state sponsorship when it receives either the explicit sanction or the tacit approval of the ultimate legal and political authorities of the sponsoring regime who, in either case, have sufficient knowledge and approval of the types of activities by its agents and who maintain effective control over these agents. (2009: 641)

While public supporters make important contributions to the resources of terrorist groups in all four categories – financing, material resources, sanctuary and intelligence – the scale of support is often much smaller than that which can be provided by states. There are some particularly wealthy individuals (e.g. Osama bin Laden) or generous public support groups (e.g. the global Tamil diaspora), but it is generally the case that states have greater resources to draw upon than individual members of the public or sub-state groups. The result is that an influx of state sponsorship carries a transformational capacity (Byman, 2005: 5; Hoffman, 2006: 259, 261). Sponsorship can increase the sophistication of terrorist groups, greatly expanding access to advanced weaponry and providing a major boost to organisational coffers (Byman, 2005: 5). It has also been argued that, although it is a minority of terrorist groups that survive their first year of operations, those groups receiving state support have much better odds than those who are not in receipt of such assistance (Cohen, 2012: 252).

The effects of an influx of state sponsorship into a terrorist group may not, however, be universally positive. While Hoffman highlights the ability of state sponsorship to reduce the dependence of a terrorist group on a local population, allowing a group to carry out deadlier attacks without having to fear the repercussions of a public backlash, Byman argues that state support comes with strings of its own (Byman, 2005: 5; Hoffman, 2006: 261). Populations may turn their backs on terrorist groups when they see them as having gone 'too far', but states often have their own agendas behind offers and provision of support. Where the actions of a terrorist group come into conflict with this agenda, or even threaten the survival of the supporting regime, support can be cut abruptly, as was the case with al-Qaeda's loss of sanctuary in both Sudan and Afghanistan (Byman, 2005: 5). Furthermore, the importance of the relationship between a terrorist group and its constituent population in and of itself should not be underestimated. For many terrorist groups this relationship with a constituent public serves as the source of its political legitimacy (Malthaner, 2011: 40). Therefore, in the long term, state sponsorship may end up working in an unexpectedly counter-intuitive fashion, making the group less effective and harming the cause (Byman, 2005: 5). Yet while the particular benefits and drawbacks of support from the perspective of the terrorist group are relatively clear, what sorts of benefits these groups offer their supporters and sponsors remain decidedly less so. Thus, the question turns to the issue of motivation: what compels individuals, groups and even states to sponsor terrorist groups?

Public support at the individual and collective level

Paul argues that there are six broad contributing factors that lie behind support for groups engaged in political violence, including: (1) intense feelings of humili-ation, exclusion or anger; (2) repression or occupation by foreign powers; (3) lack of legitimacy of the current regime or a general lack of political freedom; (4) desire for resistance, self-defence or other collective goods; (5) desire to be part of a social movement or because of shared ideology; (6) other grievances (Paul, 2010: 492–3). Underpinning the factors that Paul highlights, there is a connec-tion between individual emotions and social emotions, indicating the importance of socio-psychological approaches to explaining terrorism more broadly (see Abrahms, 2008; Sageman, 2004). What Malthaner uniquely offers in *Mobilizing the Faithful* is some initial insight into how emotional social relationships instru-mentally shape public support for political violence (2011: 38–56). The result is that, while Paul is able to relate the concrete reasons behind why individuals may provide immediate support, Malthaner is able to shine a light on why publics provide support to terrorist organisations in the long term.

The key to understanding public support for terrorist groups, Malthaner argues, lies in understanding the relationship between the group and its reference group, or constituent public (Malthaner, 2011: 39–40). He identifies four ideal-type forms of support relationships (2011: 47–50). The first form of support relationship is one based on utilitarian social exchange. In these relationships sup-port is provided in exchange for ongoing reciprocal benefits and support. Essentially they are relationships of give and take, and both parties must gain from their involvement with one another (Malthaner, 2011: 47). The second form of support relationship is one based on family, friends and kinship. He extends this category to include patron–client relationships. These relationships are more complicated than those based on reciprocal exchange, but they also extend much deeper, for these ties are particularly emotionally charged and dependent upon per-sonal trust. They are therefore difficult to disrupt through traditional counterterrorism approaches (Malthaner, 2011: 47–8). Communal solidarity and identity comprise the third form of support relationship. For these relationships to work the shared identity of the constituent public must be politicised and made salient (Malthaner, 2011: 49). This typically happens during crisis or attack from the outside and reinforce notions of collective identity and solidarity while strengthening social boundaries, or a sense of us v them (Malthaner, 2011: 50). The fourth and final form of support relationship is based on: political mobilisation; identification with the terrorist group's political, socio-cultural or religious values and perspectives; and approval of the means by which the group works to make their vision reality. This form of support relationship is dependent upon a high degree of sympathy among members of the constituent public. To reach beyond a small, committed group of hardcore activists the terrorist group must effectively convince others that their individual and collective future will be significantly better if this plan is brought to fruition (Malthaner, 2011: 50).

The root motivation behind the provision of support in each form of relationship is clear. Exchange relationships are rooted in self-interest while family/friend/kin relationships are grounded in feelings of trust, belonging and mutual protection. Trust and belonging also lie behind collective identity relationships. It is only those relationships grounded in political mobilisation and shared ideology which are inherently ideological and intrinsically dependent upon expressed sympathy. When reduced to their basic elements the relationship between the individual motivations identified by Paul and the collective motivations identified by Malthaner becomes much clearer. For instance, humiliation on a personal level can affect how one perceives his or her position within the kinship group, while on a collective level, humiliation represents an attack on collective identity. The desire to belong to something bigger than oneself, such as a social movement, can contribute to an individual's decision to zealously adopt the ideology of a terrorist group as his or her own. By recognising the different motivations behind public support at the individual and collective levels it becomes possible to paint a more nuanced picture of the support landscape.

Strategic and goal-oriented reasons for state sponsorship

Though state sponsorship has declined substantially since the end of the Cold War, its impact on the world of terrorism is potentially more significant than it was even 30 years ago. With terrorist groups competing for a piece of an ever-shrinking amount of state support, those who are able to secure it have a crucial advantage over those groups left in the cold (Bowie, 2013: 42; Watson, 2013: 4–5). In order to understand the rapid decline in support over the last quarter-century, as well as the persistence of state sponsorship even in the face of mounting international pressure, it is essential to know what benefits a state receives from sponsorship. Incurring both material and reputational costs, a state is unlikely to provide support altruistically.

For Byman, though there are a number of reasons why a particular government might choose to sponsor a terrorist group, sponsorship generally comes about either for strategic reasons or to achieve regime-specific objectives. He argues that state sponsorship serves a wide variety of strategic interests. The impression that a regime has a particular terrorist group at its disposal can provide the supporting state with additional leverage to influence the behaviour of its neighbours. In some cases a terrorist group may be used to destabilise or even topple an adversary. Because sponsoring a terrorist group is less resource intensive than expanding a state's own military capabilities, sponsorship can be a cost-effective means of expanding the international influence of a state, particularly one marginalised within the existing international political system (Byman, 2005: 4–5). Hoffman also explores the strategic advantages of state sponsorship. He argues that one particular advantage is the rare opportunity it offers for a smaller state to attack (albeit vicariously) much more powerful states without the risk of international punishment or reprisals (Hoffman, 2006: 258). Though the experience of Afghanistan in the wake of 9/11 calls into question whether it is really possible for states to avoid being held accountable for the actions of the terrorist groups they resource, in the vast majority of state-sponsorship cases, reprisals have met with only limited success (Hoffman, 2006: 263–7).

State sponsorship, Byman argues (2005: 5), can also help states meet regime-specific goals. These can be ideological, as was the case with Syria's initial decision to back Palestinian terrorist groups in their fight against Israel, though the importance of ideology has diminished over time (Byman, 2005: 138). While shared ideology is not a necessary condition of state sponsorship, nor a consistent factor, it can influence a state's decision about which specific groups to fund (Byman, 2005: 138–9; Hoffman, 2006: 261). Regime-specific goals may also be related to domestic interests or the local political climate (Byman, 2005: 138). For instance, Saudi Arabian aid to various Palestinian groups was intended to discourage attacks against Saudi interests. As mentioned earlier, this can also be seen in the Taliban's efforts to reach out to al-Qaeda in the mid-1990s during its high-stakes civil war with the Northern Alliance (Byman, 2005: 5). Where these regime-specific goals are the driving force behind state sponsorship the sponsorship arrangement may be less secure, especially if the regime is itself unstable. As objectives are met and political priorities shift, funding and other support may shift accordingly in ways detrimental to supported groups.

Conclusion

This chapter has highlighted the major issues in defining support and the key conceptual debates with regard to support, specifically on the relationship between attitudes/sympathy and behaviour/support. As will be discussed later in this book, the assumptions made with regard to this debate have led some academics to emphasise challenging sympathies to counterterrorism, while others have emphasised challenging (behavioural) support. There are four main forms of support: (1) financing; (2) material resources (including weapons, explosives and any other goods needed to carry out an attack or sustain the group); (3) sanctuary (or safe haven); and (4) intelligence. Almost all support activities, from gun smuggling to assisting with training or logistics, fit within one of these broad categories. One notable exception, however, is that of 'diplomatic support or recognition', which can only be offered by a state and has, historically, been offered relatively rarely (Cohen, 2012: 254).

Furthermore, support can be offered by states in an official capacity (state sponsorship) or by individuals and non-state groups (known collectively as public support). Because of their resources states generally have a much greater impact on a terrorist group than public supporters alone. However, as an influx of state support can reduce reliance on public support, weakening the ties between a terrorist group and its constituent public, those groups who purport to represent a specific national, political, cultural or religious group must take care to ensure that these ties do not become so weak as to cause the group to lose legitimacy. The motivational factors behind public support differ considerably from those leading to state sponsorship. With the former, the nature of the relationship between the terrorist group and its public supporters, including its emotional and social dimensions, is of particular importance, while state support can be argued to be motivated largely by strategic interests and the specific goals of the ruling regime offering its assistance.

In summary, because motivations provide important insight into the strength of the relationship between a terrorist group and its supporters and/or sponsors, understanding the reasons why individuals, groups and states support terrorism, alongside the specific details of support offered, can help those engaged in counterterrorism efforts discover the most effective means by which support can be weakened over time. Terrorist groups are known for their flexibility, adaptability and ability to thrive under pressure. They have an impact far beyond what might be suggested by the size of their bank balances or weapons stockpiles. While cutting off direct flows of support by freezing financial assets or intercepting smuggling operations may seem like the best route to defeating a given terrorist organisation, it may prove to be a very temporary (and unsuccessful) solution to a long-term problem if the bonds underpinning the support network are not similarly disrupted.

STUDY BOX CHAPTER 6

Key reading

Byman, D. (2005) *Deadly Connections: States that Sponsor Terrorism* (Cambridge: Cambridge University Press).

Malthaner, S. (2011) *Mobilizing the Faithful: Militant Islamic Groups and their Constituencies* (Chicago: University of Chicago Press).

Mascini, P. (2006) 'Can the Violent Jihad Do Without Sympathizers?', *Studies in Conflict and Terrorism* 29 (4): 343–57.

Paul, C. (2008) 'As a Fish Swims in the Sea: Relationships Between Factors Contributing to Support for Terrorist or Insurgent Groups', *Studies in Conflict and Terrorism* 33 (6): 488–510.

Study questions

1   To what extent do terrorist groups need sympathisers to sustain a campaign?

2   How important is a 'hearts and minds' approach in countering terrorism?

3   Why do states sponsor terrorist groups and is it always in their interest?

References

Abrahms, Max. (2008) 'What Terrorists Really Want: Terrorist Motives and Counterterrorism Strategy.' *International Security* 32, no 4: 78–105.

Anderson, Sean Kendall and Stephen Sloan. (2009) *Historical Dictionary of Terrorism*. Toronto: Scarecrow Press.

Aust, Anthony. (2010) *Handbook of International Law*, 2ed. Cambridge: Cambridge University Press.

Aziz, Sahar. (2003) 'The Laws on Providing Material Support to Terrorist Organizations: The Erosion of Constitutional Rights or a Legitimate Tool for Preventing Terrorism.' *Texas Journal on Civil Liberties and Civil Rights* 9, no 1: 45–92.

Baumert, Thomas. (2008) 'Review: *Terrornomics* (Costigan and Gold, Eds.).' *Democracy and Security* 4: 102–4.

Bloom, Mia M. (2004) 'Palestinian Suicide Bombing: Public Support, Market Share and Outbidding.' *Political Science Quarterly* 119, no 1: 61–88.

Bowie, Neil G. (2013) 'Trends in the use of terror by states since the end of the Cold War.' In *State Terrorism and Human Rights: International Responses Since the End of the Cold War*, Gillian Duncan, Orla Lynch, Gilbert Ramsay and Ali MS Watson (eds): 42–53. London: Routledge.

Burr, J Millard and Robert O Collins. (2006) *Alms for Jihad: Charity and Terrorism in the Islamic World*. Cambridge: Cambridge University Press.

Byman, Daniel. (2005) *Deadly Connections: States that Sponsor Terrorism*. Cambridge: Cambridge University Press.

Byman, Daniel (2006). 'Passive Sponsors of Terrorism.' *Survival* 47, no 4: 117–44.

Chugani, Sumeet H. (2008) 'Benevolent Blood Money: Terrorist Exploitation of Zakat and its Complications in the War on Terror.' *North Carolina Journal of International Law and Commercial Regulation* 34, no 2: 601–55.

Cohen, Michael D. (2012) 'Mission Impossible? Influencing Iranian and Libyan Sponsorship of Terrorism.' In *Deterring Terrorism: Theory and Practice*, Andreas Wenger and Alex Wilner (eds): 251–72. Stanford: Stanford University Press.

Cole, David. (2003) 'The New McCarthyism: Repeating History in the War on Terrorism.' *Harvard Civil Rights-Civil Liberties Law Review* 38, no 1: 1–31.

Combs, Cindy C. (2009) *Terrorism in the Twenty-First Century*, 5ed. London: Pearson.

Costigan, Sean S and David Gold. (2007) *Terrornomics*. Aldershot: Ashgate.

Croissant, Aurel and Daniel Barlow. (2007) 'Terrorist Financing and Government Responses in Southeast Asia.' In *Terrorism Financing and State Responses: A Comparative Perspective*, Jeanne Giraldo and Harold A Trinkunas (eds): 231–46. Stanford: Stanford University Press.

Cronin, Audrey. (2006) 'How al-Qaida Ends: The Decline and Demise of Terrorist Groups.' *International Security* 31, no 1: 7–48.

de Goede, Marieke. (2003) 'Hawala Discourses and the War on Terrorist Finance.' *Environment and Planning D: Society and Space* 21: 513–32.

English, Richard. (2004) *Armed Struggle: The History of the IRA*. London: Pan Macmillan.

Fair, C Christine and Bryan Shepherd. (2006) 'Who Supports Terrorism? Evidence from Fourteen Muslim Countries.' *Studies in Conflict and Terrorism* 29, no 1: 51–74.

Foley, Frank. (2013) *Countering Terrorism in Britain and France: Institutions, Norms and the Shadow of the Past*. Cambridge: Cambridge University Press.

Forest, James JF. (2006) 'Introduction.' In *Teaching Terror: Strategic and Tactical Learning in the Terrorist World*, James JF Forest (ed): 1–29 Oxford: Rowman and Littlefield.

Freytag, Andreas, Jens J Krüger, Daniel Mierriks and Friedrich Schnieder. (2011) 'The Origins of Terrorism: Cross-country Estimates of Socio-economic Determinants of Terrorism.' *European Journal of Political Economy* 27: S5–S16.

Gardella, Anna. (2004) 'The Fight Against the Financing of Terrorism between Judicial and Regulatory Cooperation.' In *Enforcing International Law Norms Against Terrorism*, Andrea Bianchi (ed): 415–452 Oxford: Hart.

Gerges, Fawaz A. (2005) *The Far Enemy: Why Jihad Went Global*. Cambridge: Cambridge University Press.

German, Mike. (2007) *Thinking Like a Terrorist: Insights of a Former FBI Undercover Agent*. Washington: Potomac Books.

Giraldo, Jeanne K and Harold A Trinkunas (eds). (2007) *Terrorism Financing and State Responses: A Comparative Perspective*. Stanford: Stanford University Press.

Glynn, Mary Ann. (1996) 'Innovative Genius: A Framework for Relating Individual and Organizational Intelligences to Innovation.' *Academy of Management Review* 21, no 4: 1081–111.

Hayes, Bernadette C and Ian McAlister. (2001) 'Sowing Dragon's Teeth: Public Support for Political Violence and Paramilitarism in Northern Ireland.' *Political Studies* 49: 901–922.

Hayes, Bernadette C and Ian McAllister. (2005) 'Public Support for Political Violence and Paramilitarism in Northern Ireland and the Republic of Ireland.' *Terrorism & Political Violence* 17: 599–617.

Hellmich, Christina. (2011) *Al-Qaeda: From Global Network to Local Franchise*. New York: Zed Books.

Hewitt, Christopher. (1990) 'Terrorism and Public Opinion: A Five Country Comparison.' *Terrorism & Political Violence* 2, no 2: 145–170.

Hoffman, Bruce. (2006) *Inside Terrorism*, revised and expanded edition. New York: Columbia University Press.

Jones, Seth and Martin C Libicki. (2008) *How Terrorist Groups End: Lessons for Countering al Qa'ida*. Santa Monica: RAND.

Kalyvas, Stathis N. (2006) *The Logic of Violence in Civil War*. Cambridge: Cambridge University Press.

Khalil, James. (2012) 'Insurgent–Populace Relations in Nepal: An Analysis of Attitudinal and Behavioural Support.' *Small Wars and Insurgencies* 23, no. 2: 221–44.

Khashan, Hilal. (2003) 'Collective Palestinian frustration and suicide bombings.' *Third World Quarterly* 24, no 6: 1049–67.

Koh, Jae-myong. (2006) *Suppressing Terrorist Financing and Money Laundering*. Berlin: Springer.

LaFree, Gary and Nancy A Morris. (2012) 'Does Legitimacy Matter? Attitudes Toward Anti-American Violence in Egypt, Morocco, and Indonesia.' *Crime & Delinquency* 58: 689–719.

van Linschoten, Alex Strick and Felix Kuehn. (2012) *An Enemy We Created: The Myth of the Taliban-Al Qaeda Merger in Afghanistan*. New York: Oxford University Press.

Lutz, James and Brenda Lutz. (2011) *Terrorism: The Basics*. London: Routledge.

McAllister, Bradley and Alex P Schmid. (2011) 'Theories of Terrorism.' In *The Routledge Handbook of Terrorism Research*, Alex P Shmid (ed): 201–71. New York: Routledge.

Malthaner, Stefan. (2011) *Mobilizing the Faithful: Militant Islamic Groups and their Constituencies*. Chicago: University of Chicago Press.

Mascini, Peter. (2006) 'Can the Violent Jihad Do Without Sympathizers?' *Studies in Conflict and Terrorism* 29, no 4: 343–57.

Moloney, Ed. (2007) *A Secret History of the IRA*. Toronto: Penguin.

Normand, Roger and Sarah Zaidi. (2008) *Human Rights at the UN: The Political History of Universal Justice*. Bloomington: Indiana University Press.

Passas, Nikos. (2007) 'Terrorism Financing Mechanisms and Policy Dilemmas.' In *Terrorism Financing and State Responses: A Comparative Perspective*, Jeanne Giraldo and Harold A Trinkunas (eds): 21–38. Stanford: Stanford University Press.

Paul, Christopher. (2009) 'How Do Terrorists Generate and Maintain Support?' In *Social Science for Counterterrorism: Putting the Pieces Together,* Paul K. Davis and Kim Cragin (ed.): 113–150 Santa Monica: RAND.

Paul, Christopher. (2010) 'As a Fish Swims in the Sea: Relationships Between Factors Contributing to Support for Terrorist or Insurgent Groups.' *Studies in Conflict and Terrorism* 33, no 6: 488–510.

Sageman, Marc. (2004) *Understanding Terror Networks.* Philadelphia: University of Pennsylvania Press.

Stampnitzky, Lisa. (2013) *Disciplining Terror: How Experts Invented 'Terrorism'.* Cambridge: University of Cambridge Press.

Vincent, Steve. (2005) *Being Empathetic: A Companion for Counsellors and Therapists.* Oxford: Radcliffe.

Watson, Ali MS. (2013) 'Introduction.' In *State Terrorism and Human Rights: International Responses Since the End of the Cold War*, Gillian Duncan, Orla Lynch, Gilbert Ramsay and Ali MS Watson (eds): 1–13. London: Routledge.

Waugh, William L. (1983) 'The Values in Violence: Organizational and Political Objectives of Terrorist Groups.' *Conflict Quarterly* 3, no 4: 5–19.

Weinberg, Leonard, Ami Pedahzur and Sivan Hirsch-Hoefler. (2004) 'The Challenges of Conceptualizing Terrorism.' *Terrorism and Political Violence* 16, no 4: 777–94.

Wellman, Carl. (2013) *Terrorism and Counterterrorism: A Moral Assessment.* London: Springer.

White, Jonathan. (2012) *Terrorism and Homeland Security*, 7ed. Belmont: Wadsworth.

7
TERRORISM, COMMUNICATION AND THE MEDIA

CRISTINA ARCHETTI

Introduction

Since 9/11 much has been said about the role of technologies like the internet and global communication networks in sustaining transnational terrorism, the spread of its ideology and its recruiting activities. Many claims have also been made about the role of the media, particularly new communication technologies, in the process of radicalisation – the embracing of extremist views that might degenerate into terrorist violence (Stevens and Neumann, 2009: 10). There is a widespread realisation that communication is crucial to terrorism, to the point that 'strategic communication' has become a buzzword in official circles, think tanks and academia. The notion of 'narrative' in particular – another 'communicative tool' – has recently both been drawn into the analysis of the roots of terrorism and advocated as an essential part of a counter-radicalisation response.

Within the deluge of literature on terrorism and security that has developed since 9/11, however, accuracy and perspective in assessing what the role of the media exactly consists of has tended to get lost among sweeping generalisations, alarmist statements and the hyperbole of a security industry that is often more oriented towards feeding its own economic interests than rigorous scientific enquiry (Mueller, 2012). Media are often mentioned, but it is clear that their role is too often taken for granted. Even academic texts by highly rated terrorism scholars, as will be illustrated in a moment, tend to address media function and effects in a surprisingly casual way.

The purpose of this chapter is not only to outline current trends in the terrorism literature about the role of communication and the media, but also to point out problematic – if not simplistic or plainly wrong – claims and to raise critical questions. At the end of this chapter you will understand:

- What communication and the media actually are
- How they are related to terrorism

- The basics of the interactions among terrorists, journalists, policymakers, publics and communication technologies
- Why several current claims about communication technologies, especially the internet and social media, are wrong

Terrorism as communication

Even without knowing that the term *communicate* comes from the Latin 'to share', we all understand what communication is about. We have an intuitive notion that it involves the exchange of information, that it can happen face to face, but that it can also be mediated through a mobile or the internet. What might not be as obvious is that we engage in communication even when we do not explicitly set out to use a communication medium. Voting, for example, is an act of communication in which we express our preference for a candidate and the political manifesto s/he represents. Protesting, no matter whether holding placards or being on a hunger strike, is about expressing support for a cause and letting others know about it. Terrorism–inflicting death and destroying property – is also a way of sending a message.

Over 20 years ago Alex Schmid (1989: 541) compared terrorism to the proverbial tree falling in the forest, the sound of which does not exist until somebody actually hears it: 'With the rise of the mass media in the 1880s reporters came to observe the falling of each "tree" and [...] their newspapers brought the story to people who would otherwise never have learned about it.' The communication of the terrorist act is, in fact, essential to terrorists' tactics, so much so that several authors have acknowledged terrorism as itself an act of communication.

Schmid and Janny de Graaf (1982: 14), for instance, have argued since the early 1980s that terrorism *is* communication: 'For the terrorist the message matters, not the victim.' In their words the casualties of terrorist attacks are 'message generators' (1982: 29), 'the skin on a drum beaten to achieve a calculated impact on a wider audience' (1982: 14). Gabriel Weimann and Conrad Winn (1994) also likened terrorism to 'theatre'.

For Ronald Crelinsten (1987) terrorism's violence is a form of political communication: 'Terrorism functions as a form of "propaganda of the deed" in which the terrorist sends messages to those in power, as well as to the general public. On a purely symbolic level, the message is equivalent to shouting "look at me!" or "listen to me!"' (1987: 419). Brigitte Nacos, who approaches terrorism as a 'mass-mediated' phenomenon, in this respect writes that mass media play a central role in what she calls the 'calculus' of perpetrators: terrorists anticipate the consequences of their actions, 'the likelihood of gaining media attention' and the possibility of entering, through the media, the 'Triangle of Political Communication' (Nacos, 2003: 11). In a triangle, the points of which are constituted by the media, policymakers and the public, as she explains, the media are not neutral. They are rather in a strategic position: they 'magnify and minimize, include and exclude' (2003: 11). In the global communication system domestic terrorists can also tap into international media and communicate their message to foreign governments and audiences (2003: 12). Access to the media, grants terrorists not only the public's attention but also recognition and a 'degree of respectability' (Nacos, 2002: 14).

The ever-present attempt by terrorists to exploit mass media to convey their political message (Gerrits, 1992) is widely illustrated in the literature by the statement of a Palestinian terrorist after the 1972 Munich Olympics attacks:

> We [Black September terrorist group] recognized that sport is the modern religion of the western world. We knew that the people in England and America would switch their television sets from any programme about the plight of the Palestinians if there was a sporting event on another channel. So we decided to use their Olympics, the most sacred ceremony of this religion, to make the world pay attention to us. We offered up human sacrifices to your gods of sport and television. And they answered our prayers. From Munich onwards nobody could ignore the Palestinians or their cause. (Quoted in Weimann, 1990: 16)

Although it is debatable whether it was really the media coverage that placed the Palestinian cause on the international political agenda (Archetti, 2012: 96–7), this example provides a clear indication of terrorists' interest in publicity. This has not changed over the years. The impact of the second plane on the North Tower on 11 September 2001, as Shlomo Shpiro (2002: 80) suggests, could have been purposely delayed to make sure that 'every television camera in New York would be focused on their murderous activities'. For a more recent example, one can think about the killing of a British soldier in London in May 2013. The two murderers, after having repeatedly stabbed the victim in a busy street in Woolwich, made every effort to be filmed and photographed by the gathering crowd while waiting for the police to arrive on the scene (BBC, 2013).

Terrorism and the media: what is the link?

While there appears to be a general agreement about the existence of a relationship between media and terrorism, a careful reading reveals that the literature presents a range of different and potentially conflicting claims. Paletz and Boiney (1992: 10) point out that 'there are two diametrically opposed camps: those that indict the media as proterrorist and those that indict the media as antiterrorist'. The 'very few works' belonging to the latter camp accuse the media of conspiring with the corporate and/or political power to support a narrow understanding of terrorism, one that is instrumental to pursuing specific interests (Paletz and Boiney, 1992: 12–13). Kevin Barnhurst (1991: 115–19) also identifies 'two schools': one which sees the media as 'culpable,' instrumental to terrorism, another which argues that the media are 'vulnerable' victims themselves of manipulation by terrorists, yet not directly responsible for their deeds. Despite this variety of views, the overall understanding of the media role in relation to terrorism in the literature appears overwhelmingly negative. Here is a brief review of the main trends.

The dependence of terrorists on the media to publicise their message has led to the assumption, more or less explicitly, of a causal link between terrorism and media coverage. In this respect Walter Laqueur (1976: 104) is often cited: 'The media are the terrorist's best friend. The terrorist's act alone is nothing: publicity is all.' Jenkins (quoted in Alali and Eke, 1991: 8) goes as far as saying that 'terrorism is a product of freedom, particularly, of freedom of the press'. For Nacos (1994: 8, my emphasis): 'Getting the attention of the mass media, the public, and decision makers is the *raison d'etre* behind modern terrorism's increasingly shocking violence.'

The relationship between media and terrorists is also often described as a 'symbiosis' (Bassiouni, 1981: 14; Martin, 1985: 127; Wilkinson, 2006: 145). On the one hand, terrorists need to publicise their motives through the media; on the other hand, media outlets constantly seek compelling stories to sell to their audiences. In her study on the causes of terrorism Martha Crenshaw (1981: 386) writes: 'The most basic reason for terrorism is to gain recognition or attention [...] Violence and bloodshed always excite human curiosity, and theatricality, suspense, and threat of danger inherent in terrorism enhance its attention-getting qualities.'

The role of the media within its symbiotic relationship with terrorism, however, can vary. Although in the literature there is a tendency to see the media as supportive of terrorism, the way in which they can actually aid terrorists can take different forms. Media can encourage terrorism through 'contagion' (Bassiouni, 1981: 19): the idea here is that media attention towards terror will encourage further incidents by providing a 'model and inspiration' for more attacks (Schmid, 1989: 558; Alexander, 1978: 105). The media can 'endorse' terrorism by romanticising or glamourising it. Yonah Alexander, for example, describes how, in reporting the kidnapping of Patricia Hearst, an American newspaper heiress, in 1974 by the urban guerrilla group Symbionese Liberation Army (SLA), the media managed to give a group of 'misfits' a modern '"Robin Hood" image' (Alexander, 1978: 103). Through their thirst for drama, media are also accused of indulging in disproportionate coverage. Schmid (1989), for instance, compares the volume of CBS coverage of the US-embassy hostage crisis in Tehran (1979) to reporting of the Vietnam war in 1972. He concludes: '50 US hostages in Iran received 3,000 times more coverage than 50 GIs in Vietnam' (Schmid, 1989: 556). Alexander (1978: 112) says that 'by providing extensive coverage the media give the impression that they sympathize with the terrorist cause', thereby granting them an aura of legitimacy. Sensationalism, in turn, can easily lead to alarmism and public panic – an outcome UK officials often refer to as 'doing the terrorists' job for them' (10 Downing Street spokesperson, 2003, quoted in Archetti and Taylor, 2005: 12–13; Straw, 2003). Media, in this perspective, can contribute to 'manufacturing' the terrorist threat. The last point is developed by Adam Curtis's documentary *The Power of Nightmares* (2004), in which the media are accomplices in policymakers' deliberate exploitation of fear to support their political agendas. This view is echoed by Nancy Snow (2005: 103), who claims that since 9/11 'we have experienced a coming together of very powerful institutions of information, the federal government and the corporate media, to create a barrier between the American public and the real environment.' Along these lines John Gray (2005: 16), in the aftermath of the 7/7 London bombings, claimed that they were 'an episode in the virtual world that is being continuously manufactured by the media'. The media create 'collective dreams', 'an alternate reality in which insoluble problems [as terrorism] can be

conjured away by displays of goodwill. But the problems never really go away'
(Gray, 2005: 17).

Media are not only seen to encourage terrorism indirectly, but through their
cameras they are thought to become co-participants in terrorist deeds (Schmid,
1989: 553; Alexander, 1978: 105); and they might interfere with governmental
crisis management. Martin Bell (2007), for example, writing for the UK broad-
sheet *The Guardian* in relation to the attempted car bombing at Glasgow airport
on 30 June 2007, wrote that the government's response to the emergency had been
'measured, welcome and reassuring'. The media's, instead, had been 'hysterical
beyond belief'. Reporters' activities around the locations of terrorist attacks are also
found to interfere with police operations (Alexander, 1978: 105). Raphael Cohen-
Almagor (2005) draws up a lengthy list of the multiple ways in which 'problematic
and irresponsible' coverage places the media on the side of terrorists rather than
governments. The 'troubling episodes' he describes range from endangering lives in
situations in which hostages are taken, through indulging in 'dangerous specula-
tions', to paying terrorists in order to get interviews and using irresponsible
terminology – for example, 'freedom fighters' rather than 'terrorists' (Cohen-
Almagor, 2005: 395).

While all of the points made so far appear perfectly plausible at first sight, they
are at closer scrutiny highly questionable. It is for this reason that, before moving
on to discussing the relationship between terrorism, the internet and new media, it
is necessary to raise a few red flags. The next section will help you think more
critically about 'the media', particularly about what they actually are, as well as
about what they can and cannot do.

The problems with 'the media'

Despite the recognition that communication and the media play an important role
in the terrorism phenomenon, their function in and effects on society are widely
misunderstood. To start with, in the literature about terrorism it is not always clear
what 'media' refers to: the term appears to be used to conflate communication technologies, content carried by media platforms (coverage) and media organisations.
One could argue that distinguishing these different meanings of 'media' is hair-
splitting. Analytical clarity, however, has far-reaching policy implications. To further
explain the relevance of the distinctions between the meanings of 'media' on tackling
terrorism let us use an example. If somebody says (as researchers actually do) that
'the media contribute to radicalisation' what does this statement actually mean?
Is the researcher suggesting that it is the availability of communication platforms
(i.e. the technology) that allows radical individuals to exchange and cultivate
extreme ideas? Or is it what media are reporting (i.e. the content) – for instance, the
focus in the coverage on civilian victims at the expense of progress in the development
of security in Afghanistan – that fuels resentment and, therefore, extremism? In yet
another of the many possibilities it could be suggested that journalists (as members
of media organisations), under the pressure of tight deadlines, do not use language
as accurately as they could. In this case they could be contributing, through rhetoric that encourages Islamophobia and the identification of Muslims as 'the enemy',

to resentment and radicalisation. These scenarios not only describe very different causal processes; each of them also implies a very different strategy to address the problem at hand. While there are always multiple solutions to the same issue, a plausible reaction to the first situation could be, for a governmental actor, monitoring access to certain websites, perhaps restricting access to extremist content – as advocated by former French president Nicholas Sarkozy in 2012 (Ackerman 2012) or, more recently, by UK Home Secretary Theresa May after the London Woolwich killing in 2013 and the beheading of hostage James Foley by Islamic State (IS) in 2014 (May, 2013; Associated Press, 2014). In the second case a course of action could be for the International Security Assistance Force (ISAF) mission in Afghanistan to attempt to balance the negative stories with more positive ones, perhaps by producing press releases, pictures and footage of good news from the theatre of operation, or by having a Twitter account directly promoting positive newsbites. In the third case training courses for journalists could be organised in collaboration with news organisations. An alternative could be developing editorial guidelines about the use of language (BBC Editorial Guidelines, n.d.).

The idea that media can be easily manipulated by governments – *The Power of Nightmares'* and conspiracy theorists' scenario – when it comes to reporting terrorism would be troubling to any researcher in political communication. The very issue of the relationship between media (more specifically understood as journalists and editors operating within organisations) and officials, particularly the extent of media independence *vis-à-vis* the political establishment, has been for decades one of the thorniest topics of debate in the field (Esser and Pfetsch, 2004). The notion that journalists can be used as mouthpieces either by terrorists or by governments dismisses an entire tradition of sociological studies of news organisations' norms, journalistic practices and newsgathering routines (for an overview of the different perspectives see Tumber, 1999). A scholar in Media Studies would be puzzled by the fact that conclusions are generally applied to 'media' without distinguishing between print, TV, internet, radio, new or mass media. The suggestion that media content can have a direct effect on potential terrorists, leading them to engage in violent behaviour – the contagion hypothesis – would be recognised by a researcher in communication as closely resembling the silver-bullet or hypodermic-needle theory of media effects (Brooker and Jermyn, 2003: 6). This is based on the belief that the media can trigger an immediate, virtually identical and predictable response in a public exposed to their messages, as if the audience had been injected with those contents. The theory was developed in the 1920s and 1930s, initially as an attempt to explain how UK propaganda had contributed to defeating German troops during World War I (Brooker and Jermyn, 2003: 5). The rise of European dictators appeared to support the idea that masses could be manipulated by leaders who were able to exploit modern communication technologies, such as radio. Despite this, the theory was quickly deemed unsatisfactory to explain media effects and replaced by more nuanced models. Lazarsfeld's 'two-step-flow', for example, later hypothesised, rather than a direct influence of the media on the public, a process in two stages in which media messages were filtered to the masses through the interpretations of opinion leaders (Lazarsfeld et al., 1944). Within the reception-studies tradition the 'uses and gratification' theory (Blumler and Katz, 1974) emphasised the way in which each individual uses media messages to satisfy psychological or social needs. A description of how these early conceptualisations evolved – for instance, by entirely abandoning the notion of a mass public or incorporating ethnic readings of media texts – could be lengthy (see Miller, 2008 for a critical review of research approaches to media audiences over time). These examples are nonetheless more than sufficient to show that a substantial part of the literature on terrorism and the media does not know much about the media and their effects. The way media are seen by most research of terrorism is stuck in the early twentieth century.

It's (not) the internet, stupid!

Most of the literature that deals with the role of media, as we have seen, tends to focus on mainstream and 'old' media (mainly national press and TV) at the expense of the internet and 'new' media. It is only for about a decade that scholars of terrorism have turned their eyes to the role of the internet. The initial focus was on which terrorist groups had an online presence, on these websites' function, content and rhetoric (Tsfati and Weimann, 2002; Weimann, 2006; Conway, 2006). Contributions now extend to the role of social media, such as Twitter (US Army, 2008: 7–10; Goodman, 2011) and YouTube (Conway and McInerney, 2009; McInerney, 2009; Seib and Janbek, 2011).

Terrorism literature is further characterised by deeply negative bias in relation to the internet. While all sort of content travels through it – including the 'good' activities of environmental activists or campaigners against child labour, for instance – the technology is described as having a crucial role when it comes to supporting terrorism, particularly in the case of Al-Qaeda and, most recently, IS. Alarmist, even sensationalist, statements characterise not only journalistic accounts but also academic literature and think tanks' assessments. *Washington Post* journalists Steve Coll and Susan Glasser, for example, wrote a few years ago that: 'Al Qaeda has become the first guerrilla movement in history to migrate from physical space to cyberspace' (Coll and Glasser, 2005). In an article published in the journal *International Security* Audrey Cronin suggested that al-Qaeda 'is in many ways distinct from its predecessors, especially in its protean ability to transform itself from a physical to a virtual organization' (Cronin, 2006: 33). More currently, the use of social media is regarded as the main driver of recruitment into the ranks of the IS terrorist organisation (Brooking, 2014).

TEXTBOX 4   AL-QAEDA IN THE ARABIAN PENINSULA

Year formed: 2009

AQAP was formed in January 2009 out of a merger of al-Qaeda's Yemeni and Saudi branches (al-Qaeda in Saudi Arabia and Islamic Jihad of Yemen). It is considered to be one of the most active of al-Qaeda's branches. Al-Qaeda was active in Yemen well before the Saudi and Yemeni branches merged, and was responsible for the October 2000 USS Cole bombing in the port of Aden, where 17 US sailors were killed, as well as the 2002 attack on a French supertanker in the Gulf of Aden, amongst others.

Aim

AQAP is a Sunni extremist group that follows al-Qaeda's brand of global jihad. It is opposed to the Al Saud monarchy in Saudi Arabia and the Yemen government. The group has targeted local, US and other Western interests in the Arabian Peninsula but is now pursuing a global strategy.

AQAP communication

A key component of AQAP's operational strategy entails reaching out to English-speaking audiences with its messages and propaganda in order to recruit new members. This material encourages Western audiences to adopt its ideology and carry out attacks against Western interests in the Arabian Peninsula and abroad. AQAP publishes the print magazines *Voice of Jihad* and *Inspire* (al-Qaeda's first ever English-language magazine, which was released in July 2010, called for followers to 'destroy' America and provided detailed instructions on using household materials to create explosives) and the online magazine *Sada al-Malahim* ('the Echo of Battles').

Despite pursuing extensive outreach and conducting many operations in Yemen, AQAP does not have deep roots in Yemeni society. Its outreach is targeted internationally and, while being successful with foreign jihadists, is limited in reaching a Yemeni population with a 54 per cent literacy rate.

The internet contributes to several activities of terrorist groups, such as fundraising, networking and coordination, as well as information gathering (Conway, 2006: 283–92). Literature on the link between terrorism and the internet is, however, currently absorbed by a focus on the role of this communication technology in information provision, including the production of training manuals and instructions on how to manufacture explosives, propaganda material (such as videos, communiqués and texts) and recruitment. The internet, in this last respect, is identified as a platform for the spreading of radical content and extremist ideology, particularly targeted at young and vulnerable individuals. In relation to Al-Qaeda, the incessant activities of *ad hoc* media-production houses like the Al-Fajr Center (including the more widely known As-Sahab as a production branch) and propaganda hubs like the Global Islamic Media Front have been regularly presented as evidence of the threat (Rita Katz, cited in Committee on Homeland Security, 2007: 18–20). The impact of the internet is portrayed in such overwhelmingly negative terms that the technology is often openly blamed for radicalisation, understood not only as the embracing of extremist ideas but also as their translation into violent action. For instance, a report by the Homeland Security Policy Institute and the Critical Incident Analysis Group entitled *NETworked Radicalization: A Counter-Strategy* stated as early as 2007 that:

> The Internet facilitates radicalization because it is without peer as a tool for both active and passive communication and outreach. Online chat rooms are interactive venues where aberrant attitudes and beliefs may be exchanged, reinforced, hardened and validated (at least in the minds of participants). (HSPI/CIAG, 2007: 5–6)

While it is true that a considerable amount of instructional content is available on the internet, it is unclear to what extent it can support actual terrorist plots. Some, in fact, would argue that manufacturing viable explosives requires more than online training (Stenersen, 2008). The myth of the radicalising function of this technology has nonetheless become deeply entrenched in the current security discourse. Akil Awan, Andrew Hoskins and Ben O' Loughlin demonstrate how radicalisation has become established as a prominent threat within security discourses in both government circles and the mainstream media (Awan et al., 2011). More specifically Hoskins and O'Loughlin point out how the notion of radicalisation conveniently matches both the news and policymakers' agendas: 'For security policymakers and journalists alike, "radicalization" can anchor a news agenda, offering a cast of radicalizers and the vulnerable radicalized, and legitimating a policy response to such danger.' It also combines with 'that major intangible of "the Internet"' (Hoskins and O'Loughlin, 2009: 107–8). As they further explain: 'It is as if society is endangered by the technology itself, which enables identity theft, the "grooming" of children by paedophiles, or indeed "grooming for jihad"' (2009: 109).

The unfortunate outcome is that both the notion of radicalisation and the role of the internet in promoting it are taken for granted. The fact that unfounded claims become the largely unchallenged basis of policy, as the following excerpt from the 2011 UK *Prevent Strategy* illustrates, is particularly worrying:

> The Internet has transformed the extent to which terrorist organisations and their sympathisers can radicalise people in this country and overseas. It enables a wider range of organisations and individuals to reach a much larger audience with a broader and more dynamic series of messages and narratives. It encourages interaction and facilitates recruitment. (Home Office, 2011: 77)

The aim here is not to argue that the internet does not play any role at all. It can and does play a facilitating function, particularly in terms of organisation, fundraising, distribution and sharing of content, and providing an initial meeting place for like-minded individuals, which can then lead to face-to-face contact. These aspects, however, are not unique characteristics of this medium. In this respect, an engagement with the history of communication and media effects – particularly the way in which the interpretation of media messages is shaped by an individual social context – contributes to placing the role of this technology into perspective (see Archetti, 2012).

To start with, the rhetoric revolving around the internet is technologically deterministic: it assumes that a communication technology will by its very existence produce certain social and political effects. This is partly related to its association with the popular notion of a communication revolution and the idea that the internet is radically changing our societies. Manuel Castells talks, for instance, about a networked society (Castells, 1996). Of course, the internet makes a difference: it changes the potential scope of social interaction from a local to a global dimension and affects the dynamics of political processes, from everyday government activities – one can think about the professionalisation of political communication (Chadwick and Howard, 2009) or e-democracy (Coleman and Blumler, 2009) – to the conduct of diplomacy and foreign policy (Potter, 2002). Look back in history, however, and we discover that the development of virtually any communication technology, from the introduction of parchment to the rise of the printing press, the telegraph and radio, was met by the same sense of amazement, uncertainty and alarmed claims that it would forever change the world as it was then known. A statement such as 'It is impossible that old prejudices and hostilities should longer exist, while such an instrument has been created for the exchange of thought between all nations of the earth' might appear to refer to the internet, but it was written in 1858 and described the development of the telegraph (Briggs and Maverick, quoted in Standage, 1998: 83).

The literature on social movements further reminds us that transnational mobilisation took place well before the internet: one can think about the anti-slavery movement (Tarrow, 1998: 47) or the International Workers' Association whose slogan, since its foundation in the nineteenth century, has been 'Workers of the World Unite!'. Studies of riots and protests over the seventeenth and eighteenth centuries also confirm that news, if certainly not instantaneously, was still able to travel surprisingly quickly, even across wide distances:

> A glance back at 1789 or 1848 will indicate how closely Europe's political centers connected with each other well before television or mass journalism provided their publicity. In 1789, English radicals and conservatives alike followed Parisian events day by day. The construction of 'Parisian' barricades became standard practice in the Germany of 1848. (Tilly, 2002: 109)

The idea that the internet's synchronous communication leads almost naturally to greater bonding among individuals (Sageman, 2004) is challenged by online activism studies, where there is a whole debate about whether exchanges among strangers in cyberspace can support the constitution of real communities or simply a superficial involvement – what's referred to as armchair activism (Karpf, 2010). If individuals committed to, let's say, environmental issues could become less involved in their cause when only interacting online why should individuals with an interest in jihad through the same mechanisms necessarily become more fixated in their beliefs and even reach the point where they are ready to take lethal action in the real world?

The fact that extremist content is online and potentially available to worldwide audiences does not necessarily mean that these audiences are actually accessing it, let alone being influenced or driven to violence by it. In relation to the UK case, Awan writes that 'the overwhelming majority of virtual jihadist forums are published in Arabic alone and so inaccessible to a large proportion of Muslims as well as other internet users. British Muslim audiences are predominantly (74 per cent) South Asian and are therefore more likely to speak Urdu, Punjabi, or Bengali, than Arabic' (Awan, 2007: 76).

Even if audiences were actually accessing the extremist material, the question of its effects would still need to be ascertained. It could appear that the internet figured in the build-up of extremist beliefs in a range of plots, from the 2004 Madrid train bombings and London 7/7 in 2005, to radical plots being developed in the Netherlands, Canada and Morocco (HSPI/CIAG, 2007: 3–5). However, at a closer look, the internet tended to provide the 'initial impetus', which was then followed by more ordinary real-world planning, meetings and training (Awan, 2007: 78).

As for the current alleged 'unprecedented' recruitment of new fighters by IS (Kerchove in BBC News, 2014), we need only to look back at past conflicts to find that today's phenomenon of volunteers joining foreign wars is neither new nor greater than it has previously been. The Spanish civil war (1936-39), for instance, attracted volunteer foreign fighters in far higher numbers: on the Franco national-ist side alone there were 8,000 Portuguese, 700 Irish, 250 French, 78,000 Moroccans, just to name some of the nationalities involved (Othen 2013: 4). On the Republican side, the biggest national contingent of the International Brigades was French with 8,500 combatants, but involved many more volunteers from as far away as Brazil, and China (ibid.: 262). Among them was also British George Orwell. We can further think of the over 210,000 Irish volunteers who fought with the British in WWI (Jeffrey, 2011). While recruitment propaganda (McGreevy, 2014) was a contributing factor to the enlisting of volunteers in past conflicts—showing that the Internet and social media are really no more effective than the old-fashioned poster—we do not tend to dismiss those volunteers' motivations (Byrne 2014) for joining foreign conflicts as the mere effect of "brainwashing" (Taylor 2014).

It is not at all clear why content available on the internet should be more responsible for radicalisation than content accessible through alternative formats. This is especially puzzling considering that what is available online, despite the much-emphasised interactivity of the internet, is still text. Besides, jihadist mate-rial has long been available through videos and publications (Awan, 2007: 78–9). Osama bin Laden, Ayman Al-Zawahiri, as well as all the individuals who first joined al-Qaeda in the late 1980s, certainly did not belong to the internet gen-eration. Ed Husain recalls in *The Islamist* how, as a young boy growing up in London's East End, he became interested in a political interpretation of Islam by reading a school textbook about religion (Husain, 2007: 20–1). To find a contem-porary example of extremism beyond that inspired by al-Qaeda one can additionally look at the case of Norwegian Anders Breivik. In his manifesto of over 1500 pages he discusses at length the ideological reasons for his bombing of Oslo city centre (which caused eight fatalities) and his killing on Utøya island of 68 young political activists in the summer of 2011 (Breivik, 2011). The sources he cites, particularly 'the cultural Marxists' who gathered around the Frankfurt School – he specifically mentions Georg Lukacs, Antonio Gramsci, Wilhelm Reich, Erich Fromm, Herbert Marcuse and Theodor Adorno (2011: 26–30, 40–5) – produced texts that are not normally regarded as extremist and are widely available in ordinary libraries.

Finally, why criminalise the internet when there are other portable and interac-tive platforms that can be used equally well for exchanging and sharing information? The UK summer riots of 2011, in this respect, have brought to the fore the potential role of BlackBerry Messenger, beyond Twitter and Facebook in the organisation of public violent disorder. These platforms were initially claimed to be drivers of vio-lent collective action, only for this view to be later toned down and corrected (Mackenzie, 2011), not least through the acknowledgment that, so far, they have not been subject to rigorous examination, mostly as a result of the inaccessibility of the information exchanged, especially in the case of BlackBerry Messenger (Ball and Brown, 2011).

Narratives and counter-narratives

Research on radicalisation, including official documents, often refers to a narrative being developed by al-Qaeda (Bergin et al., 2009; ICSR, 2008; Presidential Task Force, 2009; Stevens and Neumann, 2009). The term is used so frequently that it has truly become a buzzword. A US presidential document about preventing violent extremism, for example, states that 'Radicalization that leads to violent extremism includes the diffusion of ideologies and narratives that feed on grievances, assign blame, and legitimize the use of violence against those deemed responsible' (White House, 2011: 6). The (Dutch) National Coordinator for Counterterrorism (2010) released a whole collection of contributions about *Countering Violent Extremist Narratives* in 2010. The UK *Prevent Strategy* states the current highest priority in counterterrorism is constituted by 'activity which challenges the terrorist ideology, for example speakers challenging terrorist narratives' (Home Office, 2011: 29).

In most of the literature the 'narrative' is a 'story', often a synonym of 'ideology'. As such, it is regarded as a device exploited by terrorists not only to maintain internal cohesion within a violent extremist group and give direction to cells that might be operating on their own, but also for publicising their political cause, recruit new followers, and provide a rationale for their activities (Quiggin, 2009: 23).

Progress in counterterrorism appears to be related in the literature to both establishing a credible narrative and damaging 'their' narrative. William Casebeer and James Russell, for instance, suggest that the most effective way to counter terrorism is by developing a 'better story' to replace 'their' narrative (Casebeer and Russell, 2005). For this purpose a special communication unit, the Research, Information and Communication Unit (RICU) was set up in Whitehall in 2007. Its task was specifically to 'use messaging to disrupt the Al Qaida narrative' (Home Office, 2009: 153; Home Office 2011: 51–2). A US Presidential Task Force report (2009) also argues for 'rewriting the narrative'.

While several sources stress that countering the extremist narrative should not be limited to words but also include engagement with local communities and a consistency between words (rhetoric) and deeds (policy), there is a strong emphasis on 'messaging' (Cornish et al., 2011: 33–5; Presidential Task Force, 2009: 13–20). This approach to the narrative as a script – particularly the attention to the delivery of the 'right' message – contradicts the deeply social nature of stories in our society. These assumptions are also an obstacle to understanding the nature of global communications in the digital age. The field of communication studies, as I am going to explain, can again help in making sense of this.

Its first contribution alerts us to the fact that anti-terrorism messaging is based on obsolete models of communication. Steven Corman, for instance, points out that the current way in which US officials attempt to communicate with foreign publics (public diplomacy) to curb extremism is based on the notion that 'messages' are transmitted by an 'information source' through a 'transmitter' (via a 'signal') to a 'receiver', which will then convey the message to the desired 'destination' (Corman, 2009b). The implications are that communication occurs only when messages are sent, and that successful communication can be achieved by improving the skill of the communicator, by reducing the 'noise' in the system, by carefully planning the content of the message and by carefully transmitting it. This is a model that was developed by David Berlo in the 1960s and was based on the study of telephone communication systems. Corman explains its current role in shaping official think-ing: having being taught across communication and public-relations courses over decades, it has become part of the way public-diplomacy practitioners in the US read the reality of international communications (Corman, 2010). Yet this model, as he puts it, was 'cutting-edge at the time of Eisenhower' (Corman, 2009b).

The notion of messaging, additionally, does not fit the complexity of current global communications. There is no longer the possibility, as when propaganda stud-ies actually developed, at the time of the early diffusion of radio and TV, that a message can be targeted at a specific audience – for instance, in its crudest form, by physically dropping leaflets beyond enemy lines. The feature of the current informa-tion environment that makes it radically different from the past is its transparency. It is true that information does not flow randomly, and that there are blind spots rep-resented by areas where communication infrastructures are either underdeveloped (the issues with access in African countries, for example) or controlled (as in China). Nonetheless, information is far less constrained by state borders and through its digital format can travel almost seamlessly across communication platforms like the internet, TV and mobile phones (de Waal, 2007). As Corman writes elsewhere:

> Communication is not a process of transmission of messages but of dialogue with an audience. Modern media systems make exclusively targeting narrow audiences difficult or impossible. Communication systems are so complex that planning is of limited use. You can't straightforwardly assess results and tweak your tactics, as if you were a strategic communication version of a forward artillery spotter. (Corman, 2009a)

In addition, while a narrative is, in essence, a sequence of events tied together by a plot line, it does not just carry a set of facts. Narratives are '*social products* produced by people within the context of specific social, historical and cultural locations' (Lawler, 2002: 242, her emphasis). As Charlotte Linde points out, even 'an individual's life story is not the property of that individual alone, but also belongs to others who have shared the events narrated – or were placed to have opinions about them' (Linde, 1993, in Linde, 2009: 4).

The concept of narrative – understood as a collaborative construction rather than a mere script – illuminates the process through which the terrorist story is constructed by the organisation's leaders, but it manages to spread and keep on existing over time through the retelling of sympathisers, engaged supporters and new recruits. The terrorists' narrative, like any narrative, is the result of a collective construction. It is certainly promoted by specific actors – in the case of al-Qaeda by terrorist leaders – but there is evidence that it is being appropriated, most notably in what is mistakenly referred to as 'self-radicalisation', by individuals and local groups (Jenkins, 2007: 5–6). These narratives are retold by a range of different actors with varying agendas and very diverse audiences. Each of them potentially sees a different story. As Betz describes this process in relation to Al-Qaeda:

> Bin Laden and his associates do not appear endlessly on the British Broadcasting Corporation, or Cable News Network or even Al-Jazeera def-ending these talking points [basic elements of their narrative]: this work is

done (very effectively) by largely voluntary networks which have open access, share material, work collectively, and have a diversity of motives. Not everybody in the network needs to be a committed Jihadi, they may or may not like the idea of living under a restored Caliphate, they may indeed in some circumstances not be Muslim at all because the mindset of sullen resentment, which is what animates the movement, is shared by diverse groups from anti-globalists to anti-vivisectionists. (Betz, 2008: 521)

Conclusion: understanding communication and counterterrorism

A greater engagement with the impacts that communication technologies have had throughout history on society and on political mobilisation, as well as an appreciation of the complexity involved in assessing media effects on audiences, would have a far-reaching impact on the practice of counterterrorism. The following are the three implications that most immediately arise from the previous discussion.

The first is that the availability of extremist content – as also with the existence of a terrorist narrative – is not the problem *per se*. The fact that jihadi videos or terrorist websites are potentially available to worldwide audiences does not mean that these audiences are necessarily going to access them, let alone embrace their radical ideas. Reach is not impact. Even if extremist messages are accessed the key issue is the individual appropriation of those contents through the interpretative prism of the beliefs and worldview resulting from an individual's place in the social world. This explains how many readers of this paragraph will have watched terrorist propaganda videos or consulted extremist manifestos without having become radicalised.

The second implication is that attempting to target radicalised individuals with the 'right' message, to put it bluntly, is a waste of time. For a start, terrorists are already listening to what Western governments, think tanks and media are saying, as demonstrated by the fact that the Al Fajr Center –the media hub that coordinates the distribution of online communiqués, videos and statements by al-Qaeda and other jihadi groups (Iraqi insurgency groups, Palestinian, Somali, Saudi jihadi groups, etc.) – also has an 'intelligence brigade' (Katz, cited in Committee on Homeland Security, 2007: 18). This unit is in charge of monitoring the websites and outputs of organisations like the White House, the US Army, the RAND Corporation, the Jamestown Foundation, and *Time* magazine (Geltzer, 2010: 22–3). Additionally, most of those involved in terrorist plots live in Western societies, where they are constantly exposed to potential counter-narratives. Both public discourse and media coverage are overwhelmingly filled with the notion that terrorism and violence are deplorable, as are al-Qaeda and IS. The reason why 'our' narrative is not having any effect on the extremist mindset is that 'our message' is filtered through a very different personal worldview, grounded in a specific constellation of relationships that shapes an extremist's social context (Archetti, 2012). In this perspective communication, counter-intuitively, is most effective not directed at the terrorists or violent extremists but at the constellation of relationships *around* them.

Finally the narrative is not just a story. It is a story that is being continuously retold. The idea that the spreading of the al-Qaeda or IS narrative can be stopped by interfering with the group's communication channels – by taking down websites or making it illegal to access them – is based on the notion that the story is being told through a one-way process, that the message is being sent by terrorists to audiences. While terrorist organisations have an interest in promoting that narrative, this is a reductive understanding not only of communication processes but also of the way they take place in the contemporary media-saturated environment. There are too many channels to stop the narrative from being communicated. Beyond the internet the old technologies are still there; Carl Björkman, for instance, in talking about jihadi-Salafi terrorism in Italy, writes that military manuals and jihadi documents from prominent thinkers have over the last decade 'spread ... on CD-ROMs, videos and audio-cassettes' (Björkman, 2010: 242–3). In countries with poor literacy levels, such as Afghanistan, face-to-face interaction is still the most widely used form of communication between radicals and the wider population (Johnson, 2007). In addition, the narrative is only partly promoted by the terrorist leadership. The reason why the narrative continues to exist is that it is constantly re-evoked by wider audiences, which do not only involve terrorist sympathisers. A terrorist narrative might be contained in a journalistic report about its leadership's latest message, in a critique of the terrorist organisation or in an academic study about it.

STUDY BOX CHAPTER 7

Key reading

Archetti, C. (2012) *Explaining Terrorism in the Age of Global Media: A Communication Approach* (Basingstoke: Palgrave).

Conway, M. (2006) 'Terrorism and the Internet: New Media – New Threat?', *Parliamentary Affairs* 59(2): 283–98.

Paletz, D.L. and Schmid, A.P. (eds.) (1992) *Terrorism and the Media: How Researchers, Terrorists, Government, Press, Public, Victims View and Use the Media* (Newbury Park, CA: Sage).

Seib, P. and Janbek, D. (2011) *Global Terrorism and the Media: The Post-al-Qaida Generation* (London: Routledge).

Study questions

1   How could a terrorist group achieve greater visibility/publicity? Can it really 'manipulate' the media? And if so, how?

2   Does the internet really support more (or more effective) terrorism? If so, how and why?

3   Are the operations of international terrorism facilitated by the existence of global media networks? If so, how and why?

References

Ackerman, S. (2012) 'Idiotic Idea of the Day: Jailing Lurkers of Terror Websites,' *Wired*, 23 March. http://www.wired.com/dangerroom/2012/03/terror-lurker/

Alali, A. O. and K. K. Eke (eds.) (1991) *Media Coverage of Terrorism: Methods of Diffusion* (London: Sage).

Alexander, Y. (1978) 'Terrorism, the Media, and the Police,' *Journal of International Affairs*, 32(1): 101–13.

Archetti, C. (2012) *Explaining Terrorism in the Age of Global Media: A Communication Approach* (Basingstoke: Palgrave).

Archetti, C. and P. Taylor (2005) 'Managing Terrorism after 9/11: The War on Terror, the Media, and the Imagined Threat,' final report for ESRC project 'Domestic Management of Terrorist Attacks' (L147251003).

Associated Press (2014) 'Theresa May considering banning orders to combat British extremism,' 23 August, http://www.theguardian.com/politics/2014/aug/23/theresa-may-laws-tackle-extremism-killing-james-foley (Accessed in October 2014).

Awan, A. (2007) 'Radicalization on the Internet?' *The RUSI Journal*, 152(3): 76–81.

Awan, A., A. Hoskins and B. O'Loughlin (2011) *Radicalisation and Media: Connectivity and Terrorism in the New Media Ecology* (Milton Park: Routledge).

Ball, J. and S. Brown (2011) 'Why BlackBerry Messenger Was Rioters' Communication Method of Choice,' *The Guardian*, 7 December, http://www.guardian.co.uk/uk/2011/dec/07/bbm-rioters-communication-method-choice?newsfeed=true (Accessed in January 2012).

Barnhurst, K. G. (1991) 'The Literature of Terrorism: Implications for Visual Communications,' in A. O. Alali and K. K. Eke (eds) *Media Coverage of Terrorism: Methods of Diffusion* (London: Sage), pp. 112–37.

Bassiouni, M. C. (1981) 'Terrorism, Law Enforcement, and the Mass Media: Perspectives, Problems, Proposals,' *Journal of Criminal Law and Criminology*, 72 (1): 1–51.

BBC (2013) 'Woolwich Attack,' http://www.bbc.co.uk/news/uk-22644057 (Accessed in January 2014)

BBC Editorial Guidelines (n.d.) 'Language When Reporting Terrorism,' http://www.bbc.co.uk/editorialguidelines/page/guidance-reporting-terrorism-full (Accessed in January 2012).

BBC News (2014) 'Islamic State crisis: '3,000 European jihadists join fight,' 26 September, available from: http://www.bbc.co.uk/news/world-middle-east-29372494 (Accessed in September 2014).

Bell, M. (2007) 'The Frenzy of News,' *The Guardian*, 3 July, http://www.guardian.co.uk/commentisfree/2007/jul/03/thefrenzyofnews (Accessed in July 2007).

Bergin, A., S. B. Osman, C. Ungerer and N. A. M. Yasin (2009) 'Countering Internet Radicalization in Southeast Asia,' Issue 22, http://www.rsis.edu.sg/short%20reports/Countering_internet_radicalisation.pdf (Accessed in February 2010).

Betz, D. (2008) 'The Virtual Dimension of Contemporary Insurgency and Counterinsurgency,' *Small Wars and Insurgencies*, 19(4): 510–40.

Björkman, C. (2010) 'Salafi-Jihadi Terrorism in Italy,' in M. Ranstorp (ed.) *Understanding Violent Radicalisation: Terrorist and Jihadist Movements in Europe* (Oxon: Routledge), pp. 231–55.

Blumler, J. G. and E. Katz (1974) *The Uses of Mass Communication* (Newbury Park, CA: Sage).

Breivik, A. (2011) *2083: A European Declaration of Independence*, http://www.slideshare.net/darkandgreen/2083-a-european-declaration-of-independence-by-andrew-berwick (Accessed in July 2011).

Brooker, W. and D. Jermyn (2003) *The Audience Studies Reader* (London: Routledge).

Brooking, E. (2014) 'The ISIS Propaganda Machine Is Horrifying and Effective. How Does It Work?' Council on Foreign Relations Blog, 21 August, available from: http://blogs.cfr.org/davidson/2014/08/21/the-isis-propaganda-machine-is-horrifying-and-effective-how-does-it-work/ (Accessed in November 2014).

Byrne, E. (2014) 'The forgotten Irish soldiers who fought for Britain in the first world war,' The Guardian, 5 April, available from: http://www.theguardian.com/world/2014/apr/05/irish-soldiers-who-fought-for-britain (Accessed in November 2014).

Casebeer, W. D. and J. A. Russell (2005) 'Storytelling and Terrorism: Towards a Comprehensive "Counter-narrative Strategy",' *Strategic Insights*, 4(3), http://www.au.af.mil/au/awc/awcgate/nps/casebeer_mar05.pdf (Accessed in June 2010).

Castells, M. (1996) *The Rise of the Network Society* (vol. I) (Oxford: Blackwell).

Chadwick, A. and P. N. Howard (eds) (2009) *Internet Politics: States, Citizens, and New Communication Technologies* (Oxon: Routledge).

Cohen-Almagor, R. (2005) 'Media Coverage of Acts of Terrorism: Troubling Episodes and Suggested Guidelines,' *Canadian Journal of Communication*, 30 (3): 383–409.

Coleman, S. and J. G. Blumler (2009) *The Internet and Democratic Citizenship: Theory, Practice and Policy* (Cambridge: Cambridge University Press).

Coll, S. and S. B. Glasser (2005) 'Terrorists Turn to the Web as Base of Operations,' *Washington Post*, 7 August, A01.

Committee on Homeland Security (2007) 'Using the Web as a Weapon: The Internet as a Tool for Violent Radicalization and Homegrown Terrorism,' hearing before the Subcommittee of Intelligence, Information Sharing, and Terrorism Risk Assessment of the Committee on Homeland Security, House of Representatives, 6 November, Serial No. 110–83, http://www.fas.org/irp/congress/2007_hr/web.pdf (Accessed in June 2010).

Conway, M. (2006) 'Terrorism and the Internet: New Media—New Threat?' *Parliamentary Affairs*, 59(2): 283–98.

Conway, M. and L. McInerney (2009) 'Jihadi Video and Auto-Radicalisation: Evidence From an Exploratory YouTube Study,' paper presented at EuroISI 2008, First European Conference on Intelligence and Security Informatics, 3–5 December, Esbjerg, Denmark.

Corman, S. R. (2009a) 'Same Old Song from GAO on Strategic Communication,' *The COMOPS Journal*, 3 June 2009, http://comops.org/journal/2009/06/03/same-old-song-from-gao-on-strategic-communication/ (Accessed in June 2009).

Corman, S. R. (2009b) 'What Power Needs to Be Smart,' paper presented at the Digital Media and Security Workshop, University of Warwick, 21 May 2009.

Corman, S. R. (2010) 'Public Diplomacy as Narrative,' paper presented at the International Studies Association Annual Convention, New Orleans, 20 February 2010.

Cornish, P., J. Lindley-French and C. Yorke (2011) *Strategic Communication and National Strategy: A Chatham House Report* (London: Royal Institute of International Affairs).

Crelinsten, R. D. (1987) 'Power and Meaning: Terrorism as a Struggle over Access to the Communication Structure,' in P. Wilkinson and A. M. Stewart (eds) *Contemporary Research on Terrorism* (Aberdeen: Aberdeen University Press), pp. 419–450.

Crenshaw, M. (1981) 'The Causes of Terrorism,' *Comparative Politics*, 13(4): 379–99.

Cronin, A. K. (2006) 'How al-Qaida Ends: The Decline and Demise of Terrorist Groups,' *International Security*, 31(1): 7–48.

Curtis, A. (2004) *The Power of Nightmares: The Rise of the Politics of Fear* (2004), video documentary broadcast on BBC2 20 October–3 November, 180 min. (3 parts).

de Waal, M. (2007) 'From Media Landscape to Media Ecology: The Cultural Implications of Web 2.0,' *Open* 13: 20–33, http://www.skor.nl/_files/Files/OPEN13_P20-33.pdf (Accessed in October 2014).

Esser, F. and B. Pfetsch (eds) (2004) *Comparing Political Communication: Theories, Cases, and Challenges* (Cambridge: Cambridge University Press).

Geltzer, J. A. (2010) *US Counter-Terrorism Strategy and al-Qaeda: Signalling and the Terrorist World-View* (Milton Park: Routledge).

Gerrits, R. P. J. M. (1992) 'Terrorists' Perspectives: Memoirs,' in D. L. Paletz and A. Schmid (eds) *Terrorism and the Media: How Researchers, Terrorists, Government, Press, Public, Victims View and Use the Media* (London: Sage), pp. 29–61.

Goodman, M. (2011) 'Killer Apps: The Revolution in Network Terrorism,' *Jane's Intelligence Review*, 23(7) July: 14–19.

Gray, J. (2005) 'A Violent Episode in the Virtual World,' *New Statesman*, 18 July 2005: 16–17, http://www.newstatesman.com/200507180006 (Accessed in September 2006).

Home Office (2009) *The United Kingdom's Strategy for Countering International Terrorism* (London: The Cabinet Office).

Home Office (2011) *Prevent Strategy* (London: The Cabinet Office).

Hoskins, A. and B. O'Loughlin (2009) 'Media and the Myth of Radicalization,' *Media, War and Conflict*, 2(2):107–10.

HSPI (Homeland Security Policy Institute) and CIAG (University of Virginia Critical Incident Analysis Group) (2007) *NETworked Radicalization: A Counter-Strategy*, http://www.gwumc.edu/hspi/policy/NETworkedRadicalization.pdf (Accessed in January 2008).

Husain, E. (2007) *The Islamist* (London: Penguin Books).

ICSR (International Centre for the Study of Radicalization) (ed.) (2008) *Perspectives on Radicalisation and Political Violence* (London: ICSR).

Jeffery, K. (2011) 'Ireland and World War One,' *BBC History*, available from: HYPERLINK "http://www.bbc.co.uk/history/british/britain_wwone/ireland_wwone_01.shtml"www. bbc.co.uk/history/british/britain_wwone/ireland_wwone_01.shtml (Accessed in November 2014).

Jenkins, B. M. (2007) *Building an Army of Believers: Jihadist Radicalization and Recruitment*, testimony presented before the House Homeland Security Committee, Subcommittee on Intelligence, Information Sharing and Terrorism Risk Assessment on April 5, 2007, Rand Corporation, http://www.rand.org/pubs/testimonies/2007/RAND_CT278-1.pdf (Accessed in June 2007).

Johnson, T. H. (2007) 'The Taliban Insurgency and an Analysis of Shabnamah (Night Letters),' *Small Wars and Insurgencies*, 18(3): 317–44.

Karpf, D. (2010) 'Online Political Mobilization from the Advocacy Group's Perspective: Looking Beyond Clicktivism,' *Policy and Internet* 2(4), article 2 (n.p.).

Laqueur, W. (1976) 'The Futility of Terrorism,' *Harper's Magazine*, March, 99–105.

Lawler, S. (2002) 'Narrative in Social Research,' in T. May (ed.) *Qualitative Research in Action* (London: Sage), pp. 242–58.

Lazarsfeld, P. F., B. Berelson and H. Gaudet (1944) *The People's Choice: How the Voter Makes Up His Mind in a Presidential Campaign* (New York: Columbia University Press).

Linde, C. (2009) *Working the Past: Narrative and Institutional Memory* (Oxford: Oxford University Press).

Mackenzie, I. (2011) 'Is Technology to Blame for the London Riots?' *BBC News Technology*, 8 August, http://www.bbc.co.uk/news/technology-14442203 (Accessed in August 2011).

Martin, L. J. (1985) 'The Media's Role in International Terrorism,' *Terrorism: An International Journal*, 8(2): 127–46.

May, T. (2013) Interview with Andrew Marr, *The Andrew Marr Show*, BBC 1, 26 May.

McGreevy, R. (2014) 'New figures show almost 20,000 Irishmen fought for Canada in WW1,' *The Irish Times*, 1 August, available from: http://www.irishtimes.com/news/social-affairs/new-figures-show-almost-20-000-irishmen-fought-for-canada-in-ww1-1.1885044 (Accessed in November 2014).

McInerney, L. (2009) 'The Iraq War "YouTube Style": Mobilising en Masse?,' paper presented at the International Studies Association annual convention, New York, 15–18 February.

Miller, T. (2008) '"Step Away from the Croissant": Media Studies 3.0,' in D. Hesmondhalgh and J. Toynbee (eds) *The Media and Social Theory* (Milton Park: Routledge), pp. 213–30.

Mueller, J. (2012) 'New Year Brings Good News on Terrorism: Experts Wrong Again,' *The National Interest*, 3 January, http://nationalinterest.org/blog/the-skeptics/experts-predictions-wrong-6334 (Accessed February 2012).

Nacos, B. L. (1994) *Terrorism and the Media: From the Iran Hostage Crisis to the Oklahoma City Bombing* (New York: Columbia University Press).

Nacos, B. L. (2002) 'Terrorism, the Mass Media, and the Events of 9–11,' *Phi Kappa Phi Forum*, 82(2): 13–19.

Nacos, B. L. (2003) 'The Terrorist Calculus Behind 9–11: A Model for Future Terrorism?,' *Studies in Conflict and Terrorism* 26 (1): 1–16.

National Coordinator for Counterterrorism (ed.) (2010) *Countering Violent Extremist Narratives* (The Hague: National Coordinator for Counterterrorism).

Othen, C. (2013) Franco's International Brigades: Adventurers, Fascists, and Christian Crusaders in the Spanish Civil War (New York: Columbia University Press).

Paletz, D. L. and J. Boiney (1992) 'Researchers' Perspectives,' in D. L. Paletz and A. Schmid (eds) *Terrorism and the Media: How Researchers, Terrorists, Government, Press, Public, Victims View and Use the Media* (London: Sage), pp 6–28.

Potter, E. H. (ed.) (2002) *Cyber-diplomacy: Managing Foreign Policy in the Twenty-first Century* (London: McGill-Queen's University Press).

Presidential Task Force (2009) *Rewriting the Narrative: An Integrated Strategy for Counterradicalization* (Washington, DC: The Washington Institute for Near East Policy).

Quiggin, T. (2009) 'Understanding al-Qaeda's Ideology for Counter-narrative Work,' *Perspectives on Terrorism*, 3(2): 18–24.

Sageman, M. (2004) *Understanding Terror Networks* (Bristol, England: University of Pennsylvania Press).

Schmid, A. P. (1989) 'Terrorism and the Media: The Ethics of Publicity,' *Terrorism and Political Violence*, 1(4): 539–65.

Schmid, A. P. and J. de Graaf (1982) *Violence as Communication: Insurgent Terrorism and the Western News Media* (London: Sage).

Seib, P. and D. M. Janbek (2011) *Global Terrorism and New Media: The Post-al-Qaeda Generation* (Milton Park: Routledge).

Shpiro, S. (2002) 'Conflict Media Strategies and the Politics of Counter-Terrorism,' *Politics*, 22(2): 76–85.

Snow, N. (2005) 'Truth and Information Consequences since 9/11,' *Peace Review: A Journal of Social Justice*, 17(1): 103–9.

Standage, T. (1998) *The Victorian Internet: The Remarkable Story of the Telegraph and Nineteenth Century's Online Pioneers* (New York: Walker Publishing).

Stenersen, A. (2008) 'The Internet: A Virtual Training Camp?' *Terrorism and Political Violence*, 20(2): 215–33.

Stevens, T. and P. R. Neumann (2009) *Countering Online Radicalization: A Strategy for Action* (London: ICSR/Community Security Trust).

Straw, J. (2003) 'House of Commons Hansard Debates for 11 November 2003,' Column 168, http://www.publications.parliament.uk/pa/cm200203/cmhansrd/vo031111/debt-ext/31111–04.htm (Accessed in December 2003).

Tarrow, S. (1998) *Power in Movement: Social Movements and Contentious Politics*, 2nd edn. (Cambridge: Cambridge University Press).

Taylor, M. (2014) 'Isis militant's mother pleads for return of "brainwashed" son,' The Guardian, 22 June, available from: http://www.theguardian.com/world/2014/jun/22/isis-mother-reyaad-khad-video-plea-return.(Accessed in November 2014).

Tilly, C. (2002) *Stories, Identities, and Political Change* (Oxford: Rowman and Littlefield).

Tsfati, Y. and G. Weimann (2002) 'www.terrorism.com: Terror on the Internet,' *Studies in Conflict and Terrorism*, 25(5): 317–32.

Tumber, H. (1999) *News: A Reader* (Oxford: Oxford University Press).

US Army (2008) 'Supplemental to the 304th M Bn Periodic Newsletter,' http://www.fas.org/irp/eprint/mobile.pdf (Accessed in January 2009).

Weimann, G. (1990) '"Redefinition of Image": The Impact of Mass Mediated Terrorism,' *International Journal of Public Opinion Research*, 2(1): 16–29.

Weimann, G. (2006) *Terror on the Internet: The New Arena, the New Challenges* (Washington, DC: Unites States Institute of Peace).

Weimann, G. and C. Winn (1994) *The Theater of Terror: Mass Media and International Terrorism* (White Plains, NY: Longman).

White House (2011) 'Empowering Local Partners to Prevent Violent Extremism in the United States' (Washington, DC: Government Printing Office), http://info.publicintelligence.net/WH-HomegrownTerror.pdf (Accessed in August 2011).

Wilkinson, P. (2006) *Terrorism Versus Democracy: The Liberal State Response*, 2nd edn. (New York: Routledge).

Essay 4

IEDs, MARTYRS, CIVIL WARS AND TERRORISTS

CAROLINE KENNEDY-PIPE

... and then the huge peaceful wilderness of outer London, the barges on the miry river, the familiar streets, the posters telling of cricket matches and Royal weddings, the men in bowler hats, the pigeons in Trafalgar Square, the red buses, the blue policemen – all sleeping the deep, deep sleep of England, from which I sometimes fear that we shall never wake till we are jerked out of it by the roar of bombs. (George Orwell, *Homage to Catalonia*)

Introduction

In this chapter I explore the Iraq War in terms of the way in which the improvised explosive device (IED) has shaped both the conduct of the war and Western responses. I wish to demonstrate the importance of the IED and especially the use of suicide bombing (so-called people-borne IEDs) as central to contemporary war and politics. In relation to the quotation above I argue that the Iraq War and the prevalence of IEDs 'jerked' some Western governments out of any complacency that the war could be won easily and without consequence for domestic politics and public unease over the conflict.

During the 1990s the Western way of war was defined by avoiding traditional war and predominantly about ustilising technology to make war less 'costly' to 'our' side but more costly to the other. This was risk-transfer warfare. The culmination of this type of warfare was the Kosovo War of 1999, in which Western forces suffered not one single combat fatality whilst inflicting massive damage on the enemy.

The events of 9/11 changed some of the calculations about how to fight. The original US intervention to displace the Taliban, the war in Iraq and the continuing conflict in Afghanistan demonstrated clearly that, contrary to the views of some distinguished commentators, such as Joseph Nye and John Mueller, the great powers, or at least some of them, had not lost their appetite for war. Part of the rediscovery of traditional war was rooted in a general puzzlement as to why al-Qaeda wished to damage the USA and a shock that primitive, ghastly attacks on civilians were not simply the staple of the developing world. It had been recognised throughout the 1990s by intelligence agencies that sub-state groups and transnational actors posed a direct and enduring threat to Western and especially US interests, but few had predicted that the terrorists would take their fight to New York and Washington in quite such spectacular style. On 9/11, we learnt that even planes and men with box cutters could be transformed into a dramatic large-scale IED.

While much thought has been expended on why individuals or groups would wish to mount attacks on US assets and, indeed, its homeland itself, the idea of an inevitable confrontation between 'Islam and the rest' gained momentum. Scholars and policymakers pondered the nature of radical Islam and its threat to global politics. Some, such as Fawaz Gerges, pointed to the complex and multifaceted nature of Muslim sentiment, arguing that many Muslims condemned 9/11, the views of bin Laden generally and attacks on non-combatants (Gerges, 2011: 83). Despite this approach, however, there was and remains much speculation about processes of radicalisation and their effect domestically, especially on what appeared to be the growth of angry and radicalised groups of youths. Radicalisation across the globe may indeed be a trend of the early twenty-first century; but, as we go on to discuss, political struggle and violence is not just about the effects of capitalism and globalisation, although the processes of globalisation does facilitate the rapid movement of people and ideas around the world in a way that would have been unthinkable in earlier periods of history.

There are, though, many factors facilitating radicalization. One may indeed be an increasingly connected global community inspired by the internet, as well as more prosaically the failure of communism in the Soviet Union. The collapse of the USSR meant that one exceptionally powerful antidote to US-style capitalism suddenly and remarkably vanished, leaving a void for those opposed to the ideals and actions of the remaining hegemonic power.

We may also wish to ponder ideas of justice. One root of violent political activity is the perception (real or imagined) of injustice. Historically, this may explain, for example, the activities of the original IRA in the campaign against the oppression of UK rule in Ireland, or the Palestinians in their struggle with Israel. More latterly, though, explanations for political violence and the processes of radicalisation have cited not only injustice but also the opposition to Western military intervention in countries such as Iraq and Afghanistan. In this argument bin Laden and his group highlighted an explicit opposition to the US presence in the Middle East. All of these explanations are interlinked. In the case of the UK much was made of the fact that the horrific events of 7/7 in London took place at the same time as leaders of the G8 met in the face of popular resistance in Scotland. The 7/7 bombers also claimed a link to the commitment of the Blair government to war in Iraq. Mohammad Sidique Khan justified his participation in the London bombings in 2005 as revenge for Muslims who had been attacked, imprisoned and tortured by US and coalition forces. One former MI5 director argued that many militants were motivated by a 'sense of grievance and injustice driven by their interpretation of history between the west and the Muslim world' (Manningham-Buller, 2006). London University student Roshonara Choudhry attacked a former UK minister, Stephen Timms, with a knife arguing that he was personally accountable for having voted in favour of the Iraq War (Gerges, 2011: 157). So the war in Iraq and the US-led invasion has antagonised sentiment both at home and abroad.

Iraq 2003

The invasion of Iraq began on 20 March 2003, preceded by a so-called 'decapitation' strike against senior military and political figures (including Saddam himself) that was only partially successful. The initial military campaign, however, was relatively swift. Unlike previous engagements (for example the Gulf War of 1990–1 and the Afghan campaign of 2001) there was no long period of aerial bombardment followed by a ground campaign. This time there was a simultaneous combination of both. The ground campaign lasted just over three weeks and the Iraqi military crumbled quickly, outgunned by allied firepower, skill and kit. Baghdad itself fell in April 2003 and President Bush declared 'mission accomplished' on board the aircraft carrier Abraham Lincoln on 1 May 2003.

The problem was not the military campaign itself; the issue which very rapidly became apparent was that there was less than coherent planning for the post-war scenario. A series of bungled decisions taken in the immediate aftermath of the military victory – the action to disband the Iraqi army, the reluctance to 'stamp out' local looting, and a host of others – helped to turn a chaotic and patchwork post-conflict Iraq into a hotbed of dissent and insurgency, aside from the anger and emotion of the native peoples at the civilian casualties inflicted by the invading forces. In turn the issue of casualties inflamed sentiment against the US and its allies, sucked in Muslims and sympathisers from outside Iraq, and acted as a recruiting sergeant for al-Qaeda, which was, to all intents and purposes, one of the chief beneficiaries of the post-invasion shambles. The terrorist group established a presence in Iraq for the first time and, as we will see, it would take nearly four years to persuade the tribes to operate against the group. By the end of 2004 bin Laden had publicly proclaimed a war of attrition against the USA and voiced the ambition that Iraq would become the first Islamic state to be established after the loss of Taliban-ruled Afghanistan.

US foreign policy remained bullish. Even after it became clear that President Bush had been – to put it mildly – over-optimistic when he declared 'mission accomplished', the administration still rallied popular support to it. In the presidential election – unlike in 2000 – foreign policy and the record of the administration in the post-9/11 climate was a major campaign issue and the incumbent beat the Democratic Party challenger (Senator John Kerry) in a convincing manner.

However, problems began to multiply for the Bush administration, its allies and those serving in the conflict. The situation in Iraq went from bad to worse and popular support for the occupation in the USA itself began to ebb away. As Emma Sky, an authority on Iraq explains, the US strategy of attempting to transfer responsibility for security to the Iraqi security forces (ISF) was, in the words of US Army Colonel H. R. McMaster, 'a rush to failure' (quoted in Sky, 2011). Some elements in Washington depicted Iraq as a new Vietnam. Increasing US casualty figures also took a toll on domestic opinion, especially when the battlefield death rate exceeded 3000, more than the number of those actually killed in the events of 9/11. That figure was reached at the very end of 2006 when, while on patrol in Baquah, two soldiers were killed by a roadside bomb and a third was killed in Baghdad.

The nature of the war had also changed. In Iraq the 'descent into chaos' was relatively rapid. The USA and its allies found themselves in the midst of an emergent and bloody civil war fought between the Sunnis and Shias. Most conflicts have some elements that may be described as civil war and most, as in Northern Ireland, exhibit degrees of sectarian violence. Iraq was to become a classic and bloody case.

Following the invasion of Iraq and the replacement of Saddam Hussein, resentment had rapidly gathered pace amongst the Sunnis. The grievances were numerous, not least their political exclusion from the Shia-controlled government and a loss of access to their country's considerable oil wealth. Sectarianism was rife. The Iraqi police, infiltrated by Shia militia (backed by Iran), became involved in murders against anyone suspected of connections with the former regime. To put it simply, the Sunnis, unable to gain protection from either Iraqi forces or indeed coalition security forces, turned to al-Qaeda. The situation was complicated yet further when, throughout 2004, foreign fighters flooded in, motivated by anger at attacks on Iraqi civilians, especially women and children (coalition air strikes had been reported in graphic detail by Al Jazeera). Many such fighters travelled through Kuwait or Syria, helped by smugglers and travelling in groups of friends or neighbours from the same mosques abroad. Many had never held guns before and were given a form of rudimentary training before being deployed to fight US forces in Fallujah or elsewhere (Filkins 2009).

This movement of young men across borders to fight may be seen as part of a broader pattern of religious revival which had been something of a trend from the late 1980s onwards. The end of the Cold War, the collapse of the Soviet Union and the discrediting of ideologies such as communism seem to have increased the appeal of other forms of belief. Specifically amongst many restless young men, the allure of a certain understanding of Islam spread. This was not confined to the Middle East and Asia: the UK and Europe more generally proved vulnerable to radicalisation. Already in 2001 two young men, from the UK but of Pakistani origin, had been killed in a missile strike in Kabul after joining the Taliban. In the spring of 2003 two UK men tried to bomb a nightclub in Tel Aviv in the name of Allah. As Jason Burke has argued, while the riots in Bradford in 2001 had revealed deep fissures within UK society, these terrorist attacks, and others in the Netherlands and France, sounded alarm bells, but few at the time grasped the implications and scale of the threat for Europe or indeed the UK itself (Burke, 2011: 192).

Iraq in the years between 2004 and 2006 was hell. Meanwhile in Afghanistan – as the coalition gaze was firmly fixed on the chaos unfolding in Mesopotamia – the

Taliban infiltrated provinces in the south and east of the country. Western forces, accustomed from the 1990s to fighting wars waged with airpower, special forces and general 'shock and awe', found that they were rapidly embroiled in insurgency and counter-insurgency. As Ricks has argued it, by the beginning of 2007 the streets of Baghdad seemed to grow bloodier by the day. On January 16, two bombs were detonated during the after-school rush at a Baghdad university, killing in excess of 60 people, and two more bombs went off at a street bazaar, killing at least another 79 people. At the end of January, in one indication of the nature of the raging civil war, 60 Shi'ites were killed in multiple attacks across central Iraq (Ricks, 2009: 149).

Civil wars

So events in both Iraq and Afghanistan did not play out according to the script. What were meant to be post-conflict state-building scenarios, typified by gradual stabilisation and nation building, moved in the opposite direction. Iraq was beset by the ugly spectre of sectarian strife, death squads, beheadings of foreign hostages who had been working in the country (such as that of US citizen Nick Berg), IEDs and suicide attacks. Much was also made of the human-rights abuses both on the streets and in the prisons of Iraq (Ricks, 2009). But let us turn to the impact of IEDs on the conflict.

Dexter Filkins, who reported from Iraq over a number of years, has pithily described the way in which the insurgents and terrorists were always looking for novel ways to deliver bombs and take on their militarily superior opponents (Filkins, 2009). First there were the car bombs, then the suicide bombers, some even delivering their devices mundanely by bicycle. IEDs were also hidden: sometimes planted under dead animals, especially dogs on the street or in the countryside. Even then some insurgents had the imagination to strap bombs to living dogs and send them on a deadly mission. In the autumn of 2005 a donkey wearing a suicide vest was discovered and had to be shot; it exploded (Filkins, 2009: 173). And there was always the opportunity provided by crowded groups, the public gatherings such as weddings, all presenting opportunities for acts of terror. Filkins argues that actually many of the bombers 'cruised' the streets simply looking for an opportunity to cause mayhem amongst civilians. In colourful language, comparing such activities to watching porn, Filkins also points to the 'showcasing' of such missions, as insurgents produced videos of bombings and suicide bombings. In the summer of 2005 one of the insurgent groups posted a top-ten video of bombings on the internet. In this case the staging and filming of attacks appeared prearranged, with a camera man waiting for the explosion from the suicide bomber. We do not have to agree with Filkins that the bombers 'got off on it', pointing to a certain explanation of the activities, but we will return to the multiple causes of suicide bombing (Filkins, 2009: 174–5).

Since the invasion of Iraq the combat between insurgencies and coalition forces was a classic case of asymmetric warfare (Nader, 2007). We talk of asymmetry when there is a serious imbalance between military resources, requiring insurgents to retaliate with unconventional or novel attacks, such as IEDs. Rather ironically, though, in Iraq the prevalence of IEDs was aided by the attempts by foreign companies to reconstruct the national infrastructure. One example was the mobile-phone operators who moved in to

Iraq in early 2004. In the centre of the country, including Baghdad, a mobile-phone company, Iraqna, began operations and grew nationally at over 100,000 new subscribers a month. Phones become a classic way of triggering IED devices. Modernisation of the country thus became one route for terrorists and insurgents to step up the campaign against coalition forces and also rival factions.

One specific challenge for coalition forces was to gather intelligence on multiple groups and individuals planting IEDs. The US military throughout the first eighteen months of the conflict emphasised the imperative of destroying the very networks of bomb makers. This was a tricky task as local knowledge was sparse and there was an over-reliance on technical communications intelligence. As in Ireland in 1971 and 1972, but on a much larger scale, suspects were swept up by indiscriminate operations: doors were kicked in and men taken away from their homes on flimsy pretexts. Large numbers were detained and held in prisons such as Abu Ghraib, one of Saddam's 'facilities' and a byword for brutality. The chaotic nature of the prisons or detention facilities meant that suspects from the war were held alongside criminals in poorly administered circumstances. Overcrowding (some 7,500 prisoners were held in Abu Ghraib alone), poor sanitation and poor food became the everyday living conditions of those detained. This is not, of course, the reason why and how Abu Ghraib has become controversial; that was the sustained use of 'interrogation' in a bid to garner useful intelligence on terrorist groups. Techniques included physical violence but also sexual humiliation, chaining, electrical shocks and sensory deprivation – and Abu Ghraib was merely the most notorious of the many prison facilities in Iraq. The hooded man, the slavering dog oppressing inmates: these were the iconic symbols of the Western war effort. The effect of such images was arguably a continued process of radicalisation both in Iraq and outside (Burke: 2011).

The 9/11 wars were also fuelled by resistance to perceived occupation, serving to heighten passions. Western forces, finding themselves embroiled in conflicts they had not anticipated, searched for solutions in works that had previously been classics of counter-insurgency. Drawing inspiration from these classics, but revising them for a very different age, one of the authors of the US Army's new *Field Manual on Counterinsurgency, FM 3–40*, General David Petraeus, assumed the role of counter-insurgency expert (Ricks, 2009). The subsequent Iraq surge between 2007 and 2008 became the exemplar of how to fight a new war. At the time, however, as one astute commentator has noted, there was no guarantee of success. The surge was contested by US politicians such as Joe Biden, and was actually in military terms a pretty 'audacious' venture (Ricks, 2009: 149). The surge was, basically, a commitment of additional ground troops. It was announced by President Bush in January 2007 as a strategy which would help the Iraqis carry out the mission to eradicate sectarian violence. General Petraeus, who took over as commanding general of the multi-national task force in Iraq in that very month, was tasked with the development and implementation of this new strategy for Iraq. Counter-insurgency of any variety is not for the faint-hearted, but the twin surges of Iraq in 2007 and in Afghanistan in 2009/10 suggested that the war-at-a-distance, risk-free paradigm of the 1990s had been discarded and 'real' war had returned. The contrast with the 'technology-led' engagements of the 1990s was palpable. The fighting in, for instance, the Iraqi city of

Fallujah had already been a stark manifestation of a return to visceral warfare (McCarthy and Beaumont, 2004). The surge underlined the continued willingness of some Western states to commit troops and continue to bear casualties. Note here some, but not all, Western states. We can highlight the views of Frank Ledwidge, who after serving in Iraq and Afghanistan wrote a book about his experiences of the UK's counter-insurgency in Basra. At the same time the US was preparing for a surge the UK was bloodied and bowed and left to try to recover a military reputation for counter-insurgency in Afghanistan (Ledwidge, 2011). Ledwidge in no uncertain terms condemns both the strategy and the tactics adopted by UK commanders in the Iraq theatre. He is especially scathing of the attempts to clear IEDs using men and women in high-risk environments.

General Petraeus devised a different type of strategy for US troops, which reversed the original policy of fighting insurgents but then withdrawing, leaving the rather inadequate Iraqi forces to hold territory. Rather, additional US troops were deployed to the Sunni-dominated Anbar region in a bid to break the hold of al-Qaeda, and additional forces were deployed in the suburbs of Baghdad. This strategy, familiar to many studying traditional counter-insurgency, was to wean the people away from the terrorists and insurgents by providing a military presence amongst the people. In addition, the tribes were 'coaxed' to align with the US military against al-Qaeda.

The surge allowed the US military to ride a wave of purpose and self-belief that had so nearly been buried in the rubble of the Iraqi Sunni triangle. With the so-called Anbar Awakening, many within the Sunni community protested against the imposition by al-Qaeda of a form of radical Islam in their communities, but they also feared losing ground to the Shiite militias. The Sunni tribes, in preference to either al-Qaeda or the Iranian-backed militias, turned to the USA. So the surge transformed the political environment, not least in muting the civil war, and the conflict in Iraq entered a new phase in 2007. This, of course, was not without huge challenges for the USA and the Iraqi government in terms of national reconciliation between the Sunnis and Shiite groups, and difficulties remained in terms of ensuring that the Iraqi army adequately represented the multiple groups.

However, death rates and general rates of violence began to decline. This was partly due to the willingness of the tribes to cooperate against al-Qaeda and its allies, but the nature of the IED, in terms of roadside bombs, had also changed. Under pressure from intelligence agencies and coalition forces the insurgents had less sophisticated remote-controlled devices and were increasingly using pressure-plate IEDs. More pragmatically, as troops began to move amongst the people insurgents simply had less time to dig holes and secrete the IEDs; in short, they acted with greater haste and less firepower. The emphasis on intelligence gathering and on attacking the network – that is, finding and intercepting the groups which were assembling, planting and setting off the roadside bombs, which had been the greatest danger to troops as they moved across the country – did not dispel the threat but it did dilute it. This aspect of the surge has perhaps been underestimated as has the use of drone warfare in both Iraq and Afghanistan to kill militants as they planted their deadly weaponry. Although not a perfect 'technological fix' to the IED roadside bomb, the use of drones certainly helped answer some of the concerns expressed by Frank Ledwidge as to the vulnerabilities of troops clearing IEDs by hand.

Schools for suicide

Along with roadside bombs and car bombs, person-borne improvised explosive devices (PBIEDs) became a weapon of choice in Iraq in a variety of guises. As Diego Gambetta, an authority on suicide bombing has explained, it is notable that the number of suicide attacks in Iraq was much greater than in any other insurgency (Gambetta, 2005: 311). In fact, Gambetta has highlighted the existence of a proto- industry within Iraq for suicide missions. In this world, individuals train 'wannabe' bombers to get to the best spot for the best attack at a time to inflict the most damage (Gambetta, 2005: 310).

The suicide bomb is a simple method, often allowing the bomber to release the detonation at the point of greatest threat. Between January 2004 and June 2010 a total of 24,004 insurgent attacks occurred within Iraq, of which 5.2 per cent can be classed as suicide terrorism. However, the average number of deaths per suicide attack was ten, whilst for a non-suicidal attack it equated to only one and a half. Suicide terrorism is an effective means of communicating a message of strategic and military resilience, making it particularly effective in the case of asymmetric combat.

For this very reason suicide terrorism developed rapidly in Iraq. Following the invasion, between January 2004 and June 2010 Iraq witnessed more than 1300 suicide bombings, causing 13,249 fatalities and leaving 33,793 individuals with serious injuries (National Counterterrorism Center, 2010). The rate at which suicide attacks increased was an interesting phenomenon for other reasons, which we will now explore.

The Iraqi attacks since 2003 differ from the suicide attacks executed by organisations such as Hezbollah, Hamas and the Liberation Tigers of Tamil Eelam. Many of those responsible for the Iraqi bombings are not Iraqi nationals; they come from places as far afield as Africa and Europe. When recruited, or as volunteers, they were moved from their country of origin to a 'staging area' as rapidly as possible. Once infiltrated into Iraq they were used quickly 'since their presence and non-Iraqi features might make them vulnerable to detection' (Gambetta, 2005: 311)

However, this is not the whole story. Evidence suggests that Iraqis actually become increasingly willing to perpetrate such attacks. It is also the case that a significant majority of attacks focused on Shia civilians rather than coalition forces, again pointing to the sectarian nature of the conflict. We should not be surprised by this internal struggle. It has characterised conflicts such as those in the former Yugoslavia and, more pertinently in terms of IEDs, in Northern Ireland. One need only think about the IRA attack in October 1993 on the Protestant Shankill Road in Belfast. The bombing took place at a fish shop. Nine Protestants were killed, as was one of the terrorists who planted the bomb. The device exploded early. Its target was not the security services or the British Army but a rival group and a rival leader – Johnny Adair of the Ulster Freedom Fighters, the paramilitary wing of the Ulster

Defence Association (English, 2003: 281). Bomb making and the delivery of such devices, even for those not on a suicide mission, is a hazardous occupation.

The range of groups using IEDs in Iraq constituted a deadly mix. We noted earlier the presence of Sunni Islamist extremists along with Shi'ite extremists and militias. As part of the Sunni group a large degree of attention has to be placed on al-Qaeda in Iraq (AQI), but we should also note the focus many groups, such as Islamic Army in Iraq, ISI-al-Qaeda and Ansar Al-Sunnah, have placed on attacking Iraqi forces, Shi'ite groups and militias opposed to the presence and actions of US and coalition forces.

The Sunnis within the insurgency can basically be separated into three groups (Hafez, 2007b), which include Iraqi nationalists, Iraqi Ba'athists and foreign jihadists. Amongst these three groups there were multiple objectives in the use of IEDs and terror generally. The nationalists demanded the removal of coalition forces and the opportunity to reintegrate into the Shia-controlled government. However, although prepared to compromise and share power amongst the Shia and Kurds, two demands not immediately satisfied fed the escalation of violence.

First, the demand for a greater share of political power. Although the nationalists relied on suicide bombings, these incidents have been less frequent and intense than those by the Ba'athists and jihadists. When analysing the suicidal attacks by Sunni insurgents their strategic reasoning can be identified by the targets attacked. With widespread violence amongst Iraqi and foreign security forces, in addition to serious disruption amongst Kurdish and Shia politicians, government employees and civilians, the aim of hurting and discrediting the government was clear. Further turmoil caused by such attacks focused on the physical and economic infrastructure, engendering public unrest and maintaining high levels of sectarian violence. The situation enabled the insurgents to portray themselves as the sole protectors of the Sunnis (Hafez, 2007b).

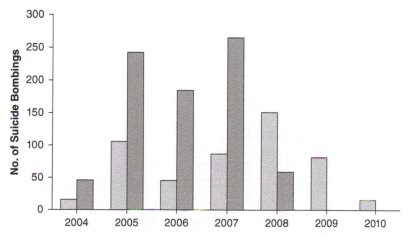

Figure E4.1 Nationality of suicide bombers between January 2004 and June 2010

Have IED – will travel

It is, though, the sheer number of foreigners that has in part defined the conflict in terms of suicide IEDs. Some have claimed that foreigners account for over 90 per cent of attackers (Gambetta, 2005: 312). According to jihadist websites that have posted information on those killed in Iraq from September 2004 to 2005, the vast majority came from Saudi Arabia, Syria and Kuwait. Indeed, nationals from 26 countries have been identified as taking part in the insurgency in Iraq. Not all became suicide bombers, but the attraction of fighting in the Iraq War is highly interesting. Gambetta in his work compares it somewhat controversially to the appeal of the Spanish Civil War, and less controversially to the foreigners who fought the Soviet Union during the Afghan War.

Arguably, then, the very nature of suicide attacks provides a political and psychological impact much greater than that of other terrorist bombings. Due to widespread media coverage, often global coverage, extensive civilian unrest can be generated as fear pervades ordinary activities such as travelling to mosques and shopping malls, or the use of public transport. When viewed from the eye of the political, national or coalition forces already fighting against the insurgents, there is the added challenge of safeguarding civilians to prove that the troops are in charge and that civilian life can continue. When we look at the targeting of Iraqi victims as opposed to coalition forces, Shia civilians were the prime target, alongside a pronounced focus on attacking police stations, private security officials and political figures, whether Kurdish, Shia or Sunni, especially those engaged in the new political processes after the removal of Saddam.

When targeting foreign individuals there was a focus on US and coalition forces, which were often attacked by vehicle or on foot, along with foreign government representatives, diplomats and, again, private security forces.

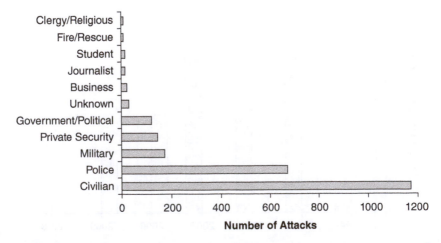

Figure E4.2 Iraqi nationals targeted by suicide bombings in Iraq

Martyrs: blowback?

The Iraq case demonstrates the importance of the insurgent message emanating from the conflict. The arrival of foreign volunteers into the furnace of war is crucial to our understanding of the attraction of that message. Bernard-Henri Lévy wrote shortly after 9/11 that there is a tendency in the West to ignore the voices throughout the developing world antagonised by a succession of US policies over a considerable period: 'There are other kamikazes ready to say to the nations of the world, you ignored us while we were alive: now we are dead; you didn't want to know about our deaths as long as they happened in our own countries; now we throw them at your feet, into the same fire that is consuming you' (quoted in Chan, 2005: 50). In this respect, some of Osama bin Laden's appeal to Muslims worldwide was rooted in the skilful highlighting of grievances, such as the question of Palestine, the treatment of the Bosnian Muslims and the humiliations many of his audience feel, just as communism as an ideology genuinely appealed to the many who were, or felt themselves to be, at odds with a rich and perhaps decadent West, especially a USA prone not only to steadfast support of Israel but to military intervention in Arab states.

To acquire support and justify violent acts, insurgents often draw on the common bonds of religion and culture. Images and videos are often displayed showing dramatic events, such as the 2003 invasion or assaults by US prison guards at Abu Ghraib prison. The point is to encourage anger and humiliation by showing the fear and pain suffered by other people. There may also be a focus on the culture of masculinity, which pervades Iraq (and, indeed, Afghanistan). Insurgent propaganda emphasises female suffering through fear and violence, or with incidents as serious as murder and rape. Such images will not always be restricted to events that have taken place within Iraq, as the aim is to justify suicide attacks across the globe. In a video released in 2005 Abu Musab al-Zarqawi, a leader of AQI, argued that 'Our Jihad in Iraq is the same as in Afghanistan, Kashmir, Chechnya, and Bosnia, an honourable jihad' (Hafez, 2007a).

In addition to portraying suffering in order to develop a bond of humiliation amongst potential bombers, insurgents also point to the links between invading forces and corrupt Muslim governments. Images of coalition forces in magazines or on websites highlight arrogance and aggression against Iraqis, including the declarations of victory against the Iraqi nation or depictions of the US occupation of symbolic locations, such as Saddam Hussein's palace. Hostility may be provoked further by revealing Arab and post-invasion leaders of Iraq in close and friendly collusion with officials and leaders of coalition forces and heads of invading and occupying states. Muslim and Western leaders may be depicted in friendly contact in comfortable surroundings whilst this image is contrasted with images of Iraqi fighters on the battlefield or suffering in deserted towns and villages.

When recruiting people to act as martyrs great importance lies in the mythology of the act. AQI are adept at displaying propaganda through web postings, videos and online journals, which reveal exceptional faith, willingness and enthusiasm to sacrifice, as well as the 'life of paradise' that will follow the act. A suicide bomber who detonated a bomb on board a lorry at a US site in Baghdad in December 2004 made a final statement to his family: 'To my mother, father, wife and brothers … I did not leave you to punish you, but instead to heed God's call to jihad. How can I live happily knowing that this country is being violated, usurped and raped, and that the infidels are storming our homes and sanctuaries and violating our religion? If we do not meet again on this earth, we shall meet in heaven' (Jaber et al., 2005). Following the statement, the video shows the bomber making an enthusiastic goodbye to his friends before self-destruction. The film ends showing his body, remarkably still intact, and a voice claiming that this is evidence that God was pleased with his sacrifice.

So martyrs…

Martyrdom may be carefully cultivated. Operations usually are depicted to greatly exaggerate the number of injuries and fatalities. Direct images of terrified and injured Muslims are used to induce anger and again help recruit potential suicide bombers. The exhibiting of countless images of injured coalition soldiers, distressed leaders and explosions, often with direct impact on the lives and bodies of foreign forces, was commonplace to emphasise the damage inflicted by the successful jihadi operations. When adapting new recruits to take the role of a martyr the focus is on the happiness and enthusiasm of the operation. This helps to counter allegations that many suicide bombers are forced or deceived into their operations. One man explained in an interview how he was captured and disarmed when his nervous reactions began to provoke suspicion. Prior to this he had been locked in a room with Ansar Mullah for three days who had continuously discussed paradise with him whilst feeding him a 'special' soup to make him strong (Gambetta, 2005). One of the sources interviewed for our IED project at the University of Hull also argued that there was direct evidence that some would-be suicide bombers had to be 'drugged' and medicated before the deadly mission (Hull University IED Project, 2013).

Although other conflicts such as Afghanistan, at least initially prohibited the use of female bombers for a multiplicity of reasons; we have seen an increase in female suicide bombers since 2005, with 44 bombings causing 2,351 injuries and fatalities. In addition to allaying the suspicions of security forces as women go about their business, the use of females has the added 'bonus' of creating an additional pool of resources if male reserves decrease. Martin van Crevald, the military historian, has argued that women are only ever used in battle when men are not available, or reluctant to take part (van Crevald, 2001), and it appears that his thesis may also be applicable in terms of female-borne IEDs. A greater use of the suicide IED requires more recruits whether they be women or children. Or it may be that the female IED has an especially shocking resonance in societies where women have traditionally inhabited a 'private', not 'public' role.

Conclusion

Despite the fact that IEDs have been present in many, indeed all, military conflicts they now occupy a central place in thinking about security generally and counter-insurgency in particular. While historically IEDs were certainly disruptive in many theatres of war they did not pose a significant strategic threat sufficient to really dent the Western way of war in the twentieth century. This was predominantly about using technological advances to make war less costly to 'our' side but more costly to the 'other' – so-called 'risk-transfer warfare'. In contemporary theatres, though, after 'invasion' by Western forces, the IED becomes the weapon of choice for the insurgents. This is true for the ongoing Syrian crisis and hence a growing realisation from Iraq onwards that military campaigns will prove to be complicated because of the proliferation of the IED. These devices 'raise' the costs both materially and in manpower for Western forces and perhaps psychologically in terms of public opinion at home.

The phenomenon of IEDs therefore posed many questions about the way the West wages war. While debates took and still take place about the nature of counter-insurgency doctrine, throughout the decade after 9/11, one feature grew ever stronger, which was that a traditional 'hearts and minds' approach was stymied by the proliferation of IEDs across the landscape of Iraq and Afghanistan. Moving amongst the people was highly problematic, and tracking, mapping and destroying IEDs became the primary task. Investment in 'force protection' became a priority and the public became aware of many of the technical issues associated with war. Home populations also of course became brutally aware of the insurgent terrorist nexus with a transfer of knowledge and ideology from sites of conflict abroad into European cities. In this sense the current preoccupation with the movement of citizens into war zones to fight and die is urgent as is the potential for the phenomenon of suicide bombers to expand further, whether it be in Africa, Europe or Asia. One thing does seem certain, however, which is that IEDs after Iraq remain a potent threat.

References

Burke, J. (2011) *The 9/11 Wars*. London: Penguin.

Chan, S. (2005) *Out of Evil, New International Politics and Old Doctrines of War*. London: I.B. Tauris.

English, R. (2003) *Armed Struggle, A History of the IRA*. Basingstoke: Macmillan.

Filkins, D. (2009) *The Forever War: Dispatches from the War on Terror*. USA: Vintage Books.

Gambetta, D. (2005) *Making Sense of Suicide Missions*. Oxford: Oxford University Press.

Gerges, F. A. (2011) *The Rise and Fall of Al-Qaeda* Oxford: Oxford University Press.

Hafez, M. M. (2007a) *Martyrdom Mythology in Iraq: How Jihadists Frame Suicide Terrorism in Videos and Biographies*. Kansas City: Taylor and Francis Group.

Hafez, M. M. (2007b) *Suicide Bombers in Iraq: The Strategy and Ideology of Martyrdom*. Washington: United States Institute of Peace.

Hull University IED Project, 2013.

Jaber, H., Rifat, A. and Allen-Mills, T. (2005) *Suicide Bombers Stream into Iraq. The Sunday Times*, 8 May. Retrieved 27 September 2010, from http://www.timesonline.co.uk/tol/news/world/article520004.ece?token=null&offset=0&page=1

Ledwidge, F. (2011) *Losing Small Wars: British Military Failure in Iraq and Afghanistan*. New Haven: Yale University Press.

Manningham-Buller, E. (2006) Speech at Queen Mary's College, London, 9 November. Retrieved 13 September 2014 from https://www.mi5.gov.uk/home/about-us/who-we-are/staff-and-management/director-general/speeches-by-the-director-general/the-international-terrorist-threat-to-the-uk.html

McCarthy, R. and Beaumont, P. (2004) Civilian Cost of Battle for Falluja Emerges *The Observer*, 14 November.

Nader, R. (2007) Asymmetrical Warfare in Iraq. *Common Dreams*, 26 February. Retrieved 14 September 2010 from http://www.commondreams.org/views07/0226-29.htm

National Counterterrorism Center (2010) *Worldwide Incidents Tracking System*. Retrieved 5 October 2010 from https://wits.nctc.gov/FederalDiscoverWITS/index.do?N=0

Ricks, T. E. (2009) *The Gamble: General Petraeus and the Untold Story of the American Surge in Iraq, 2006–2008*. London:Allen Lane.

Sky, E. (2011) *Iraq from Surge to Sovereignty: Winding Down the War in Iraq. Foreign Affairs* March/April.

van Crevald, M. (2001) *Men, Women and War*. London: Cassell.

Essay 5

TOWARDS GLOBAL JIHADISM[1]

WILLIAM BRANIFF AND ASSAF MOGHADAM

Introduction

Approaching the tenth anniversary of the 9/11 attacks, there is a growing sense among counterterrorism analysts from the policy community and academia that al-Qaeda has substantially weakened in the last decade and is destined to lose the battle against its enemies, and in particular the USA. Indeed, signs that al-Qaeda is flagging are ample, and include its loss of Osama bin Laden and important operational leaders; defeat or near defeat of various al-Qaeda franchises outside of Pakistan; a large number of ideological challenges levelled against the group by some of its former allies; and the series of protests that shook several Middle Eastern and North African states beginning in early 2011. Because the revolts in Tunisia, Egypt, Yemen, Bahrain, Syria, and other countries were mostly non-violent, they provided a striking counter-example to al-Qaeda's emphasis on violent regime change in the Middle East.

These organizational setbacks are significant, but must be viewed in the context of al-Qaeda's success in spawning an expansionist global jihadist movement.[2] Ten years into the fight against al-Qaeda, that movement's overarching narrative continues to attract followers from a multitude of countries. All the while, the interplay of al-Qaeda Core (AQC) with its affiliated groups, associated groups, and inspired adherents provides an increasing number of pathways to violence (Jenkins, 2010). A number of successful and unsuccessful plots in the past decade, and especially the last two years, serve as a stark reminder that the global jihad remains devoted to striking its enemies, often with ingenuity. The examples listed below span the breadth of the movement; taken together, these representative plots allude to the tactical, geographic, and organizational variability of the violence emanating from the global jihad.

Al-Qaeda

The August 2006 plot to blow up transatlantic airliners using liquid explosives – an attack most likely timed to coincide with the fifth anniversary of 9/11 – served as a striking example of al-Qaeda's ongoing attempts to inflict significant pain on the USA five years after 9/11. Its interdiction may have forced al-Qaeda's external operations branch to be more risk averse, but not to desist. In November 2009 this branch trained three separate cell leaders, all from separate Western nations, on bomb-making techniques. After training them AQC redeployed them to the USA, the UK, and Norway, where the operatives led terrorist cells in a geographically distributed, complex suicide attack – an adaptation of al-Qaeda's trademark complex attack. The successive deaths of al-Qaeda's primary external operations planners at the time, Saleh al-Somali and Rashid Rauf, did not prevent the plots from progressing, albeit unsuccessfully.

Affiliated organizations

On 27 August 2009 Abdullah Hassan Talea Asiri, a Saudi national and member of al-Qaeda in the Arabian Peninsula (AQAP), attempted to assassinate Assistant Interior Minister of Saudi Arabia, Prince Muhammad bin Nayef, using a Pentaerythritol tetranitrate (PETN)-based explosive device hidden in his underwear (Bergen and Hoffman, 2011: 9). On Christmas Day 2009, AQAP-trained Nigerian citizen Umar Farouk Abdulmutallab used the same compound when he attempted to detonate explosives hidden in his underwear on Northwest Airlines flight 253. A third variation of the AQAP attack placed PETN within printer cartridges shipped in cargo planes intended to detonate over the continental USA in a plot discovered in late 2010.

Associated organizations

On 30 December 2009 a Saudi national named Humam Khalil al-Balawi wore a bomb vest into a CIA outpost in Khost, Afghanistan, killing himself, seven CIA employees and one Jordanian intelligence officer. Balawi, a formerly imprisoned al-Qaeda devotee and an infamous jihadist blogger known by the pen name Abu Dujana al-Khorasani, had been recruited as an informer for the Jordanian General Intelligence Directorate (GID), but played a sophisticated double game on behalf of the Tehrik-i-Taliban Pakistan (TTP). In a second TTP plot in May 2010 a Pakistani-American citizen, Faisal Shahzad, demonstrated effective operational security and planning but poor bomb-making skills when he targeted New York's Times Square with a crude vehicle-borne improvised explosive device (VBIED).

Adherents

In November 2009 Nidal Malik Hasan, a US Army officer with only tangential personal ties to a radical cleric and no known organizational affiliation to al-Qaeda, conducted a firearms attack at a deployment centre in Fort Hood, killing 13 individuals and wounding over 30 others. Al-Qaeda and its Yemen-based affiliate both endorsed the action, but neither entity claimed the alleged assailant as a group member. In 2010 in Portland, Oregon, Mohamed Osman Mohamud, a naturalized Somali-American citizen, attempted to detonate a VBIED at a Christmas-tree-lighting ceremony. In March 2011 authorities in the USA arrested Khalid al-Dawsari, a Saudi Arabian student who, acting alone, procured explosive materials for use against targets in the USA.

This anecdotal survey of plots illuminates the contours of a multifaceted threat fostered by, but not unique to, the al-Qaeda organization. To describe how this multifaceted threat has evolved over the last decade, this paper will first recount some of the more salient examples of al-Qaeda's post-9/11 strategic, ideological, and structural adaptations. It will then offer a balance sheet of al-Qaeda's contemporary strengths and weaknesses. Ultimately, the aggregation of al-Qaeda's adaptations since 9/11 has brought about an evolutionary change in the landscape of anti-Western Islamist militancy, ushering in an era of global jihadism beyond al-Qaeda.

Al-Qaeda post-9/11: strategic, ideological, and structural evolution

In the years following the 9/11 attacks al-Qaeda adapted – by necessity as well as design – to a new reality in which the USA and its allies were determined to defeat the group militarily.

Strategic evolution after 9/11: changes in emphasis

Al-Qaeda's strategic adaptations have been numerous, but are frequently a matter of degree rather than type. For that reason these adaptations tell a story of both organizational continuity and organizational change.

First, al-Qaeda increased its media production in the years following 9/11 to compensate for the loss of its training-camp infrastructure and its corresponding centrality among jihadist groups. This increase also reflected its maturation as a terrorist organization seeking to capitalize on its newly found brand recognition (Brown, 2007). Spurred on by the thoughts and actions of fellow travelers such as Abu Musab al-Suri and Younes Tsouli (aka Irhabi007), AQC embraced the agenda-setting power of the internet, hence Ayman al-Zawahiri's assertion that at least half of the overall battle against the 'Crusader-Zionist foe' takes place in the media (Global Security, 2005). A look at the number of official al-Qaeda releases demonstrates the steadily growing output of media productions on the part of the group, from six in 2002 to 11 in 2003, 13 in 2004, 16 in 2005, 58 in 2006, peaking in 2007 with 97 releases. The number of media releases dropped to 49 in 2008 and picked up slightly to reach 79 in 2009, but seemed to drop again in 2010 (Bergen and Tiedemann, 2010; Bergen and Hoffman, 2011: 21). After 2003 al-Qaeda proved particularly skillful at exploiting widespread negative sentiment about the US invasion and occupation of Iraq. It would seize upon the Ethiopian occupation of Mogadishu in a similar way, urging the erstwhile Islamist militia-turned-jihadist group al-Shabaab to 'fight on' as 'champions of Somalia'.

The second element of al-Qaeda's strategic evolution after 9/11 was its determination to exploit the West's perceived weaknesses. Al-Qaeda and its scions have increasingly monitored, identified, and exploited gaps in Western defenses by reading Western literature and downloading materials from Western websites. This new jihadi tactic was exemplified by a new genre of jihadi publications termed jihadi strategic studies – writings that draw on Western secular-rationalist sources; identify and analyze weaknesses of both parties; consider political, economic, and cultural factors in the conflict; and recommend realistic strategies (Lia and Hegghammer, 2004; Stout et al., 2008; Adamsky, 2010).

Inspire, an English-language jihadist magazine produced by AQAP, illustrates this trend. The first edition of *Inspire* featured a 'Message to the American People and Muslims in the West' by Anwar al-Awlaki, a dual US and Yemeni citizen – an article that points to a future of religious intolerance for Muslims in the USA. Al-Awlaki contextualizes this prediction with examples of racism from US history (al-Awlaki, 2010). In follow-on editions *Inspire* amplified examples of Islamophobia in the West, such as proposed Qur'an burnings and protests over the establishment of mosques, to underline al-Awlaki's argument and reify al-Qaeda's narrative of a war against Islam.

Third, since 9/11 al-Qaeda has become more political in terms of its communiqués as well as the timing and targeting of its attacks. The group has attempted to create a rift between the USA and its allies, conducting attacks against Spanish, UK, German, and other forces to undermine popular support for the war efforts in Afghanistan, Iraq, and other theaters. Osama bin Laden's offer of a truce to European countries in April 2004 served a similar goal, as he withheld that offer to the USA. Further, the group began exploiting the Western political calendar, as was most clearly evident in the timing of the 11 March 2004 attacks in Madrid, which were carried out just prior to the Spanish presidential elections. Peter Nesser and Brynjar Lia assess a plot disrupted in Oslo, Norway, in July 2010 as another indicator of al-Qaeda's interest in attacking 'peripheral' Western nations allied with the USA and Israel (Nesser and Lia, 2010).

A fourth strategic adaptation in the post-9/11 period is al-Qaeda's emphasis on economic jihad, foremost by targeting oil facilities in Middle Eastern and Gulf states. Prior to the 9/11 attacks bin Laden acknowledged the strategic importance of the energy sector, as is evident in his 1996 declaration of war, where he called upon the mujahideen to 'protect this (oil) wealth and [do] not... include it in the battle as it is a great Islamic wealth and a large economical power essential for the soon to be established Islamic state'. The shift in al-Qaeda's strategy to emphasize these targets was complete by December 2004, when bin Laden declared the 'bleed-until-bankruptcy' strategy. He called the purchase by Western countries of oil at then market prices the 'greatest theft in history' and concluded that there was now 'a rare and golden opportunity to make America bleed in Iraq, both economically and in terms of human loss and morale ... Focus your operations on it [oil production] especially in Iraq and the Gulf area, since this [lack of oil] will cause them to die off [on their own]' (Gartenstein-Ross, 2010). Within a year an al-Qaeda cell attempted to hit a key energy facility in Dammam, Saudi Arabia, and in February 2006 al-Qaeda's Saudi affiliate was able to breach security at the Abqaiq processing facility, the world's largest crude-processing plant. Although the attack was not able to interrupt production, it foreshadowed al-Qaeda's growing focus on strikes at the economic assets of its enemies.

In a recent example, the November 2010 special issue of *Inspire* celebrated the economic rationale of al-Qaeda's attrition strategy. Demonstrating the centrality of economic jihad, the magazine's cover-art superimposed '$4200' in large font over the blurred image of a United Parcel Service jet, referring to the low price tag of its plots targeting the cargo airline industry. It also alluded to a quote by al-Awlaki, who contrasted the low cost of Operation Hemorrhage with the high cost that the attacks were expected to exact from the West owing to stepped-up security expenses (al-Awlaki, 2010).

Ideological dilution: from elitist organization to catch-all movement

Al-Qaeda has endeavored to widen the target audience of its recruitment and propaganda campaign. Whereas before 9/11 al-Qaeda made exclusive appeals to Muslims, it gradually adopted more populist rhetoric following 9/11 in order to appeal to a wider audience, including non-Muslims. In an essay published in February 2005 titled 'The Freeing of Humanity and Homelands Under the Banner of the Quran' Ayman al-Zawahiri, for the first time, attempted to appeal to anti-globalization and environmental activists. An article from the first edition of *Inspire* magazine, attributed to Osama bin Laden, echoes this approach, placing the blame for global warming squarely on US shoulders (bin Ladin, 2010).

Some of the populist propaganda emanating from al-Qaeda is intended to increase anti-Americanism among the camp of the 'infidel' proper, tearing at the social fabric of the USA along racial lines. Examples include Ayman al-Zawahiri's co-opting of Malcolm X as a Muslim martyr who died fighting against racial injustice; al-Zawahiri's use of the term house slaves to discredit the success of prominent African-American politicians; and Abu Dujana al-Khorasani's appeal to various minority communities in the USA to fight against their oppressors (Haas and McGrory, 2008). Al-Qaeda has also made appeals to Muslim and African-American members of the military to turn their weapons against their own government, foreshadowing such incidents as the Fort Hood shooting of November 2009 (Scheuer, 2007).

Al-Qaeda has also increased its efforts to frame local grievances in accordance with its global narrative outside of the USA. While not a new characteristic of al-Qaeda propaganda, increased media production amplifies its attempts to aggregate disparate Islamist conflicts since 2001. Al-Qaeda has attempted to harmonize its propaganda with the grievance narratives associated with local and regional jihadist movements in Yemen, Somalia, the Caucasus, Pakistan, Afghanistan, Iraq, India, Central Asia, and Southeast Asia. While its ability to globalize these disparate conflicts has been limited, isolated successes across a spectrum of theaters has increased the number of ideological pathways to participation in the global jihad (Brown, 2010).

Structural adaptation: towards multipolarity

The evolution from organization to movement in the decade since 9/11 can be explained by three structural adaptations, more so than by the strategic and ideological changes witnessed over the same time period. As an organization, al-Qaeda has formally affiliated with geographically dispersed groups; it has informally partnered with geographically co-located groups; and it has fostered a virtual safe haven with few barriers to entry.

Al-Qaeda's mergers with militant groups, including Jama'at al-Tawhid wal-Jihad in Iraq, the Salafist Group for Preaching and Combat (GSPC) in Algeria, al-Shabaab in

Somalia, and the reconstitution of AQAP, have all resulted in a fundamental structural shift. Rather than an organization with cells spread in scores of countries, al-Qaeda in 2011 is better understood as a multipolar organization with a central hub in North Waziristan and a small number of autonomous regional nodes. By offering their organizational fealty to al-Qaeda, these organizations extend al-Qaeda's ideological and operational influence in their respective regions, while also allowing al-Qaeda to engage in networking, propagandizing, and resource mobilization in active conflict zones (Brown, 2010). These nodes create resilience and dynamism in the movement, amplify the world's perception of al-Qaeda, and even provide a degree of redundancy should al-Qaeda suffer a devastating blow in Pakistan.

The most consequential implication of al-Qaeda's structural transition into a multipolar entity lies in the resulting locations, targets, and tactics of terrorist violence. Thus, the most likely theaters for current and future attacks against local and Western targets are those in proximity to the main territorial hubs of AQC and its affiliates, such as Afghanistan, Algeria, Iraq, Pakistan, Somalia, Yemen, and their neighbors. It is not a coincidence that al-Qaeda tactics such as suicide bombings have been introduced precisely in these regions, where jihadist cells, including al-Qaeda affiliates, have sprung up. Algeria, Somalia, and Yemen, for example, have seen prolonged periods of localized, brutal violence, but radical Islamist groups in these countries traditionally shunned the use of suicide bombings against Western targets until al-Qaeda solidified its affiliations in these areas (Moghadam, 2008; 2009; Schweitzer, 2010). Besides the adoption of suicide attacks, the use of vehicle-borne improvised explosive devices (VBIEDs) offers additional evidence of knowledge transfer to these regional nodes.

Although patterns in attack locations, targets, and tactics can be observed in relation to al-Qaeda affiliates, the establishment of regional nodes introduces increased complexity into the demographics and travel patterns of the terrorists themselves. Perhaps unsurprisingly, tens of members of the Somali diaspora from Minnesota, Canada, Sweden, and the UK have reportedly joined al-Shabaab in Somalia, but so have many non-ethnic Somalis with no personal connections to Somalia. While one may have expected a Nigerian jihadist to join the movement through a militia in West Africa or al-Qaeda in the Islamic Maghreb (AQIM), a wealthy Nigerian named Umar Farouk Abdulmuttalab studying in England sought training in Yemen in order to attack the USA.

Al-Qaeda's merger with the Algerian GSPC serves as an example of what al-Qaeda stands to gain from regional mergers. This merger enabled al-Qaeda to leverage AQIM's existing reach into Europe, where AQIM enjoys well-established connections, as well as into the Sahel, where ungoverned spaces provide opportunities for fundraising and training. Al-Qaeda intends to use affiliates such as AQIM as force multipliers, as was evident from an intercepted message in which Ayman al-Zawahiri asked AQIM leader Abdelmalek Droukdel to help exact revenge against Denmark following the Danish cartoon controversy (Mekhennet et al., 2008).

TEXTBOX 5   CASE STUDY: AL-QAEDA IN THE ISLAMIC MAGHREB (AQIM)

Year formed: 1998

AQIM evolved from the Algerian militant group, the Salafist Group for Call and Combat (GSPC). GSPC formed in 1998 as an outgrowth of the once-powerful and extremely violent Groupe Islamique Armé (GIA). GIA's popularity declined following a series of massacres in which it killed thousands of Algerian civilians.

Aim

AQIM's primary objective is to overthrow governments and establish a theocracy in Algeria, Libya, Mali, Mauritania, Morocco, and Tunisia. AQIM also seeks to expel Westerners from historically Muslim lands. The group has declared its intention to attack European and US targets.

GSPC initially drew support from the Algerian population by vowing to continue the rebellion without killing civilians, but a government amnesty and counterterrorism campaign drove it into disarray in the early 2000s. In September 2006 the GSPC joined forces with al-Qaeda. Ayman al-Zawahiri, al-Qaeda's emir, announced a 'blessed union' between the groups, declaring France an enemy and indicating that they would fight against French and US interests. In January 2007 the group announced that it had changed its name to al-Qaeda in the Islamic Maghreb (AQIM) to reflect its alliance with al-Qaeda, from which it receives material and financial support, as well as to get legitimacy among extremists and facilitate recruitment.

2007 marked the highest point for AQIM suicide attacks and other violent incidents in Algeria.

Organizational structure and tactics

The group is divided into *katibas*, or brigades, which are often organized into independent cells. AQIM uses bombings, kidnappings (of aid workers, tourists, diplomats, and employees of multinational corporations – some of them were executed), and paramilitary operations against civilian, government, and military targets. Kidnappings are used not only to raise funds but to facilitate prisoner exchanges and discourage foreign enterprise in the region. In 2012 the US State Department said AQIM had coordinated with other terrorist groups in the region, including Nigeria's Boko Haram, Somalia's al-Shabaab, and Yemen's AQAP, through the transfer of arms and funds.

Al-Qaeda seeks to build regional alliances where it believes them to be beneficial, and rejects them when the risks are excessive. Thus, the group did not hesitate to reject an offer from the Lebanese jihadist group Fatah al-Islam – likely a result of al-Qaeda's calculation that the embattled group's chances of survival looked rather dim. Similarly, al-Qaeda does not seem to have taken seriously overtures by Salafi-jihadist factions in the Gaza Strip such as Jaesh al-Islam. Aware of the animosity Hamas harbors for these jihadist groups and its willingness to use violence to obviate competing groups or rogue behavior, al-Qaeda was careful not to ally itself with entities whose existence might be endangered. Al-Qaeda is keenly aware of perceptions of strategic competence, and therefore would like to bet on winning horses only (Forest, 2009).

Al-Qaeda has always maintained associations short of formal affiliation with militant organizations, primarily as a result of geographic co-location in training environments and conflict zones. While this tendency has not changed over the last decade, what has changed is the intensity of intelligence collection and military pressure on al-Qaeda itself. As a result, al-Qaeda has utilized these associations more aggressively in recent years, facilitating the reorientation of jihadist violence against Western interests.

Al-Qaeda attempts to reorient violence against the West by superimposing a transnational explanatory framework on local grievances. The extent to which it has been successful in instilling a global jihadist ideology into locally oriented groups is reflected in the growing involvement of such groups in attacks against Western targets. While there are many other examples, al-Qaeda's relationship with Tehriki-i-Taliban Pakistan (TTP) is perhaps the most illustrative. For example, the Islamic Jihad Union provided training to a German cell of jihadists known as the Sauerland bombers, who plotted to attack numerous targets in Germany before they were apprehended in September 2007. In addition to the above-mentioned attacks on the CIA outpost in Khost, Afghanistan, and in Times Square, New York, Pakistani citizens trained by TTP have been involved in a sophisticated plot to target the Barcelona Metro with multiple suicide bombers (BBC, 2011).

In addition to operational convergence, regional affiliates and associates have also embraced the same types of information operations for which al-Qaeda has become famous. As a result, al-Sahab media is now only one of many organizations producing propaganda. The proliferation of highly differentiated content found on dynamic jihadist websites, the empowering nature of user-generated content, and links between jihadist activity online and jihadist activity in the real world have created a third structural shift in the global jihad. Independent jihadist pundits, like Abu Dujana al-Khorasani, can articulate a new narrative, cultivate a new demographic of consumers, and move seamlessly from the e-jihad to the battlefield by building trusted relationships online that translate into mobilization networks. Further, when an iconic jihadist blogger makes this transition he is celebrated by jihadist media organs and on the virtual forums he left behind, becoming a new role model and paving a new pathway to participation in the global jihad.

An al-Qaeda scorecard

Despite much talk in recent years suggesting al-Qaeda's imminent demise, al-Qaeda capitalizes on a number of core strengths that will ensure its relevance at least for the foreseeable future. The first and most obvious strength is that, after regrouping along the Afghan–Pakistan border, al-Qaeda has been able to re-establish a limited safe haven in an active conflict zone. This allows al-Qaeda to link up with other like-minded groups either directly involved in the conflict or living parasitically off the war economies of that conflict. These associated organizations can then share training resources, fundraising and mobilization networks, and opportunities to propagandize. Al-Qaeda can facilitate violence locally, enable jihadist attacks abroad, and shape propaganda as consultants to violent jihad (Gallo, 2011).

The second of these strengths is that al-Qaeda's foundational ideological assumption remains convincing to politicized demographics; the USA is, in their perception, waging a war on Islam as evidenced by its occupation of Muslim countries. As long as the US military is present in Arab and Muslim countries – a political reality beyond Iraq and Afghanistan, given current events in Yemen, Libya, and Somalia – al-Qaeda's propaganda will resonate.

A third, and related, advantage is that al-Qaeda's Salafi-jihadist ideology has been subsumed in a more inclusive global jihadist ideology.[3] Adopting the elitist tenets of Salafi-jihadism has been a potential barrier to entry in the past, and ideologically contested components of al-Qaeda's Salafi-jihadism left it vulnerable on theological grounds. Global jihadism, in contrast, is populist and malleable. The only requirement is to identify with the basic worldview presented through various lenses by various components of the movement: the Muslim world, or one's portion of it, is in decline as a result of an anti-Islamic conspiracy, and only jihad (understood solely in militant terms) can redeem it. Recognizing the value of inclusivity, al-Qaeda has subordinated itself to the broader violent movement. Al-Qaeda now endorses lone-wolf jihadism conducted by those who may lack Salafi credentials (Gadahn, 2010); its closest affiliate, AQAP, endorses anti-regime violence by ideologically distant organizations (Koehler-Derrick, 2010); and al-Qaeda-inspired political organizations, like Hizb ut-Tahrir America, endorse jihadism while making little pretense of piety (Gruen, 2010).

The internet provides al-Qaeda with its fourth core advantage. Legally constrained and uncomfortable in the propaganda realm, the USA and its allies have largely ceded the virtual arena as a platform in the war of ideas. Al-Qaeda and its affiliates, on the other hand, have built a geographically distributed and resilient communications architecture that they have saturated with highly differentiated propaganda. In the tribal belt, for example, DVDs, movies, and other media produced by local branches of companies such as As-Sahab, Ummat Studio, and Jundullah CD Center feature jihadist propaganda in Urdu, Pashto, Arabic, English, and other languages. Al-Fajr Media Center distributes copies of such videos in German, Italian, French, and Turkish online, where web forums make them available to a broader community. Members of those forums subtitle, translate, expound upon, and further disseminate these materials on social media sites, availing new consumers of jihadist propaganda. In September 2006 jihadism scholar Reuven Paz (2006) declared, 'Global jihad has clearly won the battle over the internet. As a means of indoctrination, Al-Qaeda and its affiliates dominate this medium, while the West and the Muslim world have so far failed to devise …

a serious "counter-Jihadi" response.' As we approach the tenth anniversary of the 9/11 attacks, Paz's assessment of the digitally mediated war of ideas rings as true today as it did in 2006.

Offsetting many of al-Qaeda's advantages, however, are several signs that the group has been significantly weakened in recent days and years. Most recently, the US raid of Osama bin Laden's safehouse in Abbottabad, Pakistan, ended the life of the organization's emir and the most important unifying symbol of global jihadism. This decapitation strike will not sound al-Qaeda's death knell outright, but the symbolic void left by bin Laden's death may lead to the fracturing of a geographically distributed and ideologically fraught AQC. Furthermore, intelligence collected during the raid may amplify an existing trend for al-Qaeda – the death or capture of key operational figures. Examples include the capture of Abu Faraj al-Libi in May 2005, and the killing of others, such as: Hamza Rabia, who died in November 2005; Abu Laith al-Libi (January 2008); Abu Sulayman al-Jazairi (May 2008); Abu Khabab al-Masri (July 2008); Rashid Rauf (November 2008); Saleh al-Somali (December 2009); and Saeed al-Masri (May 2010).

Accompanying the loss of al-Qaeda's senior leaders has been the defeat, near defeat, or stagnation of a number of al-Qaeda's local affiliates. AQAP, prior to its current reincarnation in Yemen, was decimated by the Kingdom of Saudi Arabia (Hegghammer, 2010), while AQI suffered a strategic defeat at the hands of the Sunni Awakening and 'the US military surge'. At its most lethal in 2007, AQIM failed to destabilize Algiers, and its initial calls to conduct attacks in neighboring countries did not materialize in significant numbers. In the Sahel, where AQIM is currently most active, Mokhtar Belmokhtar's *katiba* engages in kidnap for ransom and counterfeiting while also engaging in a turf war with the committed AQIM jihadist Abdelhamid Abou Zeid. Al-Shabaab's popularity in Somalia saw its high-water mark during the 2007–8 Ethiopian occupation, but it now struggles to retain nationalist Islamists among its ranks as it battles African Union troops in Mogadishu and the Ahlu Sunna wal Jama Sufi militia in central and southern Somalia. Tribal rivalries and competing interests further hamstring the group, such that its relative position as the strongest group in Somalia does not mean that Somalia is or will be what Afghanistan and Pakistan have been for al-Qaeda.

Exacerbating al-Qaeda's problems in recent years are a number of underlying weaknesses and long-term challenges (Moghadam and Fishman, 2011). The first is structural. While mergers can afford al-Qaeda the benefits described above, they are not without risk. Principal-agent problems can dilute or undermine al-Qaeda's brand. The clearest example of an al-Qaeda affiliate 'going rogue' was that of AQI under Abu Musab al-Zarqawi. Although al-Qaeda needed to take credit for violence waged against US troops if it was to remain relevant, internecine violence fomented by al-Zarqawi alienated erstwhile supporters from the Muslim world and provided the impetus for Sunni tribes to mobilize against AQI. The result was not only a strategic loss for AQI, but a significant black-eye for AQC (Fishman, 2009; Shapiro, 2006). This and similar problems are inherent in al-Qaeda's structure as a decentralized organization.

Competition from state and non-state entities poses another long-term challenge. Iran's ongoing defiance of the West, and especially the USA, undermines al-Qaeda's credibility in claiming the status of the Muslim world's leading anti-US force. Iranian foreign policy 'successes', such as its determined pursuit of a nuclear weapon, its pursuit of regional hegemony, and its hostile attitude to Israel, are problematic for al-Qaeda because it reminds al-Qaeda's current and potential supporters of the mismatch between what the group preaches and what it does. It underscores al-Qaeda's failure to attack Israel and act against Iran despite the jihadist movement's extremist rhetoric *vis-à-vis* both nations.

Al-Qaeda also perceives popular Islamist movements such as the Muslim Brotherhood and Hizballah as a threat. The Brotherhood provides an Islamist alternative with a record of performance on the Arab street. With regard to the latter, Hizballah's ability to stand up to Israel in the 2006 war has presented the Shia militant group as the Muslim world's only movement capable of fighting the Jewish state. Similar to the case of Iran, the political and military success of Hizballah undermines al-Qaeda's ability to claim a leadership role for the Islamic community at large.

More recently, non-violent protests beginning with the Jasmine Revolution in Tunisia highlight another weakness. For decades jihadists have argued that violence is necessary to overthrow authoritarian, apostate regimes. The recent wave of protests across the Muslim world undermines the assertion that violence is necessary, as several have succeeded where al-Qaeda and its brethren have repeatedly failed. While significant, this setback is conditional and predicated upon the successful establishment of legitimate government in the wake of the Arab Spring.

The recantations and condemnations by individuals who were part of al-Qaeda's foundational history, meanwhile, have presented al-Qaeda with what is perhaps its most significant challenge.[4] Al-Qaeda has been plagued by a series of recantations and defections by formerly venerated jihadists, including Abdul Qadir bin Abdul Aziz, aka Dr Fadl, and the Saudi cleric Salman al-Awdah. These more recent recantations follow previous condemnations of isolated acts of extreme jihadist violence by theologians highly respected in the jihadist community, including Abu Basir al-Tartusi and Abu Muhammad al-Maqdisi, who have rejected the usefulness of the London bombings and AQI's systematic targeting of Shia civilians respectively.

While the downplaying of its elitist, Salafi rhetoric has softened the blow of these recantations to some extent, al-Qaeda has been put in an untenable position with respect to one issue. Al-Qaeda has been forced to defend itself against charges that its actions lead to the death of countless innocent Muslims. Whether al-Qaeda uses allegations of apostasy to justify these deaths ideologically; whether it argues pragmatically that the ends justify the means; or whether al-Qaeda genuinely tries to minimize Muslim fatalities – these are irrelevant. Declining opinion polls in the Muslim world reflect the indisputable fact that al-Qaeda has failed to redeem Islam, but has succeeded in killing innocent Muslims in large numbers. Despite its many adaptations, this is al-Qaeda's major weakness, and it remains an enduring weakness of the global jihad that the West should continue to expose (Helfstein et al., 2009; Fishman and Moghadam, 2010).

Conclusion

Al-Qaeda continues to enable the violence of others, orient that violence towards the USA and its allies in a distributed game of attrition warfare, and foster a dichotomous us-versus-them narrative between the Muslim world and the rest of the international community. Despite this overarching consistency, al-Qaeda shepherds a different phenomenon than it did ten years ago. The organization has adapted to changing environmental pressures at the strategic, ideological, and structural levels, and the aggregation of these adaptations has fundamentally changed the nature of the jihadist threat to the West. This evolved threat is not inherently more dangerous, as counterterrorism efforts today focus on and disrupt capability earlier and more consistently than prior to September 2001. This multifaceted global jihad will, however, continue to attempt greater numbers of attacks in more locations, from a more diverse cadre of individuals spanning a wider ideological spectrum.

Notes

1   This essay was written at the tenth anniversary of the 9/11 attacks and is hence a snapshot of the authors' assessment at September 2011.
2   For a similar argument see Leah Farrall, 'How al Qaeda Works', *Foreign Affairs*, March/April 2011. While acknowledging that al-Qaeda continues to pose a threat today, the present authors would not go as far as Farrall in arguing that 'al Qaeda is stronger today than when it carried out 9/11'. The global jihadist movement is defined here as a transnational movement of like-minded jihadists led by al-Qaeda. It includes affiliated and associated individuals, networks, and groups. The term 'affiliated' denotes groups that have formal ties to al-Qaeda, and have often adopted the al-Qaeda name, e.g. al-Qaeda in the Arabian Peninsula. The term 'associated' refers to entities with more informal ties to al-Qaeda, i.e. those that are influenced by al-Qaeda's guiding ideology but have not sworn fealty (*bay'ah*) to bin Laden. It also includes 'adherents', i.e. individuals inspired by the worldview propagated by al-Qaeda, its affiliates, and/or associates. The authors recognize that these divisions are not perfect, that some groups associated with al-Qaeda have not fully adopted al-Qaeda's ideology, and that still other groups fall into a gray area between associates and affiliates. However, for descriptive purposes in this article this division shall suffice.
3   The authors are indebted to Jarret Brachman for this observation.
4   For a dissenting view see Lahoud, 2011.

References

Adamsky, D. (2010) 'Jihadi Operational Art: The Coming Wave of Jihadi Strategic Studies,' *Studies in Conflict and Terrorism*, 33.1.

al-Awlaki, A. (2010) 'Shaykh Anwar's Message to the American People and Muslims in the West,' *Inspire*, 1.

BBC (2011) 'Spain Becoming Breeding Ground for Jihadism – Experts,' BBC, 4 January.

Bergen, P. and Hoffman, B. (2011) 'Assessing the Terrorist Threat,' Bipartisan Policy Center.

Bergen, P. and Tiedemann, K. (2010) 'The Almanac of Al-Qaeda,' *Foreign Policy*, available online at http://www.foreignpolicy.com/articles/2010/04/26/the_almanac_of_al_qaeda; last accessed 20 April 2011.

bin Ladin, U. (2010) 'The Way to Save the Earth,' *Inspire*, 1. Bin Laden's Fatwa, August 1996. Available at the Online News Hour website, http://www.pbs.org/newshour/terrorism/international/fatwa_1996.html (last accessed 20 April 2011).

Brown, V. (2007) 'Cracks in the Foundation: Leadership Schisms in Al-Qa'ida 1989–2006,' (West Point, NY: Combating Terrorism Center).

Brown, V. (2010) 'Al-Qa'ida Central and Local Affiliates', in A. Moghadam and B. Fishman (eds.), *Self-Inflicted Wounds: Debates and Divisions within al-Qa'ida and its Periphery* (West Point, NY: Combating Terrorism Center).

Farrall, L. (2011) 'How al Qaeda Works,' *Foreign Affairs*, 90(2): 128–38.

Fishman, B. (2009) 'Dysfunction and Decline: Lessons Learned from Inside Al-Qa'ida in Iraq' (West Point, NY: Combating Terrorism Center).

Fishman, B. and Moghadam, A. (2010) 'Do Jihadi and Islamist Divisions Matter? Implications for Policy and Strategy,' in A. Moghadam and B. Fishman (eds.), *Self-Inflicted Wounds: Debates and Divisions within al-Qa'ida and its Periphery* (West Point, NY: Combating Terrorism Center).

Forest, J. J. F. (2009) 'Exploiting the Fears of Al-Qa'ida's Leadership,' *CTC Sentinel*, 2.2.

Gadahn, A. (2010) 'A Call to Arms,' Al-Sahab.

Gallo, A. (2011) 'Understanding Al Qa'ida's Business Model,' *CTC Sentinel*, 4.1.

Gartenstein-Ross, D. (2010) 'Large-scale Arrests in Saudi Arabia Illustrate Threat to the Oil Supply,' *The Long War Journal*, 24 March.

Global Security (2005) 'Letter from Al-Zawahiri to Al-Zarqawi.' Available at http://www.globalsecurity.org/security/library/report/2005/zawahiri-zarqawi-letter_9jul2005.htm (last accessed 20 April 2011).

Gruen, M. (2010) 'Hizb ut-Tahrir America Uses Social Media to Promote its "Emerging World Order" Conference,' *Huffington Post*, 14 June.

Haas, B. and McGrory, D. (2008) 'Al-Qa'ida Seeking to Recruit African-American Muslims,' *CTC Sentinel*, 1.8.

Hegghammer, T. (2010) 'The Failure of Jihad in Saudi Arabia,' *CTC Occasional Paper* (West Point, NY: Combating Terrorism Center).

Helfstein, S., Abdullah, N. and al-Obaidi, M. (2009) 'Deadly Vanguards: A Study of al-Qa'ida's Violence Against Muslims,' *CTC Occasional Paper* (West Point, NY: Combating Terrorism Center).

Inspire: Special Edition (2010) November.

Jenkins, B. M. (2010) 'Would-be Warriors: Incidents of Jihadist Terrorist Radicalization in the United States since September 11, 2001,' *RAND Occasional Paper* (Santa Monica, CA: Rand Corporation).

Koehler-Derrick, G. (2010) 'Developing Policy Options for the AQAP Threat in Yemen,' *CTC Sentinel*, 3.11.

Lahoud, N. (2011) 'Jihadi Recantations and their Significance: The Case of Dr Fadl,' in A. Moghadam and B. Fishman (eds.), *Fault Lines in Global Jihad: Organizational, Strategic, and Ideological Fissures* (London: Routledge).

Lia, B. and Hegghammer, T. (2004) 'Jihadi Strategic Studies: The Alleged Al Qaida Policy Study Preceding the Madrid Bombings,' *Studies in Conflict and Terrorism*, 27.5.

Mekhennet, S., Moss, M., Schmitt, E., Sciolino, E. and William, M. (2008) 'A Threat Renewed: Ragtag Insurgency Gains a Lifeline From Al-Qaeda,' 7 June, 2012, *New York Times*.

Moghadam, A. (2008) *The Globalization of Martyrdom: Al-Qaeda, Salafi Jihad, and the Diffusion of Suicide Attacks* (Baltimore: Johns Hopkins University Press).

Moghadam, A. (2009) 'Shifting Trends in Suicide Attacks,' *CTC Sentinel*, 2.1.

Moghadam, A. and Fishman, B. (2011) (eds.), *Fault Lines in Global Jihad: Organizational, Strategic, and Ideological Fissures* (London: Routledge).

Nesser, P. and Lia, B. (2010) 'Lessons Learned from the July 2010 Norwegian Terrorist Plot,' *CTC Sentinel*, 3.8.

Paz, R. (2006) 'Qaidat al-Jihad: Moving Forward or Backward? The Algerian GSPC Joins Al Qaeda,' *PRISM Occasional Papers* 4.5 (September), p. 1.

Scheuer, M. (2007) 'Latest al-Zawahiri Tape Targets American Society,' *Terrorism Focus*, 4.13.

Schweitzer, Y. (2010) 'Al-Qaeda and Suicide Terrorism: Vision and Reality,' *Military and Strategic Affairs*, 2.2.

Shapiro, J. N. (2006) 'Theoretical Framework: The Challenges of Organizing Terrorism,' in J. Felter, J. Bramlett, B. Perkins, J. Brachman, B. Fishman, J. Forest, L. Kennedy, J. N. Shapiro, and T. Stocking (eds.), *Harmony and Disharmony: Exploiting al-Qa'ida's Organizational Vulnerabilities* (West Point, NY: Combating Terrorism Center).

Stout, M. E., Huckabey, J.M. and Schindler, J.R. (2008) *Terrorist Perspectives Project: Strategic and Operational Views of Al Qaida and Associated Movements* (Annapolis, MD: Naval Institute Press).

Essay 6

LIVING WITH TERROR, NOT LIVING IN TERROR: THE IMPACT OF CHRONIC TERRORISM ON ISRAELI SOCIETY

DOV WAXMAN

Introduction

Counting the number of terrorist fatalities and comparing this to the number of fatalities in conventional wars, or even traffic accidents, leads some to claim that the threat of terrorism is wildly exaggerated. But counting fatalities from terrorist attacks is the crudest and most simplistic way to measure the impact of terrorism. The consequences of terrorist attacks often go far beyond the deaths and destruction they cause. The effects of terrorism are not limited to its actual victims. They can be wide-ranging and far-reaching. They include the direct and indirect economic costs of terrorist attacks, the psychological effects of terrorism upon the population, and the social and political impact of terrorist attacks. This essay will discuss these different kinds of effects with the aim of presenting a fuller picture of the impact of terrorism on a society.[1] In doing so I will draw extensively upon recent research into the effects of terrorism conducted by psychologists, sociologists, economists, and political scientists. Brought together, this research into the psychological, economic, social, and political effects of terrorism enables us to develop a more comprehensive and integrated understanding of the overall impact of terrorism. This article uses the Israeli experience during the second Palestinian Intifada as a case study.

Psychological effects

The first and most immediate effects of terrorism are psychological. Terrorist campaigns can be expected to affect a sizeable portion of the population of a targeted society psychologically, either directly, by harming a person or their family, or indirectly, through coverage of terrorist attacks (Bleich et al., 2003: 11.) The greater the number of attacks and the more lethal those attacks, the more people who will be psychologically affected. Terrorism is a form of psychological warfare against a society (Crenshaw, 1983: 1). It is designed to strike fear into the heart of the targeted society, and it generally succeeds in doing so. Suicide terrorism can be particularly effective in terrifying people because it projects an aura of fanaticism (Hoffman, 2006: 142), which makes the threat of future attacks seem more likely. People's fear of terrorism is both rational and irrational; rational in that there is an ever present threat of a terrorist attack being repeated, but irrational in the probability assigned to that potential event (Ganor, 2002: 15). Since people tend to overestimate their chances of being a victim of terrorism, the fear of terrorism is widespread in a society. It does not, however, affect everyone to an equal degree. Research has shown that there is a negative correlation between a person's education and their fear of being a victim of terrorism. This suggests that the more educated a person is, the less likely they are to succumb to the irrational fear evoked by terrorism (Huddy et al., 2002: 499).

In the case of Israel, a large majority of Israeli civilians have long feared terrorism. Israelis' personal fear of terrorism has been recorded in public-opinion surveys over many years. In a 1979 survey 73 percent of respondents reported being 'afraid' or 'very afraid' that they or their close family members would be hurt in a terrorist attack (Merari and Friedland, 1980: 228). Similarly, 85 percent of Israelis expressed this fear in a poll conducted in 1995, and 78 percent in a 1996 poll (Arian, 1999, cited in Merari and Friedland, 1980: 228). Israelis' fear of terrorism reached new heights during the second Intifada. In the spring of 2002 – when Palestinian suicide bombings inside Israel were most frequent – 92 percent of Israelis reported fear that they or a member of their family would fall victim to a terrorist attack (Bar-Tal and Sharvit, 2004: 15) – almost every member of Israeli society. While this fear certainly had some basis, it was not grounded entirely in the facts, since the probability of themselves or a member of their family being killed or wounded in a terrorist attack was actually far smaller than the Israeli public believed.

Nevertheless, Palestinian terrorist attacks during the second Intifada affected a large number of Israelis. Nineteen months into the second Intifada 16.4 percent of Israeli adults said they were victims of a terrorist attack, 22.1 percent had friends or relatives who were victims, and a further 15.3 percent knew someone who had survived a terrorist attack without injury. In total a staggering 44.4 percent of the Israeli population was exposed to a terrorist attack (Bleich et al., 2003: 6). With terrorist attacks affecting so many people, it is not surprising that they resulted in widespread psychological problems. More than a third of Israelis who participated in a major psychological study reported at least one traumatic stress-related (TSR) symptom, with an average of four symptoms reported per person (Bleich et al., 2003: 9).

The number and intensity of TSR symptoms reported by the Israeli sample during the second Intifada was similar to the number and intensity reported by Americans following the terrorist attacks on 11 September 2001, even though far fewer Americans were directly exposed to the 9/11 attacks (Bleich et al., 2003: 10). This suggests that terrorism can psychologically affect people who have no direct connection to a terrorist attack. Indeed, there is no statistically significant association between psychosocial responses to traumatic events and the level of exposure (Bleich et al., 2003: 10). Being an actual victim of terrorism has little effect on the prevalence of stress-related psychological disorders, while gender and age have a far more acute effect. A person who is injured in a terrorist attack is no more likely to suffer from psychological disorders than a person whose only connection to the attack was seeing it on TV. The extensive media coverage of terrorist attacks can seriously harm people's psychological well-being.

The psychological effect of terrorism that is easiest to quantify is the prevalence of post-traumatic stress disorder (PTSD),[2] a potentially socially crippling psychological disorder. One of the major symptoms of PTSD is avoiding people or situations that remind one of the traumatic experience. PTSD can change the way people behave at home and at work; neither the private nor public sphere is immune from the harm caused by terror attacks (Pedahzur, 2005: 183). In the middle of the second Intifada 9.4 percent of Israelis suffered from PTSD; but the occurrence of PTSD varied considerably between men, women, and children, with 40 percent of Israeli children suffering from this disorder (Morag, 2006). Women are also more likely to have PTSD than men, and also have a significantly higher chance of having TSRs and depression (Bleich et al., 2003: 11). The psychological effects of terrorism are by no means uniform; different people are affected to different degrees.

The psychological effects of terrorism are not limited to PTSD. For example, those who witness terrorist attacks but are not directly harmed are generally the last to be evacuated from the scene of the attack, since medics typically focus their attention on the casualties (Eshel, 2003). These people typically replay the scenes of carnage endlessly in their heads, and many end up with 'hypertension, accelerated pulse, disassociation, and a desire to flee from the slightest noise, such as a car exhaust pipe backfiring or even a slamming door' (Eshel, 2003). In the wake of terrorist attacks people can become incapable of concentrating on their typical daily tasks. For example, following the 9/11 attacks 52 percent of Americans polled said that they could not concentrate on their work as a result of those attacks (Huddy et al., 2002: 496). Terrorism, therefore, has a significant impact on people's everyday lives, whether or not they are directly exposed to it.

The psychological effects of terrorism are well documented. What is less clear, however, is the psychological impact of repeated terrorist attacks. Do more terrorist attacks result in more psychological damage to the population or does their psychological impact diminish over time? One might think that a wave of suicide attacks would have an increasingly negative psychological impact on the targeted population. After all, it stands to reason that repeated exposure to traumatic events will make the affected public more fearful and more prone to stress-related disorders. In Israel, however, this does not appear to be the case. Despite experiencing numerous traumatic events during the second Intifada, which should, logically, cause progressively more psychological damage, the rate of PTSD symptoms among the Israeli population remained at a fairly low level (Bleich et al., 2003: 10). This was the case despite the fact that 60 percent of Israelis believed that their lives were in danger, and 68 percent believed the same about the lives of their family and friends (Bleich et al., 2003: 9).

The explanation for this lies in what is known as the accommodation effect (Kirschenbaum, 2005: 15). The accommodation effect means that the amount of stress created by recurring traumatic events actually decreases (Bleich et al., 2003: 10). As terrorism becomes a regular occurrence a process of habituation and desensitization may occur, and people become able to maintain a semblance of a normal life (Roy-Byrne, 2003). This suggests that people can learn to live with terrorism and psychologically cope with it. Further evidence of the ability of the Israeli population to cope with repeated exposure to terrorism is provided in a study of the effect of terrorism on the life satisfaction (happiness) of Israelis between 2002 and 2004 (Zussman et al., 2012). This study revealed that Palestinian terrorist attacks had a very limited effect upon the overall happiness of Israelis, and that despite living with a high level of terrorism 'Israelis were not particularly unsatisfied with their lives when compared to citizens of other, mostly terrorism-free, countries' (Zussman et al., 2012: 3).

The negligible impact that the campaign of terrorism from 2002–4 had upon the happiness of Israelis suggests that the psychological effects of terrorism should not be overstated. While they can be severe, they are generally short-lived. Despite experiencing fear, anxiety and stress in the aftermath of a terrorist attack, and even suffering from PTSD, over time most people recover well and are soon able to function normally again (at least within a matter of months).[3] Even repeated exposure to terrorism, as Israelis experienced during the second Intifada, does not have devastating psychological consequences upon a population. To be sure, there is some evidence to suggest that chronic exposure to terrorism is more psychologically harmful than the experience of a single terrorist attack (such as 9/11) (Hobfoll et al., 2009; Besser and Neria, 2009), but even in this extreme case people demonstrate a great deal of psychological resilience.

Economic effects

The economic effects of terrorism can be broken down into its direct costs, associated with the destruction caused by an act of terrorism, and its indirect costs, which affect nearly every aspect of a targeted state's economy. The most direct economic effect of a terrorist attack is the damage caused to life and property at the site of the attack. As an example, a suicide attack in a supermarket would cause direct economic damage in four different ways. First, it would damage the infrastructure of the building and destroy products. While the costs of rebuilding or repairing the building and restocking goods might be significant to the store in question, they do not have any effect on the economy at large. Second, the supermarket would probably have to shut down, at least temporarily. This would also have no major impact upon the national economy. Even in a small country like Israel there are 470 supermarkets controlled by the main three supermarket chains, and damage to one of them is not going to affect Israel's economy. Third, if the terrorist attack killed people one must also take into account the lost lifetime earnings of each individual killed. Since the numbers of people killed in individual terrorist attacks are relatively few (compared with the amount of deaths in civil wars or inter-state conflicts) this is also an insignificant cost for the national economy. Fourth, if the terrorist attack results in many casualties then the wounded both lose earnings and need to pay for medical procedures (the cost to an economy does not change if the cost of medical procedures is borne by the wounded themselves or by their government), but this too has no real impact on the national economy. Thus, the direct economic impact of a terrorist attack is minimal. Even 9/11, the most devastating terrorist attack in modern history, had a direct cost of roughly US$27 billion (Morag, 2006). In comparison, World War II cost the US government over $15 trillion, when adjusted for inflation (Morag, 2006).

The indirect economic costs of terrorist attacks, however, are potentially more significant. The indirect economic effects of terrorism are many and varied, yet they are very difficult to accurately gauge. Terrorism can affect an economy in numerous ways. A long-running terrorist campaign can impact a state's GDP, as happened to Israel during the second Intifada (according to Ekstein and Tsiddon, 2003, in the 2000–3 period, terrorism was responsible for a 10 percent reduction in per-capita production in Israel). Israel's GDP growth slowed from an average of 5 percent in the two years prior to the Intifada to –0.8 percent in the first two years of the Intifada (Morag, 2006). Only in the fourth year of the Intifada did Israel's GDP growth rebound (Morag, 2006). A terrorist campaign can make an economy more unstable, which in turn increases risk in the economy. With higher risk and the same or slightly lower potential return, foreign direct investment (FDI) in the targeted country's economy can decline. Since foreign investors have a large choice of countries to invest in, any kind of uncertainty, even one resulting from minor terrorist acts, can lead to a drop in the inflow of foreign funds (Frey et al., 2004: 11). In Israel FDI dropped sharply from $5.01 billion in 2000 to $1.72 billion in 2002 before recovering to $3.7 billion in 2003 (Morag, 2006). Finally, the perceived risk of future terrorist attacks can lower confidence in the economy, which in turn affects consumer spending, an integral part of an economy (Morag, 2006: 499).

A country's tourism industry can be particularly hard hit by terrorism since tourist destinations are easily substituted, and dangerous ones usually become instantly unattractive to foreign tourists (Frey et al., 2004: 6). Even a small risk of terrorism leads potential tourists to travel elsewhere. Thus, the more reliant a country's economy is on tourism, the more it will be affected by terrorism. In Israel's case terrorism in the second Intifada had a significant impact on the country's tourist industry. The amount of foreign tourists in Israel declined from 2.7 million in 2000 to 718,000 in 2002 before recovering slightly to 1.25 million in 2004 (Morag, 2006). Yet since tourism is only responsible for about 1.5 percent of Israel's GDP, a decline in foreign tourists (who comprise roughly 30–35 percent of tourists in Israel) does not have a great effect on the overall health of the Israeli economy.

Ultimately, the economic effects of terrorism depend upon many factors. Significant economic costs are unlikely to be incurred as a result of a single terrorist attack, but a prolonged campaign of terrorism can negatively impact a country's GDP, especially in the case of a small country in which tourism is a large sector of the national economy (Abadie and Gardeazabal, 2003). Of course, relatively wealthy countries are more able to absorb the economist costs of terrorism than poorer countries, where any loss of national income can have immediate repercussions on the population's living standards. In Israel's case, while terrorism definitely hurt the Israeli economy during the second Intifada, it soon recovered and Israel's economic development continued.

Social effects

Whereas the economic impact of terrorism ranges from minimal to moderate, the same is not necessarily the case with the social impact of terrorism. The social effects of terrorism can be pronounced and far-reaching, influencing many different aspects of a society. The starting point for the impact of terrorism on a society is the effect that terrorist attacks have upon people's beliefs and attitudes; major events influence these (Sharvit et al., 2005: 3). Shavrit et al. explain that 'terror attacks are negative, threatening events. Considerable evidence from psychological studies has shown that negative information tends to be more closely attended, better remembered, and have a stronger impact on evaluations and judgments than positive information' (Sharvit et al., 2005: 4). Since terrorist attacks are events of a highly negative nature, they can lead to changes in people's beliefs and attitudes. One such belief concerns how people view other societies, especially the society to which the terrorists belong. In a situation of inter-group conflict, terrorist attacks increase negative beliefs about and hostile attitudes toward the group the terrorists claim to represent (Bar-Tal and Labin, 2001: 6).

A sense of victimhood is common in a society experiencing terrorism (Bar-Tal and Sharvit, 2004: 17). Civilians are not expected to be victims of political violence (whereas military casualties are expected); hence, a public feels victimized when it is the target of political violence (i.e. when it experiences terrorist attacks) (Mosher, 2005: 16). The more the civilian population is targeted, the more this sense of victimhood increases. This sense of victimization in turn leads to a delegitimization of the terrorists and the people they claim to represent. Consequently, the targeted society becomes unwilling or unable to consider the other side's grievances and objectives (Bar-Tal and Sharvit, 2004: 15). No longer is the opposing group believed to have rational objectives and/or justifiable grievances; instead, the target society's worst views become 'common sense', especially those concerning its propensity towards violence. For example, while 39 percent of Israeli Jewish respondents perceived Palestinians as violent in a 1997 survey, by the end of 2000 after the onset of the second Intifada this figure had risen to 68 percent of Israeli Jews (Bar-Tal and Sharvit, 2004: 16).

The threat of terrorism increases a group's reliance on stereotypes (Huddy et al., 2002: 486), leading to more negative stereotyping by members of the targeted society (Sharvit et al., 2005: 4). There have been numerous instances of this such as the rise of Islamophobia in the USA following the 9/11 attacks (Pedahzur, 2005: 185) and the increase in anti-Arab sentiments in Spain in the wake of the 2004 Madrid train bombings (Echebarria-Echabe and Fernandez-Guede, 2006: 263). Likewise, in Israel during the second Intifada, Israelis held extremely negative stereotypes of Palestinians, viewing them as dishonest, violent, and having little regard for human life (Bar-Tal and Sharvit, 2004: 2).

Another major social effect of terrorism is a rise in ethnocentrism and xenophobia as a group increases its solidarity in the face of violence (Huddy et al., 2002: 486). Hence, identification with and support for the in-group rises as a result of terrorism, while identification with and support for any out-group decreases. This was apparent in Russia in the wake of terrorist attacks carried out by Chechen militants, when ethnic Russian identity became more salient, while xenophobia rose (Pedahzur, 2005: 184). This also took place in the USA in the aftermath of 9/11, when there was a surge of patriotic sentiment (evident, for instance, in the numerous American flags that adorned windows in New York City – a place where such overt displays of American patriotism are generally less common than elsewhere in the country). So too in Israel during the second Intifada, when repeated Palestinian terrorist attacks led to a renewed sense of national unity among Israeli Jews. A public opinion survey taken in March 2002, for example, posed the question: 'In your opinion have recent events, including terrorist attacks and operation "Defensive Shield," strengthened or weakened the sense of national unity in the Israeli-Jewish public?' Eighty-six percent of Israeli Jewish respondents answered that the events strengthened national unity (Hermann, 2002). As one Israeli commentator put it: 'Israeli (Jewish) society in Israel has returned to a state of cohesiveness' (Landau, 2001).

While Israeli Jews experienced a renewed sense of solidarity in the face of the wave of Palestinian terrorism unleashed in the second Intifada, Arab citizens of Israel became the object of intensified suspicion and hostility (Arian, 2003). Israeli Arabs were increasingly perceived as a security threat and a potential 'fifth column' in Israel's conflict with the Palestinians (Rouhana and Sultany, 2003). As more and more Israeli Jews came to view Israeli Arabs as the enemy (because of their general identification with and support for Palestinians in the West Bank and Gaza), popular support increased for policies that would promote their voluntary emigration or even force them to leave Israel. In one survey in 2003, for example, 57 percent of Israeli Jews expressed support for the government encouraging the emigration of Arabs from Israel, and 33 percent favored their expulsion (Arian, 2003: 30). Growing intolerance of Israeli Arabs was evident not only in social attitudes but in government legislation aimed at them. For example, the Knesset (the Israeli parliament) passed a bill in 2002 that curtailed the freedom of expression of Arab political parties and Knesset members by allowing the Central Elections Committee to ban parties and individuals that supported (in action or speech) 'the armed struggle of enemy states or terror organizations' against the State of Israel (Yiftachel, 2002: 40–1). Another law passed on 22 July 2002 lifted the parliamentary immunity of Knesset members who violated this restriction, thereby allowing them to be legally prosecuted.

Just as Muslims in the USA and Europe have complained about suffering from intolerance, harassment, and discrimination in the aftermath of recent terrorist attacks (most notably 9/11) so have Arabs in Israel during the second Intifada. Although official and unofficial discrimination against Israeli Arabs long predates the second Intifada and cannot simply be attributed to Palestinian terrorism, there is evidence that Palestinian terrorism during the second Intifada did increase discrimination against Arabs in the Israeli labor market (Miaari et al., 2007). More generally, Palestinian terrorist attacks increased anti-Arab attitudes within Israeli-Jewish society, the most blatant expressions of which were the calls of 'Death to Arabs' in soccer stadiums and at the sites of terrorist attacks, and in slogans like 'No Arabs – No Terror Attacks' appearing in graffiti and on car-bumper stickers (Shamir, 2006). Undoubtedly, Palestinian terrorism exacerbated the already-tense relationship between the Jewish and Arab communities in Israel.

Beyond these specific effects of Palestinian terrorism on Israeli society are the less obvious but no less real social repercussions of persistent political violence. In Israel's case it has been argued that the stress that terrorism creates manifests itself in a rise in violent crimes (homicide and robbery) and a general 'brutalization of Israeli society' (Landau, 2003). The fact that criminal homicide in Israel increased by 28 percent during 2000–1 (i.e. from the year before to the year after the beginning of second Intifada) and robberies increased by 11 percent offers some evidence – though by no means conclusive – to support this argument (Landau, 2003). Although it is difficult, if not impossible, to prove that a causal connection exists between terrorist attacks and societal violence, further support for this linkage comes from the discovery by scientists of a positive relationship between stress and aggression (American Psychological Association, 2004). Aggressive social behavior in Israel may, therefore, be linked to the high threat of terrorism Israelis face.

Political effects

The extensive social effects of terrorism described above often have political implications. The unifying effect that terrorism had upon Israeli-Jewish society during the second Intifada is typical of what is known as the rally-'round-the-flag syndrome, which is common to societies experiencing terrorism (Pedahzur, 2005: 184). The syndrome generally leads to a muting of public criticism of the government and its policies. This public reaction to terrorism is also in line with system-justification theory, according to which threats increase social conservatism (the desire to defend and maintain the status quo). The role that terrorism can play in strengthening conservatism was demonstrated in a study that compared Spanish attitudes before and after the Madrid train bombings, which found that the bombings increased adherence to conservative values (Echebarria-Echabe and Fernandez-Guede, 2006: 263).

In some cases the political effects of terrorism are clear-cut and pronounced, but often they can be difficult to assess accurately because specific political outcomes cannot be causally linked to terrorism, owing to the multiplicity of potential causes. A government's policy or a particular political decision may be the result of any number of factors, and can rarely be definitively attributed only to a terrorist attack or series of attacks. Take the case of the Sharon government's adoption of the policy of disengagement, which brought about the complete withdrawal of Israeli settlers and soldiers from the Gaza Strip in September 2005. Was this policy the result of Palestinian terrorist attacks, as many Palestinians at the time believed (Associated Press, 2005)? Even if Palestinian terrorism was a factor, it was certainly only one of a number of reasons behind the Sharon government decision to unilaterally withdraw from Gaza (Rynhold and Waxman, 2008).

TEXTBOX 6   CASE STUDY: THE YESHA (EXTREMIST SETTLER GROUPS OF JUDEA, SAMARIA AND GAZA)

The main groups include the Hilltop Youth and its offshoot, Bat Ayin, the most structured and documented of the groups. Most violence, however, remains unclaimed by any group.

Areas of operation

West Bank: Bethlehem, Hebron, Jenin, Jerusalem, Nablus, Qalqilya, Ramallah, Salfit, Tubas and Tulkarem.

Roots

Violent settler groups emerged from the wider settler movement. The movement arose from the shifting geographic boundaries and political landscape after the Israeli victory in the Six Day War in 1967 and the annexation of the West Bank, the Gaza Strip and East Jerusalem by Israeli forces that followed.

Ideological framework

The roots of the settler-movement ideology are found in religious Zionism, which emerged in the aftermath of the 1967 war. The Israeli victory, 'against all odds', was taken as a sign from God of 'messianic redemption', as Jews began to return to their Biblical homeland. Settler groups are often pitted against the state, whose views of settlement in the West Bank are often incongruent with the views of settler groups.

  The enlargement of the settler population and the geographic displacement of Palestinians have created significant friction between settlers and the indigenous Palestinian population. This in turn has created militant settler groups such as the Hilltop Youth who seek both to reduce the amount of land currently held by Palestinians and also to limit the extent to which the Israeli government can influence their objective.

Tactics

The main acts of violence are typically employed during the olive-harvest season, where shootings, arson attacks, the destruction of property, stone throwing and physical assaults are common. The media has dubbed these acts of violence as price-tag attacks. Jewish settlers perpetrate these attacks either when

(Continued)

(Continued)

they are removed from an area designated for Palestinian habitation by the Israeli security forces, or when settlers believe that Palestinians have harmed Israeli property or persons. Settlers also commonly graffiti areas with messages relating to a local conflict, affixing the term price tag to the end of the message. This price-tag addition differentiates these attacks from conventional settler violence and associates them with groups such as the Hilltop Youth and the Yesha. The Hilltop Youth and the Yesha are also willing to target Israeli security personnel and prominent settler leaders. The willingness to employ violence against the state and fellow settlers distinguishes these groups from other settlers, groups that attack Palestinians in order to annex further territory. Between 2007 and 2011 violence directly attributable to settlers has increased by 315 per cent.

While the political impact of terrorism is often hard to pinpoint, it can hardly be doubted that terrorism has political effects and also influences the political process, at least in democratic and partially democratic states. The most obvious way in which terrorism can influence the political process is by bringing about changes in public opinion, which governments then tend to take into account when formulating their policies (Shamir, 2007). It can be very hard for governments to resist the pressure from public opinion for a strong reaction in the wake of a terrorist attack. For an elected policymaker the political costs of underreacting to a terrorist attack are always higher than the political costs of overreacting. The failure to prevent future attacks due to inaction can be fatal to a politician's career, while failing to prevent them after having taken strong measures can be justified as having done everything possible (Ignatieff, 2005).

The impact of terrorism on public opinion, however, is not as straightforward or predictable as one might imagine. There is no uniform public response to a terrorist attack. Numerous factors affect how a public responds to a terrorist attack, such as the nature and scale of the terrorist attack, and the context in which it occurs. Moreover, different groups within the general public respond in different ways to a terrorist attack. People with different political orientations are likely to have different responses since existing political orientations serve as a mechanism through which new information is received and processed (Sharvit et al., 2005). Nor do terrorist attacks necessarily change people's political opinions. The greater a person's confidence in their views, the less likely they are to change as a result of a major event (Petty and Krosnick, 1995, cited in Sharvit et al., 2005). Finally, people's views are more likely to be influenced by a terrorist attack when it receives a lot of media coverage, since this serves to increase its perceived importance (Petty and Krosnick, 1995, cited in Sharvit et al., 2005).

In Israel's case Palestinian terrorism during the second Intifada definitely had an impact on Israeli public opinion concerning the conflict with the Palestinians and the prospects for peace with them (although, of course, it was not the only factor affecting Israeli public opinion). Prior to the second Intifada, while the Oslo peace process was ongoing, a large majority of the Israeli public was optimistic about the possibility of achieving peace with the Palestinians (according to one survey in 1999 68 percent of Israeli Jews believed that peace between Israel and the Palestinians would be achieved within three years) (Bar-Tal and Sharvit, 2004: 18). Israeli hopes for peace were dashed by the collapse of the peace process and especially the outbreak of the second Intifada. The surge of Palestinian terrorist attacks in the years 2001–4 contributed to a significant change in Israeli-Jewish beliefs about Palestinian intentions and the prospects for peace. Whereas in 1999 less than 50 percent of Israeli Jews thought that the Arabs wanted to conquer the State of Israel, in 2002 this number had risen to 68 percent, and by 2004 it reached 74 percent (Bar-Tal and Sharvit, 2004: 14).

Palestinian terrorism helped convince Israeli Jews that, in the oft-repeated phrase first used by their Prime Minister, Ehud Barak, they had 'no partner for peace'. Although a majority consistently continued to support a two-state solution to the Israeli–Palestinian conflict, there was little hope that such a solution could be reached in the foreseeable future. In a March 2001 survey, for instance, 72 percent of Israeli Jews thought that the Palestinian Authority (PA) was not interested in a peace treaty with Israel (Peace Index Survey, 2001). Similarly, in a 2002 survey 68 percent of Israelis thought that it was impossible to reach a peace agreement with the Palestinians, and only 26 percent thought that signing peace treaties would mean an end to the Arab–Israeli conflict (compared to 30 percent in 2001, 45 percent in 2000, and 67 percent in 1999) (Arian, 2002: 10).

Accompanying the change in Israeli views of the Palestinians, and the possibility of achieving peace with them, was greater public support for the use of more aggressive military measures against the Palestinians and less support for continuing peace negotiations. Prime Minister Barak's premiership became a casualty of this change in Israeli public opinion. He was attacked by his political opponents on the right for not responding to the Intifada with the force necessary to quell it (slogans like 'Let the IDF win' and 'Barak is humiliating Israel' became popular) at the same time as he was accused abroad (and by some in Israel) of excessive use of force against the Palestinians. Increasingly unpopular with the Israeli public, Barak eventually suffered a massive defeat in the February 2001 election for prime minister at the hands of right-wing Likud party leader Ariel Sharon. Disillusioned with the Oslo peace process and convinced of the futility of further negotiations with the Palestinians (at least with its current leadership), the Israeli public elected a strong, hard-line leader who they hoped could bring them greater security (by implementing a policy of severe military retaliation for Palestinian terrorist attacks).

Palestinian terrorism during the second Intifada clearly affected the political preferences of the Israeli electorate (Berrebi and Klor, 2008). Sharon's resounding victory in the 2001 election was one indication of this effect. Another was the Likud party's decisive win in the 2003 Knesset elections, doubling the number of its seats in parliament (from 19 to 38), while the rival center-left Labor party lost seven seats (dropping from 26 to 19). Not only did Palestinian terrorism boost the electoral appeal of the political right in Israel (Berrebi and Klor, 2008); it also helped to bring about a rightward shift in the political positions of the Israeli public. In general, more Israelis identified themselves as right-wing and fewer as left-wing (Shamir, 2007). On the specific issue of land for peace (that is, the idea of returning territories in exchange for peace), Israeli-Jewish support dropped from 50 percent in 2000 to only 37 percent in 2002 (Ben Meir and Bagno-Moldavsky, 2010: 75–6). This shift to the right was also evident in the increased number of Israeli Jews opposed to removing any Jewish settlements in the event of a peace agreement – a 10 percent increase in just one year from 2000–1 (from 26 percent to 36 percent of Israeli Jews) (Ben Meir and Bagno-Moldavsky, 2010: 77). Nevertheless, these changes in Israeli-Jewish public opinion were not lasting – support for the principle of land for peace gradually rose after 2002 as the level of violence decreased, reaching 48 percent in 2005 at the end of the second Intifada (2010: 74–5). Likewise, opposition to the removal of Jewish settlements also declined after 2002 (2010: 77). This suggests that Palestinian terrorism only had a temporary impact on the political views of Israeli Jews (2010: 83). It initially had a pronounced effect on Israeli-Jewish public opinion, but gradually this effect lessened over time.

Although Palestinian terrorism only had a short-term impact on Israeli-Jewish political opinion (concerning things like their willingness to compromise for the sake of peace, and their positions regarding a permanent solution to the conflict with the Palestinians), it had a major impact on their attitudes towards the use of force against Palestinians. Israeli Jews became much more militant and 'hawkish'. Terrorist attacks increased Israeli public support for strong military actions. The militancy of Israelis rose during periods when there was an upsurge in terrorism, and declined in periods of relative quiet (Canetti-Nisim, 2005). The rise in militant attitudes among Israelis was clearly apparent during the early years of Sharon's tenure as prime minister at the height of the second Intifada. Angry and embittered by the seemingly endless series of gruesome Palestinian suicide bombings inside Israel, the vast majority of the Israeli public staunchly supported the Sharon government's offensive military measures against the Palestinians. In 2001, for instance, 89 percent of Israeli Jews supported the Sharon government's policy of 'targeted assassinations' of Palestinian militants involved in terrorism against Israel; the following year the number was 90 percent; and in 2003 it had risen to 92 percent (Arian, 2003). The overwhelming public support for Prime Minister Sharon's tough policies towards the Palestinians revealed the emergence of a new national consensus in Israel. According to Ephraim Yuchtman-Yaar: 'This consensus is reflected in widespread mistrust of the Palestinians' commitment to make peace with Israel, and in the common conviction that so long as Palestinian terror continues, Israel must resort to arms in order to protect the lives of its citizens' (Yuchtman-Yaar, 2002: 23). Palestinian terrorism undoubtedly played a role in creating this new national consensus in Israel.

The powerful influence that Palestinian terrorist attacks could have upon Israeli public opinion and consequently Israeli government policy toward the conflict with the Palestinians during the second Intifada was most evident in the spring of 2002. March 2002 was the bloodiest month of the second Intifada for Israelis. During that month Palestinian suicide-bombing attacks killed at least 80 Israeli civilians and wounded or maimed some 420 people (Human Rights Watch, 2002). In one week alone Palestinian suicide bombers struck at a restaurant in Haifa, a Jerusalem supermarket, a café in Tel Aviv, and a hotel in Netanya, the latter during a meal for the Jewish holiday of Passover (this last attack killed 30 people and wounded over 140). This devastating series of suicide bombings unleashed a wave of public shock, fear, and anger. The militancy of the Israeli public reached new heights. In a poll taken in April 2002 71 percent of Israeli Jews agreed with the statement 'Every military action that Israel initiates is justified', and 80 percent believed that 'All means are justified in Israel's war against terror' (Canetti-Nisim, 2005: 109). It was in this climate of opinion that the Sharon government initiated two large-scale military operations in the West Bank (Operations Defensive Shield and Determined Path). These military offensives into the West Bank – in which Israel's military reoccupied large parts of the territory – received overwhelming support from the Israeli public (Bar-Tal and Sharvit, 2004).

The massive Israeli public support for the construction of a security barrier between the West Bank and Israel (Arian, 2003) was also a direct result of Palestinian terrorism during the second Intifada, as Israelis became desperate to find a way to stem the relentless tide of Palestinian suicide-bombing attacks. The idea of building a wall or fence to separate Israel from the Palestinian territories was not new, but it was Palestinian terrorist attacks that propelled the idea to the top of the political agenda. In October 2001 a new political movement called Fence for Life emerged with the aim of increasing public support for a security barrier (Rudge, 2001). The Israeli public enthusiastically embraced the idea of a security barrier between the West Bank and Israel. Faced with a steadily mounting civilian death toll from suicide-bombing attacks, Israelis fervently hoped that such a barrier would at least greatly reduce the chances of successful suicide attacks by making it much harder for suicide bombers to enter Israel (not only would there be a high concrete wall or electrified fence for them to surmount, but also ditches, razor wire, electronic motion sensors, and armed guard posts). Growing public support for a security barrier eventually led the Sharon government in June 2002 to adopt the idea and announce its plans to begin building the barrier, despite Prime Minister Sharon's initial opposition (Ben-Aroya, 2002).

Conclusion

This article has discussed the different effects of terrorism and described how many of these effects occurred in Israel as a result of Palestinian terrorist attacks during the second Intifada. In doing so it has sought to emphasize the many effects of terrorism – psychological, economic, social, and political. To varying degrees terrorism can affect the psychological health and well-being of a country's population, its economy, its societal beliefs and attitudes, and its politics. These effects can range from minimal to severe, depending on a host of other factors. As discussed here, Palestinian terrorism during the second Intifada had a profound and far-reaching impact upon Israeli society. The frequency of terrorist attacks, especially at the height of the second Intifada in 2002–3, spread fear and anxiety among Israelis, hurt the Israeli economy, affected social attitudes and intra-societal relations, and influenced not only Israeli public opinion and domestic politics but also the actions and policies of Israeli governments.

Notes

1 For a full version of this essay see Waxman, 2011.
2 According to the Anxiety Disorders Association of America, PTSD is 'a condition that results from experiencing or witnessing an unusually distressing event; symptoms range from repeatedly reliving the trauma, such as in dreams or flashbacks, to general emotional numbness, which often causes sufferers to withdraw from family and friends' (Anxiety Disorders Association of America).
3 Two recent studies have demonstrated the psychological resilience of populations in the aftermath of terrorist attacks: Bonanno et al., 2006, and Miguel-Tobal et al., 2006.

References

Abadie, A. and Gardeazabal, J. (2003) 'The Economic Cost of Conflict: A Case Study of the Basque Country,' *American Economic Review* 93: 113–32.

American Psychological Association (2004), 'Stress and Aggression Reinforce Each Other at the Biological Level,' 5 October, http://biopsychiatry.com/aggression/index.html (Accessed 4 March 2008).

Anxiety Disorders Association of America (n.d.) http://www.adaa.org/gettinghelp/glossary.asp. (Accessed 4 March 2008).

Arian, A. (1999) *Security Threatened: Surveying Israeli Opinion on Peace and War* (New York: Cambridge University Press).

Arian, A. (2002) *Israeli Public Opinion on National Security 2002* (Tel Aviv: Jaffee Center for Strategic Studies), 10, 16–17.

Arian, A. (2003) *Israeli Public Opinion on National Security 2004* (Tel Aviv: Jaffee Center for Strategic Studies).

Associated Press (2005) 'Palestinians Believe Armed Struggle Led to Pullout,' 12 September.

Bar-Tal, D. and Labin, D. (2001) 'The Effect of a Major Event on Stereotyping: Terrorist Attacks in Israel and Israeli Adolescents' Perceptions of Palestinians, Jordanians and Arabs,' *European Journal of Social Psychology* 31, no. 3: 265–80.

Bar-Tal, D. and Sharvit, K. (2004) 'Psychological Foundations of Israeli Jews' Reactions to Al Aqsa Intifada: The Role of the Threatening Transitional Context,' in V. M. Esses and R. Vernon, eds, *Explaining the Breakdown of Ethnic Relations: Why Neighbors Kill* (Oxford: Wiley-Blackwell, 2008), 147–170.

Ben-Aroya, A. (2002) 'Sharon: The Separation Fence is a Populist Idea,' *Haaretz*, 12 April.

Ben Meir, Y. and Bagno-Moldavsky, O. (2010) 'The Second Intifada and Israeli Public Opinion,' *Strategic Assessment* 13, no. 3: 75–6.

Berrebi, C. and Klor, E. F. (2008) 'Are Voters Sensitive to Terrorism? Direct Evidence from the Israeli Electorate,' *American Political Science Review* 102, no. 3: 279–301.

Besser, A. and Neria, Y. (2009) 'PTSD Symptoms, Satisfaction with Life, and Prejudicial Attitudes toward the Adversary among Israeli Civilians Exposed to Ongoing Missile Attacks,' *Journal of Traumatic Stress* 22, no 4: 269–75.

Bleich, A., Gelkopf, M. and Solomon, Z. (2003) 'Exposure to Terrorism, Stress-related Mental-health Symptoms, and Coping Behaviors among a Nationally Representative Sample in Israel,' *Journal of the American Medical Association* 290, no. 5: 612–20.

Bleich, A., Gelkopf, M., Melamed, Y., and Solomon, Z. (2006) 'Mental Health and Resiliency following 44 Months of Terrorism: A Survey of an Israeli National Representative Sample,' *BMC Med* 4, http://www.pubmedcentral.nih.gov/articlerender.fcgi?artid=1560155. Accessed 22 March 2008.

Bonanno, G. A., Galea, S., Bucciarelli, A., and Vla, D. (2006) 'Psychological Resilience After Disaster: New York City in the Aftermath of the September 11th Terrorist Attack,' *Psychological Science* 17, no. 3: 181–86.

Canetti-Nisim, D. (2005) 'Militant Attitudes among Israelis throughout the al-Aqsa Intifada,' *Palestine-Israel Journal* 11, nos. 3-4: 104–11.

Crenshaw, M. (1983) 'Introduction: Reflection on the Effects of Terrorism,' in Martha Crenshaw, ed., *Terrorism, Legitimacy and Power: The Consequences of Political Violence* (Middletown, CT: Wesleyan University Press), 1–37.

Echebarria-Echabe, A. and Fernandez-Guede, E. (2006) 'Effects of Terrorism on Attitudes and Ideological Orientation,' *European Journal of Social Psychology* 36: 259–65.

Eckstein, Z. and Tsiddon, D. (2004) 'Macroeconomic Consequences of Terror: Theory and the Case of Israel,' *Journal of Monetary Economics* 51, no. 5: 971–1002.

Eldor, R. and Melnick, R. (2004) 'Financial Markets and Terrorism,' *European Journal of Political Economy* 20, no. 2: 367–86.

Eshel, D. (2003) 'Post-traumatic Stress in Emergency Rescue Teams: The Israeli Experience,' *Journal of Homeland Security* 3, no. 3: 1–17.

Frey, B. S., Luechinger, S., and Stutzer, A. (2004) 'Calculating Tragedy: Assessing the Costs of Terrorism,' Cesifo Working Paper no. 1341.

Ganor, B. (2002) 'Israel's Counter-terrorism Policy 1983–1999: Efficacy versus Liberal Democratic Values,' unpublished PhD dissertation, Hebrew University.

Hermann, T. (2002) 'Tactical Hawks, Strategic Doves: The Positions of the Jewish Public in Israel on the Israeli-Palestinian Conflict,' *Strategic Assessment*, 5, no. 2.

Hobfoll, S. E., Canetti-Nisim, D., Johnson, R.J., Palmieri, P.A., Varley, J.D. and Galea, S. (2009) 'Trajectories of Resilience, Resistance, and Distress During Ongoing Terrorism: The Case of Jews and Arabs in Israel,' *Journal of Consulting and Clinical Psychology* 77, no. 1: 138–48.

Hoffman, B. (2006) *Inside Terrorism* (New York: Columbia University Press).

Huddy, L., Feldman, S., Capelos, T., and Provost, C. (2002) 'The Consequences of Terrorism: Disentangling the Effects of Personal and National Threat,' *Political Psychology* 23, no. 3: 485–509.

Human Rights Watch (2002) 'Erased in a Moment: Suicide Bombing Attacks Against Israeli Civilians,' October 2002.

Ignatieff, M. (2005) *The Lesser Evil: Political Ethics in an Age of Terror* (Edinburgh: Edinburgh University Press).

Jost, J. T., Banaji, M. R., and Nosek, B. A. (2004) 'A Decade of System Justification Theory: Accumulated Evidence of Conscious and Unconscious Bolstering of the Status Quo,' *Political Psychology* 25, no. 6: 881–917.

Kirschenbaum, A. (2005) 'Surviving Terror Threats through Adaptive Behaviors: The Israeli Experience,' paper presented at the European Sociological Association Conference, Torun, Poland, 9-12 September.

Landau, D. (2001) 'Carpe Diem,' *Haaretz*, 6 April.

Landau, S. (2003) 'Societal Costs of Political Violence: The Israeli Experience,' *Palestine-Israel Journal* 10, no. 1: 28–35.

Merari, A. and Friedland, N. (1980) *Memorandum: Public Positions on Terrorism*, The Center for Strategic Studies, Tel Aviv [Hebrew].

Miaari, S., Zussman, A., and Zussman, N. (2007) 'Labor Market Segregation in the Shadow of Conflict,' unpublished manuscript, Hebrew University.

Miguel-Tobal, J. J., Cano-Vindel, A., Gonzalez-Ordi, H. and Iruarrizaga, I. (2006) 'PTSD and Depression after the Madrid March 11 Train Bombings,' *Journal of Traumatic Stress* 19, no. 1: 69–80.

Morag, N. (2006) 'The Economic and Social Effects of Intensive Terrorism: Israel 2000-2004,' *Middle East Review of International Affairs* 10, no. 3: 120–141.

Mosher, K. (2005) 'Public Interpretations and Reactions to Terror Related Casualties: The Effects of Numbers and Identities,' paper presented at the annual meeting of the International Studies Association, Hawaii.

Peace Index Survey (2001) The Peace Index: December 2014 http://www.peaceindex.org/defaultEng.aspx

Pedahzur, A. (2005) *Suicide Terrorism* (Cambridge: Polity Press).

Petty, R. E. and Krosnick, J. A. eds., (1995), *Attitude Strength: Antecedents and Consequences* (Hillsdale, NJ: Lawrence Erlbaum Associates).

Rouhana, N. and Sultany, N. (2003) 'Redrawing the Boundaries of Citizenship: Israel's New Hegemony,' *Journal of Palestine Studies* 33, no. 1: 15.

Roy-Byrne, P. (2003) 'Effects of Terror and Violence Vary by Culture,' *Journal Watch Psychiatry*, 8 October.

Rudge, D. (2001) 'New Movement Calls for Unilateral Separation from Palestinians,' *The Jerusalem Post*, 15 October.

Rynhold, J. and Waxman, D. (2008) 'Ideological Change and Israel's Disengagement from Gaza,' *Political Science Quarterly* 123, no. 1: 1–27.

Shamir, S. (2006) 'The Arabs in Israel – Two Years after the Or Commission Report,' Tel Aviv University, Konrad Adenauer Program for Jewish-Arab Cooperation.

Shamir, J. (2007) *Public Opinion in the Israeli-Palestinian Conflict: From Geneva to Disengagement to Kadima and Hamas* (Washington, DC: United States Institute of Peace).

Sharvit, K., Bar-Tal, D., Gurevich, R., Raviv, A. (2005) 'Jewish-Israeli Attitudes Regarding Peace in the Aftermath of Terror Attacks: The Moderating Role of Political Worldview and Context,' paper presented at the annual meeting of the Israeli Sociological Society, Tel-Hai, Israel.

Statement by Prime Minister Ehud Barak (200) Jerusalem, 7 October, http://www.mfa.gov.il/MFA/Government/Speeches+by+Israeli+leaders/2000/Statement+by+Prime+Minister+Ehud+Barak+-+07-Oct-20.htm (Accessed 18 March 2008).

Waxman, D. (2011) 'Living with Terror, Not Living in Terror: The Impact of Chronic Terrorism on Israeli Society,' *Perspectives in Terrorism* 5: 5–6.

Yiftachel, O. (2002) 'The Shrinking Space of Citizenship: Ethnocratic Politics in Israel,' *Middle East Report*, no. 223: 40–1.

Yuchtman-Yaar, E. (2002) 'The Oslo Process and Israeli-Jewish Public: A Story of Disappointment?', *Israel Studies Forum* 18, no. 1: 11–25.

Zussman, A., Zussman, N., and Romanov, D. (2012) 'Does Terrorism Demoralize? Evidence from Israel,' *Economica* 79, no. 313: 183–198.

PART 3
HOW TERRORISM ENDS

Part 3 considers how terrorism campaigns come to an end, whether through negotiations, internal dissent, policing and prisons or military means. Chapter 8 provides a contextual overview by outlining how terrorist groups in the past have ended, analysing which factors are more salient. It also discusses the extent to which the use of terrorism can be considered successful. Following on from this chapter's observation of peace negotiations, Chapter 9 analyses terrorism from a conflict-studies perspective; terrorist groups can often become spoilers in peace processes and can undermine attempts to combat terrorism through political engagement. Having explored the group level, Chapter 10 questions why individuals might leave terrorist groups and what approaches can be used to facilitate their disengagement. Essay 7 follows on from the discussion in the previous chapter, considering counterterrorism attempts to de-radicalize terrorists and examining the benefits of such a strategy from a societal perspective. Essay 8 discusses recent controversies stemming from the use of drones to combat terrorism and political violence.

8

HOW TERRORISM ENDS

SARAH MARSDEN

Approaching the question of how terrorism ends appears relatively straightforward as there are, after all, only a limited number of options. Either groups are destroyed by the military or counterterrorism efforts, they implode, they transition into mainstream politics, or, very rarely, they succeed and disband. However, as with many seemingly straightforward questions in terrorism studies, scratch the surface and we find more questions than answers. For example, we have only a limited understanding of the nature of the interaction between counterterrorism initiatives and factionalization; the differences between leadership and cadre outcomes; and the relationship between political and organizational outcomes. Even the best way of conceptualizing the outcomes of violent political groups is subject to debate. It is at the boundaries of the seemingly straightforward dichotomies that characterize much of the literature on how terrorism ends that some of the most interesting questions lie.

Our understanding of why and how terrorism ends is underdeveloped, both empirically and methodologically. Much of the literature takes an aggregate approach to describing how terrorism ends, rather than offering cogent explanations or setting out causal mechanisms that might tell us why particular outcomes come about. Similarly, our understanding of the effectiveness of counterterrorism efforts is demonstrably weak. There is, therefore, much left to learn about how and why terrorism ends. What follows reviews some of the main findings to date and looks forward to the questions that remain to be answered. We begin by looking at some of the ways in which the question of how terrorism ends has been approached in the literature, and go on to set out what we know about the main organizational outcomes of militant groups, before considering some of the precipitants of these outcomes. We will first look at external drivers, including the impact of different counterterrorism efforts, moving on to examine factors internal to groups, such as factionalization and burn-out, before reviewing some of the debates over whether terrorism is successful at achieving the political aims of its enactors.

Conceptualizing how terrorism ends

Before beginning our exploration of how terrorism ends, we need to first establish what it is we are seeking to explain. The end of terrorism can be understood as the cessation or dramatic decrease in the use of terroristic violence.[1] Groups may become incapable of using terrorism, choose to move away from violence, or their violence may come to be perceived as legitimate. For example, if a group gains political power their violence is no longer that of an illegitimate opponent but can instead be seen as the appropriate use of force to defend the people; alternatively, it may be interpreted as the repressive behavior of a brutal regime. Similarly, where the context changes, such that a campaign of terrorism evolves into an insurgency or civil war, violence may no longer be conceptualized as terrorism. Interpreting how to appropriately categorize violence is, of course, wrapped up in the thorny issue of defining terrorism, and is not something we will consider here. What is important to note, however, is that there are a number of paths away from terrorism, and these relate to capacity, coercion, agency, and position in the political context.[2]

A number of further dimensions are useful when approaching the question of how terrorism ends. Clark McCauley helpfully delineates between actors, actions and outcomes when conceptualizing how and why groups move away from terrorism (McCauley, 2011). Relevant actors include the militant group, its supporters and competitors, as well as state opponents, their sympathizers, and those in competition for state power. These actors may engage in a variety of actions that influence how terrorism ends. On the militant side, these relate to the degree of violence and its target, and the extent of political engagement, including developing alliances or engaging in negotiations. On the government side, a range of counterterrorism responses might be important, including target hardening, attacking militant groups, and reducing levels of support (through repression or incentivization), as well as negotiations and inducements for individual defection or group cessation. Finally, a range of outcomes can emerge from the interaction between actors and actions: militant groups may choose to desist from using terrorism, or the organization can break down, either due to a split or because of loss of support, members, or leadership, disabling the organization.

Using these three dimensions to conceptualize how terrorism ends brings valuable clarity. McCauley's approach delineates the actions that lead to particular outcomes, for example, differentiating between decapitation (action) and organizational disablement (outcome). Second, it draws a distinction between political outcomes (e.g. success) and organizational outcomes (e.g. disbandment, or a shift into politics). Finally, setting out actors, actions and outcomes highlights the dynamic and complex range of factors we need to be aware of, taking into account different levels of analysis and their interactions. Hence, whilst the focus of this chapter is on outcomes, it is vital to take into account the range of actors that affect outcomes, and the actions that precipitate them. In exploring this complexity what follows first establishes the organizational outcomes of militant groups, before going on to consider some of the actions that inform these outcomes.

How does terrorism end?

In setting out what we know about how terrorism ends we will rely on three major studies that have catalogued the outcomes of a large number of militant groups.

The first of these was carried out by Seth Jones and Martin Libicki (2008). Their study analysed 648 groups operating between 1968 and 2006. Of these only 10 percent ended because they had achieved their ultimate goals. The majority of militant groups ended by joining the political process, an outcome accounting for 43 percent of their sample. Other outcomes catalogued by Jones and Libicki were that 136 groups splintered into factions, a figure equating to 21 percent of groups in the RAND-MIPT database from which they drew their sample. The other major outcome was disruption by the police (40 percent), or, much less frequently, by military forces (7 percent). Jones and Libicki's account focuses most heavily on organizational outcomes, and less on the actions that brought them about, instead setting out the range of end games for violent oppositional groups.

The second, and perhaps most comprehensive, account of how terrorism ends is Audrey Kurth Cronin's book of the same name (Cronin, 2009). Cronin reaches a similar conclusion to Jones and Libicki regarding the extent to which militant groups achieve their ultimate objectives. Based on analysis of 457 groups active from 1968 onwards, only 4.4 percent fully achieved their aims, 2 percent achieved substantial concessions, with a further 6.4 percent managing to achieve limited strategic objectives. This means 87 percent of groups failed to achieve any of their primary aims. In addition to political success, the final outcomes of the groups in Cronin's study are categorized according to whether they were decapitated, by losing their leadership; reached a negotiated settlement; experienced repression resulting in defeat and elimination; transitioned to different forms of violence; or failed owing to group collapse or a loss of support. Exact figures for these various outcomes were not provided in Cronin's account, which focused most heavily on the impact of negotiations, the groups' lifespans, and the extent to which they achieved their political objectives. Although an important analysis of how terrorism ends, the categories of decapitation, negotiation, repression, transition, and failure conflate organizational and political outcomes and the actions that precipitate them, making it harder to develop clear causal accounts of what influences particular outcomes, although these are explored further in individual case studies.

The third and most recent of the major studies into the ultimate fate of militant groups, by Leonard Weinberg (2012), finds little to contradict Jones and Libicki or Cronin. Of the 268 groups Weinberg looked at, 40 percent ended through policing, 43 percent by politicization, 7 percent by military force, and 10 percent achieved victory. It is perhaps not surprising that Jones and Libicki and Weinberg reach exactly the same findings – displayed in Figure 8.1. Although they used different datasets, both studies are likely to be looking at a similar sample of groups, using a similar framework for interpreting outcomes, and, therefore, reaching similar conclusions. What is perhaps a more striking finding, across all three studies, is the abysmal failure of terrorism to achieve the political goals it was ostensibly employed to promote. On the basis of these analyses it is difficult to disagree with an earlier assessment by Ariel Merari (1993) which, using a different dataset, led him to conclude that 'the overwhelming majority of the many hundreds of terrorist groups which have existed in the second half of this century have failed miserably to attain their goal' (Merari, 1993: 384–5). We will return to this issue towards the end of

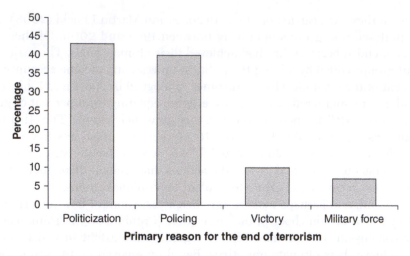

Figure 8.1 Primary reasons for how terrorism ends, drawn from Jones and Libicki (2008) and Weinberg (2012)

the chapter. For now it is enough to note that, according to the most comprehensive accounts of how terrorism ends, the majority of groups cease violence, either because they enter the political process, or as a result of policing.

Having laid out the broad sweep of organizational and political outcomes identified in the literature, we now turn our attention to some of the actions that have informed these outcomes. Clark McCauley delineates between internal factors impacting groups, for example related to membership and organization, and external factors, for example military offensives against the group (McCauley, 2011). Reflecting this approach, what follows describes some of the external reasons for why and how terrorism ends, before looking at internal causes for group dissolution or a cessation of violence. Our discussion concentrates on groups that have ended, rather than transitioned into other forms of opponent, such as political organizations or organized crime. Through the ensuing discussion it is important to remain aware that the distinctions between internal and external factors are employed more for the purposes of presentational clarity than to claim to represent an empirical 'truth' about how terrorism ends. Even though, as Weinberg helpfully emphasizes, analysts are generally looking for central tendencies rather than single factors (Weinberg, 2012), there are significant challenges in identifying the primary cause for a particular outcome. The reasons groups fail or move away from violence are complex, and intra- and extra-group factors are likely to interact in most cases.

External factors

In looking at some of the external factors that can inform how terrorism ends, we focus primarily on state actions. Although a number of external actors may impact how terrorism ends, including competition from other non-state groups, the primary external determinant of how terrorism ends is generally the state. There are a number of ways states may respond to terrorism that can be delineated along two continua. First, there is the level of force involved, from the most severe form of violence, including assassination, through to arrest, and, at the least forceful end of the spectrum, covert surveillance. Second, we can delineate counterterrorism operations based on the specificity of the tactic, determined by the number of people it affects, ranging from targeting militant leaders to widespread violence or surveillance affecting whole communities. For example, large-scale violent repression of those perceived to support a militant group is both the most forceful and least specific form of response, whereas intelligence gathering against named militant leaders is the least forceful and most specific.

The range of options available to states is obviously wide-ranging; we will focus on those counterterrorism tools most commonly discussed in the literature. Methods involving the use of force include repression and military operations against militant organizations, and decapitation, either through the killing or arrest of leaders. At the less forceful end of the counterterrorism spectrum we will examine counter-intelligence and law-enforcement options for responding to violent oppositional groups.

Repression

Given the disproportionate capacity for violence between state and non-state actors, it might appear that of all the possible counterterrorism responses repression is most likely to destroy militant groups and secure state control. However, using military force can have a range of effects that go beyond disrupting the group. These can include impacting the perceived legitimacy of the state, consolidating support for the militant organization, the substitution of one type of target for another, and provoking a violent backlash (Duyvesteyn, 2008). Despite this, repression has remained a well-used tool against violent opposition throughout history. Generally understood to include the threat or use of physical sanction against opponents, repression continues to be employed in the response to terrorism today.[3]

Cronin suggests a number of reasons why states respond to terrorism with violent repression: catharsis; assuaging domestic pressure to 'do something'; retributive 'justice'; deterrence; to demonstrate resolve, both to the home audience and to allies; and to destroy a group's capacity to act against the state (Cronin, 2009). Cronin describes a range of cases of state repression against militant groups, including Russia's move against Narodnaya Volya in the 1850s and Chechen separatists in the 1990s, Peru's violent repression of Sendero Luminoso, and Egypt's response to the Muslim Brotherhood (Cronin, 2009).

Empirical evidence suggests a number of dimensions of repression that are important to take into account when examining coercive force by states. These include the timing and the target of violence, the timeframe for assessing violent responses in the face of repression, and the extent to which state behavior accords with militant aims to provoke a disproportionate response. There are also a number of actors that can be involved in violence directed at oppositional groups. Although perhaps most commonly associated with military intervention, paramilitaries can also be involved in counterterrorism operations. The Autodefensas

Unidas de Colombia (AUC) famously received plentiful support from the Colombian government to fight the Fuerzas Armadas Revolucionarias de Colombia (FARC) (Mazzei, 2009). As well as being deployed domestically, as in Colombia, militaristic responses can be international in scope. The global war on terror is perhaps the most famous such operation, designed to destroy al-Qaeda and – as originally conceived – international terrorism anywhere in the world (Burke, 2011). Alternatively, the scale of deployment can be relatively limited, as was the case with the comparatively smaller-scale US air strikes against Libya in 1986, retaliating against bombings directed at US targets in Greece and Germany (Prunckun and Mohr, 1997).

TEXTBOX 7   CASE STUDY: THE FUERZAS ARMADAS REVOLUCIONARIAS DE COLOMBIA – EJÉRCITO DEL PUEBLO [THE REVOLUTIONARY ARMED FORCES OF COLOMBIA – PEOPLE'S ARMY] (FARC-EP/FARC)

Year formed

Originated in May 1964 as the military arm of the Colombian Communist Party. Formally recognized as a guerrilla army in 1966.

Area of operation

Colombia is a mountainous and tropical state with a highly dispersed population. In keeping with traditional guerrilla tactics the FARC's operations were originally restricted to the countryside and mountainous areas. Its core zones of operation are divided into seven 'blocs' across the country, with FARC-related violence occurring across and between these delineated areas.

By the 1980s the FARC began expanding its operations in the coca-rich departments of Caquetá, Meta, and the Magdalena Valley to begin extracting new sources of revenue from the drug trade. Involvement in the cocaine industry and their declining support base in the countryside has brought the FARC closer to the urban centres of Colombia, and since the 1990s they have sporadically attacked large towns and cities.

Ideological framework

Explicitly Revolutionary Socialist, with its doctrine largely focused on the protection of peasants' land from business and landowners, the equal distribution of Colombia's countryside to the peasants, and the rejection of the privatization of Colombia's natural resources. The social unrest and disorder that emerged from Colombia's bloodiest civil war, La Violencia (1948–58), provided the nascent Communist guerrilla movement with an opportunity to establish 'independent republics' in Colombia's political vacuums. However, once the war ended, the communists became the target of Colombia's major political parties, backed by the USA, who needed to reassert their control over the state. Since then the FARC has waged a guerrilla insurgency against the political and military institutions of Colombia.

Whilst the FARC continues to reassert its political position *vis-à-vis* land reform, its involvement in the drug trade has prompted debate as to whether the FARC's motivation has transitioned from political grievance to criminal greed. The killing and kidnapping of civilians who refuse to cooperate in coca growing has also besmirched their image as protectors of the peasant class. In the current peace talks with the Colombian government the key issue for the FARC has been land reform and the regulation, rather than prohibition, of coca cultivation.

Disengagement

To encourage the decline of the FARC the Colombian state has offered 'rehabilitation programmes' to members since the 1960s. However, these initiatives have failed to result in the collective disengagement of combatants, largely due to the guerrillas' mistrust of the government and fear of reprisals. Colombia's current rehabilitation programme provides disengaged combatants with political amnesty, healthcare and education – if they prove that they haven't participated in acts of terrorism or human-rights violations. Peace talks have gone as far as offering the FARC the chance to retain territory they already control, but these have failed and resulted in a surge in violence in 1999. The Colombian government is currently offering the FARC an opportunity to join the legal political process if they demobilize entirely.

More recently there have been increasing numbers of individual disengagements as a result of ideological disillusionment. Nonetheless, the Colombian government will continue to face difficulties in encouraging the impoverished younger members to disengage while the drug trade continues to be so lucrative for them.

Given these various dimensions of scope, target, timing, and measures of success, what do we know about the effectiveness of repressive tactics against violent opponents? Given that repression is rarely the only form of response states use when responding to terrorism, it is difficult to separate out the effect of repression from other forms of counterterrorist action. Omar Ashour, in a detailed account of how a number of Islamist movements moved away from terrorism, argues that repression plays an important part in the renunciation of violence (Ashour, 2009). In the case of Al-Gama'a al-Islamiyya (in Egypt), the role of repression was seen at two stages in the movement's history. Initially, it was important in the radicalization of individuals in the early days of opposition, and, latterly, long-term, more severe repression in prisons led to a change in attitude and ideology. The leadership reached the conclusion that the torture, stigma, discrimination, and ill health suffered by members and their families was unlikely if God was 'on their side' (Ashour, 2009: 100). This played a significant part in the de-radicalization of the movement.

In a similarly rigorous account, Mohammed Hafez uses the timing and target of repression to explain Islamist rebellions (Hafez, 2003). Distinguishing between preemptive and reactive, and indiscriminate and selective repression, Hafez finds that 'if state repression is reactive and indiscriminate, it will likely induce rebellion. If, on the other hand, state repression is preemptive and selective, it will likely deter mass rebellion' (Hafez, 2003: 77). Selective repression signals to supporters and sympathizers that only those at the core of the rebellion will be punished, and encourages latent supporters to avoid becoming too heavily involved. Indiscriminate repression leads those on the periphery to seek protection and those more heavily involved to harden their resolve. Further support for the importance of discrimination and the timing of military actions comes from Israel, where Efraim Benmelech and colleagues found that house demolitions targeting the families of suicide bombers resulted in fewer martyrdom operations, whilst preventative home demolitions saw a significant increase in the same (Benmelech et al., 2010). Similarly, Laura Dugan and Erica Chenoweth found that indiscriminate repressive actions against Palestinian militants led to an increase in terrorism, whilst indiscriminate conciliatory actions saw a decrease (Dugan and Chenoweth, 2012).

The timeframe by which any impact on militancy is judged is also important to take into account. For example, Walter Enders and Todd Sandler found that military retaliations against Libya by the USA in 1986 led to a short-term increase in attacks, but had little appreciable impact in the longer term (Enders and Sandler, 1993). Similarly, in an assessment of attacks in Israel between 1968 and 1989 Bryan Brophy-Baermann and John Conybeare found that only one major retaliation against Palestinian militants had any effect on reducing the number of terrorist attacks, the remainder having no observable impact (Brophy-Baermann and Conybeare, 1994).

Taking account of the empirical record assessing repressive and militaristic responses to terrorism, several points are worth underlining. The first is that states respond to terrorism using military force for a variety of reasons, and whilst decreasing the number of attacks may be an important measure – and is the one that has primarily been assessed in the literature – it is not the only issue we should take into account. Other metrics, such as assuaging domestic pressure, or demonstrating resolve to a wider audience, are also relevant when assessing the success or failure of military retaliation against terrorism. Secondly, looking at a tactic as broad as repression demands a careful approach, taking account of a number of important dimensions. The timing of an operation is relevant, as is the level of discrimination employed. Similarly, the timeframe by which we assess the effect of any military action needs to be considered. Finally, it is vital to assess how repressive responses interact with other forms of counterterrorism in order to develop a clearer account of its effects and the extent to which they accord with the aims of those instigating the operation.

Decapitation

Assassinating or capturing leaders, or core members of militant groups, has a long history in statecraft. The logic is simple: remove those who provide ideological or strategic leadership and the organization will be weaker, with a greater chance of failing entirely, or, at the very least, posing less of a threat. It is perhaps not difficult to see the appeal of targeted killing – it is more proportionate than the types of repressive military intervention we have just discussed; it is less resource intensive, more discriminatory; and it minimizes the number of civilians and military personnel likely to be killed or injured. It is, therefore, often seen as the 'least–bad option' (David, 2002). It certainly appears to be an attractive strategy for states; since the ban on assassinations by the USA was lifted following 9/11, targeted killing has become a central part of US counterterrorism strategy, with thousands killed in drone strikes in recent years, primarily in Pakistan, Yemen, and Somalia.[4] However, important ethical and legal challenges face advocates of targeted killings, as well as the need to consider the potential impact on relations between states, and the possibility of bolstering support for militant groups when civilians are mistakenly killed (Plaw, 2008). Whilst these debates are played out, one of the questions determining the utility of attempting to 'decapitate' organizations is its efficacy.

Efforts to assess the effectiveness of targeted killing as a strategy face significant challenges. The mechanism by which targeted killings may work to reduce the likelihood of terrorism is uncertain and differs across cases; as Cronin suggests, 'Charismatic leadership is not important to all groups at all stages and at all times' (Cronin, 2009: 15). As this point acknowledges, the role of leaders, and the impact of their removal from the field, are highly dynamic factors, subject to shifting perceptions, intra-group processes, and the wider political context. A robust account of why terrorism ends (or continues) following decapitation promises a response to these issues, but much of the existing empirical work falls short of this.

Increasing attention has, nevertheless, been directed towards the question of whether and how targeted killings end terrorism. Three major studies have addressed this issue in recent years.[5] Jenna Jordan, Bryan Price, and Patrick Johnston have looked across hundreds of cases to determine the efficacy of 'targeting top terrorists' (Jordan, 2009; Johnston, 2012; Price, 2012). No consensus has emerged from this work. Jenna Jordan looked at 198 cases where the leader or senior figure of authority was killed (Jordan, 2009). Jordan's primary measure of success was whether or not the group remained inactive for two years following the strike. Compared with a baseline figure of militant-group decline, Jordan concluded that decapitation does not make it more likely that an organization will collapse. In fact, Jordan found that those groups that lost their leader were actually likely to survive longer than those that had not.

In contrast to Jordan's findings, Bryan Price, who looked at 207 groups and 299 leadership changes, concluded that groups that lost their leader had a higher mortality rate than those that did not (Price, 2012). Price's analysis also revealed that the longer a group lasts, the less impact leadership decapitation has – when groups had been around for twenty years or more, losing their leader made little difference.

Further results from Price's research suggest that groups are negatively impacted by the loss of their leader regardless of whether they are arrested, killed, or arrested then killed. Finally, Price found that group size was not a relevant factor in determining the effect of leadership decapitation, and that groups adhering to a religious ideology experienced a greater negative effect than those following nationalist ideologies when they lost their leader.

The third of the major recent studies, by Patrick Johnston, analysed 118 efforts to decapitate militant groups across 90 counter-insurgency campaigns. Johnston found that killing senior leaders supported counter-insurgency aims across a range of measures (Johnston, 2012). In particular, Johnston's results suggest that decapitation serves to increase the chance that an insurgency will be defeated, and decreases the number of attacks, as well as bringing the overall level of violence down. However, Johnston is careful to point out that decapitation is not a silver bullet, and that the probability of killing senior leaders having a positive impact (i.e. in line with state aims) on an insurgency is around 25 to 30 percent. Importantly, Johnston's analysis compared successful and failed decapitation attempts, making it a valuable addition to the literature. However, he and Price both differ from Jordan on leadership decapitation, which raises the question of why this might be the case.

A number of challenges face efforts to interpret the effectiveness of decapitation that perhaps help to explain these diverging conclusions, not least of which is how we might most appropriately measure success. For example, we could look at the number and position of those killed, changes in the number of terrorist attacks, the failure of the organization, impact on group numbers, and a willingness to engage in ceasefires. Jordan sets the bar extremely high by demanding that groups remain inactive for two years following the death of their leader, whilst Price makes the case for looking at a longer timeframe. A second issue that is relevant to explaining these differing findings is sample selection. Johnston is alone in looking at insurgent organizations, rather than what are generally described as terrorist groups, which target civilians. Notwithstanding the difficulties associated with differentiating between these groups, using this selection criterion means he is using a different sample, which in turn should caution against making direct comparisons across studies. A further difference is the measure by which leaders are identified – Jordan and Price consider leaders and the 'upper echelon', whilst Johnston only looks at cases where the most powerful individual was removed. The challenges in interpreting definitions of success, sample selection and the criteria for defining leaders are compounded by the difficulties of accessing reliable data. Even the most rigorous analysis can face problems of accuracy when looking across hundreds of cases, particularly given the limits on open-source data. Hence, it is important to approach the conclusions of such studies – particularly where there is disagreement – with care.[6]

Alongside these broader studies, it remains important to look at individual cases of decapitation to try to understand its effects. In her analysis of the question Cronin points out that the effectiveness of a decapitation strategy depends on the extent to which the group relies on the leader, the group's popularity, and its level of mobilization. Whilst this does not perhaps offer the generalizations of the broader studies described above, these issues go some way to demonstrating the complex nature of the leader's role in militant groups, and the differing ways particular groups are likely to respond to their loss. Broad level analyses such as those of Jordan, Price, and Johnston have laid out the landscape of the impact of targeted killings; it is now necessary to look at the contours of these issues. Given the import of any ensuing policy prescriptions, we need to develop our understanding of particular cases, as well as carefully assessing the moral and legal arguments associated with decapitation as a strategy.

Policing and intelligence

Moving down our continuum of force, governments have developed a plethora of responses to terrorism that preclude violence, ranging from pre-emptive arrest to promoting community cohesion.[7] The most pertinent strand of UK counterterrorism policy for our discussion is called Pursue, which focuses on stopping attacks. The others are prevent – stopping people engaging in terrorism; protect – strengthening protection against attacks; and prepare – mitigating the impact of attacks (HM Government, 2011). The focus, therefore, is on detecting, investigating, and disrupting terrorism, both domestically and internationally.

A number of organizations are involved in this type of counterterrorism work, most notably the police, security, and intelligence services. One of their core roles is intelligence gathering, something widely considered vital in counterterrorism efforts (Wilkinson, 2011). Broadly speaking, intelligence can be derived from people (known as HUMINT) and from electronic sources (SIGINT, or signals intelligence). Reviewing some of the attempts to define intelligence, Michael Warner concludes that intelligence is concerned with producing and disseminating information, is reliant on confidential sources and methods employed by state agents for state purposes, and – perhaps controversially – is primarily concerned with foreign entities (Warner, 2009). Many would argue that domestic intelligence gathering is as relevant as that focused on threats from overseas; however, perhaps the central point is that intelligence is covert and confidential.

David Charters describes counterterrorism intelligence in terms of three facets: warning intelligence, operational intelligence, and criminal-punishment intelligence (Charters, 1991). Warning intelligence aims to identify attacks and thereby safeguard targets; operational intelligence works to develop a picture of militant activity, including recruitment routes, group membership, leaders, associates, patterns of behavior, sources of funding and weapons, as well as developing knowledge of plans and plots; whilst criminal-punishment intelligence provides the information that enables successful prosecution. None of these are without controversy; debates over appropriate limits to state surveillance have most recently been seen in the context of the National Security Agency's surveillance program, the extent of which was revealed by former employee and whistleblower Edward Snowden (Byman and Wittes, 2014). Similarly, debates in the UK over 'closed material procedures', where secret information can be used against a defendant in court, but may not be seen by them, illustrate the sensitivities over releasing confidential information into normally public settings.[8] It is perhaps in this realm that the tension between the principles of liberal democracy and the need for security is most commonly seen, raising the question of the most appropriate balance between individual rights and liberties, and security (Wilkinson, 2011).

Martha Crenshaw sets out a number of further issues facing counterterrorism efforts (Crenshaw, 2010). The first is the cross-border nature of terrorism operations, no more emblematically exemplified than in al-Qaeda's global jihad. A further issue is the extent of state involvement in terrorism – the ongoing uncertainty over responsibility for the bombing of Pan Am Flight 103 over Lockerbie is just one case in point. These issues make cross-border cooperation and international consensus on how best to respond to particular threats both extremely important and deeply problematic. Differing levels of commitment to the rule of law are just one challenge facing criminal-justice approaches to counterterrorism. The process of deporting Abu Qatada from the UK to Jordan took eight years, in part because of the possibility that evidence extracted under torture would be used against him. A further question Crenshaw raises, which has received differing responses from agencies within and across borders, is the stage at which the state should intervene in the 'causal chain' of terrorism. This raises questions about when freedom of speech becomes a license to incite violence, when freedom to worship without fear of surveillance becomes a price worth paying for security, and when it is appropriate to restrict someone's movements without testing the evidence against them in a court of law. A relatively limited evidence base from which to develop appropriate policy responses compounds these challenges.

Inevitably, the secrecy associated with counterterrorism work makes assessing its process and outcome something of a challenge. Indeed, our knowledge about the effectiveness of counterterrorism policy is relatively poorly developed. In a major review of the literature on counterterrorism published in 2006 Cynthia Lum and colleagues found that only seven of 20,000 studies evaluated the effect of counterterrorism empirically (Lum et al., 2006). Little has improved in the intervening years; as John Horgan suggests, 'counterterrorism is rarely evidence or outcome-based' (Horgan, 2005: 161). This is against the background that counterterrorism and intelligence – particularly warning intelligence – needs to be effective all the time to avoid devastating consequences. As the IRA famously stated following the Brighton bombing in 1984, which targeted the governing Conservative party and attempted to kill its leader, Margaret Thatcher: 'Today we were unlucky, but remember we only have to be lucky once. You will have to be lucky always' (BBC, n.d.).

Assessing the effectiveness of counterterrorism faces the challenge that relevant information is often classified, whilst appropriate criteria for assessing effectiveness is difficult to determine and can change depending on the political context (Freese, 2014). Similarly, the most appropriate way of framing counterterrorism evaluation is problematic. In a review of evaluative work in the field Nick Adams and colleagues found efforts were either trying to look across entire national counterterrorism programs, which had the effect of conflating successes and failures, or research examined individual cases in detail, offering few comparative insights (Adams et al., 2011). In response, Adams et al. looked at individual policies, and held them against their stated aims, alongside considering second-order effects of counterterrorism policy. They concluded that the least-controversial approaches to counterterrorism are likely to be the most effective. Most plots were foiled by routine police work, including information from the public and from overseas intelligence. Conversely, Adams et al.'s study found no evidence to support the use of controversial counterterrorism tactics such as 'enhanced interrogation' and ethnic and religious profiling. Indeed, they argued that, given the importance of community intelligence, such controversial tactics can actually alienate those who are in a position to provide valuable information, and so may actually be counterproductive. Whilst these conclusions should be interpreted in light of the relatively weak evidence base on which there is to draw, Adams et al.'s study underlines the importance of clearly specifying appropriate evaluative criteria, and the need to consider unintended consequences of counterterrorism policies.

To supplement the above discussion on warning and operational intelligence, we will conclude this section by looking at Christopher Hewitt's research on arrest after an attack, which falls under criminal-investigation intelligence (Hewitt, 2014). Here, the appropriate measure of success is relatively straightforward: effective counterterrorism work is seen in the successful arrest and prosecution of those who have carried out an attack. In evaluating the main tools used by US police when investigating fatal terrorism attacks, Hewitt identified seven types of police action: crime-scene investigation, questioning witnesses, routine policing, informers, surveillance, tips from the public, and rewards. When looking at all fatal terrorist attacks since 1968, in which the attacker had not been killed or immediately surrendered, Hewitt found that there were differences between the most effective forms of policing against militant organizations and unaffiliated individuals. Informers and surveillance were more important against organizations, whilst witness identification and information from the public were more effective against unaffiliated individuals. Overall, routine policing, the use of informers, and information from the public were the most important factors in successfully identifying and capturing those responsible for attacks. Hewitt also looked, more briefly, at some of the main factors implicated in detecting plots, finding that undercover agents and informants had a substantial role in many operations, as did surveillance, although to a lesser extent. Indeed, a number of these have been something closer to entrapment than undercover policing.

The police and security services play a vital role in counterterrorism work. Preventing terrorism and arresting those who have carried out attacks are central to national security. However, as we have seen, there are important debates over the extent of state powers, and, given the necessarily covert nature of this work, appropriate forms of oversight are particularly important – not only to ensure that counterterrorism work is effectively managed, but also so that the public, and the community which often provides vital intelligence and information, does not feel alienated from the broader project of enhancing national security. In light of the wider question as to whether terrorism is successful, one of its most important victories, arguably, is when terrorism plays a role in undermining those liberal democratic principles to which many states aspire. As the Norwegian Prime Minister said on the anniversary of Anders Behring Breivik's attack: 'The bomb and the gun shots were meant to change Norway. The Norwegian people answered by embracing our values. The perpetrator lost. The people won' (Associated Press, 2012). However, before looking at whether terrorism is effective we will first consider some of the internal reasons why terrorism ends.

Internal

Internal reasons associated with how terrorism ends have been characterized as either leading to an organization becoming disabled or splitting up (McCauley, 2011). A group may become disabled for a number of reasons, most obviously due to a loss of personnel. Members may burn out owing to the fatigue associated with high-risk underground activism. If members defect in sufficiently large numbers this can also signal the end of the group. Internal processes such as disagreements or consistent failure to achieve political gains can also lead to defection (Horgan, 2009a). The state can play a role in encouraging disengagement, for example, through amnesties. Groups may also end because of a loss of support, or due to a failure to inspire the next generation to continue violent action. Alternatively, groups can splinter into different factions because of ideological, strategic, or personality differences.

It is important to stress that these factors are likely to interact with external actions. Pressure from counterterrorism efforts can impact internal group dynamics, whilst attempts to discredit a group's political message can affect the transmission of ideas between generations. Our knowledge of these issues is growing but still relatively limited, and cogent explanations for how and why internal group processes impact how terrorism ends are relatively limited. With this in mind, what follows sets out some of the literature on internal factors associated with how terrorism ends, beginning with organizational disabling and decline, then moving then on to look at factionalization and split.

Organizational decline

Describing the circumstances under which 'terrorism defeats itself', Cronin describes a number of features that can cause a group to implode (Cronin, 2009). The first of these is a failure of generational transition. Taking a longer-term view, and looking across campaigns and cycles of protest, a changing political context or an inability to frame issues in a way that encourages ongoing militancy can mean a group fails to pass the cause on to the next generation. A further cause of organizational decline described by Cronin sees leaders lose operational control. Al-Qaeda's ongoing struggles with its affiliates and adherents, perhaps most emblematically seen in the debates over appropriate levels and targets of violence between al-Qaeda leaders and the then head of al-Qaeda in Iraq, Abu Musab al-Zarqawi, exemplify these problems (Hafez, 2007; Moghadam and Fishman, 2010). Zarqawi's excessive violence was one of the reasons for the failure of his project in Iraq, resulting in a backlash that ultimately led to the Awakening movement, involving previously allied groups fighting against al-Qaeda in Iraq (Haykel, 2010; McCary, 2009).

Voluntary exit from militancy is a further reason why terrorism ends. Individual disengagement from terrorism has been characterized as involving push and pull factors (Bjørgo, 2009). Push factors relate to unpleasant aspects of being part of the extremist group, whilst pull factors refer to factors that become increasingly attractive when compared with ongoing involvement in violence. Tore Bjørgo suggests that push factors include negative social sanctions – for example, social stigma and societal disapproval; losing faith in the ideology or politics of the group; the feeling that things are going too far; a sense of disillusion; a loss of status; and a sense of exhaustion. With respect to pull factors, these are thought to include the desire for a 'normal life'; the feeling of getting too old; potentially negative effects on career and personal prospects; and the desire to establish a family or serious relationship. Individuals can also be incentivized to leave organizations voluntarily – for example, when defection is encouraged through the offer of reduced sentences or more favorable conditions in prison, as was the case with the Brigate Rosse in Italy (della Porta, 2013).

Disenchantment, because of a dissonance between what motivated the person to become involved and the actual experience of involvement, can play a role in why people leave militant groups, as can burn-out (Horgan, 2009a). When it becomes impossible to maintain the momentum necessary to continue a campaign through fatigue and exhaustion, individuals can leave. Clandestine violence can be highly stressful, exacting a significant emotional toll. It can also be physically exhausting, as one member of Brigate Rosse described: 'I got between three and four hours' sleep a night ... when they [police] knocked on my door that morning, my first thought was "I knew it"; the second was "thank goodness, more sleep"' (della Porta, 2013: 279). Tore Bjørgo noted a similar experience in an account of disengagement from skinhead and extreme-right militant nationalists (Bjørgo, 2009). Whilst the excitement of being involved in a violent underground movement can be highly stimulating, over long periods of time it can also be exhausting and, ultimately, unsustainable.

Disillusion because of internal conflict over tactics, strategy, politics, or ideology can lead to significant internal group divisions, which can be an important reason why terrorism ends. For example, John Horgan suggests that differences of tactics, alongside difficulties in the relationship between Mohammed Nassir Bin Abbas and Jemaah Islamiya leaders, led to the former's disengagement form the movement (Horgan, 2009b). As well as infighting leading to individuals leaving an organization, in some cases comrades or leaders can kill members – for example, if the bonds of trust break down to such an extent that group members are no longer believed to be trustworthy or sufficiently committed to the cause. At its most extreme this can lead to the dissolution of the group – for example, Abu Nidal lost many of his men over the years as he tortured, dismissed, killed, or demoted his followers. In a particularly brutal purge in the late 1980s up to 150 cadre were killed, ultimately leading to a loss of state support, which precipitated the decline of the Abu Nidal Organization (Wege, 1991; Seale, 1992). Internal division can lead to individuals leaving a group, but it can also result in breakaway groups forming, a phenomenon which we will now look at in a little more detail.

Factionalization

Both intra- and inter-group dynamics can lead to factionalization and the dissolution of organizations into splinter groups (Wieviorka, 1993). Depending on the source of the disagreement, the result can be more extreme factions, or a shift of some elements of the group into the political process, a not uncommon driver of internal division (Cronin, 2009; Jones and Libicki, 2008). Constituting over a fifth of all the groups in their dataset, Jones and Libicki's study identified 136 groups that splintered into factions, making factionalization a common outcome for militant groups. However, it is important to note that this dataset includes groups that, in some settings, have memberships and administrative leaderships that can be fluid and difficult to pin down. This is true of the Taliban, for example, where links to the central Taliban leadership are characterized as complex and dynamic, and 'in which the leadership seeks to increase its control, local commanders seek to retain their independence... and rivals seek to undermine each other through strategic affiliations' (van Bijlert, 2009: 169).

A group's size and organizational form can present challenges to leaders, which can inform how terrorism ends. 'Networked' organizations represent particular challenges to leaders seeking to unite conflicting groupings – something perhaps most emblematically seen in the ideological and strategic debates that exist in the 'global jihad'.[9] However, it is important to note that factionalization does not always lead to a decline in violence. Often splinter organizations instigate more extreme violence, and can play a crucial role in undermining efforts to move towards peace (Stedman, 1997). Nevertheless, many splinter groups do wither, making it important to consider in the context of how terrorism ends. This is particularly the case with militant groups. Victor Asal and colleagues' investigation of 121 ethno-political organizations in the Middle East found that, along with those exhibiting factional leadership, organizations using violence are more prone to split (Asal et al., 2012).

Perhaps two of the most high-profile militant organizations to have suffered from factionalization are the Groupe Islamique Armé (GIA) in Algeria and the Irish republican movement. In an account of dissident Irish republicanism John Morrison (2013) described splits as one of the movement's 'most persistent phenomena'.[10] Although Morrison emphasizes that these splits did not constitute the end of terrorism, they are important in understanding the dynamic way movements rise and fall. Omar Ashour (2009) offers a similarly interesting comparative account of why the Armé Islamique de Salut (AIS) demobilized and reintegrated into Algerian society, whilst the GIA split. Of the minority of the AIS that did not engage in the reintegration process some remained part of the GIA, to be destroyed following government repression, whilst a splinter group broke away to become the Groupe Salafist pour la Prédication et le Combat (GSPC), which split again when much of the group became al-Qaeda in the Islamic Maghreb (AQIM) in 2007. Ashour explains the differences between these factions' outcomes by looking at the role of state repression, social interaction with the 'other', selective inducements, and charismatic leadership. He argues that whilst all four were present when elements of the AIS moved away from violence, and state repression and selective inducements were constant features, there was often a lack of charismatic leadership and/or social interaction that resulted in continuous factionalization within the militant Islamist groupings in Algeria.

Examining how terrorism ends demands analysis that takes account of individual, group, and wider social factors. Ashour's study of de-radicalization in

Islamist groups is particularly valuable in taking this into account. A similar approach, employed by Lorenzo Bosi and Donatella della Porta (forthcoming) explains how the IRA and the Brigate Rosse moved away from political violence. Both groups have experienced significant factionalization and split, but were also influenced by wider socio-political conditions and shifts in repressive policies enacted by the state. Similarly, changes in organizational strategy as well as activists' perceptions led to disengagement from political violence. In Italy the result was disengagement predominantly at the individual level, which led to a lack of armed activists. In Ireland changes in constituency perceptions and organizational strategy saw disengagement from violence at the meso – or organizational – level, with many activists co-opted into the political process (Bosi and della Porta, forthcoming). The important point to note is the interaction between individuals, leaders, the group, and wider socio-political circumstances, and, relatedly, the relationship between internal and external drivers in informing the end of terrorism. Having looked at some of the main reasons why terrorism ends, it remains to consider how effective it is – a question about which there has been considerable debate.

Is terrorism 'successful'?

Having set out the range of reasons why groups fail, we now turn our attention to the question of terrorism's effectiveness. Inevitably, any discussion of outcomes is going to be determined by the metric we use.[11] If terrorism is primarily a communication strategy then we would need to look at measures such as the reach of political messages. If, however, terrorism is understood as a form of political coercion then we instead need to look at how effective it is at achieving political goals. Increasing attention has been paid to this question, making it important to consider in some detail.

The political goals of militant groups have been described as falling into the following areas: policy change, social control, territorial change, regime change, and maintaining the status quo (Kydd and Walter, 2006). The debate over how successful terrorism is at furthering these goals is characterized by diverse and contradictory views. Some argue terrorism enjoys considerable success (Pape, 2003), others that it is partially successful (Merari, 1993), whilst others pronounce it a failure (Abrahms, 2006). Equally, a variety of methods have been applied to understanding terrorism's political achievements, including formal models (Lake, 2002) and detailed examination of individual cases (Hoffman, 2011). Others draw out a few notable successes (Kydd and Walter, 2006). Repeated reference is made, for example, to a relatively small number of examples in support of terrorism's effectiveness. These include the FLN in Algeria, in their fight for independence; the Irgun in Israel, whose violence contributed to the end of the British Mandate in Palestine; and Hezbollah, who effectively pushed peacekeepers from Lebanon in 1984 and 2000. However, as Max Abrahms points out, these analyses generally fail to hold the relatively limited number of successes against a broader selection of cases (Abrahms, 2012).

We have already seen in our earlier discussion that analyses looking across many hundreds of cases have found that terrorism succeeds only around 10 percent of the time. Smaller-scale analyses have confirmed terrorism's failure rate. Most notably, Max Abrahms has devoted considerable attention to this issue and he too finds terrorism is largely unsuccessful. In a study published in 2006 Abrahms found that of the 42 policy objectives held by 28 groups on the USA's list of foreign terrorist organizations only 7 percent were achieved. He compares this unfavorably with the literature on economic sanctions, considered effective 34 percent of the time (Hart, 2000), concluding that terrorism is an inefficient way of achieving political goals.

One apparent exception to the growing consensus around terrorism's failure to achieve political goals is Robert Pape's analysis of suicide bombing (Pape, 2003). Pape looked at all suicide attacks from 1980 to 2001, disaggregated into eleven campaigns of terrorism. Of these, six led to some of the groups' goals being addressed. However, exploring this analysis a little more carefully, it seems that the reason for this apparent disparity is the measure of effectiveness Pape uses. Most of the gains Pape sets out are partial successes and do not constitute a complete victory – the standard used for most of the other analyses. Pape also compares effectiveness before and after the implementation of terrorism, rather than holding achievement steady against pre-specified group goals, as for example Abrahms does. Similarly, the measures by which Abrahms and Pape understand success are different; for example, Pape sets Hamas' victory in pushing Israel out of Gaza as a success, whereas Abrahms marks down their failure to achieve an independent Palestinian state. Also, as Abrahms points out, whilst the Israeli Defense Force withdrew from parts of the Gaza Strip in 1994 – classified as a success by Pape – there was a simultaneous increase in the number of settlers, constituting a failure for Hamas (Abrahms, 2006).

Reviewing work to date on terrorism's ability to achieve militant groups' political ambitions, there is still support for Schelling's view expressed in 1989 that 'acts of terrorism almost never appear to accomplish anything politically significant' (Schelling, 1989: 20). Given the high costs associated with involvement in terrorism, this finding seems surprising. Why would people engage in such a risky form of political action given the relatively limited chances of success? Inevitably, our interpretation of this question is determined by the measure of success we employ. As discussed, most efforts to understand the success of terrorism have taken policy measures as the primary outcome. In making the case for this metric, Abrahms argues that they represent a 'stable and reliable indicator of their actual intentions' (Abrahms, 2006: 47). However, it is not difficult to think of groups that have significantly changed their goals over the course of a campaign. For example, Thomas Hegghammer has observed that jihadist groups have undergone a process of ideological hybridization which has significantly changed the extent to which the various currents focus on the 'near' or 'far' enemy (Hegghammer, 2009). Indeed, only two years after championing policy change as an ideal measure of outcome Abrahms published another article which characterized the protean and shifting nature of violent group goals as one of the fundamental puzzles of terrorism research, arguing: 'Some of the most important terrorist organizations in modern history have pursued policy goals that are not only unstable but also contradictory' (Abrahms, 2008: 88). If this is the case, and it seems likely that it applies to at least some militant groups, then using policy outcomes as a measure is missing something more funda-mental about what those using terrorism seek to achieve.

A further important issue, which encourages us to think again about how to conceptualize outcomes, is the potentially fluid nature of perceptions of success and failure. Rather than fixed, static notions, progress and regress are perhaps best understood as dynamic concepts. Shifts in leader attitudes (or leader), changes in aims and aspirations, or changes of government can all alter perceptions of success and failure. What was once an unassailable goal may become a matter for debate or compromise. A static rendering of outcomes neglects these issues. Furthermore, the agenda-setting nature of terrorism, which attracts attention and forces govern-ments to confront the groups' aims, may be a necessary precursor for political engagement. The notion of the vanguard that makes real political change possible is relatively well established in the terrorism literature; however, this insight has not yet been applied to discussion of terrorism's outcomes. It suggests that we should perhaps be looking at the extent of political representation, or longer-term-outcome measures. Again, though, there are problems trying to apply single measures to a varied collection of actors. Whilst this may be useful in assessing some cases, it is not appropriate for those who are more interested in encouraging popular revolt than gaining official political representation, such as the Movimiento Revolucionario Túpac Amaru. It seems that by solely using policy goals to assess success and failure the challenges of developing cogent explanations as to why ter-rorism ends and what it achieves are not being met.

Explaining terrorism's outcomes

When trying to interpret terrorism's outcomes it is important to set out the scope and subject of what we are attempting to explain. Efforts to explain why terrorism ends have generally taken one of three approaches: setting out broad-level explana-tions, proposing a series of lower-order factors argued to influence outcomes, or examining individual cases in detail. Abrahms reflects the first approach, suggest-ing that whilst group size, its capabilities, and those of its opponent are all factors influencing success, target selection is the most important reason why violent groups fail (Abrahms, 2006; 2012). Through a robust series of tests he finds that groups which select civilian targets are almost never successful compared with those that focus on military targets. Abrahms puts this down to the perception, by governments, that when groups are minded to use a tactic as extreme as terrorism they are likely to have equally extreme, radical political intentions. He argues that because of this flaw in communicating their aims governments perceive such groups as untrustworthy and incorrigible, thereby reducing the bargaining space available to the actors.

Abrahms' explanation, although based on rigorous analysis, only incorporates the group-state dyad and fails to consider the impact of the wider social context. Targeting civilians may, for example, impact group support from the organization's constituency, perhaps to the extent it can no longer operate. It also neglects the impact of group dynamics on targeting preferences, which can have similar negative effects. Finally, it doesn't clearly specify how governments develop their responses based on interpretations of extreme demands. Indeed, there is evidence that governments clearly recognize the aims of those who use violence against their civilians. A number of groups have entered into negotiations with governments. In doing so they went through the process of setting out preconditions, agreeing the parameters for talks etc., all of which demand that the government, to some extent, acknowledges their wider aims. Abrahms seems to conflate governments' stated positions and their actual policy decisions. For example, the UK government has a policy of 'not negotiating with terrorists', despite engaging in back-channel negotiations over many years with the IRA (Ó Dochartaigh, 2011). In short, Abrahms' explanation is perhaps best understood as one possible reason why groups fail, falling short of a broader account of why terrorism is politically ineffective.

Drawing out central tendencies rather than offering robust explanations, Jones and Libicki consider group size to be the most powerful variable in determining group success (Jones and Libicki, 2008). They found it explained 32 percent of the variance in outcome, with additional variables offering little in explanatory power. Based on this, and the finding that groups in democratic settings tend to be smaller and achieve fewer of their aims, they offer a number of observations about the relationship between group size, level of host-country development, and terrorism's success rate. They propose that democratic political contexts offer a more stable environment with less likelihood of large-scale disaffection amongst their peoples. A more methodological response to their findings focuses on the Global Terrorism Database from which they developed their analysis. As its primary source is media reporting, it privileges high-income countries with media that are better established and operate more freely. As such, it is likely to under-represent smaller groups in countries with more restrictive media coverage, thereby failing to incorporate their relative success rates. As for explanations as to why group size is the most powerful variable affecting success rates, the authors suggest that somewhat tautologically, it is because they 'have stood the test of time and can stand on their own' (Jones and Libicki, 2008: 40).

Weinberg proposes that organizations succeed when terrorism is used sparingly and alongside other tactics, but almost never when it is the only form of coercion (Weinberg, 2012). Terrorism, Weinberg argues, is only likely to bring about tactical or strategic successes that fall short of achieving the ultimate goals of the group. Cronin agrees that terrorism rarely 'works' (Cronin, 2009). She suggests that when it does there are clear and attainable goals, a wider socio-political environment conducive to the group's cause, other methods alongside terrorism are applied, and powerful actors become convinced of the legitimacy of the group's aims.

In reviewing existing explanations for why terrorism ends and what it achieves, two main approaches have been considered: large-scale explanations aiming to account for most cases of non-state terrorism and its outcomes through reference to a limited number of variables (Jones and Libicki, 2008), and a range of more focused explanations that specify trends related to group and policy outcomes (Weinberg, 2012). As this discussion revealed, the causal processes implicated in specific organizational, political, and social outcomes are less clearly specified. With a phenomenon of such broad scope, setting out a range of potential pathways and influencing factors, as Weinberg and Cronin do, is a valuable move towards explaining different outcomes. However, compartmentalizing them into aggregate categories, such as 'failure', is insufficiently specific about the causal processes at work and seems to confound an array of potentially important influential factors.

One of the main challenges, as Charles Tilly points out, are the multiple internal and external influences that impact the claims of political opponents (Tilly, 1999). This is something analyses to date recognize but do not entirely address. Indeed, Cronin and Abrahms sidestep this issue entirely in important elements of their analyses (Abrahms, 2006; Cronin, 2009). Where policy goals were achieved both wholly or partially, code groups as successful regardless of who or what may have actually contributed to the outcome.[12] To some extent this reflects a genuine problem in larger-scale analyses. Identifying exactly what carried the causal weight, when examining hundreds of groups, as Cronin does, is a significant practical challenge. However, the extent to which applying such an approach advances our understanding of when, and under what conditions, terrorism is successful is debatable.

Where, then, does this leave us in trying to understand militant-group outcomes? It might appear that in highlighting the challenges facing large-scale studies this discussion has merely reiterated some of the debates contrasting such approaches with case studies (Burnham et al., 2008). Is the only alternative to engage in detailed examinations of specific cases, expanding our knowledge of those groups, but offering little in the way of more generalized conclusions? As Richard English puts it in reviewing Cronin's book, the challenge 'is to harmonize the insights of the hedgehogs and the foxes: for case-study specialists to do more than they have tended to do to reflect on wider patterns, and for wide-angled students [foxes] of the subject to be sure to learn fully from case-study hedgehogs as they proceed' (English, 2011: 10). There is much to be done to respond to this call. However, recent work from political sociologists has begun to address these issues.

As we have seen, Lorenzo Bosi and Donatella della Porta applied a multi-level approach to the demise of the Provisional IRA and the Italian left-wing (Bosi and della Porta, forthcoming). It incorporates micro, meso, and macro levels of analysis, and offers a cogent account of how similar mechanisms operated across both contexts, but in crucially different ways, influencing the groups' shift away from political violence. Further recognition of the potential for such an approach has been seen in Domenico Tosini's mechanism-led account of campaigns of terrorism (Tosini, 2011) and the call for a greater focus on the causal processes and mechanisms that inform how violence emerges and declines (Bosi and Giugni, 2012). These tools afford the opportunity not only to set out how terrorism ends but also to explain why these outcomes unfold as they do.[13]

Conclusion

In this chapter we have reviewed some of the ways in which the question of how terrorism ends has been addressed in the literature, making the case for clearly conceptualizing the influence of actors, actions, and outcomes. We also examined the primary actions that inform how terrorism ends, focusing on internal group dynamics and external, generally state-led responses, to elucidate a wide range of factors that influence the decline of groups. Finally, we asked whether terrorism is successful, setting out our current understanding about how and why terrorism succeeds or fails.

In explaining terrorism's outcomes it is vital to take account of the complex, nuanced, and dynamic reasons terrorism is used – and against which criteria it should be assessed. Using a single lens, be that organizational, strategic, or policy-oriented, risks imposing a top-down interpretation of militant-group goals that does not hold up to close examination of individual cases. Rather, we need to look far more closely at the causal mechanisms and processes that inform how terrorism ends. These almost always stretch further than mono-dimensional constructs such as strategic interaction with the state, continued organizational survival, or achieving specific policy concessions. Finally, it is important to remember that multiple levels of analysis are implicated in how terrorism ends. Individuals can leave terrorism, groups can demobilize or be repressed by the state, and, at the societal level, wider cycles of violence can come to an end. It is really only by taking account of the range of reasons, the interactions between internal and external factors, and the different levels of analysis that are implicated in this phenomenon, that we are likely to understand how to assess outcomes and the most appropriate way of explaining how and why terrorism ends.

STUDY BOX CHAPTER 8

Key reading

Abrahms, M. (2006). 'Why Terrorism Does Not Work', *International Security*, 31(2): 42–78.

Ashour, O. (2009). *The Deradicalization of Jihadists: Transforming Armed Islamist Movements* (New York: Routledge).

Cronin, A. K. (2009). *How Terrorism Ends: Understanding the Decline and Demise of Terrorist Campaigns* (Princeton: Princeton University Press).

Jones, S. G. and Libicki, M. C. (2008). *How Terrorist Groups End: Lessons for Countering al-Qa'ida* (Santa Monica, CA: RAND).

Weinberg, L. (2012). *The End of Terrorism?* (Padstow, Cornwall: Routledge).

Study questions

1   How effective is repression and decapitation at ending a terrorist group's campaign?

2   To what extent does addressing the root causes of terrorism lead to its decline?

3   Does terrorism work?

Notes

1 As Erin Miller points out (2012), it is difficult to specify at which point, after the cessation of violence, terrorism may be safely declared over, as violence can re-emerge; hence the focus on the significant decline of the use of terrorism.

2 Some of the earliest treatments of the question of how terrorism ends set out a similar list of factors to take into account. For example, Martha Crenshaw (1996) emphasizes the likely interaction between the choices militant groups make based on the perceived effectiveness of terrorism; the increasingly high costs continuing violence is likely to produce as a result of government response to militancy; and alternative routes that do not necessarily involve violence, for example amnesty or other forms of collective action.

3 For a review of work on state repression see Davenport (2007).

4 Figures compiled by The Bureau of Investigative Journalism suggest that a conservative figure of 340 drone strikes have killed at least 2,600 people between 2002 and 2014. See www.thebureauinvestigates.com

5 Earlier work that is more limited in scope – primarily because it uses small samples or individual cases (notably Israel) – includes that by Hafez and Hatfield (2006), Byman (2006), Kaplan et al. (2005), Mannes (2008), and Langdon et al. (2004).

6 For a discussion of some of these issues see Carvin (2012). Particular issues facing targeted killing include the likelihood of 'blowback', and the potentially increased likelihood that militant groups will target political leaders for assassination in retaliation. Also, the next generation of leaders who replace those killed may be more extreme and violent. Finally, the unpredictability of the tactic in particular situations makes it a potentially risky strategy for states to pursue. For a collection of essays engaging with the legality and morality of targeted killings see Finkelstein et al. (2012).

7 As the focus of this chapter is how terrorism ends, it does not cover anti-terrorism, i.e. efforts to prevent terrorism, for instance through the use of target hardening or other defensive or deterrent measures. For a short review of some of the work on this see Sandler (2014).

8 For more on these debates see *The Guardian* (2012).

9 For comprehensive accounts of these issues see Moghadam and Fishman (2010) and Paz (2009).

10 Four main splits have shaped the republican movement. In the late 1960s the IRA and Sinn Fein split to form the Original IRA and Official Sinn Fein, and the Provisional IRA and Provisional Sinn Fein. A short while later the Irish National Liberation Army split from the official movement. In 1986 the Continuity IRA split from the Provisional movement, and in the late 1990s the Real IRA and the 32 County Sovereignty Committee were formed, also from the Provisional movement (Morrison, 2013).

11 For a discussion of the various ways successful terrorism can be conceptualized and interpreted see Marsden (2012).

12 Cronin states: 'Achievement is indicated if the group's goals were wholly or partially achieved during the group's life span, *regardless of who directly achieved or negotiated that outcome*. Usually the strategic goal of a group is shared by various actors in a conflict, and this database does not attempt to claim which group enjoys primary responsibility for the outcome' (2009: 211, italics in original). Similarly, Abrahms clarifies that 'all policy successes are attributed to terrorism as the causal factor, regardless of whether important intervening variables, such as a peace process, may have contributed to the outcome' (2006: 51).

13 For more on this mechanism- and process-led approach to interpreting the dynamics of violent political contestation see Tilly (2003; 2005), McAdam et al. (2001), and Tilly and Tarrow (2007).

References

Abrahms, M. (2006). Why terrorism does not work. *International Security, 31*(2), 42–78. doi: 10.1162/isec.2006.31.2.42

Abrahms, M. (2008). What terrorists really want: Terrorist motives and counterterrorism strategy. *International Security, 32*(4), 78–105. doi: 10.1162/isec.2008.32.4.78

Abrahms, M. (2012). The political effectiveness of terrorism revisited. *Comparative Political Studies, 45*(3), 366–93. doi: 10.1177/0010414011433104

Adams, N., Nordhaus, T. and Shellenberger, M. (2011). *Counterterrorism since 9/11: Evaluating the efficacy of controversial tactics.* Breakthrough Institute: Oakland, CA.

Asal, V., Brown, M. and Dalton, A. (2012). Why split? Organisational splits among ethnopolitical organisations in the Middle East. *Journal of Conflict Resolution, 56*(1), 94–117.

Ashour, O. (2009). *The deradicalization of jihadists: Transforming armed Islamist movements.* New York: Routledge.

Associated Press. (2012). *Norway remembers victims on massacre anniversary.* CBS News. Retrieved from: http://www.cbsnews.com/news/norway-remembers-victims-on-massacre-anniversary/ (Accessed 14 May 2014).

BBC (n.d.). *1984: Memories of the Brighton bomb.* Retrieved from: http://news.bbc.co.uk/onthisday/hi/witness/october/12/newsid_3665000/3665388.stm (Accessed 17 April 2014).

Benmelech, E., Berrebi, C. and Klor, E. (2010). Counter-suicide terrorism: Evidence from home demolitions. Working Paper No. 16493. National Bureau of Economic Research: Cambridge, MA.

Bjørgo, T. (2009). Processes of disengagement from violent groups of the extreme right. In T. Bjørgo and J. Horgan (Eds.), *Leaving terrorism behind* (pp. 30–48). London: Routledge.

Bosi, L. and della Porta, D. (forthcoming). Processes out of political violence: A comparative historical sociology of Italian left-wing underground organisations and the Provisional IRA. In J. Gunning (Ed.), *How does 'terrorism' end?* London: Routledge.

Bosi, L. and Giugni, M. (2012). The study of the consequences of armed groups: Lessons from the social movement literature. *Mobilization, 17*(1), 85–98.

Brophy-Baermann, B. and Conybeare, J. A. (1994). Retaliating against terrorism: Rational expectations and the optimality of rules versus discretion. *American Journal of Political Science 38*(1), 196–210.

Burke, J. (2011). *The 9/11 wars.* St Ives, Cornwall: Penguin.

Burnham, P., Gilland Lutz, K., Grant, W. and Layton-Henry, Z. (2008). *Research methods in politics* (2nd ed.). China: Palgrave Macmillan.

Byman, D. (2006). Do targeted killings work? *Foreign Affairs, 85*(2), 95–111.

Byman, D. and Wittes, B. (2014). Reforming the NSA: How to spy after Snowden. *Foreign Affairs*, May/June, 2014, 127–38.

Carvin, S. (2012). The trouble with targeted killing. *Security Studies, 21*(3), 529–55.

Charters, D. A. (1991). Counter-terrorism intelligence: Sources, methods, process and problems. In David A. Charters (Ed.), *Democratic responses to international terrorism*, (pp. 227–66). Transnational Publishers: New York.

Crenshaw, M. (2010). Introduction. In M. Crenshaw (Ed.), *The consequences of counter-terrorism* (pp. 1–30). New York: Russell Sage Foundation.

Cronin, A. K. (2009). *How terrorism ends: Understanding the decline and demise of terrorist campaigns.* Princeton: Princeton University Press.

Davenport, C. (2007). State repression and political order. *Annual Review of Political Science, 10*(1–23). doi: 10.1146/annurev.polisci.10.101405.143216

David, S. R. (2002). Fatal choices: Israel's policy of targeted killing. *Mideast Security and Policies Studies, 51*(1–26).

della Porta, D. (2013). *Clandestine political violence.* New York: Cambridge University Press.

Dugan, L. and Chenoweth, E. (2012). Moving beyond deterrence: The effectiveness of raising the expected utility of abstaining from terrorism in Israel. *American Sociological Review, 77*(4), 597–624.

Duyvesteyn, I. (2008). Great expectations: The use of armed force to combat terrorism. *Small Wars and Insurgencies, 19*(3), 328–51. doi: 10.1080/09592310802228666

Enders, W. and Sandler, T. (1993). The effectiveness of antiterrorism policies: A vector-autoregression-intervention analysis. *The American Political Science Review 87*(4), 829–44.

English, R. (2011). *H-Diplo/ISSF roundtable on Audrey Kurth Cronin. How terrorism ends: Understanding the decline and demise of terrorist campaigns.* Retrieved from: http://www.h-net.org/~diplo/ISSF/PDF/ISSF-Roundtable-2-8.pdf (Accessed 3 March, 2014).

Finkelstein, C., Ohlin, J. D. and Altman, A. (Eds.) (2012). *Targeted killings: Law and morality in an asymmetrical world.* Croydon: Oxford University Press.

Freese, R. (2014). Evidence-based counterterrorism or flying blind? How to understand and achieve what works. *Perspectives on Terrorism, 8*(1), 37–56.

The Guardian (2012). *Secret courts: The essential guide.* Retrieved from: http://www.theguardian.com/law/2012/sep/25/secret-courts-the-essential-guide (Accessed 3 March, 2014).

Hafez, M. M. (2003). *Why Muslims rebel: Repression and resistance in the Muslim world.* Boulder, CO: Lynne Rienner Publishers.

Hafez, M. M. (2007). Al-Qa'ida losing ground in Iraq. *CTC Sentinel, 1*(1).

Hafez, M. and Hatfield, J. M. (2006). Do targeted assassinations work? A multivariate analysis of Israeli counter-terrorism effectiveness during Al-Aqsa uprising. *Studies in Conflict and Terrorism, 29*(4), 359–82.

Hart, R. A. (2000). Democracy and the successful use of economic sanctions. *Political Research Quarterly, 53*(2), 267–84. doi: 10.1177/106591290005300203

Haykel, B. (2010). Jihadis and the Shi'a. In CTC, *Self-inflicted wounds: debates and divisions within al-Qa'ida and its periphery* (pp. 202–23). Westpoint, VA: Combating Terrorism Center.

Hegghammer, T. (2009). Jihadi-salafis or revolutionaries? In R. Meijer (Ed.), *Global Salafism: Islam's new religious movement* (pp. 244–66). India: Hurst and Co.

Hewitt, C. (2014). Law enforcement tactics and their effectiveness in dealing with American terrorism: Organisations, autonomous cells, and lone wolves. *Terrorism and Political Violence, 26*(1), 58–68.

HM Government. (2011). *CONTEST: The United Kingdom's strategy for countering terrorism.* London: HM Stationery.

Hoffman, B. (2011). The rationality of terrorism and other forms of political violence: Lessons from the Jewish campaign in Palestine, 1939–1947. *Small Wars and Insurgencies, 22*(2), 258–72. doi: 10.1080/09592318.2011.573394

Horgan, J. (2005). Analysis, integration, response. In J. Horgan, *The psychology of terrorism* (pp. 158–68). Padstow, Cornwall: Taylor and Francis.

Horgan, J. (2009a). Individual disengagement from violent groups of the extreme right. In T. Bjørgo and J. Horgan (Eds.), *Leaving terrorism behind* (pp. 17–29). London: Routledge.

Horgan, J. (2009b). *Walking away from terrorism: Accounts of disengagement from radical and extremist movements.* London: Routledge.

Johnston, P. B. (2012). Does decapitation work? Assessing the effectiveness of leadership targeting in counterinsurgency campaigns. *International Security, 36*(4), 47–79.

Jones, S. G. and Libicki, M. C. (2008). *How terrorist groups end: Lessons for countering al-Qa'ida.* Santa Monica, CA: RAND.

Jordan, J. (2009). When heads roll: Assessing the effectiveness of leadership decapitation. *Security Studies, 18*(4), 719–55.

Kaplan, E. H., Mintz, A., Mishal, S. and Samban, C. (2005). What happened to suicide bombings in Israel? Insights from a terror stock model. *Studies in Conflict and Terrorism, 28*(3), 225–35.

Kydd, A. H. and Walter, B. F. (2006). The strategies of terrorism. *International Security, 31*(1), 49–80. doi:10.1162/isec.2006.31.1.49

Lake, D. A. (2002). Rational extremism: Understanding terrorism in the twenty-first century. *Dialog-IO,* Spring, 15–29. Retrieved from: http://journals.cambridge.org/action/displayIssue?iid=148134 (Accessed 13 April 2014).

Langdon, L., Sarapu, A. J. and Wells, M. (2004). Targeting the leadership of terrorist and insurgent movements: Historical lessons for contemporary policy makers. *Journal of Public and International Affairs, 15,* 59–78.

Lum, C., Kennedy, L. W. and Sherley, A. (2006). Are counter-terrorism strategies effective? The results of the Campbell systematic review on counter-terrorism evaluation research. *Journal of Experimental Criminology, 2*(4), 489–516.

Mannes, A. (2008). Testing the snake head strategy: Does killing or capturing its leaders reduce a terrorist group's activity? *Journal of International Policy Solutions, 9,* 40–9.

Marsden, S. (2012). 'Successful terrorism': A framework and review. *Behavioral Sciences of Terrorism and Political Aggression, 4*(2), 134–50.

Mazzei, J. (2009). *Death squads or self-defense forces?: How paramilitary groups emerge and challenge democracy in Latin America.* North Carolina: University of North Carolina Press.

McAdam, D., Tarrow, S. and Tilly, C. (2001). *Dynamics of contention.* New York: Cambridge University Press.

McCary, J. A. (2009). The Anwar Awakening: an alliance of incentives. *The Washington Quarterly, 32*(1), 43–59.

McCauley, C. (2011). Group desistance from terrorism: The dynamics of actors, actions and outcomes. In R. Coolseat (Ed.), *Jihadi terrorism and the radicalisation challenge: European and American experiences* (2nd ed., pp. 187–204). Bodmin, Cornwall: Ashgate Publishing Ltd.

Merari, A. (1993). Terrorism as a strategy of insurgency. *Terrorism and Political Violence, 5*(4), 213–51. doi: 10.1080/09546559308427227, pp. 384–5.

Miller, E. (2012). Patterns of onset and decline among terrorist organisations. *Journal of Quantitative Criminology, 28,* 77–101.

Moghadam, A. and Fishman, B. (Eds.) (2010). *Self-inflicted wounds: Debates and divisions within al-Qa'ida and its periphery.* Westpoint, NY: Combating Terrorism Center. Retrieved from: https://www.ctc.usma.edu/v2/wp-content/uploads/2011/05/Self-Inflicted-Wounds.pdf (Accessed 13 May 2014).

Morrison, J. (2013). *Origins and rise of dissident Irish republicanism: The role and impact of organizational splits.* India: Bloomsbury Academic.

Ó Dochartaigh, N. (2011). Together in the middle: Back-channel negotiation in the Irish peace process. *Journal of Peace Research, 48*(6), 767–80. doi: 10.1177/0022343311417982

Pape, R. A. (2003). The strategic logic of suicide terrorism. *American Political Science Review, 97*(3), 13–14. doi: 10.1017.S000305540300073X

Paz, R. (2009). Debates within the family: Jihadi-Salafi debates on strategy, Takfir, extremism, suicide bombings and the sense of the apocalypse. In R. Meijer (Ed.), *Global salafism: Islam's new religious movement* (pp. 267–80). India: Hurst Publishers.

Plaw, A. (2008). *Targeting terrorists: A license to kill?* Farnham, Surrey: Ashgate Publishing Ltd.

Price, B. C. (2012). Targeting top terrorists: How leadership decapitation contributes to counterterrorism. *International Security, 36*(4), 9–46.

Prunckun, H. W. and Mohr, P. B. (1997). Military deterrence of international terrorism: An evaluation of operation El Dorado Canyon. *Studies in Conflict and Terrorism, 20*(3), 267–80. doi: 10.1080/10576109708436039

Sandler, T. (2014). The analytical study of terrorism: Taking stock. *Journal of Peace Research, 51*(2), 257–71.

Schelling, T. (1989). What purposes can 'International Terrorism' serve? In R. G. Frey and C. W. Morris (Eds.), *Violence, terrorism and justice* (pp. 18–33). New York: Cambridge University Press.

Seale, P. (1992). *Abu Nidal: A gun for hire*. New York: Random House.

Stedman, S. J. (1997). Spoiler problems in peace processes. *International Security, 22*(2), 5–53.

Tilly, C. (1999). From interactions to outcomes in social movements. In M. Giugni, D. McAdam and C. Tilly (Eds.), *How social movements matter* (pp. 253–70). Minneapolis, MN: University of Minnesota Press.

Tilly, C. (2003). *The politics of collective violence*. New York: Cambridge University Press.

Tilly, C. (2005). Terror as strategy and relational process. *International Journal of Comparative Sociology, 46*(1–2), 11–32. doi: 10.1177/0020715205054468

Tilly, C. and Tarrow, S. (2007). *Contentious politics*. Boulder, CO: Paradigm Publishers.

Tosini, D. (2011). Agents and mechanisms of terrorist campaigns: A contribution to a general theory of rationality. *Revue européenne des sciences ssociale, 29*(2), 43–70. doi: 10.4000/ress.973

van Bijlert, M. (2009). Unruly commanders and violent power struggles: Taliban networks in Uruzgan. In A. Giustozzi (Ed.), *Decoding the new Taliban: Insights from the Afghan field*, (pp. 155–79). India: Hurst Publishers.

Warner, M. (2009). Wanted: A definition of intelligence. In C. Andrews, R. J. Aldrich and W. K. Wark (Eds.), *Secret intelligence: A reader*, (pp. 3–11). Suffolk: Routledge.

Wege, C. A. (1991). The Abu Nidal Organization. *Studies in Conflict and Terrorism, 14*(1), 59–66. doi: 10.1080/10576109108435857

Weinberg, L. (2012). *The end of terrorism?* Padstow, Cornwall: Routledge.

Wieviorka, M. (1993). *The making of terrorism*. Chicago, IL: University of Chicago Press.

Wilkinson, P. (2011). *Terrorism versus democracy: The liberal state response* (3rd ed.). Chippenham: Routledge.

9

CONFLICT RESOLUTION AND TERRORISTS AS SPOILERS

SOPHIE A. WHITING

Introduction

The previous chapter discussed a number of ways that a terrorism campaign may come to an end, one of which is through negotiations as part of a peace process. The aim of this chapter is to place the decline of terrorism in a conflict-studies perspective. Some of the biggest groups labelled as terrorists have sought to end their campaign through negotiation and by taking a political direction. Yet insights from conflict studies show this is not always clear-cut, with many groups maintaining a military dimension, or ceasefires being vulnerable to disruption, especially if negotiations prompt a split in the terrorist group.

A peace process is a term used to describe 'any sustained political and diplomatic efforts to resolve either international or internal conflicts' (Wilkinson, 2007: 77). Attempts to find solutions to armed conflict are often lengthy, complicated and vary greatly from one conflict situation to another. The label of peace process has been applied to situations as diverse as those in South Africa, Israel/Palestine, Sri Lanka, Northern Ireland, the Basque Country, Bosnia and Lebanon. Steps towards finding peace typically involve the ending of violence, negotiations to reform constitutional and political arrangements and, finally, post-settlement peace building and reconciliation. However, in reality these stages are indistinct and less succinct. The origins and concluding phase of a peace process may be hard to identify without the benefit of hindsight. Darby describes how the path taken towards addressing the root causes of violence and division is not simply a linear route to a lasting peace but a cyclical process along which steps occur simultaneously and at different speeds (Darby, 2001). A peace process extends beyond the signing of any peace agreement, which tends to set out general principles and is often purposefully designed to contain elements of ambiguity. Therefore, after signing a peace accord, implementation is more often than not a drawn-out period during which contentious issues may emerge and renegotiations may occur. A peace process does not necessarily mark the end of violence but rather its transformation.

When mediation occurs to find a conclusion to violent conflict the policy agenda shifts rapidly from military containment of the actors involved towards addressing a new set of problems, such as disarmament of combatants and the implementation of new institutional and constitutional arrangements. Pursuing an official end to political violence is never unanimous within the parties involved. Continuing support by combatants of a peaceful path depends on gaining tangible rewards, such as prisoner releases and a role within reformed institutional structures. However, such returns are never immediate; it can take years for the agreement and implementation of such contentious decisions. As a result, the sensitive issues within a negotiated settlement often produce leaders or factions who are unsatisfied with the outcome and continue to pursue political violence (Stedman, 1997). Ceasefires rarely signify a definitive end to conflict; as Darby and MacGinty note, 'violence precedes peace processes and continues as an unavoidable background during them' (Darby and MacGinty, 2000: 8). Those who use violence to undermine negotiated peace, often referred to as 'spoilers' or splinter groups, can be identified in almost all peace processes (Heidelberg Institute for International Conflict Research, 2012).

This chapter examines political violence surrounding peace processes. Initially, discussion focuses on the nature of modern-day conflict and the utility of comparing global conflict situations. Building upon Steven Stedman's (1997) seminal work on spoiler theories, this chapter continues to explore the motivation of actors during phases of mediation and negotiation, and questions how this threat of political violence can be managed and contained. The aim of this chapter is therefore twofold. Firstly, to explore the nature of political violence surrounding peace processes and, secondly, to question how, if at all, armed groups can be managed and brought in to the political process. The context in which political violence is discussed is within armed intra-state civil conflict where at least one of the parties to the conflict is committed to or involved in a peace process.

Protracted conflict and intra-state violence

In order to understand the presence of political violence surrounding the transition to peace it is first necessary to discuss the nature of conflict from which political violence emerges. The ending of the Cold War marked a seismic shift in the nature of global conflict. Previous frameworks and theories of understanding and predicting international politics became antiquated as conflict moved away from relations among states (inter-state) to order within states (intra-state). It should be noted that the boundaries of a state may be contested, therefore blurring the lines between whether a conflict should be classed as inter- or intra-state.

The number of conflicts classed as intra-state rose from 303 in 2011 to 314 in 2012, whist the number of inter-state conflicts decreased by two from 84 to 82 (Lacina, 2006). In 2012, then, 80 per cent of all global conflicts were domestic. Between 1999 and 2002, civil wars accounted for 90 per cent of combatant and civilian related deaths. Internal conflict can be deep rooted, with disputes reaching back centuries over the issues of sovereignty, territory or resources, such as oil in the Middle East or scarce cropland in areas such as Rwanda (Darby and MacGinty, 2000). Rasmussen argues that the difference between international war and inter-group fighting within states is the manner in which they are conducted. For example, international wars are typically fought between professional state armies that are expected to follow internationally agreed standardised rules of engagement (Rasmussen, 1997). However, internal conflicts tends to involve paramilitary formations that are less likely to adhere to the same standardised rules, making the domestic setting more susceptible to human-rights violations, guerrilla warfare and the targeting of civilians (Rasmussen, 1997). As a result, the typical nature of modern-day conflict is protracted, entrenched and runs along ethnic or identity-based lines. Finding a solution to conflict involves bringing together sides that are likely to possess deep-rooted feelings of mistrust and suspicion towards one another. Therefore, a successful peace process does not just have to focus on organising a post-conflict political settlement but on addressing grievances and divisions across society.

Searching for a solution to violent conflict

Practitioners, policymakers and academics have searched to find a new paradigm of conflict resolution in order to address the intractability of intra-state violence within deeply divided societies. In order to find a solution to modern-day conflict, separate cases are often brought together in the attempt to form a comparative perspective. For example, the commonalities between the ethno-national conflicts in Northern Ireland, South Africa and Israel/Palestine, such as high civilian casualties, inter-communal violence and human-rights violations, mean that they are often used to investigate the possibility of identifying comparable features between different conflict situations (Gidron et al., 2002; Knox and Quirk, 2000). The hope is that by identifying similarities and points of divergence between the various contexts it will be possible to provide a positive lesson for reducing violence and offer encouragement to finding a durable solution to conflict elsewhere.

The increase in global peace processes has been accompanied by debate in relation to the practical value of studying them, particularly in relation to the benefit and utility of comparing distinct conflict settings. For example, the peace process in Northern Ireland is often compared to the situation in the Basque Country in the hope of transferring successful elements from one context to another. Guelke and Cox both examine the importance of international influences upon the peace process in Northern Ireland and the signing of the 1998 Good Friday Agreement (GFA), and in reducing violence in other global peace processes. Cox suggests that the larger changes in the international system, when the end of the Cold War caused a shift in the focus of global politics towards intra-state tensions, provided a significant influence on the Northern Irish conflict (Cox, 2006). With a conflict as ostensibly parochial and deep rooted as

Northern Ireland's, it may be hard to see what relationship it may have to events elsewhere. Bearing this in mind, Cox is careful not to argue that the peace process was a result of the cessation of the Cold War alone, but contends that whilst 'the IRA may well have been a quintessentially Irish phenomenon it could, however, not escape the world or ignore what was happening outside of Ireland. Nor I think did it try to' (Guelke, 2006).

Whilst Cox emphasises the importance of the international perspective to Northern Ireland, Guelke takes this argument a step further by highlighting the connections between various peace processes. Guelke goes about demonstrating a chain of events linking one process to another. For example, South Africa embraced a peace process in the 1990s, which culminated in the country's transition to a non-racial democracy, this in turn providing encouragement and a positive basis for comparison in Northern Ireland. By the late 1990s the GFA 'came to be seen as a model for the resolution of conflict in other deeply divided societies', especially in the Basque region, and 'despite the difficulties and implications the GFA encountered, the example of the settlement ... was seen as particularly relevant to the continuing quest for peace between Israelis and Palestinians' (Kidd and Walters, 2002: 264). Therefore, whilst the comparison of peace processes helps to provide a framework or predictive function, according to Cox and Guelke it also provides encouragement to the process of change in other seemingly intractable violent conflicts.

The importance and practicality of this comparative function being able to transfer the lessons learnt from one situation to another in reducing violent conflict has been disputed. Whilst conflict resolution does not happen in a vacuum and is inevitably touched to some extent by international events, it is necessary to question exactly how much weight should be attached to the importance of international comparisons. For example, Darby and MacGinty (2008: 1) argue that 'peacemaking processes cannot be lifted wholesale like templates and applied to other locations'. Peace processes display an extensive set of variables and defy neat categorisation. Attempting to implement an accord is highly reliant on the situation in hand and details vary greatly from one conflict to another. It is vital to remember that each conflict is essentially parochial, with its own distinct culture, history and social development. The possibility of implementing a peace agreement is dependent upon the understanding of contextual realities where culture, history and infrastructure vary greatly.

There is a danger that concentrating too much on finding a blueprint of conflict resolution could blind us to vital differences and the root causes of violence. Such diversity makes the study and comparison of peace processes seem rather futile; however, it is possible to look beyond certain variables to see how techniques used in one location may be adapted and applied in another location (Stedman, 1997: 8). Whilst there is no one-size-fits-all approach to resolving violent conflict, commonalities do occur, especially in relation to the emergence of splinter groups and the continued presence of violence.

TEXTBOX 8   CASE STUDY: PKK (KURDISTAN WORKERS' PARTY)

Kurdistan is an area of land that crosses the borders of four states: Turkey, Iran, Iraq and Syria. The Partiya Karkerên Kurdistani (PKK) fight for the liberation of the Kurdish population in Turkey and operate primarily in southeast Turkey (northwest Kurdistan). At the time of the PKK's formation in 1978 the Turkish military were carrying out large-scale arrests of those associated with nationalist groups and leftist (Marxist–Leninist) politics, and the organization was forced to base itself in Syria. Following the increased autonomy gained by the Kurds in northern Iraq (southern Kurdistan) in 1991, the PKK used this region to launch cross-border attacks. The PKK still maintains a stronghold in the Qandil Mountains of northern Iraq. In the formation of states following the collapse of the Ottoman Empire after World War I the nation of Kurdistan was overlooked. When the Turkish state was formed in 1923 the Kurdish population was disregarded and their autonomy was assumed unnecessary, owing to the close historical ties of the Turkish and Kurdish populations. The PKK was founded with the intention of establishing a united, independent and socialist Kurdish nation through armed rebellion, capitalising on the widespread unrest following the 1971 military coup and the reintroduction of democracy in the mid-1970s. Despite an original doctrine of armed rebellion there has been a greater flexibility in the group's stance and a greater willingness to negotiate with the Turkish government since the capture of Öcalan, the group's founder and ideological leader, in 1999.

Disengagement

The activity of the PKK has come in a clear series of waves. The first wave reached a climax in the 1990s, which witnessed the highest casualty rate of the conflict. Following the capture of Öcalan, there was a short-lived upsurge in attacks, but this did not last long and a ceasefire was announced soon after. This ceasefire was largely observed but was announced to be over by the PKK in 2004; it regrouped and commenced its militant activity in protest to the government's stagnation on the Kurdish issue and as a response to the increased autonomy granted to the Kurds in Iraq.

With a perceived lack of military progress, another unilateral ceasefire was announced by the PKK in 2007 but this was short-lived.

By 2012 the clashes between the Turkish military and the Kurdish militants had increased dramatically and had resulted in the highest death rates since before the capture of Öcalan. This came despite the Turkish government's attempted 'democratic openings', which sought to bring the PKK to the negotiating table. However, direct negotiations between the government and Öcalan towards the end of 2012 led the PKK leader to use the Newroz celebrations of March 2013 to announce a ceasefire and call for the withdrawal of armed militants from Turkey.

In May 2013, following the orders of Öcalan, the military faction of the PKK began their withdrawal, mostly to the Qandil Mountains of northern Iraq (southern Kurdistan).

Further disengagement, notably the disarmament of the fighters, rests on whether Öcalan's demands are met in the new constitution that is currently being written. Reportedly the pro-Kurdish BDP, which forms part of the four-party constitutional committee tasked with producing a new draft constitution in 2013, was pushing for reforms backed by Öcalan himself. If these demands are met then this may ultimately pave the way for the disbanding of the PKK as it currently exists.

Spoiling the peace

Understanding the nature and threat of violence that surrounds the negotiation and implementation of a peace agreement is an important area of analysis for understanding contemporary conflict and the factors that inhibit the transition from violent conflict to peace. One of the immediate goals of a peace process is to put an end to physical violence. However, many attempts at peace fail to reach the negotiation phase owing to the continuation of armed fighting. A ceasefire is often demanded as a precondition for allowing militant groups to enter into negotiations. The term ceasefire acknowledges that there has been a pause in the use of force, as opposed to a complete surrender, where parties involved have kept open the option to return to violence. If successful a cessation of physical violence may develop into a peace process. However, many ceasefires and peace agreements give way to renewed and escalating hostility and rarely indicate a complete end to violence.

The violence committed by groups during peace negotiations is not indiscriminate or random – rather it is timed and tactically calculated. For example, whilst discussing the scale of opposition surrounding peace negotiations, Kydd and Walter argue that violence in the Middle East and Northern Ireland over the past two decades has shown a reoccurring pattern: violence has been timed to coincide with major events in a peace process (Kydd and Walter, 2002). For example, in Israel–Palestine the agreement of Israeli Prime Minister Yitzhak Rabin and the Palestinian Liberation Organization's (PLO) Yasir Arafat to the Oslo Peace Accord in 1993 was followed by an increase in the intensity of attacks by Hamas as an expression of their opposition to Arafat's more 'moderate agenda' and the legitimacy offered by the Oslo Accord to the Israeli state.

When violence lowers in scale, focus turns towards issues such as decommissioning, the reform of policing, prisoner releases and the embedding of a new justice system. Approaching the sensitive issues of amnesties, human rights and democratic reform within a negotiated settlement often produces leaders or factions who are unsatisfied with the outcome. As Stedman argues, 'Even the best designed settlements must be prepared for violence from leaders and organisations who decide that the kind of peace in question is not in their interest' (Stedman, 1997: 6). Spoilers, who use violence to undermine negotiated peace, can be identified in almost all peace processes.

Identifying spoilers

According to Stedman, the greatest source of risk to peace negotiations and mediation comes from spoilers. Spoilers are defined by Stedman as 'leaders or parties who believe that the peace emerging from negotiations threatens their power, world view, and interests, and who use violence to undermine attempts to achieve it' (Stedman, 1997: 5). Crucially, spoilers are contextual: they can only exist where there is an emerging or existing peace to spoil. During conflict there are numerous labels given to those engaged in the struggle for power, such as terrorists, rebels, militia, radicals and dissidents; only once there is a movement towards peace can the label of spoiler be applied.

The utility of spoiler theory is to allow for comparison between conflict areas and to 'evaluate the appropriateness and effectiveness of different strategies of spoiler management' (Stedman, 1997: 6–12). The literature on spoiler groups and spoiler management therefore focuses on creating a typology for categorising the different actors based on their motivations and tactics. Spoiler management asks important questions such as: How have these groups emerged? What do they want to achieve? How might preventative action be taken?

Peace processes create spoilers who perceive their political interests as being undermined by accommodations falling short of their traditional goals. Having invested heavily in armed struggle, there may be a desire to continue this path. Armed conflict commonly experiences a rise in organised groups, individuals and politicians who are able to exploit positions of power and profit from war-related activities, and who may not want organisational or political change (Stedman, 1997). Even the most carefully crafted settlements must be prepared for the continuation of violence by factions that decide that the direction of the peace is not in their interest. Spoilers exist in many forms with different goals and strategies. Dealing with the threat of continued violence is dependent on the appropriate diagnosis of spoiler type. Stedman identifies different spoiler types by considering their position in the peace process, the goals they seek and their commitment to achieving those goals (Stedman, 1997).

The position of spoilers is defined by Stedman as being inside or outside the process. An inside spoiler 'signs a peace agreement, signals a willingness to implement a settlement, and yet fails to fulfil key obligations to the agreement' (Stedman, 1997: 6–7). Such groups utilise strategies of stealth and are willing to keep the peace process going as long as it is beneficial to them. Outside spoilers use strategies of overt violence in an attempt to undermine peace; they are described by Stedman as 'outside parties who are excluded from a peace process or excluded themselves' (Stedman, 1997: 7–11). Such strategies involve the targeting of moderates where violence tactically coincides with progress in negotiations.

Spoiler groups also differ by the goals they seek and their determination to achieve those goals. Whilst some spoilers are more likely to engage in a reasoned judgement towards the cost and benefit of their action, others are more immune to the price of their activities and irrevocable goals. Therefore, spoilers occupy different positions on a spectrum depending on their aims and willingness to use pragmatic considerations in achieving these aims. As Stedman notes, 'some spoilers have limited goals; others see the world in all or nothing terms and pursue total power' (Stedman, 1997: 6–11). Managing spoiler groups and responding to the violent threat they pose requires the correct identification of spoiler type. Stedman applies a typology of limited, greedy and total spoilers to accommodate the variations between spoiler goals and their commitment to achieving these goals. Firstly, limited spoilers are described as possessing limited goals and could conceivably be included in the peace process given the right concessions, such as a share of power and the guaranteed security of their followers. At the other end of the spectrum total spoilers are seen to be radical and devoid of the pragmatism necessary for compromise and instead pursue total power and exclusive recognition of their authority. In such a case any recognition of peace is tactical. For a peace process to move forward, total spoilers must either be suppressed or marginalised. Greedy spoilers sit somewhere in the middle of this spectrum and are thought to have goals and aims that contract and expand in relation to risk and cost. Greedy spoilers can therefore be accommodated in peace processes if the incentives are right and the costs constrain them from making additional demands (Greenhill and Major, 2006/07).

The work of Stedman is useful in explaining opposition to peace processes and resistance to accommodation, yet labelling militant groups into one of three categories and their position in the process does not necessarily take into account the evolving nature of the parties involved. It is easy for external observers or third parties to assume that spoilers are fixed in their views and behaviour and that they are compelled by their ideology and identity to a pre-determined course of action. Spoiler theories do not consider the tactical considerations of actors – for example, the category of total spoilers suggests that they are actors who are immune to logic and rationale. Actors within conflict are rational in the sense that they will deploy tactics in response to the situation they find themselves in to achieve a certain goal. Therefore, the existence of a group that fits Stedman's definition of a total spoiler as rigid and dogmatic or a limited spoiler as pragmatic and realistic has been brought into question. Stedman's definition of spoilers has attracted criticism for not considering factors such as intra-group dynamics and tactical strategy which determine the different roles spoilers play.

Structural influences on spoiler behaviour

An over-reliance on the framework set out by Stedman runs the risk of greatly underestimating the considerable influence that structural factors such as intra-group relationships and inter-group dynamics continue to exert on the trajectory and implementation of a peace process (Greenhill and Major, 2006/07). Greenhill and Major argue that, whilst such profiling may be helpful in structuring behaviour towards certain parties in the peace process, it is the opportunity structure and not the actors' overall intention that determines their behaviour. They therefore propose a reversal of Stedman's spoiler model by suggesting that 'the type of spoiler does not determine the kinds of outcomes that are possible; instead, the kinds of outcomes that are possible determine the type of spoiler that may emerge at any given time' (Greenhill and Major, 2006/07). Parties to a peace process adjust their goals according to prevailing opportunities.

It is not the case that all spoilers act the same and for the same reasons across the various contexts where peace is being negotiated. Zahar warns that the profiling of groups who use violence (as spoilers who want to derail peace) is analytically inaccurate and practically harmful to the efforts of mediators seeking to build the foundations of sustainable peace (Zahar, 2010). Instead, she develops the profiling of spoilers further by linking action to the costs and risks available to actors based on their position in the peace process. Whilst Stedman's typology characterises outside spoilers as those more likely to use violence, Zahar argues that there is no *a priori* logical reason why actors who want to derail the peace would necessarily use violence. Rather, violence is one of several strategies used by spoilers that are both inside and outside the process in an attempt to undermine the mediation process or renegotiate terms of the agreement. Therefore, 'to simply say that an actor resorted to violence tells us little about their attitudes towards peace' (Zahar, 2010: 270). Violence does not necessarily signify an opposition to peace; it can also be tactical in order to express discontent with the means of implementation.

Actors may become involved in mediation in order to improve upon their position and prospects, not necessarily as an honest indication of their willingness to compromise with their opponent. Within Stedman's definition of spoiler-group positioning, this suggests that inside spoilers may involve themselves within a peace agreement for tactical reasons. Newman and Richmond argue that the negotiation process of a peace agreement may provide assets that the actors involved may value. As a result, they suggest that 'disputants may therefore harbour devious objectives, unrelated to the attainment to a compromise solution' (Newman and Richmond, 2006: 2). The motives for involvement in a peace process may include the attainment of time to regroup and reorganise, avoid sanctions, a recognition of their cause and to escape responsibility for the continuation of the conflict. Therefore, Stedman's description of inside spoilers as using strategies of stealth and outside spoilers engaging in overt violence and the targeting of moderates should not be applied to indicate the overall goals of a group. As Zahar warns, 'Observing the non use of violence should not automatically comfort us in believing that an actor is favourable to peace. Peace processes can be sapped in multiple nonviolent ways' (Zahar, 2010: 270). Whilst the use of violence may be tactical, likewise, those inside the process may not be involved in order to negotiate an end to the conflict.

Intra-party dynamics

In parallel with structural factors, spoiler behaviour may also be determined by intra-group dynamics. Most peace processes generate organisational divisions. The Irish Taoiseach at the time of the Good Friday Agreement, Bertie Ahern, commented, 'It is an observable phenomenon in Northern Ireland, and elsewhere, that tension and violence tend to rise when compromise is in the air' (Ahern, 1997). Groups involved in negotiations are rarely a single united front but are instead described by Darby and MacGinty as 'complex organisms performing different functions and providing umbrellas for different interests' (Darby and MacGinty, 2004: 275). It is during sensitive periods such as ceasefires and negotiations that these interests diffuse and the unity of the group breaks down.

The dividing lines between the actors involved in conflict are not necessarily well defined. In addition, actors in an ever-evolving situation such as intra-state conflict are susceptible to changing their stance, demands and allegiance. Whilst discussing general trends between spoiler-group violence and intra-party dynamics, Darby states that the involvement of paramilitaries in peace negotiations implies that the purity of their cause has been compromised, causing a strain on the movement. He states that during these negotiations 'it is difficult to find any instances when such a move was not accompanied by a split between two main groups – zealots and dealers' (Darby, 2006: 219). The zealots represent the less compromising and more theological groups who 'picked up the torch – sometimes literally – they believed had been surrendered by the dealers' (Darby, 2006: 219). One example is that of Hamas who continued a struggle they believed the PLO had abandoned. Zealots also existed on the Israeli side, demonstrated by the assassination of Prime Minister Rabin in 1995 by a right-wing Israeli 'radical' opposed to the signing of the Oslo Accords. According to Darby's definition, it is not the aim of such groups or individuals to influence the content of any agreement but to disrupt negotiations and prevent any agreement being reached. Dealers, on the other hand, incorporate those militant groups that take the decision to engage in negotiations for reasons such as war weariness or mounting external pressure (Darby, 2001).

The conventional understanding of conflict resolution is that parties act as peacemakers or spoilers primarily to achieve objectives against their external opponent. However, Pearlman suggests that, during conflict, parties do not simply act against their opponents who are sitting across the negotiating table: they act also in response to internal political imperatives (Pearlman, 2008/09). Internal communal dynamics are likely to play as significant a role in the emergence of spoiler violence as inter-party competition. According to Pearlman, 'for competing factions in a non-state group ... participation in or spoiling of negotiations offers an opportunity to advance their struggle for political dominance' (2008/09: 79). Therefore, actors turn to negotiations or spoiler behaviour to contest both what the peace agreement entails and also to decide who has the balance of power within their own community.

Internal dynamics are relevant not only in terms of understanding the intra-party politics within a single group, but also in situations where multiple actors present a single community or identity. As Nilsson and Kovacs explain, the internal politics of one side in the armed conflict is an explanatory factor in the emergence of spoiler behaviour, demonstrated by situations such as in Lebanon, South Africa and Palestine. For example, in the later stages of the Lebanese Civil War (1975–90) two Shia Muslim factions, Hezbollah and the more secular and reformist Amal movement, fought to secure the community heartlands in the south of the country and in Southern Beirut. The struggles between Amal and Hezbollah between 1988 and 1990 determined to a great extent the borders and regions of influence of the two movements as well as the balance of power between them in the Lebanese system. Hezbollah's defeat of Amal in Beirut brought with it military and political recognition whilst Amal suffered a drop in status in the eyes of both the Shia community and the powers active in Lebanon, leading to the further erosion of its influence and internal unity (Azani, 2011).

Not all factions on the same side will benefit equally from a peace deal. Leaders of dominant groups are more likely than subordinate groups to benefit from a peace settlement in terms of receiving external recognition, political influence and peace dividends. According to this logic, it is the group that wins the competition for dominance within a community that is most likely to receive larger gains from the peace negotiations – and the minor groups who are considered more likely to act as spoilers.

Are spoilers anti-peace?

Stedman's typology has attracted criticism for being reductionist towards a highly complex issue and ascribing pejorative characteristics to those labelled as spoilers. For example, Cochrane is critical of the 'over-simplification' of the spoiler discourse that connotes anybody resistant to a peace process as an 'extremist who prefers violence to peace' (Cochrane, 2008: 109). Newman and Richmond continue this debate by stating that 'the very notion of "spoilers" suggests a binary between those "for" and "against" conflict settlement, but most evidence shows that peace processes are not so simple' (Newman and Richmond, 2006: 4). Rather than ascribing set characteristics by spoiler type the capacity to engage in spoiler behaviour is in fact evident within most actors during various stages of the process. The labelling of actions as spoiler behaviour assigns negative connotations to those involved as being anti-peace, whereas according to an alternative rationality such actions may be perceived as legitimate. In asymmetrical disputes negotiations may occur on an uneven basis and actions which may be labelled as spoiling by some may appear justified and legitimate to others. The labelling of actors as spoilers may reflect subjective criteria of evaluation and 'external' rationality and power (Stephanova, 2006). It is therefore unclear who has the right to make a judgement about whether the spoiler's demands are legitimate and should be accommodated within the peace process.

Gunning also warns against the negative connotations that are attached to the label of spoiler. Characterising groups as spoilers may at times be a political act (as opposed to an impartial description) that uncritically assumes that all of the blame for a failed peace process is the responsibility of the spoilers, leaving any further limitations of the procedure unexamined (Gunning, 2007). A lack of trust between the parties involved, stunted progress towards a settlement or the inability to advance on key issues are likely to be central in explaining the failure of a peace process. Therefore, it is more likely that the spoiler problem will be indicative of the conflict's deeper, unaddressed issues.

As part of its subjectivity the term spoiler also insists that the liberal peace-building framework is the best way to organise post-conflict societies. Peace agreements differ between contexts in order to address the root causes of the violence within different conflict situations. However, they all generally include aspects of the liberal peace framework such as democratisation, human-rights safeguards, return and resettlement of refugees and the free market (Newman and Richmond, 2006). Applying the label of spoiler in reference to those groups who do not conform to this framework is based on prior assumptions.

Greenhill and Major warn against demonising certain types of actor, dubbed extremists, who are then excluded from the political process and peace negotiations (Greenhill and Major, 2006/07). The approach of labelling armed non-state actors as terrorists or dissidents, for example, has become much more dominant in the post-9/11 context. For those who support a no-negotiation policy with groups termed spoilers or terrorists, isolation and delegitimisation is seen as the only way forward to avoid justifying armed non-state actors. An alternative line of reasoning says that dialogue with groups deemed to be spoilers does not legitimise means and ends but rather stresses the importance in keeping the channels of communication open.

Spoiler management: inclusion or exclusion?

Should peace negotiations encourage inclusion and facilitate the participation of all parties involved or exclude actors that are deemed to be spoilers? Including groups engaged in spoiler behaviour runs the risk of undermining democratic principles and the legitimacy of peace negotiations. The nature of intra-state conflict typically involves the violation of human rights and inter-communal violence, the result being a deeply polarised society. Höglund argues that there is a serious risk involved in incorporating actors that do not adhere to democratic principles of non-violence and respect for human rights, as their inclusion may challenge the legitimacy of the democratic process (Höglund, 2008). Inclusion of spoilers who continue to use violence may run the risk of undermining public belief in the new political arrangements.

However, it is also possible to argue that the more excluded parties are from peace negotiations, the greater the chances of the agreement being unsuccessful. Such a position rests on the assumption that a group's tendency to act as a total spoiler is less of an influencing factor than the political context in which it operates. The hope is that the incentives that accompany inclusion and participation within a democratic system may turn such groups into moderates. Zahar argues that peace processes provide insiders with a voice as well as material and political dividends associated with peace implementation: 'All else being equal, the use of violence by insiders is expected to be more costly than the use of violence by outsiders.

Mediators trying to minimise the risk of violence might thus want to ensure that the mediation process is as inclusive as possible' (Zahar, 2010: 273). Inside actors assessing whether to use violence involves them weighing up not only the cost of fighting but also the loss of inclusion.

Excluding parties from the process means that those who are outside negotiations have less to lose by returning to war, and the main costs to consider are in military terms. In some peace processes, such as Northern Ireland and South Africa, inclusion in negotiations and being offered a place at the table in response to the abandonment of violence have served as incentives to the factions involved in conflict. Jonathan Powell, Tony Blair's chief negotiator in the Northern Irish peace process, stressed the importance of keeping contact open with all sides involved in negotiations:

> One of the lessons that comes most starkly out of the Northern Ireland experience is the importance of maintaining contact. It is very difficult for governments in democracies to be seen to be talking to terrorists who are killing their people unjustifiably. But it is precisely your enemies, rather than your friends, you should talk to if you want to resolve a conflict (Powell, 2008: 313).

According to this judgement the process of mediation and implementation should be as inclusive as possible as actors outside of the process have a greater motivation to act as spoilers.

Research evaluating the management of spoiler violence highlights the significance of third parties to conflict management. Third parties act as an external broker to mediation and can be international organisations, such as the UN or European Union, as well as major global powers that are able to provide expertise and influence and offer substantial economic rewards and resources, such as the USA in Northern Ireland. External actors are also involved in knowledge transfer as they can apply their experience and expertise from acting as a broker in one conflict situation to another conflict situation. For example, Senator George Mitchell acted as a mediator for the talks in the build-up to the GFA then went on to become the US peace envoy to the Middle East.

TEXTBOX 9   EXTERNAL BROKERS

External brokers or third parties have become a standard feature of peace negotiations. The involvement of third parties, such as the UN, international organisations and large or regional powers, can help restore trust, build confidence and change the perceptions and behaviour of disputing parties. For third parties to have a positive impact they are expected to operate as an 'honest broker', who requires contextual historical knowledge, as well as an ability to mediate and facilitate deals and to act as enforcers of deadlines and targets.

As well as knowledge transfer a key advantage of involving third parties in the mediation process is that unofficial actors are largely unencumbered by the political baggage their official counterparts carry and can therefore be more effective (Rasmussen, 1997). In many cases external mediators can provide invaluable support and direction to the process. Stedman notes that the crucial difference between the success and failure of spoilers 'is the role played by the international actors as custodians of peace' (Stedman, 1997: 6). Hampson also singles out the role of third parties as the most important factor in determining success: 'Peace processes that enjoy high levels of third party assistance and support during the entire course of the peacemaking and peace building process are arguably more likely to succeed than those that do not' (Hampson, 1996: 13). An external actor can act as a bridge between rival forces, as they may not be prepared to engage directly with each other. Therefore, in some instances the successful implementation of a peace agreement is dependent upon the presence or availability of third parties that can help restore trust, build confidence and change the perceptions and behaviour of disputing parties. The role of third parties can be seen as a major incentive to parties to encourage rebuilding and recovery within a post-conflict context.

The positive interpretation of third parties as having the potential to encourage and guide a peace agreement considers their involvement from a neutral and unbiased position. However, a number of peace processes have been touched by regional and international powers that have had a negative impact on the progress of mediation. The electoral and strategic interests in Israel–Palestine have meant that events in the Middle East have always gained attention in the US. In addition, the input of regional powers in Lebanon has meant that the influence of Syria and Iran has never been far away. In both these contexts the partiality of external parties has heightened the insecurity of some actors to the process who do not see the outside party as a custodian of peace but as a hostile presence. It is therefore necessary to warn that the mere presence of a third party is not sufficient to overcome the divisions within society, manage spoiler behaviour and generate commitment to the peace process. Ultimately, the presence of a third party cannot guarantee transformation and management – such actors can only referee rather than resolve the causes of violence (Tonge, 2014).

Conclusion: spoiling the peace?

In order to understand spoilers and spoiler activity it is essential to first comprehend the nature of modern-day conflict. The specific characteristics of violent conflict are contextual with distinct differences that reflect the variations in socio-economic development, culture, history and identity from one situation to another. It is therefore questionable the extent to which academics and practitioners are able to develop a tick-box list identifying common characteristics to conflict resolution. Despite a need to look beyond a common framework of conflict mediation the continuing presence of violence is an extremely common feature surrounding global peace processes. There will always be the presence of groups or individuals who profit financially and/or politically from armed conflict, and it is in their interest to prevent a cessation of violence. It is also likely that there will be groups and individuals ready and willing to pick up the torch put down by actors moving away from armed conflict and towards mediation.

In the post-9/11 context the use of politically loaded terms such as extremists, terrorists and spoilers comes with subjective assumptions about the intentions and rational judgement of the actors involved. The reality is that violent acts are rational in the sense that they have a calculated purpose. Distinctions need to be made between political players using spoiling tactics and groups that can be labelled total spoilers. It is more beneficial to focus analysis on spoiler behaviour as opposed to characterising groups depending on their position and aims.

Stedman's work on spoiler groups allows us to contemplate the behaviour and motivations of actors in conflict situations and begin to understand ways of limiting such threats. Understanding spoiler behaviour is important because isolation can strengthen hardliners whilst inclusion and engagement within conflict mediation can strengthen moderates. Spoiler behaviour is dependent on and shaped by circumstantial variables such as structural factors and the socio-political background. Stedman's typology has since been developed to consider the unique influences of intra-group dynamics, tactical strategy and inter-group competition within distinct contexts. Spoiler theories therefore serve an example as to why it is impossible to present a universal framework of conflict resolution.

STUDY BOX CHAPTER 9

Key reading

Darby, J. (2001) *The Effect of Violence on Peace Processes* (Washington, DC: United States Institute for Peace).

Darby, J. and MacGinty, R. (2000) *The Management of Peace Processes* (Basingstoke: Palgrave).

Newman, E. and Richmond, O. (2006) (Eds.) *Challenges to Peacebuilding: Managing Spoilers During Conflict Resolution* (New York and Tokyo: United Nations University Press).

Stedman, S.J. (1997) 'Spoiler Problems in Peace Processes', *International Security* 22(2): 5–53.

Wilkinson, P. (2007) 'Politics, Diplomacy and Peace Processes: Pathways out of Terrorism?', *Terrorism and Political Violence* 11(4): 66–82.

Study questions

1 To what extent should states negotiate with terrorists?

2 What impact do spoilers have during peace processes?

3 To what extent can negotiations and a peace process lead to the successful end of a terrorism campaign? What is the role of external actors?

References

Ahern, B. (1997) cited in *The Observer*, 22 September.

Azani, E. (2011) *Hezbollah: The Story of the Party of God* (Basingstoke, Palgrave Macmillan).

Cochrane, F. (2008) *Ending Wars* (Cambridge, Polity Press).

Cox, M. (2006) Rethinking the International and Northern Ireland: A Defence, in M. Cox, A. Guelke and F. Stephens (eds.), *A Farewell To Arms? Beyond the Good Friday Agreement* (Manchester, Manchester University Press), pp. 427–442.

Darby, J. (2001) *The Effect of Violence on Peace Processes* (Washington, United States Institute for Peace).

Darby, J. (2006) A Truce Rather than a Treaty? The Effect of Violence in the Irish Peace Process, in M. Cox, A. Guelke and F. Stephens (eds.), *A Farewell To Arms? Beyond the Good Friday Agreement* (Manchester, Manchester University Press), pp. 212–225.

Darby, J. and R. MacGinty (2000) *The Management of Peace Processes* (Basingstoke, Palgrave).

Darby, J. and R. MacGinty (2004) Coming out of Violence: A Comparative Study of Peace Processes, in O. Hargie and D. Dickson (eds.), *Researching the Troubles: Social Science Perspectives on the Northern Ireland Conflict* (London, Mainstream Publishing), pp. 273–288.

Darby, J. and MacGinty R. (eds.) (2008) *Contemporary Peacemaking: Conflict, Peace Processes amd Post-War Reconstruction* (Palgrave, London).

Gidron, B., Katz, S. N. and Hasenfeld, Y. (2002) (eds.) *Mobilizing for Peace: Conflict Resolution in Northern Ireland, Israel/Palestine and South Africa* (Oxford, Oxford University Press).

Greenhill, K. M. and Major, S. (2006/07) The Perils of Profiling: Civil War Spoilers and the Collapse of Intrastate Peace Accords, *International Security* 31, no. 3: 7–40.

Guelke, A. (2006) Political Comparisons: From Johannesburg to Jerusalem, in M. Cox, A. Guelke, and F. Stephens (eds.), *A Farewell To Arms? Beyond the Good Friday Agreement* (Manchester, Manchester University Press), pp. 367–376.

Gunning, J. (2007) Hamas: Socialisation and the Logic of Compromise, in M. Heiberg, B. O'Leary and J. Tirman (eds.), *Terror, Insurgency and the State* (Philadelphia, University of Pennsylvania Press), pp. 123–156.

Hampson, F. O. (1996) *Nurturing Peace: Why Peace Settlements Succeed or Fail* (Washington, DC, United States Institute of Peace Press).

Heidelberg Institute for International Conflict Research (2012) *Conflict Barometer 2012*, available at http://www.hiik.de/en/konfliktbarometer/pdf/ConflictBarometer_2012.pdf (Accessed on 9 October 2013).

Höglund, K. (2008) Violence in War-to-Democracy Transitions, in A. K. Jarstad and T. D. Sisk (eds.), *From War to Democracy* (Cambridge, Cambridge University Press), pp. 80–102.

Knox, C. and Quirk, P. (2000) *Peace Building in Northern Ireland, Israel and South Africa* (Basingstoke, Palgrave Macmillan).

Kydd, A. and Walters, B. (2002) Sabotaging the Peace: The Politics of Extremist Violence, *International Organisation* 56, no. 2: 263–96.

Lacina, B. (2006) Explaining the Severity of Civil Wars, *Journal of Conflict Resolution* 50, no. 2: 276–89.

Newman, E. and Richmond, O. (2006) *Obstacles to Peace Processes: Understanding Spoilers*, in E. Newman and O. Richmond (eds.), *Challenges to Peacebuilding: Managing Spoilers During Conflict Resolution* (New York and Tokyo: United Nations University Press), pp. 23–39.

Pearlman, W. (2008/09) Spoiling Inside and Out: Internal Political Contestations and the Middle East Peace Process, *International Security* 33, no. 3: 79–109.

Powell, J. (2008) *Great Hatred, Little Room: Making Peace in Northern Ireland* (London, Random House).

Rasmussen, J. L. (1997) Peacemaking in the Twenty-first Century: New Rules, New Roles, New Actors, in Zartman, W. I., *Peacemaking in International Conflict* (Washington, United States Institute of Peace Press), pp. 23–50.

Ryan, S. (2000) United Nations Peacekeeping: A Matter of Principles, *International Peacekeeping* 7, no. 1: 27–47.

Stedman, S. J. (1996) Negotiation and Mediation in International Conflicts, in M. E. Brown (ed.), *The International Dimensions of Internal Conflict* (Cambridge, MA, MIT Press), pp. 369–71.

Stedman, S. J. (1997) Spoiler Problems in Peace Processes, *International Security*, 22, no. 2: 5–53.

Stephanova, E. (2006) Terrorism as a Tactic of Spoilers in Peace Processes, in E. Newman and O. Richmond (eds.), *Challenges to Peacebuilding: Managing Spoilers During Conflict Resolution* (United Nations University Press), pp. 78–104.

Tonge, J. (2014) *Comparative Peace Processes* (Cambridge, Polity Press).

Wilkinson, P. (2007) Politics, Diplomacy and Peace Processes: Pathways out of Terrorism?, *Terrorism and Political Violence*, 11, no. 4: 66–82.

Zahar, M. J. (2010) SRSG Mediation in Civil Wars: Revising the 'Spoiler' Debate, *Global Governance*, 16: 265–280.

10

INDIVIDUAL DISENGAGEMENT FROM TERRORIST GROUPS

PAUL GILL, NOEMIE BOUHANA AND JOHN MORRISON

Introduction

In his 2005 account of the psychology of terrorism, Horgan provides a process model of terrorist involvement that comprises three main stages: becoming a terrorist, being a terrorist and disengaging from terrorism. In the opening paragraphs of the disengagement chapter Horgan notes that this particular subject matter 'would appear to have been the basis for the shortest chapter of this book for one simple reason – we simply know too little about what happens for the individual terrorist to leave terrorism behind' (2005: 140). The reasons for this lack of academic enquiry are multiple. First, some researchers may be reluctant to interview former members (Ferguson, 2010). Second, many may not realize the potential of these interviews and instead regard the disengaged as unworthy of study (Horgan, 2005). Third, the availability of disengaged terrorists varies drastically from country to country. For USA-based academics the opportunities afforded are far less compared to UK-based or Spanish academics, owing to recent conflicts. Fourth, obtaining ethical approval for interviewing former offenders can be an onerous process in some academic settings.

Despite these issues, we have seen a small rise in empirically focused analyses of former terrorists that utilize both primary interview techniques and secondary data analysis. Indeed, almost a decade after Horgan's *Psychology of Terrorism* we can identify eight empirical studies of terrorist disengagement spanning groups such as ETA (Reinares, 2011), the (Greek) Revolutionary Organization 17 November (17N) (Kassimeris, 2011), FARC (Rosenau et al., 2013) and ELN (Rosenau et al., 2013) in Colombia, al-Qaeda and its affiliates (Jacobson, 2010), various groups in Northern Ireland including the IRA, UVF and the Red Hand Commandos (Ferguson, 2010; Ferguson et al., forthcoming), and various offenders across a range of ideological and geographical domains (Horgan, 2009).

This chapter summarizes the main findings of these studies across a number of themes identified as key to understanding the disengagement process. Table 10.1 identifies these key themes, and highlights which authors are in agreement with one another.

As can be seen from the table, the key themes that emerge from these studies can be clustered into two types of factors. The first type is thought to lead people down the path of psychological disengagement. The second is made up of a much smaller number of factors thought to encourage actual physical disengagement.

A point of note: some of the factors listed below may turn out to be merely indicators or predictors of disengagement, while others may turn out to be necessary or sufficient causal mechanisms.

Table 10.1 Factors related to disengagement

Author(s)	Rosenau et al. (2013)	Jacobson (2010)	Reinares (2011)	Kassimeris (2011)	Ferguson et al. (forthcoming)	Horgan (2009)
Group	FARC and ELN	al-Qaeda	ETA	17 November	Northern Ireland Loyalists	Various
Desire for or experience of life change	X			X	X	
Mistreatment	X	X	X			
Pressure of military ops	X			X		
Family reasons	X	X				
Demoralized about armed struggle	X		X	X		
Ideology	X	X	X			
Tactical differences		X	X	X		X
Strategic differences		X	X			X
Disillusionment with group's hypocrisy		X	X			X
Unmet expectations		X				
Cognitive dissonance		X				
Environment change		X		X	X	X
Socio-political environment change			X			
Loss of social support			X			
Role migration			X			

Mechanisms are processes by which an effect is produced by its cause. As explained by Campbell (2005: 42), 'Mechanisms are the nuts, bolts, cogs, and wheels that link causes with effects. The specification of causal mechanisms involves more than just establishing correlations [associations] among variables. The identification of a correlation may demonstrate that a relationship exists between variables, but unless we understand the underlying mechanism that caused it, we will not know why the relationship exists.' Whereas variable-based methods of explanation seek to identify predictive (but not necessarily causal) relationships between dependent and independent variables, mechanism-based analyses seek to uncover the pathways that link causes to their effects (McAdam et al., 2008). They provide a rationale for considering any given factor as causal or non-causal. The distinction between variable-based (often called statistical) and mechanism-based explanations matters, because preventing a problem from occurring, or, in the case of disengagement from terrorism, encouraging a particular outcome to happen, requires the manipulation of actual causes, not just symptoms or predictors. (Consider this: treating a fever does not actually cure the disease; eradicating the virus does.)

Given the methodological state of disengagement studies at present, however, it may not always be possible to distinguish one from the other. Often, all that supports the interpretation of a mechanism is a 'good story', which suggests how a given factor could have reasonably brought about a particular outcome. At this stage much of our understanding of the causal processes of disengagement from terrorism remains theoretical or speculative – something to keep in mind when going through the remainder of this chapter.

Over the course of this chapter we outline different aspects of both psychological and physical disengagement, drawing on first-hand accounts from previously published research. Together, the sections outline the state of knowledge with regards to terrorist disengagement and also highlight what we know very little about.

Factors that encourage psychological disengagement

Although few empirical studies are available on terrorist disengagement, this section highlights the wide range of factors identified by researchers as associated in some way with this phenomenon. They show that psychological disengagement is a complex process and may differ dramatically both between and within terrorist groups. Although some common themes are apparent, it seems that disengagement is a highly personal experience that may not be readily generalizable across cases. Context is likely to play a key moderating role across each of the core themes.

Desire for or experience of life change

Being a member of a terrorist organization is obviously a stressful, intense and fraught experience. No wonder, then, that many former members relate their disengagement to a desire for life change. Of the 15,308 accounts of disengagement from Colombian terrorist groups preliminarily analysed by Rosenau et al. (2013) a third stated a desire for a change of life as the primary motive. This was the most commonly occurring narrative within the transcripts. A former Greek terrorist elaborates upon this aspect further: 'As a member of this group, I had no private life. I couldn't start a family. I had to be secretive and constantly hiding' (Kassimeris, 2011: 562). The majority of Loyalists interviewed in the Ferguson et al. study (forthcoming: 11) cited life-changing experiences such as 'getting older, gaining an education, realising they had family responsibilities, and beginning to think about the next generation'.

Pressures of military life

Related to the desire for life change was the fact that many combatants felt pressured by the demands of military life. Almost 14 per cent of the former Colombian militants said that pressure from military operations was their primary motive for exiting the terrorist group. A former member of the Greek 17N group elaborated upon this factor: 'My biggest problem... was that I could no longer comprehend the possessiveness on the part of some members for constant violent activity. This, in the language of the left, is called militarism. There was, in other words, a need for violent activity being carried out constantly but for no objective reason... My complaints over the necessity and regularity of our actions led to ill feelings between myself and the rest of the group and that became obvious when they stopped asking me to take part in operations' (Kassimeris, 2011: 562).

Demoralization

A very small number (4 per cent) of Rosenau et al.'s (2013) sample of former Colombian militants cited demoralization (loss of courage or commitment, due to the belief that the struggle cannot be won) as the key reason for their exit.

Mistreatment

A quarter of the 15,308 accounts of former Colombian militants analysed by Rosenau et al. (2013) highlighted mistreatment as the primary motive for disengagement. Much of this mistreatment came in the form of physical abuse from co-ideologues. An ex-ETA militant evokes similar sentiments: 'You start to see what some of these people are really like and you say to yourself, well, if this is the way they are treating me, who is someone who is playing on the same team they are, and you think that with this kind of treatment and this kind of thinking and we win this war ... this is well, really serious' (Reinares, 2011: 792).

Accumulative mistreatment, as in the case of ex-ETA militants, can also lead to a sense of distrust in superiors within the organization. 'I began to feel scared of the organization. All these bad vibes... I didn't trust the organization anymore. That was when I told myself: no way, there's just no way for this to go on. I can't go on risking my life and to hell with everything. By that I mean they aren't playing fair with me so I don't want to be playing with them anymore. I'm out of here and that's all there is to it' (Reinares, 2011: 790–1).

The second-largest primary motive for leaving Colombian groups in the sample of 15,308 was mistreatment. This was particularly high amongst those under the age of 18. Mistreatment included issues such as 'hunger and extreme fatigue, the relentless nature of the government's counterinsurgency campaign, and physical abuse by commanders' (Rosenau et al., 2013 :8). For example, 'Jorge', a former member of the ELN, disengaged soon after a botched kidnapping he conducted, earned him a death threat and the job of laying land mines from his commander (Rosenau et al., 2013). For many others the realization that lower-level recruits like themselves are expendable also leads to disillusionment. Jacobson (2010: 14) cites the case of Hanif Qadir, a UK citizen who on his journey to join the insurgency in Afghanistan met a group of wounded fighters. One of them said, 'These are evil people ... We came here to fight jihad, but they are just using us as cannon fodder.' Qadir immediately returned to the UK. For others the disengagement process is not so linear. Rosenau et al. (2013) cite the case of 'Alejandro', who originally joined the ELN but left following mistreatment at the hands of others. Two weeks later he joined FARC in order to ensure his protection from an ELN commander who was looking for him. At the FARC camp 'Alejandro' experienced worse conditions, including starvation, and left a few months later.

Ideological differences

Jacobson's study of al-Qaeda highlights that many of the key players who left the organization cited al-Qaeda's 'inaccurate interpretation of Islam as a major factor in their decision' (Jacobson, 2010: 8). For example, Dr Fadl was one of al-Qaeda's elite members from its conception and is highly respected in Islamist circles. Decades ago Dr Fadl authored one of the main texts used by al-Qaeda to legitimize its violence, 'The Essential Guide for Preparation'. Some Arab governments regarded the book as so dangerous that simply possessing it was an offence. Fadl has now authored a second book that deeply criticizes political violence and the strategies originally adopted by Osama bin Laden. He questions the legitimacy of committing aggressive acts irrespective of the violence the enemy is engaged in or their nationality. Al-Qaeda's chief ideologue, Ayman al-Zawahiri, felt compelled to issue a 200-page rebuttal of Fadl's book. According to some intelligence sources, Fadl's book has the potential to undermine al-Qaeda's violent strategy and its ability to recruit volunteers (Wright, 2008; Blair, 2009). Other high-profile former-al-Qaeda-linked individuals have cited similar issues, such as disagreement with fatwas that seek to legitimize the targeting of civilians, Americans and Jews (Jacobson, 2010: 8). Many former FARC members also cited 'ideological disenchantment, and in particular, the FARC's perceived deviation from the revolutionary principles that had first attracted these young people to the movement' (Rosenau et al., 2013: 8). One former ETA member noted that the group was 'losing sight of our goals ... [and] ... you begin to sense that the process is being redirected towards objectives that are not the same as the ones you began fighting for' (Reinares, 2011: 790).

Differences in tactical preferences

Many members accumulate a sense of disillusionment with the general pattern of violence. For example, Jacobson (2010) highlights the case of Hassan Hattab, who began his militant career with the Armed Islamic Group (GIA) in 1992. Hattab quickly rose through the ranks of the group, becoming emir of the eastern part of Algiers in 1994. In 1996 he left the GIA. In an online interview Hattab outlines his reasoning behind leaving the GIA as being largely due to tactical differences with the GIA's new leader, Djamel Zitouni. In Hattab's eyes, Zitouni led the GIA into 'more violence and extremism and bloodshed. He would eliminate anyone suspected of treason ... He was surrounded by dangerous people who later became his advisers ... The image of Zitouni then deteriorated in the eyes of all because of his entourage.' The same year he left the GIA Hattab set up a rival group, the Salafist Group for Preaching and Combat (GSPC). In its first communiqué the GSPC differentiated itself from the GIA by announcing that the Algerian government, not the Algerian people, would be the sole target of its violence. This is also a factor in groups that engaged in far less violence than these jihadist groups. A former member of the Greek 17N relayed that he 'couldn't understand why somebody's life had to be taken when a different type of action or the release of a communiqué would have achieved the same' (Kassimeris, 2011: 562).

Differences in strategic preferences

The case of Hassan Hattab (above) becomes even more interesting when we consider the fact that he also later disengaged from the GSPC, the group he founded. His exit from the group occurred in 2003 after his colleagues failed to support his recommendation for conciliation with the government. It is common for the questioning of the continuation of political violence to lead to individual disengagement from a terrorist group. One ex-ETA member noted: 'That's when you start thinking things through for yourself until you say: wait, wait a minute, this whole thing is absolutely useless' (cited in Reinares, 2011: 785). Reinares' (2011) study of ETA showed similar forces at play:

> The thing was that we reached this point where... elections are held, and you say to yourself: okay, what comes next? We got what we wanted, so what sense is there in going on shooting people and planting bombs? That's the starting point for a thought process, and at the end of it, you are left with not a whole lot of arguments for justifying this armed struggle business... Some others will insist that the primary goal ever since we first decided to take up the armed struggle was total independence ... [but] ... no matter how you look at it, independence is not something that was ever going to be achieved by a handful of kill-happy morons... you're not going to get very far at all... down that path. (Reinares, 2011: 782)

Another former ETA member noted that violence was the sole obstacle to political progression: 'If the nationalists in Euskadi can reach agreement among themselves, a lot of things can be accomplished. So what is preventing them? One of the things separating them is the violence. There are other issues, sure, different matters of emphasis, different viewpoints, you're on the right and I'm on the left, but one can accommodate them in order to achieve a common purpose... The real problem that is keeping them divided is the violence' (cited in Reinares, 2011: 787).

Disillusionment with group hypocrisy

Jacobson (2010) highlights the case of several former jihadists who became disillusioned with their group leaders in terms of their greed, lack of religiosity and engagement with criminality to fund their violent activities. Criminality also emerged in Reinares' study of former ETA militants:

> There was the question of whether we wanted to get involved with... drug dealers and that scene. Even though that whole thing ... well, I suppose it can be justified, but it just didn't square with the military view we had of ETA at that time. If the idea is to send me out on a job like that, well, who's in charge here? That is when, one way or another, you first start to think about the idea of cutting loose, you know? The thing is you could see that people were having doubts about what was going on. Until then, everything was absolutely unquestionable. (2011: 791–2)

Unmet expectations

Jacobson (2010) outlines that some Western recruits to jihad become disillusioned with their surroundings in terrorist training camps, their insecurity, the food, the expense, the disciplining and the level of training. One of the most high-profile and public examples of this in recent years is that of Abu Mansoor al-Amriki. Prior to his death in 2013 the US-born jihadist publicly distanced himself from his former group, al-Shabaab, and their leader, Moktar Ali Zubeyr (aka Ahmed Abdi Godane). The disgruntled jihadist spoke of how he believed that Zubeyr 'had left the principles of our religion and he is trying to change al-Shabaab into an organisation that oppresses every single Muslim in an effort to make him the next Siad Barre of Somalia' (Sabahi Staff, 2013). His further discontent with Zubeyr and the group was highlighted when he stated that the group's leaders wanted to be the 'leader of Somalia regardless of whether he is ruled by sharia or any other laws', and that he had been 'one of the few people in Somalia who stood out against al-Shabaab blowing up innocent civilians' (Voice of America, 2013).

Whether true or exaggerated the public statements of al-Amriki illustrate the dichotomy between the original expectations of what organizational membership would mean and the reality on the ground. This could be the result of an overly idealistic perception of the group, its members and the cause prior to joining. When these ideals are dashed by the reality this can result in the disengagement of members such as al-Amriki. These problems could also stem from recruitment processes that involve a great deal of deception. Rosenau et al. (2013) cite the case of 'Alexander', who had previously worked on a rice plantation. One night he was offered a more promising position at a feedlot. Upon arriving at the apparent feedlot some days later 'Alexander' was informed he would instead be joining the AUC. Three months later he fled.

TEXTBOX 10   AL-SHABAAB

Who

Al-Shabaab: literally translated as 'The Youth'.

Ideological framework

Al-Shabaab's main objectives are to undermine the Transitional Federal Government (TFG) and its foreign allies and create an Islamic state within Somalia, governed by strict Sharia law. However, since their declaration of obedience to al-Qaeda in 2012 there is reason to believe that al-Shabaab may be moving toward becoming a global jihadi group. Furthermore, since territorial defeats in 2011 an evidential ideological split has weakened the organization, with some leaders believing the aim of the organization is to counter the threat of foreign occupation and unite Somalia, whilst other more ambitious leaders aim to establish an Islamic Caliphate that unites Greater Somalia with an area that reaches Egypt and stretches across East Africa.

Formation

Al-Shabaab was initially the armed militia of the Islamic Courts Union (ICU) but became an autonomous organization in 2006 following an intervention headed by the TFG and African Union Mission in Somalia (AMISOM) that subsequently displaced the ICU as head of state.

Area of operation

Al-Shabaab has managed to control vast regions of lawless Somalia. During the golden years of the group, 2009–10, al-Shabaab controlled most of southern Somalia including the capital Mogadishu. Since 2010 operations backed by the TFG and AMISOM have regained control of the capital and much of al-Shabaab's former southern territories. Whilst clearly weakened, al-Shabaab still maintains territorial control of a number of significant regions and ports. Attacks have also stretched beyond Somalia's borders; the double suicide-bomb attack in Kampala, Uganda, in 2010, as well as the more recent attack on a Nairobi shopping centre in Kenya, highlight al-Shabaab's widening of area of operation.

Popular support

As an opposing force to Western-backed foreign intervention and an alternative to the corrupt control of warlords, al-Shabaab was initially popular in Somalia amongst the people. It is important to note that Somali society runs on a clan system which is central to authority within the country; many have argued that this is why a centralized state was never successful in Somalia.

Al-Shabaab successfully managed to merge a number of clans and created stability in many of Somalia's southern regions through strict Sharia law.

Al-Shabaab's heavy-handed governance has led many to criticize it for human-rights abuses, and during 2011 al-Shabaab lost much of its support when it withheld Western aid during a famine.

Resources and external relations

Somali culture and trade networks are more closely associated with the Middle East than with Africa, largely because the Horn of Africa bridges the two continents. Support between Middle Eastern Islamists and Somali Islamists is prevalent; during the 1979–89 war in Afghanistan many Somali jihadists travelled to help their brethren fight the occupation of the Soviet 'infidels'. Al-Shabaab has received similar support in return; fighters from across the Middle East as well as the West have travelled to Somalia to join al-Shabaab's fight. Al-Qaeda has also consistently helped al-Shabaab in a number of ways, namely providing training.

Organizational structure and tactics

Like all organizations, al-Shabaab should not be assumed to be a homogeneous entity; within its organizational structure there are different branches in which the leadership tends to change fairly regularly.

Al-Shabaab's area of operation changes frequently as they are constantly fighting to win territory from the TFG and AMISOM forces. The lack of stability within the group makes it difficult to ascertain who the leaders and members are at any given time. The group is also highly secretive, organized in a regimented structure with apparent transnational linkages. Since 2011 and the strengthening of opposing African Union forces the organizational structure of al-Shabaab has been dramatically weakened owing to the killing of leaders.

The group has also experienced a change in the nature of its tactics. Initially the group used hit-and-run tactics, occupying small areas and then moving on. Firearm attacks have become a favourite tactic for al-Shabaab; the most recent attack that gained worldwide media attention was the 21 September 2013 attack on the Westgate shopping mall in Kenya in which 67 civilians were killed. Al-Shabaab has also recurrently used suicide bombs both in Somalia and neighbouring states; as well as being cheap and strategically logical, suicide attacks serve as a useful propaganda tool to be broadcast online as symbols of martyrdom and jihadist struggle.

Disengagement

In recent years al-Shabaab has experienced various waves of disengagement. Following the withdrawal of Ethiopian troops in 2008, some members

(Continued)

(Continued)

of al-Shabaab became discontent with the ongoing struggle, believing the expulsion of foreign forces to be an aim fulfilled. Moreover, since 2011 AMISOM and TFG's strengthened military capacities have led to huge losses of al-Shabaab territorial occupation which has severely weakened al-Shabaab's ability to impose authority in the region. Whilst al-Shabaab still constitutes a serious threat to regional stability and international security, the increasing pressure of the TFG, AMISOM and US-sponsored drones have led to the loss of key members of the organization, which has resulted in the overall weakening of the group.

Cognitive dissonance

Whilst some members such as 'Alexander' and al-Amriki may leave a group because of unmet expectations others may be influenced by what psychologists refer to as cognitive dissonance. Cognitive dissonance is a theory first put forward by Leon Festinger in the 1950s (Festinger, 1957). It refers to an individual's cognitive (mental) struggle when presented with new information or experiences that conflict with their existing beliefs, values or ideals. It can also be the result of an individual holding two or more contradictory beliefs at one time. In relation to terrorist disengagement, cognitive dissonance can occur when there is a disconnection between the reasons why an individual joined and his/her subsequent experiences. One example is sympathetic treatment by the security forces of the 'enemy' (Jacobson, 2010). As with each of the factors introduced in this short chapter, cognitive dissonance on its own will not lead to an individual's disengagement. However, when new ideas or experiences challenge their existing worldview this can lead to an individual moving closer to organizational exit. Even if it does not lead to complete exit it may result in the individual being less committed to the cause than they were previously. In essence cognitive dissonance can play the role of cultivating a sense of doubt in an individual member in relation to their continued commitment.

Family

For those who maintain contact with their family, news from home can alter the individual's value hierarchy. Jacobson (2010) cites examples of former jihadists who left because of family illness. In many groups new recruits are socially isolated from primary friends and family for a variety of reasons, but largely due to what the leadership believe to be the necessary clandestine nature of the terrorist organization. This management decision can lead to disillusionment later down the line. For example, 5 per cent of Rosenau's sample of former Colombian militants stated that the imposed absence from family was a primary driver for them leaving the organization.

Socio-political change

Some individuals leave terrorist organizations when the socio-political climate that inspired them to join in the first place changes. Reinares' (2011) study of disengaged ETA militants highlights the fact that many joined to help overthrow an authoritarian regime. Once Spain democratized and began to decentralize territorially, the grievances that motivated many ebbed away. One disengaged female militant notes that by the time she left the group in 1976:

> I had this feeling that things had really changed ... that the situation was objectively different than when I first became a militant. You had this feeling a new era was dawning for Euskadi and for the Spanish state. Fascism had come to an end with Franco, and there was this pervading feeling of things finally opening up... that my ideas might even be ... you know? Everything that had led me to become a member was at least starting to change. (Reinares, 2011: 781–2)

Loss of social support

Research has shown that social support is a key pull factor into terrorist groups in the first place (Horgan, 2005). The loss of social support has understandably also been suggested as a driver of disengagement. For example, an ex-ETA member stated that: 'I could just feel it... with everyone, like two years before, people would offer you their homes, their this, their that, and now I was getting just the opposite. Nobody offered you anything; everyone made some kind of excuse. That was when I really first began feeling all this' (cited in Reinares, 2011: 785). Related to these notions, a second ex-ETA member stated: 'In that case... you see that the support from society in the zone of conflict is dropping off... and you say to yourself: "All right, that's it. That's all, that's the end of political violence in Euskadi, and it's all over, over and done with"' (cited in Reinares, 2011: 787). A third ex-ETA member expressed similar sentiments:

> And then you had to come to terms with the fact that society was really closing ranks against the armed struggle we were carrying out, you know? Even back then it was ordinary people who turned out to protest the actions ... people saying: 'listen, man, this is not, repeat not, the way to go about it'. (cited in Reinares, 2011: 785)

Factors that encourage physical disengagement

Change in environment

For some, this change may result from incarceration. One former Loyalist terrorist outlined that 'Prison just gives you an opportunity to be detached from the conflict; it's a dubious way to be detached but you're detached from it and it gives you time to think; you come out with pretty clear ideas in your head' (Ferguson et al., forthcoming: 14). One of his colleagues similarly commented that 'it should come as no surprise that people in prison do develop because you've been removed from the conflict' (Ferguson et al., forthcoming: 14). Prison life may open up new social networks and activity fields for those incarcerated terrorists. As one former right-wing extremist explains: 'Prison was a good thing because I was moved away from the movement. Prison was the best thing that happened to me then. I didn't meet people in the movement and was not around them anymore … I did make some new friends in the prison from at least two other different countries. Normal people. One was from Sierra Leone… I discovered that everything I had done, and everything that I was thinking about before, was completely wrong. In prison, meeting these people, I realised how very wrong I was … It was a different world' (cited in Horgan, 2009: 45).

For others, meaningful change could result from moving to a new location and not being surrounded by like-minded peers. Jacobson (2010) cites examples of individuals whose commitment to the cause waned in the absence of their co-ideologues, following a change in environment. For example, Abdelghani Mzoudi, a member of the Hamburg network, told others that his level of commitment to the cause varied depending on his location. 'Mzoudi described himself as a strong Muslim when he was in Germany with his radical friends, but a weak Muslim when he was at home in Morocco, away from these influences' (Jacobson, 2010: 20). This was also apparent in the case of a former 17N member, who suspended his activities to look after his dying father. During this time he 'had time to think things through, to reflect, and reached the conclusion that it was no longer necessary to continue with armed action as it made no sense' (Kassimeris, 2011: 568).

Family

Family can also act as a mechanism for disengagement – for example, by physically impeding the individual from returning to the group. This has been highlighted in analogous research, including with Somali pirates (Gjelsvik and Bjorgo, 2012).

Role migration

Terrorist groups are made up of a plethora of roles. Numerous terrorist groups have a political wing and many transfer away from illegal violent activities to much more mundane and legal political activities. An ex-ETA member expressed these sentiments:

> So what you have to do is get a political party up and running and to do that you have to start with the rank and file, right? We were already used to that. Setting up these small groups… Well, this was one job that we couldn't get out of, and I don't need to tell you that it's a dreary business. But someone had to do it. And that's when you say to yourself, shit, what is the really useful thing here? Carry on doing this or cross on over to the other side? That is sort of what the dynamic is like that leads you to decide one way or another, and what's more, you would take care of members who are blown to the

police... that's when you have to decide on whether you go over to the other side and go into exile or keep on doing what you're doing and work in a whole different way. (cited in Reinares, 2011: 786)

Where to next?

In the past number of years great strides have been taken in conceptualizing terrorist disengagement. The literature is broadly in agreement that disengagement is often a gradual process, involving a plethora of push and pull factors (Horgan, 2005). Yet there is still plenty of room for progress.

First, there is an implicit tendency within the literature to treat all offenders homogeneously. In other words, it is assumed that the disengagement pathway for a terrorist is always the same, with similar events or instances occurring that affect the journey. Yet it is very easy to imagine that people become less involved in terrorism in a number of different ways and this may be due to some aspect of the terrorist's role, personal circumstances or level of embeddedness within the wider milieu that supports the movement. More comparative studies may tease out such differences. Empirically, we are not yet in a position to carry out studies which would look in close detail at the disengagement process of large numbers of offenders (e.g. have large-n samples); therefore, we cannot state with certainty how common (or uncommon) a pathway (or series of events) is in the disengagement process.

To address this problem it may be worth turning to alternative approaches that emulate the rigour of multiple-case analysis, investigating events instead of variables and using sequence methodologies to analyse data (Taylor et al., 2008). Although not commonplace, research adopting process-driven or sequential approaches has enjoyed success in such diverse fields as economics, linguistics, political science and psychology (Abbott, 1995; Roe, 2008; Taylor et al., 2008). These techniques show that analysing behaviour as part of a sequence or chain of events can reveal important aspects of the unfolding development that leads to an end point, such as engaging in terrorism.

Second, the studies listed in Table 10.1 reveal that research has tended to focus upon ethno-nationalist groups, rather than jihadist groups. This could be due to easier access, language barriers or the fact that many of these campaigns have ended whereas many jihadist campaigns continue. It also shows a predilection for interviews with terrorists whose offences were developed, planned and instigated within a wider group. We know nothing of how or why lone actors may disengage. Empirically researching disengagement beyond ethno-nationalist group settings is, therefore, a definite area for development.

Third, it is clear that a lot of knowledge is available on the types of experiences that aid an individual's disillusionment with life in the group. In fact, a disproportionate number of factors have been identified, given that empirical studies number so few (n=8). It is likely that more studies will only lead to a greater number of factors, given the complexity involved in outlining individual life trajectories. We may, therefore, gain much from working to identify specific but generalizable mechanisms of disengagement other than involuntary processes (e.g. group desistance from violence; rejection of the individual by the group). We cannot stop at documenting the variety of individual pathways and experiences associated with disengagement. While mapping the diversity of disengagement trajectories is a necessary endeavour (as stated above), it is not the end of the road. To return full circle to our introduction, scholarship with ambitions to support intervention (e.g. to inform disengagement programmes) must pursue the search for causes and causal mechanisms.

In this undertaking, our fourth and final point, it will be worthwhile to draw from neighbouring problem domains, such as research on desistance from crime (Bottoms et al., 2004), including disengagement from criminal gangs (Disley et al., 2011). On the one hand, these research domains tend to have access to relatively more abundant data (there is more crime than terrorism) and, therefore, the opportunity to implement more sophisticated research designs. On the other, a rational case can be made that the processes and mechanisms which lead to disengagement from criminal groups are likely to be analogous to processes and mechanisms implicated in disengagement from terrorism. In matters of scientific progress, some clever bit of knowledge transfer can often be invaluable.

STUDY BOX CHAPTER 10

Key reading

Bjørgo, T. (2009) 'Processes of Disengagement from Violent Groups of the Extreme Right'. In T. Bjørgo and J. Horgan (Eds.), *Leaving Terrorism Behind* (London: Routledge), pp. 30–48.

Ferguson, N. (2010) 'Disengaging from Terrorism'. In A. Silke (Ed.), *The Psychology of Counter-terrorism* (London: Routledge), pp. 111–23.

Horgan, J. (2009) *Walking Away from Terrorism: Accounts of Disengagement from Radical and Extremist Movements* (London: Routledge).

Kassimeris, G. (2011) 'Why Greek Terrorists Give Up: Analyzing Individual Exit from the Revolutionary Organization 17 November', *Studies in Conflict and Terrorism*, 34(7): 556–71.

Reinares, F. (2011) 'Exit from Terrorism: A Qualitative Empirical Study on Disengagement and Deradicalization Among Members of ETA', *Terrorism and Political Violence*, 23(5): 780–803.

Study questions

1 To what extent do the reasons for individual disengagement vary according to the typology of a group?

2 Do de-radicalized former terrorists reoffend less than former terrorists who are not de-radicalized?

3 What impact does individual disengagement have on terrorist groups? To what extent can it lead to the group's decline?

References

Abbott, A. (1995). Sequence Analysis: New Methods for Old Ideas. *Sociology, 21*, 93–113.

Blair, D. (2009) Al-Qaeda Founder Launches Fierce Attack on Osama Bin Laden. *The Telegraph*, 20th February 2009.

Bottoms, A., Shapland, J., Costello, A., Holmes, D. and Muir, G. (2004). Towards Desistance: Theoretical Underpinnings for an Empirical Study. *The Howard Journal of Criminal Justice, 43*(4), 368–89. doi:10.1111/j.1468–2311.2004.00336.x

Campbell, J. (2005). Where Do We Stand? Common Mechanisms in Organizations and Social Movements Research. In G. Davis, D. McAdam, R. Scott and M. Zald, eds., *Social movements and organization theory* (pp. 41–68). Cambridge: Cambridge University Press

Disley, E., Weed, K., Reding, A., Clutterbuck, L. and Warnes, R. (2011). *Individual Disengagement from Al Qa'ida-influenced Terrorist Groups: A Rapid Evidence Assessment to Inform Policy and Practice in Preventing Terrorism*. London: Home Office.

Ferguson, N. (2010). Disengaging from Terrorism. In Silke, A. (Ed.), *The Psychology of Counter-terrorism* (pp. 111–23). London: Routledge.

Ferguson, N., Burgess, M. and Hollywood, I. (forthcoming). Leaving Violence Behind: Disengaging from Politically Motivated Violence in Northern Ireland, *Political Psychology*

Festinger, L. (1957). *A Theory of Cognitive Dissonance*. Stanford, California: Stanford University Press.

Glelsvik, I. M. and Bjorgo, T. (2012). Ex-Pirates in Somalia: Processes of Engagement, Disengagement and Reintergration. *Journal of Scandinavian Studies in Criminology and Crime Prevention, 13*(2), 94–114.

Horgan, J. (2005). *The Psychology of Terrorism*. London: Routledge.

Horgan, J. (2009). *Walking Away from Terrorism: Accounts of Disengagement from Radical and Extremist Movements*. London: Routledge.

Jacobson, M. (2010). *Terrorist Dropouts: Learning from Those Who Have Left*. The Washington Institute for Near East Policy. Policy Focus Paper #101.

Kassimeris, G. (2011). Why Greek Terrorists Give Up: Analyzing Individual Exit from the Revolutionary Organization 17 November. *Studies in Conflict and Terrorism, 34*(7), 556–71

McAdam, D., Tarrow, S. and Tilly, C. (2008). Methods for measuring mechanisms of contention. *Qualitative Sociology, 31*(4), 307–331.

Reinares, F. (2011). Exit From Terrorism: A Qualitative Empirical Study on Disengagement and Deradicalization Among Members of ETA. *Terrorism and Political Violence, 23*(5), 780–803

Roe, R. A. (2008). Time in Applied Psychology: The Study of 'What Happens' Rather than 'What Is'. *European Psychologist, 13*, 37–52.

Rosenau, W., Espach, R., Ortiz, R. and Herrera, N. (2013). Why They Join, Why They Fight, and Why They Leave: Learning From Colombia's Database of Demobilized Militants, *Terrorism and Political Violence, 26*(2), 277–285.

Sabahi Staff (2013). Al-Amriki Blasts Al-Shabaab Leader in Final Communications to the World. *Sabahi*, September 20, 2013. Available online http://sabahionline.com/en_GB/articles/hoa/articles/features/2013/09/20/feature-01?change_locale=true (last accessed October 3, 2014).

Taylor, P. J., Jacques, K., Giebels, E., Levine, M., Best, R., Winter, J., and Rossi, G. (2008). Analysing Forensic Processes: Taking Time into Account. *Issues in Forensic Psychology, 8*.

Voice of America (2013). Al-Shabab Militants Kill American Who Cut Ties With Group. *Voice of America*, September 12, 2013. Available online http://www.voanews.com/content/sources-alshabab-militants-kill-american-who-cut-ties-with-group/1748177.html (last accessed October 3, 2013).

Wright, L. (2008). The Rebellion Within: An Al Qaeda Mastermind Questions Terrorism. *The New Yorker* (June 2, 2008).

Essay 7

DE-RADICALIZATION, DISENGAGEMENT AND THE ATTITUDES–BEHAVIOR DEBATE

GORDON CLUBB

We do not merely destroy our enemies; we change them. (George Orwell, 1984)

Introduction

A relatively new counterterrorism strategy has emerged that attempts to challenge the motivations and beliefs that supposedly cause people to engage in terrorism; this strategy has been broadly labelled de-radicalization. The term de-radicalization emerged in the context of the post-9/11 counterterrorism environment – like radicalization it is in a sense a zeitgeist buzzword that reflects the assumed importance of the religious and ideological dynamics of terrorism campaigns. De-radicalization has emerged as a government counterterrorism strategy in South- east Asia, the Middle East, and Europe, although the huge differences in these programs reflect the fact that policymakers and academics differ on what such de-radicalization programs entail. Broadly, de-radicalization programs aim to change the attitudes of captured terrorists to ensure that they do not return to terrorism upon release (known as recidivism reduction). De-radicalization can also occur organically within a terrorist group, whereby a group experiences a shift in attitudes and voluntarily ends its terrorism campaign (see Chapters 8 and 10). However, a substantial problem with de-radicalization as a concept is that it tends to be underpinned by assumptions with regard to the causal relationship between attitudes (and ideology more broadly) and terrorist behavior. As a result, the concept of de-radicalization, despite the initial excitement associated with it (especially in policy circles), has been lambasted for being unrealistic, insignificant, and, at worst, an Orwellian attempt by the state to change the beliefs of people. Therefore, a debate has emerged whereby disengagement (behavioral change) is emphasized over de-radicalization (attitudinal and behavioral change), and between the types of attitudes that ought to be changed in order to change behavior. The aim of this chapter is to provide an exposition of the attitudes–behavior problem that underpins de-radicalization, thus overcoming some of the criticisms it has recently faced.

The chapter firstly outlines the two different types of definitions of de-radicalization, which provides a foundation for the argument presented below. It then provides an overview of research on de-radicalization, highlighting how it has been critiqued in academic debate, both as a concept and as a policy. The chapter then presents its argument that this critique is partly undeserved, having its root in the failure to develop de-radicalization conceptually, especially in terms of recent psychological findings on the relationship between attitudes and behavior. The chapter outlines this new approach and applies it to the counterterrorism context, arguing a position that goes beyond the dichotomy of disengagement or de-radicalization.

De-radicalization: broad and narrow definitions

As Chapters 9 and 10 discussed disengagement, the following section will define de-radicalization. At the heart of the concept of de-radicalization is the assumption that a change in attitudes will lead to a durable change in behavior. This is typically contrasted with a case where a militant (group) stops using terrorism (disengagement) because of short-term, tactical reasons, but when the conditions become favorable again the militant (group) re-engages in terrorism. If the militant (group) is de-radicalized, however, they will not re-engage in violence when the conditions change, because as the attitudes have changed they do not want to engage in terrorism anymore. Yet the problem with de-radicalization is that, conceptually, it is unclear what it means (Schmid, 2013) and there is little agreement (and little explicit discussion) on what types of attitude need to be changed in order to reduce the risk of a return to violence (known as recidivism). There are two types of definition in the literature: one which identifies a broad range of attitudes that inform behavior, and another which identifies a narrow range of attitudes that inform behavior. The 'opposing' approach – the disengagement perspective – claims that neither narrow nor broad de-radicalization is necessary to inform behavior, and instead places emphasis on targeting behavioral change, through coercion, surveillance, or incentives.

A broad definition of de-radicalization expects a change in a wide range of attitudes. In this definition de-radicalization implies a cognitive shift, a fundamental change in understanding (Fink and Hearne, 2008). It has been taken to refer to 'a complete shift in the [individual's] mindset, sympathies and attitudes' (Silke, 2011), with some scholars specifically stating that de-radicalization is 'the transformation of ideology' (Morris et al., 2010). This transformation in ideology then has an impact upon views toward and motivations for using terrorism and political violence.

A narrow definition of de-radicalization refers to a change in attitudes toward the use of terrorism and political violence, not necessarily taking ideology or general attitudes into account. Horgan refers to it as a softening of views whereby an individual accepts that the pursuit of his/her objectives using terrorism was illegitimate, immoral, and unjustified (Horgan, 2008). Ashour (2009) argues that de-radicalization is separate from a change in ideology and instead refers to the de-legitimization of violence, although ideology may be used to strengthen its de-legitimization. Yet even the narrow definition of de-radicalization has problems identifying whether this de-legitimization should be against the use of terrorism and political violence past, present, and future. For example, the failure of former Provisional IRA members to de-legitimize past violence (prior to the 1994 ceasefire) despite de-legitimizing the use of violence today leads some scholars to argue that they are not de-radicalized (broadly or narrowly) (Silke, 2011; Horgan, 2008), and that the Provisional IRA only disengaged (they just changed their behavior), implying that the motivation for ending violence was tactical and not 'genuine' (Rabasa et al., 2010). Thus, de-radicalization has been underdeveloped as a concept, with no study clarifying the distinction in narrow and broad approaches that have been identified – and the consequence of this is that de-radicalization has been substantially critiqued in academic research and by counterterrorism policymakers.

To sum up, broad and narrow de-radicalization refers to changing attitudes to create a better quality of behavioral change, whereas the disengagement perspective underplays the significance of attitudinal change because, for example, former militants can still attitudinally support terrorism but not 'do' terrorism. As will be discussed later, these perspectives are based on the assumption (or lack thereof) that there is a causal link between attitudes and behavior, but this link has not been made clear and is implicitly based on assumptions that are outdated in terms of research in psychology. To demonstrate the problem resulting from this the following section will outline the debates with regard to de-radicalization programs, specifically whether they reduce the risk of recidivism. The chapter will then seek to provide greater conceptual clarity on the attitudes–behavior debate.

De-radicalization programs and recidivism reduction

The article will now turn its attention to discussing the effectiveness of de-radicalization at reducing the risk of recidivism. As will be shown, the mainstream perspective is critical of de-radicalization in this regard, to the point that there have been calls for its abandonment as a counterterrorism strategy. De-radicalization can be a result of a cognitive process in which the individual's attitudes change because of social stimuli or a counterterrorism program that overtly seeks to change attitudes – and, of course, there are many causes that operate somewhere in between. The causes of de-radicalization are similar to the causes of disengagement (see Chapter 10), but the push and pull factors that cause disengagement do not often lead to de-radicalization (Schmid, 2013). The literature on de-radicalization has two, at times overlapping, aspects. The first aspect looks at the de-radicalization of individuals within a group and the knock-on effect it has, using either a broad or narrow definition of de-radicalization. The second aspect – and the focus of this chapter – looks at the extent to which the state can de-radicalize militants, reducing the risk of them re-engaging and defeating a terrorism campaign from the bottom up.

A number of states (e.g. Saudi Arabia, Indonesia) have intervened through prisoner programs to try incentivizing and facilitating de-radicalization in the hope that this provides a more durable end to terrorism once prisoners are released. The prisoner programs have been concerned with ensuring that, once released, terrorist prisoners disassociate themselves from radical movements, provide intelligence, meet victims as part of a reconciliation initiative, distance themselves publicly from terrorism, take part in activities aimed at reducing recruitment, and do not re-engage in terrorist activities (whether directly or by providing material support) (Horgan and Braddock, 2010). On one of the most famous state initiatives – the Saudi Arabian program – Islamist prisoners take a six-week course and at the end are given an exam and a psychological evaluation, where the expectation is that they will renounce terrorism. If they pass they proceed to the program's after-care phase, where on release they are helped to secure employment, transportation, funds, and a place to live (Boucek, 2008; Horgan and Braddock, 2010). Other programs, however, do not have an ideological or attitudinal component, such as Northern Ireland's Early Release Scheme. In this scheme prisoners were released but could be re-imprisoned if they violated the conditions of their release, or if the affiliated group broke the ceasefire. There was no requirement to denounce violence, therefore, but to simply remain disengaged. Furthermore, unlike the Saudi program there was little effort to integrate former prisoners back into society (Horgan and Braddock, 2010). This difference between the programs is seen as important because the whole justification for attempting to de-radicalize prisoners is that it creates a better quality of behavioral change – by changing attitudes (whether broadly or narrowly defined) the risk of recidivism should be lower because the former terrorist will not want to re-engage in terrorism, even when opportunities re-emerge.

Yet the dominant view in the literature (see Schmid, 2013) is that there is little difference in the rate of recidivism between the programs. On average, the risk of recidivism is generally low for ex-prisoners convicted of terrorism in comparison to 'ordinary criminals': the Saudis claim that their program has a 3 percent recidivism rate while in Northern Ireland this figure is about 4 percent (Horgan and Braddock, 2010). Thus, the difference in terms of quality between programs focused on changing attitudes and those solely concerned with behavioral change remains unclear. Furthermore, the literature tends to suggest that recidivism reduction is dependent upon a mix of incentives and coercive tools applied by the state to the individual rather than any change in attitudes, and this may explain the high recidivism of 20 percent amongst ex-Guantanamo Bay prisoners for example, where the US government cannot monitor them (Rabasa et al., 2010; Horgan and Braddock. 2010). For many scholars, the limited success of the prisoner programs suggests that de-radicalization 'is a misleading term to encompass what are context-specific and culturally determined efforts to reduce the risk of involvement or re-engagement in terrorism' (Horgan and Taylor, 2011, cited in Schmid, 2013: 49). Increased recognition of the context that shapes the risk of recidivism – for example, the extent to which a state monitors former prisoners, or the emergence of conflicts further afield (e.g. Syria) (Beaumont, 2014) – has meant there has been a shift away from attempting to de-radicalize individuals, to identifying risk factors more broadly (Horgan and Altier, 2010).

However, while accepting the argument that assessing the risk of recidivism requires a broader, more contextualized approach, this has led attitudes and de-radicalization to become the proverbial baby that has been thrown out with the bath water. As argued above, there has been little analysis of what the concept of de-radicalization means and there have been assumptions made about the link between attitudes and behavior. One source of the lack of conceptual clarity is the failure to distinguish between de-radicalization program and de-radicalization process. Silke (2011) states that Martin McGuinness, a senior figure in the Provisional IRA, did not go through a de-radicalization program but still supports the peace process. Yet this argument does not preclude the possibility that McGuinness underwent de-radicalization himself; Silke, therefore, is too quick to dismiss the importance of attitudinal change. Furthermore, what little conceptual engagement with de-radicalization has occurred has tended to focus on observing the distinction between behavior and attitudes without expanding on how the two interact (Horgan and Braddock, 2010). Finally, while assessing the rates of recidivism is a useful means of identifying the success of specific programs, it does not capture the reasons for low rates of recidivism – for example, are they low because former prisoners are 'red flags' who militant groups keep at the fringes of activity (Silke, 1999)? Also, recidivism rates do not say anything about recruitment rates and whether former prisoners encourage or discourage young people to join a militant group. Therefore, research on de-radicalization would benefit by (a) engaging with the attitudes–behavior debate, which implicitly informs the entire debate, and (b) placing de-radicalization within context, recognizing that de-radicalization can be nuanced, rather than expecting de-radicalization programs to turn terrorists into pacifists. The remainder of the chapter will engage with the attitudes–behavior debate, given how crucial it is to the concept of de-radicalization and how it has not been substantially discussed. This will then be applied to counterterrorism as an alternative to the disengagement or de-radicalization dichotomy.

The attitudes–behavior debate: between disengagement and de-radicalization

At the core of the de-radicalization-versus-disengagement debate is the assumption that certain attitudes lead to certain behavior. With regard to the behavior, it generally refers to involvement in or support for groups who use political violence and terrorism, or in the use of political violence and terrorism itself. This chapter highlights a lack of agreement on what the attitudes encompass, with one perspective emphasizing radical ideology, beliefs, goals and tactics, while another perspective emphasizes tactics only. The distinction is important. In the first perspective (the broad approach), an actor believing in, for example, Irish Republicanism, the removal of UK influence from Ireland, and the validity of armed struggle will be likely to engage in or support armed struggle. In the second perspective (the narrow approach), an actor believing only in the validity of armed struggle will be likely to engage in or support armed violence. So in the narrow approach, someone can remain committed to the goals of Irish Republicanism but will denounce the use of terrorism and political violence. The narrow approach would lead one to argue that de-legitimizing such violence is sufficient to reduce the risk of recidivism and spread disengagement to others, while not challenging the actors' ideological commitment to the cause (Ashour, 2009). There is a lack of consensus on whether the narrow approach should even be considered de-radicalization in academia and in policy circles. Silke (2011) refers to the public de-legitimization of armed violence by European leftist militants as disengagement and not de-radicalization, despite this surely being the core aspect of de-radicalization rather than ideological change. Schmid (2013) argues that continuing to hold a radical ideology can be a factor in radicalizing others, hence the importance of the broad approach to de-radicalization. One senior UK counterterrorism policymaker referred to the de-legitimization of armed violence as disengagement (Clubb, 2014) rather than de-radicalization (Ashour, 2009). The desire of states to combat (Islamist) ideologies that contradict the values the state wishes to promote (Clubb, 2014) has led to an unhelpful over-emphasis on the broad approach in academic research.

However, given that research on attitudes–behavior in psychology has widely criticized broad approaches (Fishbein and Ajzen, 2011), it should not come as a surprise that the broad approach to de-radicalization has been found to have little bearing on participation in violence. Building on a range of theories that seek to explain the relationship between attitudes and behavior, Fishbein and Ajzen's Reasoned Action Theory identifies three 'attitudinal objects' that need to be ascertained in order to identify a correlation with behavior (Fishbein and Ajzen, 2011). This model has been used widely to explain how attitudes on consumer spending and tourism habits correspond with behavior quite consistently, yet terrorism studies is still based on assumptions that the Reasoned Action Theory dismissed decades ago. Applied to political violence, the following attitudes would be important: the perceived (strategic) benefit or attraction of political violence, the perceived control over being able to use political violence in a specific time and location, and the perceived norms surrounding the use of political violence. Therefore, ideological beliefs, which the broad approach emphasizes, are not necessarily a substantial factor in shaping behavior; one's ideology may shape all of these factors but they are not contingent upon ideology. Fishbein and Ajzen's approach provides a better framework for ascertaining the connection between attitudes and behavior than has been offered in the terrorism literature.

There are some clear problems in applying Fishbein and Ajzen's approach to the field of terrorism, namely that people are unlikely to identify how they feel about terrorism, when they plan to engage in terrorism, how easy they think it would be to use terrorism, and what their loved ones think about them using terrorism. However, it demonstrates that (narrow and broad) de-radicalization and disengagement are much more nuanced than presented, and their current dichotomization does not capture the types of attitudes that actually correspond to behavior. If all that is left from the de-radicalization-versus-disengagement debate is a narrow definition of de-radicalization – i.e. the public de-legitimization of armed violence – and if social norms are more significant than ideological change, then de-radicalization is a social process as much as an individual one. Therefore, the false dichotomization of the debate has led de-radicalization to become all or nothing. Former terrorists are expected to oppose and renounce violence everywhere, and when they do not (like with former Provisional IRA members) this is taken as a sign that changing attitudes is not important. However, this chapter has argued – by drawing on contemporary psychology research on attitudes–behavior – that attitudes do not correspond to behavior in this way. Therefore, affecting attitudinal change is important to reduce the risk of recidivism, but this should be targeted toward the three types of attitudes with regard to using terrorism and political violence. These will briefly be discussed.

Perceived utility/attraction

The focus on Islamist groups has meant that group strategies that justify the use of terrorism have been conflated with ideology and religion, but the wider cultural and ideological frames that motivate and justify violence are far more fluid than assumed in the de-radicalization literature. Reasoned Action Theory shows that it is not only the case when actors perceive terrorism as an effective means to achieve goals, but also when they view it as attractive. Therefore, de-glamorizing violence may be effective at challenging these attitudes, especially if there are difficulties in challenging an ideology that justifies violence in terms of its utility. As discussed, former Provisional IRA members do not renounce violence in the past and still view it as legitimate in that context, which leads some young people to view violence as an attractive option to achieve goals. Subsequently, a program was launched by prisoner groups, community workers and academics in which former Provisional IRA members de-glamorized violence, although this may be more effective at preventing others from becoming involved in violence than reducing the risk of recidivism (Clubb, 2014).

Perceived control

Counterterrorism approaches that take a disengagement perspective – affecting the immediate costs and benefits of behavior rather than attitudes – have been broadly correct but this is only one part of the picture. Reasoned Action Theory also highlights that there is more to these types of attitude than a mechanical cost–benefit rationalist analysis that informs whether they will be translated into terrorist behavior. Firstly, state counterterrorism efforts to limit material opportunities to engage in terrorism are important, but these have to be perceived as being so, and, more importantly, the success of these counterterrorism efforts depends on whether the loss of perceived behavioral control impacts upon the perceived benefit. The Real IRA and Provisional IRA both recognized the limited ability to engage in violence in the current climate, but the former still sees it as an attractive option when the opportunity re-emerges, while the latter saw that it was better to trade in violence for political influence. Therefore, the perception of the same object – behavioral control – can be framed in different ways, leading to less chance of a return to violence in some cases. While tactical forms of disengagement are presented as having a higher risk of recidivism than renouncing violence publicly, the loss of perceived control can lead to greater de-radicalization if it is managed correctly. Many members of the Provisional IRA justified their support for the peace process as a tactic, returning to violence when it suited them, but this was primarily to legitimize their support for the peace process, and over the years they have gradually de-radicalized (Clubb, 2014).

Perceived norms

De-radicalization programs have, to varying degrees, recognized the importance of perceived norms. For example, the Saudi and Indonesian programs emphasize bringing on board ex-terrorists' families, who play a normative role in discouraging recidivism. Reasoned Action Theory reminds us that counterterrorism efforts should not assume that the family will always play the same normative role, or, even if they do, that other networks, such as friends or even imagined communities, can have a higher perceived normative value. Furthermore, this indicates that de-radicalization efforts need to be done at a societal level to encourage norms against terrorism and political violence. Given the contested nature of the state's legitimacy in many conflicts, the consequence of this may be that a hands-off approach is more effective at challenging perceived norms. For example, former Provisional IRA members have been crucial in discouraging inter-community violence, which can often erupt into far more deadly forms of violence (Clubb, 2014). Finally, norms against violence can emerge among former militants over time, but the concept of de-radicalization is unrealistic in expecting this to occur so comprehensively and quickly. For example, one former militant may be normatively opposed to terrorism and political violence today, but normatively supportive of it in the past. Thus, the concept of de-radicalization has been too ambitious, and a focus on perceived norms provides a middle ground between it and the disengagement perspective.

These three types of attitudes toward violence – its perceived utility, the perceived ability to use violence, and the perceived views of loved-ones toward the use of violence – when changed, can lead to a reduction in the risk of recidivism, and they can also be useful in discouraging others from becoming involved in violence. One critique against using this theory to explain attitudes and behavior is that it does not represent 'genuine' de-radicalization (Rabasa et al., 2010) – that de-radicalization should refer to a complete renunciation of terrorism to reduce the risk of recidivism, rather than short-term tactical considerations or mixed messages. There are two reasons why de-radicalization as the complete renunciation of terrorism can be an unhelpful idea. Firstly, Reasoned Action Theory shows that there is far more nuance than the binary assumptions of de-radicalization versus disengagement suggests, and that short-term tactical considerations can also lead to wider attitudinal change where terrorism is renounced. Secondly, there is an inherent flaw in the argument that a former terrorist has to renounce terrorism totally in order to reduce the risk of recidivism. For example, if Provisional IRA members had been asked to renounce terrorism past and present, the risk of recidivism would have been higher. The major reason why the end of the Provisional IRA's campaign was successful was because its leaders had credibility within the movement. This credibility was based on their role in the conflict, and to renounce past violence would have undermined that credibility. Thus, by renouncing current violence but legitimizing past violence the Provisional IRA was able to reduce the risk of recidivism. It is this nuance that the application of the Reasoned Action Theory brings to the study of disengagement and de-radicalization.

Conclusion

De-radicalization, as a concept and counterterrorism policy, has been quickly and roundly dismissed, but it is important not to underplay the importance of fostering attitudinal change to reduce the risk of recidivism and end terrorism. This chapter has shown that the debate between de-radicalization and disengagement approaches has been based on simple assumptions of the relationship between attitudes and behavior – assumptions that were dismissed decades ago in the field of psychology. One of the most contemporary theories identifies three types of attitudes which correspond with behavior. While the application of this theory to terrorism studies is difficult for practical reasons, it can provide a framework which goes beyond the dichotomy presented in the disengagement and de-radicalization debate. The utilization of this model overlaps with both of these approaches, showing which type of attitudes a counterterrorism policy should attempt to challenge.

References

Ashour, O. (2009) *The De-radicalization of Jihadists: Transforming Armed Islamist Movements* (London: Routledge).

Beaumont, P. (2014) '"Living suicide bomb" Rejoins al-Qaida after Saudi Deprogramming', *The Observer* 18 January.

Boucek, C. (2008) 'Saudi Arabia's "Soft" Counterterrorism Strategy: Prevention, Rehabilitation, and Aftercare' (Washington: Carnegie Endowment for International Peace).

Clubb, G. (2014) '"From Terrorists to Peacekeepers": The IRA's Disengagement and the Role of Community Networks', *Studies in Conflict and Terrorism* 37(10): 842–861.

Fishbein, M. and Ajzen, I. (2011) *Predicting and Changing Behavior: The Reasoned Action Approach* (New York: Psychology Press – Taylor Francis Group).

Horgan, J. (2008) 'Deradicalization or Disengagement?', *Perspectives on Terrorism* 2(4): 3–8.

Horgan, J. and Altier, M. B. (2010) 'The Future of Terrorist De-Radicalization Programs', *Georgetown Journal of International Affairs* 13: 1–12.

Horgan, J. and Braddock, K. (2010) 'Rehabilitating the Terrorists? Challenges in Assessing the Effectiveness of De-radicalization Programs', *Terrorism and Political Violence* 22(2): 267–91.

Morris, M., Eberhard, F., Rivera, J., and Watsula, M. (2010) 'Deradicalization: A Review of the Literature with Comparison to Findings in the Literatures on Deganging and Deprogramming', (Institute for Homeland Security Solutions).

Rabasa, A., Pettyjohn, S., Ghez, J., and Boucek, C., (2010) *Deradicalizing Islamist Extremists* (Santa Monica: RAND).

Schmid, A. (2013) 'Radicalisation, De-radicalization, Counter-Radicalisation: A Conceptual Discussion and Literature Review', ICCT Research Paper, The Hague.

Silke, A. (1999) 'Rebel's Dilemma: The Changing Relationship Between the IRA, Sinn Fein and Paramilitary Vigilantism in Northern Ireland', *Terrorism and Political Violence* 11(1): 55–93.

Silke, A. (2011) 'Disengagement or Deradicalization: A Look at Prison Programs for Jailed Terrorists', *CTC Sentinel* 4(1): 18–21.

Essay 8

DRONE WARFARE

MICHAEL BOYLE

Introduction

Over the last decade, the USA has made the use of unmanned aerial vehicles (UAVs), otherwise known as drones, a cornerstone of its counterterrorism response to al-Qaeda and other terrorist groups. Today, the US government uses drones over ungoverned spaces in countries like Pakistan, Yemen, and Somalia to locate and kill suspected terrorist operatives. It also uses drones as a form of combat support when battling the Taliban insurgency in Afghanistan and when assisting other governments with their homegrown insurgencies and secessionist movements. By any conventional measure, the US drone program has grown at an exponential rates. In the late 1990s the US drone program had only a few drones, with limited surveillance capabilities. By 2001 it had begun using drones for combat operations in Afghanistan. By 2002 the US had conducted its first drone-based targeted killing outside a warzone, killing a prominent al-Qaeda commander in Yemen (Williams, 2013). By 2011 the US government was estimated to have approximately 7,000 drones in its fleet, with plans to build up to a thousand more (Finn, 2011). The embrace of drone warfare by the Obama administration has led a number of critics to charge that the USA has become overly reliant on drones for counterterrorism at the expense of other tools and approaches.

Drones have been adopted as a counterterrorism tool by the USA and a growing number of other states, including the UK and Israel, for at least three reasons. First, the capabilities of drones, especially their surveillance abilities and range, have grown with remarkable speed over the last 15 years to the point where they can be flown at great distances and strike with high levels of accuracy. Sophisticated drone models, such as the popular MQ1/Predator model produced by Boeing, can remain in the air for up to 40 hours at a time and have a range of 770 miles.[1] As a result, drones can hover for long periods over ungoverned spaces inaccessible to ground forces, and monitor the movements of targets over time, allowing for some precision in identifying and striking targets. Second, drones are flown by pilots located hundreds or even thousands of miles away from the theater of operations. This means that governments can engage in drone strikes without the risk of casualties on their own side, thus producing a seductive illusion of riskless and clean warfare, at least for those attacking. This advantage is particularly important given the aversion to casualties that the USA and other liberal democracies have exhibited over the last several decades. Finally, drones are relatively cheap: the Predator model can cost as little as $10.5 million, compared to the $150 million price tag of a single F-22 fighter jet (Wan and Finn, 2011). Confronted with an amorphous but enduring terrorism threat, the USA and other states have turned to drones as a way of eliminating terrorist operatives without engaging in ground campaigns or paying for a costly occupation.

A number of critics have argued that much of the conventional wisdom over the utility of drones needs to be re-examined in light of the evidence of the backlash effect produced by the US drone campaign in places like Pakistan and Yemen (Boyle, 2013). According to data produced by the New America Foundation, the USA has engaged in 370 drone strikes in Pakistan, killing between 2,040 and 3,428 people between 2004 and 2013. In Yemen, the US has engaged in 109 drone strikes between 2002 and May 2014, killing between 781 and 1024 people (New America Foundation, n.d.). In both countries, the US drone campaign against al-Qaeda and its affiliates has been a flashpoint of controversy, as local officials have decried the attacks for violating the sovereignty of these countries and for inflaming anti-US sentiment. The extent to which the USA is 'normalizing' extra-judicial killing has also been controversial, as a number of other states (such as Israel and China) have begun to consider using drones for similar purposes (Boyle, 2012). For an array of practical, legal, and moral reasons, there are reasons to suspect that drones will be an increasingly controversial tool which will offer no clear resolution to the dilemmas of counterterrorism that the USA and other states face.

Effectiveness of drones

The US government has consistently argued that drones are a remarkably effective counterterrorism tool and that al-Qaeda has been pushed to the point of strategic collapse due to the strikes. In 2011 former Secretary of Defense Leon Panetta argued that drones had vastly improved US counterterrorism operations and left the prospect of 'strategically defeating al-Qaeda' in reach (Miller, 2011). Many believe that the core of al-Qaeda – the central command, now led by Ayman al-Zawahiri in the Afghanistan–Pakistan region – has been decimated by drones, leaving the al-Qaeda affiliates or offshoots in North Africa and the Arabian Peninsula as the only elements capable of attacking. Before his death Osama bin Laden allegedly encouraged his colleagues to flee this region in order to avoid the drones (CNN, 2012). He also recommended a range of operational security measures, such as traveling by road infrequently, carefully monitoring movements to not attract attention, and moving on overcast days to avoid the gaze of drones. By one independent estimate, over 50 senior al-Qaeda and Taliban leaders have been killed by drone strikes (Byman, 2013). The operational pressure placed on al-Qaeda and the number of leaders removed from the battlefield has convinced many in the Obama administration that drone strikes are effective, or, in the words of Panetta, the 'only game in town' (CNN, 2009). In an important address defending his drone-strike policies in May 2013, President Obama said that:

> To begin with, our actions are effective. Don't take my word for it. In the intelligence gathered at bin Laden's compound, we found that he wrote, 'We could lose the reserves to enemy's air strikes. We cannot fight air strikes with explosives.' Other communications from al-Qaeda operatives confirm this as well. Dozens of highly skilled al-Qaeda commanders, trainers, bomb makers and operatives have been taken off the battlefield. Plots have been disrupted that would have targeted international aviation, U.S. transit systems, European cities and our troops in Afghanistan. Simply put, these strikes have saved lives. (The White House, 2013)

Senior administration officials have pointed out that the absence of terrorist attacks in the USA and Europe is at least in part due to the pressure that drones have placed on amorphous terrorist networks in other countries.

The argument for the effectiveness of drones, however, is less clear-cut than this description suggests. While it is clear that al-Qaeda has been placed under severe pressure in the so-called AfPak region, it is far from being destroyed as an organization. In Afghanistan and Pakistan, al-Qaeda has a diminished role but nevertheless can cooperate with other militant networks, such as the Haqqani network and the Taliban, to attack US, Afghan, and Pakistani military forces. In Yemen the al-Qaeda regional affiliate, al-Qaeda in the Arabian Peninsula (AQAP), has been responsible for a number of terrorist attacks even while under pressure from a growing US drone-strike campaign. Since the drone war in Yemen began, AQAP has launched three major attacks: a foiled plot to blow up an airliner bound for Detroit on Christmas Day in 2009, a plot to destroy UPS cargo planes in 2010, and a coordinated series of attacks against the Yemeni army in 2012. These examples suggest that the argument that drones are sufficient to decimate terrorist organizations is too simple, as they may weaken them but will also cause them to reorient their strategic priorities and adapt. Moreover, as Micah Zenko has noted, drones tend to force operatives to leave one theater for another, thus leading to the diffusion of the threat (Zenko, 2012). The use of drones in South Asia and Yemen has forced operatives to move to Somalia and other parts of the Levant, especially Syria, therefore seeding their insurgencies with capable operatives and making these local wars more deadly.

Another key question about the effectiveness of drone warfare revolves around how one should measure the political costs associated with their use in countries like Pakistan and Yemen. Until the Obama administration put the drones program on hold in Pakistan in late 2013 drones had become highly controversial within Pakistani politics, leading to demands that the USA cease the use of the strikes in the Federally Administered Tribal Regions (FATA) of the country. To some extent, Pakistan's position on drone strikes has always been ambiguous: its government has cheered when US drones target its own domestic enemies, but it has publicly condemned unpopular US strikes. It has also allowed the USA to launch drones from Pakistani territory while claiming that the drones are a violation of its sovereignty.

Nevertheless, public hostility towards the drones program is substantial and politically salient. According to a 2012 survey by the Pew Global Attitudes Project, 97 percent of informed Pakistani respondents viewed the drones program as 'bad' or 'very bad' (Pew Global Attitudes Project, 2012). Another Pew poll in 2012 revealed that 74 percent of Pakistanis now consider the USA an enemy (Pew Research Center, 2012). Similarly, anecdotal evidence from Yemen and firsthand accounts of the drone attacks suggest that they are unpopular there as well (Mothana, 2012). Critics have noted that opposition to drone strikes varies in response to media coverage of the events, and opposition to drone strikes in regions where the militant groups are active may be less strong and consistent than in areas dominated by the urban elite (Fair et al., 2013; Swift, 2012). Yet broad public opposition to drone strikes is important if it makes it difficult for the government to say yes to the USA or other states on key counterterrorism demands or important foreign-policy priorities. In other words, drones might be effective in removing terrorist operatives but only at the expense of creating a hostile climate which raises the costs of political cooperation over the long term.

Finally, the effectiveness of drones needs to be re-evaluated in light of the casualties caused by drone strikes. The administration has consistently argued that civilian casualties are relatively low, and that the vast majority of those killed by drone strikes are hardened terrorist operatives. John Brennan, the Obama administration's chief counterterrorism advisor, has said that civilian casualties from drone strikes have 'typically been in the single digits' (Pilkington, 2013). More recently the administration has argued that it has tightened the standards for civilian casualties so that, in the words of President Obama, 'before any strike is taken, there must be near-certainty that no civilians will be killed or injured – the highest standard we can set' (The White House, 2013). Yet the evidence of low civilian casualties and high standards for targeting individuals is hard to find and to verify. On some level, this is due to the methodological problems associated with collecting data on who was killed in drone strikes in areas with little independent media coverage. But it is also due to the fact that the US government has not released public data on the drone strikes, and has refused to lay out publicly much of its targeting standards for drone strikes in foreign countries. Despite promises to the contrary, much of the drones program remains in the shadows. Independent estimates suggest that civilian casualties from drone strikes can vary but be as much as 10 percent of the total of those killed (Boyle, 2014). Moreover, an estimate by the New America Foundation suggests that only 2 percent of the casualties from drone strikes are from 'high-value targets' or key commanders of Islamist groups (Bergen and Rowland, 2013). If drone strikes are killing more civilians or low-ranking militants than the administration implies, it is possible that they may be creating more future terrorists than they kill. If so the assumption that the drones are effective because they remove 'bad guys' from the battlefield should be challenged, as a comprehensive analysis of their effectiveness would also have to measure those advantages against the increase in the membership of terrorist organizations due to opposition to the US strikes.

Legal basis

Another key area of concern with drone strikes is the legal basis for conducting such strikes. In terms of international law there is a key difference between drone strikes conducted inside a declared theater of war and outside a declared theater of war. In declared theaters of war, such as Afghanistan and Iraq, drone strikes can be used by the USA as part of recognized hostilities with an enemy force and, in many ways, are no different than conventional air strikes. The use of drones in active combat theaters is governed by the same laws of war that apply to other types of military activities – for example, targeting only combatants and avoiding civilian casualties whenever possible. So long as a human pilot is in charge of a weapon of war the legal basis and limitations on use, based on international humanitarian law, remain the same even if that pilot is thousands of miles away in a bunker.

Yet the USA has also begun to deploy armed drones outside of formal war zones in its global war with al-Qaeda, which raises a new set of perplexing legal questions. In particular, the Obama administration has used drones in the ungoverned spaces of states (such as Pakistan and Yemen) against whom the USA has not declared war. It has pointed to the Authorization to Use Military Force (AUMF), passed by Congress after the 11 September attacks, as a legal justification for drone strikes in these areas. The AUMF authorizes the USA 'to use all necessary and appropriate force against those nations, organizations, or persons he determines planned, authorized, committed, or aided the terrorist attacks that occurred on September 11, 2001, or harbored such organizations or persons, in order to prevent any future acts of international terrorism against the United States by such nations, organizations, or persons' (Golan-Vilella, 2013). According to the Obama administration's interpretation, drones are permissible in places like Pakistan and Yemen because the AUMF declared a global war against al-Qaeda which allows the USA to use force wherever al-Qaeda exists. Moreover, administration officials have cited Article 51 of the UN Charter, which permits self-defense under an attack, as a supplementary legal justification for the use of drone strikes abroad (Zenko, 2013).

Critics have charged that the AUMF, as interpreted by both the Bush and Obama administrations, leaves the USA in the midst of a perpetual war against an amorphous enemy that may never be decisively defeated. At points, even President Obama has acknowledged that an over-expansive definition of the AUMF is dangerous, and in his May 2013 speech on drones he promised to 'refine, and ultimately repeal, the AUMF's mandate' (The White House, 2013). The problem, as some critics have noted, is that the AUMF is being stretched to include not just direct al-Qaeda forces, but their associates and even 'associates of associates' (Golan-Vilella, 2013). In the case of drone warfare, this has been in evidence with the US targeting of Islamist forces that are predominantly local in nature and only loosely affiliated with al-Qaeda. For example, US drone strikes have targeted the Afghan and Pakistani Taliban, the Haqqani network, Ansar-al-Sharia, al-Shabaab, Lashkar-e-Taiba, and other, even smaller, Islamist groups whose chief quarrel is with their local government. Because there is no precise definition of what it means to be 'associated' with al-Qaeda, the AUMF leaves the door open for the USA to take on an ever expanded array of enemies (Boyle, 2014).

At present no state has accepted the US interpretation of the AUMF as granting it the right to strike anywhere a declared enemy is located. But some states are following suit: Israel has begun to strike at militants in the Sinai and in the Palestinian territories, and China seriously considered using a drone strike to kill a notorious drug lord in Myanmar (Associated Press, 2013; Perlez, 2013). Further, there have been questions raised about how the laws of war should apply to cases in which the USA engages in a drone strike outside a recognized war zone. The UN Human Rights Council has called for independent investigations of US drone strikes in Pakistan and Yemen to ensure that the standards for targeting, legal accountability, and other safeguards are the same in these classified strikes as they are in normal war zones (MacAskill and Bowcott, 2014). The USA has hereto refused to engage with the UN over these strikes, claiming that such an international investigation would jeopardize classified information and weaken its campaign against al-Qaeda. Ben Emmerson, the UN Special Rapporteur leading the charge for the investigation of the US drone program, has warned that drone strikes intentionally targeting civilians may be considered war crimes even if they are conducted outside a declared theater of war (Bowcott, 2012).

Ethical dilemmas

Aside from the legal issues surrounding their use, there are serious ethical questions over the use of drones in combat in declared war zones and in targeted-killing programs. No one disputes that the fundamental ethical requirements for the use of force derived from the *jus in bello* tradition – including proportionality, necessity, and the distinction between combatants and non-combatants – remain in place for the use of drones. Yet drones may present special ethical problems because they are remotely piloted and removed from the battlefield, thus potentially making the determination of combatants and non-combatants more difficult than it would be otherwise. Critics of drones have argued that deciding who to target from a drone flying thousands of feet high is necessarily imprecise and allows for more civilian casualties than other forms of warfare (Chatterjee, 2014). The inevitable mistakes that pilots of all kinds can make – such as mistaking civilians for military targets and false positives in identifying proper targets – may be magnified in drones because the pilots are a few extra steps removed from the battlefield. Moreover, there are serious questions over proportionality and necessity, especially given that some drone strikes can kill large numbers of civilians and be directed against what would normally be considered civilian targets, such as funeral processions and even hospitals (O'Connell, 2010). Whether the normal standards of proportionality, necessity, and humanity can be maintained in a war solely conducted by vehicles flying thousands of feet above the target remains to be seen.

Defenders of drones have responded that drones are actually more precise than many of the available alternatives, such as ground operations and conventional air strikes, and that fewer civilians are being killed with drones than with the alternatives (Shane, 2012). The Obama administration has argued that civilian casualties are rare and that the number of civilians killed by drones is 'in the single digits' (Pilkington, 2013). John Brennan has even gone as far as to assert that there have been no collateral deaths associated with the drones program (Shane, 2011). Yet the Obama administration's tallies of civilian casualties cannot be taken at face value because it has adopted a classification scheme which counts any male between the ages of 18 and 70 killed in a drone strike as a 'militant' unless posthumous evidence is presented to clear their name (Becker and Shane, 2012). The ultimate problem, as many have noted, is transparency: so little data is in the public domain that it is nearly impossible to tell how many civilians have been killed and whether US drone strikes in places like Pakistan and Yemen have been proportionate and humane. Until there is reliable data on civilian drone strikes no one will know whether drones are more discriminate than the military alternatives.

A second problem arising from the use of drones revolves around the problem of moral distancing during warfare. According to some critics, drone pilots at a safe distance from the actual killing could become indifferent to civilian casualties and more willing to pull the trigger than those caught in a direct confrontation on the ground. There is some evidence that drone pilots can be morally distanced from the strikes themselves, and some drone pilots have described their targets as 'bug splats' (Greenwald, 2012). The US military has contributed to this problem by redesigning the controls for drones to more closely resemble the controllers for video games. This development has raised the prospect that the USA and others are increasingly treating war as a virtual experience, removing the threat of harm from their own soldiers while viewing their enemies in less than human terms, as mere images scattering across a drone's video feed. Among the most serious consequences of such a development would be moral hazard: if war is cheap and riskless – if it seems like a video game even to those pressing the trigger to kill – then there is a danger that drone-wielding states like the USA and Israel will be willing to engage in it more often.

Yet drone pilots argue that this depiction of their work is a gross simplification that overlooks the fact that continuous video feeds from drones breed a degree of intimacy with the target that one does not have in conventional aircraft. In the words of one US drone pilot, with the drone feed 'I see mothers with children, I see fathers with children, I see fathers with mothers, I see kids playing soccer' (Bulmiller, 2012). Far from being desensitized to the experience of those killed, drone pilots are often intimately acquainted with their victims, seeing them as they go about their daily life, and also seeing the blood and chaos when the strikes occur. Drone pilots categorically reject the notion that drones make war seem like a video game to them, and often report feelings of post-traumatic stress after strikes (Mullen, 2013). The question remains open: do drones remove individuals from the battlefield morally as well as physically, or do they breed a level of intimacy between the pilot and the target that cannot be accomplished by those flying manned aircraft at 30,000 feet or more? The fear that drones will become a tool in a bloodless, almost robotic form of killing may reflect a deeper societal unease with forms of violence that do not conform to the traditional notions of honor and heroism.

Conclusion

The use of drones for counterterrorism is controversial for an array of practical, legal, and ethical reasons, but it is clear that drones will be the way of the future. Since 2004 the number of states with active drone programs doubled from 40 to over 80 (Government Accountability Office, 2012). Many developed states now have their own drone programs, ranging from relatively small boutique programs to growing multi-purpose drone programs used for combat, surveillance, and civilian uses. Israel and China are investing heavily in the drones export market and selling their models to governments with which the USA is unwilling to do business. Even non-state actors, such as Hezbollah, have begun to experiment with rudimentary drones. The race for drones – one which will involve governments and non-state actors, terrorist groups, and private companies – is now on and it will gradually begin to reshape how counterterrorism operates in the twenty-first century.

The consequences of this explosion of interest in drones are hard to predict, but it is likely that more states will follow the US model of using drones to eliminate terrorist operatives, possibly in their own undeclared wars across the globe. Terrorists will be forced to adapt and to find countermeasures that allow them to survive when facing governments equipped with high-quality surveillance and attack drones. There is some evidence that this adaptation has already begun, as al-Qaeda has looked into ways in which it might blunt the effect of US drones and even hijack some for its own purposes (Whitlock and Gellman, 2013). This example suggests that drones will not be a silver bullet that eliminates terrorism in the long run; rather the growing use of drones will produce a new cycle of innovation and adaptation that will mark the interactions between governments and terrorists groups for the foreseeable future.

Note

1   The estimate of 40 hours is General Atomics International (n.d.). The estimate of range is US Air Force (n.d.).

References

Associated Press (2013) 'Israeli Drone Kills Suspected Islamic Militants in Egypt,' 9 August.

Becker, J. and Shane, S. (2012) 'Secret "Kill List" Proves a Test of Obama's Principles and Will,' *The New York Times*, 29 May.

Bergen, P. and Rowland, J. (2013) 'Drone Wars,' *The Washington Quarterly* 36:3 (summer), pp. 7–26.

Bowcott, O. (2012) 'Drone Strikes Threaten 50 Years of International Law, Says UN Rapporteur,' *The Guardian*, 21 June.

Boyle, M.J. (2012) 'Obama's Drone Wars and the Normalization of Extrajudicial Murder,' *The Guardian*, 11 June.

Boyle, M.J. (2013) 'The Costs and Consequences of Drone Warfare,' *International Affairs* 89:1., pp. 1–29.

Boyle, M.J. (2014) 'Is the US Drone War Effective' *Current History* (April), pp. 137–143.

Bulmiller, E. (2012) 'A Day Job Waiting for A Kill Shot a World Away,' *The New York Times*, 29 July.

Byman, D. (2013) 'Why Drones Work,' *Foreign Affairs*, July/August, available at: http://www.foreignaffairs.com/articles/139453/daniel-byman/why-drones-work (accessed 16 October 2014).

Chatterjee, P. (2014) 'The True Cost of Remote Control War,' *The Nation*, 12 May.

CNN (2009) 'US Airstrikes in Pakistan Called 'Very Effective,'' 18 May.

CNN (2012) 'Bin Laden Documents: Fear of Drones,' 3 May.

Fair, C., K.C. Kaltenhaler, and W. J. Miller, (2013) 'You Say Pakistanis All Hate the Drone War? Prove It,' *The Atlantic*, 23 January, available at: http://www.theatlantic.com/international/archive/2013/01/you-say-pakistanis-all-hate-the-drone-war-prove-it/267447/, accessed 16 October 2014.

Finn, P. (2011) 'Rise of the Drone: From a Calif. Garage to Multibillion Defense Industry,' *The Washington Post*, 23 December.

Government Accountability Office (2012) 'Agencies Could Improve Sharing and End-use Monitoring on Unmanned Aerial Vehicle Exports,' GAO 12-536, July.

General Atomics International (n.d.) 'Predator UAS,' available at: http://www.ga-asi.com/products/aircraft/predator.php, accessed 21 May 2014.

Golan-Vilella, R. (2013) 'Time to Narrow the AUMF,' *The National Interest*, 18 September.

Greenwald, G. (2012) 'Bravery and Drone Pilots,' *Salon*, 10 July.

MacAskill, E. and Bowcott, O. (2014) 'UN Report Calls for Independent Investigation of Drone Attacks,' *The Guardian*, 10 March.

Miller, G. (2011) 'US Officials Believe al Qaeda on the Brink of Collapse,' *The Washington Post*, 26 July.

Mothana, I. (2012) 'How Drones Help al Qaeda,' *The New York Times*, 13 June.

Mullen, J. (2013) 'Report: Former Drone Operator Shares His Inner Torment,' CNN.com, 25 October (accessed 16 October 2014).

New America Foundation, 'Drone Wars Pakistan: Analysis,' available at: http://natsec.newamerica.net/drones/pakistan/analysis, accessed 25 May 2014.

O'Connell, M.E. (2010) 'Unlawful Killing with Combat Drones: Case Study of Pakistan 2004–2009,' Working Paper. University of Notre Dame Law School, July 2010.

Perlez, J. (2013) 'Chinese Plan to Kill Drug Lord with Drone Highlights Military Advances,' *The New York Times*, 20 February.

Pew Global Attitude Project (2012) 'Little Support in Pakistan for American Drone Strikes Targeting Extremist Leaders,' Pew Research Center, 29 June, available at: http://www.pewresearch.org/daily-number/little-support-in-pakistan-for-american-drone-strikes-targeting-extremist-leaders/, accessed 16 October 2014.

Pew Research Center (2012) 'Pakistani Public Opinion Ever More Critical of the U.S.' 27 June , available at: http://www.pewglobal.org/2012/06/27/pakistani-public-opinion-ever-more-critical-of-u-s/, accessed 16 October 2014.

Pilkington, E. (2013) 'Does Obama's "single digit" civilian death claim stand up to scrutiny?' *The Guardian*, 7 February.

Shane, S. (2011) 'CIA Is Disputed in Civilian Toll on Drone Strikes,' *The New York Times*, 11 August.

Shane, S. (2012) 'The Moral Case for Drones,' *The New York Times*, 14 July.

Swift, C. (2012) 'The Drone Blowback Fallacy,' *Foreign Affairs*, 1 July, available at: http://www.foreignaffairs.com/articles/137760/christopher-swift/the-drone-blowback-fallacy (accessed 16 October 2014).

US Air Force (n.d.) 'MQ-1B Predator,' available at: http://www.af.mil/AboutUs/FactSheets/Display/tabid/224/Article/104469/mq-1b-predator.aspx, accessed 21 May 2014.

Wan, W. and Finn, P. (2011) 'Global Race to Match U.S. Drone Capabilities,' *The Washington Post*, 4 July.

The White House (2013) Remarks by the President at the National Defense University, 23 May, available at: http://www.whitehouse.gov/the-press-office/2013/05/23/remarks-president-national-defense-university (accessed 16 October 2014).

Whitlock, C. and Gellman, B. (2013) 'U.S. Document Details Al Qaeda's Efforts to Fight Back Against Drones,' *The Washington Post*, 3 September.

Williams, B.G. (2013) *Predators: The CIA's Drone War on Al Qaeda* (Washington, DC: Potomac Books).

Zenko, M. (2012) 'The Seven Deadly Sins of John Brennan,' *Foreign Policy*, September 18, available at: http://www.foreignpolicy.com/articles/2012/09/18/the_seven_deadly_sins_of_john_brennan, accessed 16 October 2014.

Zenko, M. (2013) 'Reforming U.S. Drone Strikes Policies,' Council on Foreign Relations Report 65, pp. 1–28.

PART 4
RESOURCES

The final part of the book seeks to provide students of terrorism studies with the resources to engage in a deep analysis of the subject, with a solid theoretical grounding. To this end Part 4 is split into two. The first resource provides guidance on how to approach essay and dissertation writing. As terrorism studies gradually expand in terms of original data and fieldwork, there are opportunities for researchers to conduct fieldwork in more focused projects, especially when contextualized approaches to terrorism studies provide original avenues to explore. The second resource offers guidance on how best to undertake this fieldwork.

Resource 1

Study Skills for Dissertations, Essays and Exams

TERRY HATHAWAY

Introduction

University-level assessed work on terrorism, and politics more broadly, is primarily evaluated on the degree to which it presents a coherent, logical, informed and well-ordered argument. Creating good assessed work involves using a variety of skills that are rarely explicitly discussed, and that take a lot of practice to develop. This chapter is for students faced with assessed work. It clearly defines many important academic skills, gives some useful pointers for approaching various forms of assessments, and highlights some of the common mistakes in assessed work. It encourages a basic three-stage process of writing for assessed work – planning, writing and redrafting – and is ordered accordingly.

Plan

Planning and preparation are under-appreciated parts of good writing generally, and academic writing in particular. Spending more time planning what you intend to write helps cut down on the time spent writing and redrafting, particularly if you have a clear idea of your argument prior to writing. In exams there is a lot less time to spend on this stage, but it would still be time well spent if it ensures you are on target with your response. Planning can also help organise points so that fewer words are wasted in the writing stage.

Approaching a question

The foundation of any good response comes from the initial assessment of possible answers and the degree to which such answers correspond, or can be made to correspond, to the question. Rarely, if ever, do university-level essay questions entirely limit the scope of an answer or have an expected response containing required knowledge that your essay will be marked against. Indeed, many marking schemes reward essays with the highest marks when they demonstrate the capacity to contribute to academic debates or be published in an academic journal. As such, there is a wealth of possible ways in which an essay question can be answered.

That said, some questions are more open than other questions – with more restrictive questions usually being used in exams. For instance, the question 'Explain three reasons why terrorism should be dealt with by law enforcement agencies' is reasonably limiting in comparison to 'Can states commit terrorist acts?' In the former example, a (three-reason) structure is forced by the question and a position (that terrorism should be treated as a criminal act) is implied, whereas in the latter question the structure and position are left to the author.

In this respect, it is important to pay close attention to the question and to ensure that, if the question has specific requirements (such as writing of three differences), the work meets these requirements; often, students slip up in exams because they paid insufficient attention to the question and spent little time in thinking through their answer. Generally, however, questions for assessed work are open and allow a range of arguments to be made.

When approaching an open question the first step is to think of the points made in the readings, seminars and lectures and to lay out all the points that come to mind, perhaps in a spider diagram, mind map or word storm. This collection of points can be added to when new points are uncovered or when good examples that illustrate a specific point are found. Next, think of how the points can fit together, which points are strongest and, ultimately, what overarching **argument** based on linking several points together makes the most sense. In essays and research projects this process should not occur alone; at the same time as thinking of points and an argument, continue to read and research the topic. Often, during this interplay between planning and research, different arguments and points will seem more or less strong and relevant, which is just part of the natural process of researching and writing. A similar iterative process of planning and research also occurs when designing a research question and attempting to plan your own research project, as is expanded upon in the next section.

> The *argument* of an essay is the overall evaluative position (yes/no/maybe) of the piece in response to the question. It should be present throughout the essay from start to finish and points made in the body of the essay should support the argument.

Additionally, at this stage it may become apparent that the strongest argument actually involves rejecting elements implied by the question. This approach is perfectly legitimate but must be done well. Central to such a move is ensuring that the assumption you are rejecting is fully explained and its relation to any wider argument (such as a particular theory that the question mentions) is apparent. So, for instance, 'Was the war on terror a success?' could be answered by an argument that, because the war on terror had such an ill-defined remit that was lacking in particular aims, success or failure were never possibilities. A definition of success that mentions the achievement of aims as an integral part of judging success would be a useful way of showing the reader how you are turning the question.

Designing a research question

For research projects and dissertations, designing your own research question is often a requirement. There are two elements that are important to consider in such an endeavour: scope and significance. Scope refers to how broad or specific the question you are asking is. Generally, the broader the question the more difficult it is to give a considered response to it. For instance, 'What factors cause terrorist groups to disarm?' is a much broader question than 'What factors caused the IRA to disarm?' The latter question is much more answerable in 12,000 or 15,000 words than the former.

Significance is the other side of the coin; it involves thinking about what the question can tell us that is important or useful. For instance, a question could work with a very limited scope – 'What did Osama bin Laden eat for breakfast on the day he died?' – that would make it much more answerable but tell us little about the world. So, going back to the example in the previous paragraph, answering 'What factors caused the IRA to disarm?' could be understood as significant because it helps give a partial answer to the question 'What factors cause terrorist groups to disarm?'.

Determining significance can be tricky. There are two general approaches for dissertations. First, a review of the literature on your broad topic of interest should throw up questions or issues that others have found significant and important. Some texts even highlight topics that, in the author's view, are worthwhile investigating and which you can design your question around. Second, from reviewing the literature you may find that questions have been asked of one area but not of another relevant area. So, continuing the example, the literature may focus on factors surrounding IRA disarmament, but not ETA's, leaving a gap that you can explore. In this case you can reformulate the research questions of others to your specific case.

As can be seen, designing a research question relies on reviewing the literature, which means the literature review is the first chapter that will need to be worked upon. In the same way that approaching a question involves an iterative interplay of research and thought, designing a research question and conducting the literature review are simultaneous exercises that complement one another. During these simultaneous exercises your thoughts will change and your conception of the structure of the research project may shift. Also remember that a literature review is not simply a background commentary on what the literature has said, but is part and parcel of your original inquiry into a particular topic; it should highlight where you stand in relation to the literature and lay the groundwork for your research question by showing the question's significance.

One final element worth considering in addition to scope and significance is the wording of the question. Aim for as neutral a position as possible in the question itself so that your answer isn't overly reliant on assumptions in the question. For instance, 'Is the effective counterterrorism tactic of waterboarding against human rights?' is a loaded question that assumes waterboarding is effective, which could then allow an argument to be made about waterboarding involving the trade-off of a suspected terrorist's rights with those of the victims of a terrorist attack. If you want to make that particular argument the effectiveness of waterboarding would need to be explicitly discussed in the text.

Research

Textbooks (and lectures) are a useful starting point for research. The purpose of a textbook is to provide a clear overview of the literature, which can help with a broad understanding of important authors, ideas and debates. Yet the textbook focus on breadth and clarity can often result in a lack of depth and nuance in its presentation of such a broad range of material. Also, since textbooks are introductory texts there is a tendency to recount the debates of the past – to make readers aware of the history of the discipline's major debates – and in doing so de-prioritise the current state of research. This point is particularly important if you are designing a research question, since textbooks may direct you towards a question that has already been answered.

Instead, consider textbooks as the tourist office of academic literature. They are a place you visit for the purpose of visiting other, more exciting places; they offer you a map of the literature. Reading the map involves following the references and citations. Starting with a textbook, check its bibliography for the writers it has flagged as important, and read their work. In turn, you can trace the references of these works as well. In this manner you are moving back through the literature and seeing what and who has informed its arguments. To move forward in the literature, and see who the work has influenced, use academic internet-research databases such as Google Scholar or Web of Science. These instruments often have a 'cited by' function that will show who has subsequently cited the work, and this can bring you up to date with the literature.

Beyond literature research, assessed work may involve the use of primary data. Good primary data sources available online include the Global Terrorism Database (http://www.start.umd.edu/gtd/), the US National Counterterrorism Center (http://www.nctc.gov/), Jihadica (http://www.jihadica.com/) and the International Crisis Group (http://www.crisisgroup.org/). Other useful databases may be national legislative records (such as *Hansard* in the UK and

FDsys in the US), WikiLeaks or similar sites, and LexisNexis, which is a database of news articles.

A further step for research projects would be to go into the field and create your own primary data. Interviews, surveys and participant observation can all help with a research project. Yet use of these methods may not be possible due to safety concerns, failure to obtain ethical approval, lack of access to relevant people and lack of financial resources, although it is increasingly possible to conduct research interviews through Skype, which removes many of the geographic and financial barriers that existed previously. One important element to consider when conducting primary research is how much time you have to properly analyse and make use of the information; uncovering lots of primary data is a pointless exercise unless you then analyse it. For more guidance on possible research methods (and on thinking through a research methodology), consult the further-reading section at the end of the chapter.

Writing

With most of the research done and with an idea of your argument, start putting pen to paper (or, more likely, fingers to keyboard). Writing is a difficult process and everyone approaches it differently. Some are able to produce large amounts of text rapidly whereas others are slower (but may end up with less redrafting). Whatever your style it can be very helpful to set targets for your writing, particularly with much longer pieces such as dissertations. A good minimum daily target is 750 words: while it is only one or two pages, it is just big enough to feel like

> Being a writer is a very peculiar sort of a job: it's always you versus a blank sheet of paper (or a blank screen) and quite often the blank piece of paper wins.
> Neil Gaiman

you've achieved something significant and will, if done daily, accumulate into a larger number quickly (if you can set the number higher do so!). It can also be useful to set a further goal beyond the minimum that you can push yourself for. The purpose of setting goals is that it breaks a larger task down into smaller, more readily achievable goals and helps you grind through the tough times when the words aren't flowing and hours can drift by without noticeable gain. If the words are flowing, stop counting and just enjoy ploughing through the work as quickly as your fingers can move. Do remember to question, though, if your central argument is being advanced in your writing.

Analytical writing style

Good academic writing is clear, **analytical** and concise. There are examples, far far too many examples, of bad academic writing by prominent academics. Often this writing is overly complex, full of jargon and not parsed well, involving long rambling sentences. The problem with such writing is that it defeats the point of writing itself; writing is a means of communication and, as such, should be reader-friendly.

> **Analysis** is the breaking down of an object of study into its constituent parts in order to gain understanding of the object. **Critical analysis** is breaking an issue down and then asking probing questions of the constituent parts.

Being reader-friendly involves laying out your thoughts, clearly explaining your premises and walking the reader through your argument. In this respect, it is not the same as trying for a conversational or rhetorical tone. Conversation is interactive and can proceed with unstated assumptions that can be queried by other participants. In writing you get one chance to communicate your ideas and must do so in a manner accessible to the reader, who, in the case of assessed university work, is an academic. Likewise, a rhetorical tone often allows unproven assertions or leaps in your logic.

To write in a reader-friendly manner use simple, short sentences (as much as possible) and make sure a paragraph is focused on one particular topic. Also, use simple words, and only use a thesaurus for remembering synonyms, rather than discovering new words. Think about what specific background knowledge or information is important for helping a reader to understand a point or an example. Equally, be wary of going into great detail on a comparatively small point; keep in mind that the ultimate purpose of your writing is to answer the question as best you can within a set word limit.

One very important element for reader-friendly writing is signposting. Signposting involves being explicit in the text about the structure the essay follows, about the argument or aim of the work, and about how sentences or points follow one another. The purpose of putting signposts throughout a piece of work is to ensure that the reader can see the interrelations between your points and that the bigger picture isn't lost. Subheadings are a very useful way of signposting. Often students are wary of subheadings because of a notion that an essay should be one continuous block of text – that part of the test of a piece of work is writing 3,000 words that flow together. This notion is strange since most textbooks and journal articles (and this very chapter) are split according to subheadings for the sake of both reader clarity and ease of writing. When it comes to dissertations the standard procedure is to split your writing into chapters, which serves the same purpose as subheadings but on a larger scale. Normally, dissertation chapters also have subheadings throughout.

Structuring

While writing, it is vital to think of the **structure** of the argument you are making. The structure of an argument is always organic – it is dependent upon the argument you wish to make, rather than being something that can be universally applied. Commonly adopted structures are thematic, chronological, comparative and, for certain research projects, linear deductive.

Despite being organic, essay structure should have an introduction, body and conclusion, all of which would likely benefit from the broad advice below.

In the introduction a bit of relevant history or a quick explanation of the importance of the topic is a nice way to open. Other elements in a good introduction are an overview of your argument and an explanation of how the argument is made in the body of the text. A useful part

> **Structure** refers to the overall shape of the text and the underlying ordering principles. The structure should reflect the chosen argument.

of most introductions (or early in the body) is the definition of a word or key concept, as a definition helps to establish the topic you are discussing. But, it should be remembered, a definition is meant to work as an integral part of the argument – it is something that helps inform the argument and is referred back to. Sometimes a question is entirely about the definition (or definitions) of a term and at other times a definition is not necessary. For example, the question 'To what extent does the 24/7 news media support more (or more effective) terrorism?' does not necessarily require a definition of a word or concept; a definition of the news media or terrorism could help certain arguments but would not necessarily help all. Again, the structure is organic and should reflect your particular argument.

Moving to the body of the text, make sure that the points you want to make are as well organised as possible so that sequential points (points relying on other points) are clustered to reduce repetition in the text and to provide greater narrative flow. Another element to consider if you find that you wish to make a lot of different points is whether

> **Evaluation** is the process of determining the worth of a point or argument. If done in relation to competing arguments it can help cut through heavily contested debates by giving greater weight to one argument over another.

you can fully explain, exemplify and then reconcile all these points with the central argument. Reconciliation of points can be achieved through their **evaluation**.

One frequently occurring problem in student essays is the inclusion of counterpoints (often to be instantly refuted) in an effort to 'balance' the argument. Balance is impossible because you are not able to judge points entirely neutrally or objectively, nor is it possible to balance many different competing, arguments and positions. There are rarely two sides to an argument and, when there are, people can hold very divergent views as to why they chose a particular side. The inclusion of counterpoints often leads either to a contradictory structure or one that needlessly fights with other literature. If you find your structure is contradictory evaluate the points. If you spend most of your words refuting the views of others remember that doing so does not push forward your own argument; proving one argument wrong does not make your argument right.

In the conclusion make brief reference back to the points made in the body of the essay and try to show how, together, they support your argument. It can also be useful to restate why points counter to your argument were considered weaker than others. Most importantly, be explicit in answering the essay or research question. In a dissertation the conclusion can also be used to discuss the limitations of the research – what topics were not covered and what the dissertation cannot say – and where further research would be useful.

When writing dissertations different structures can be used for different chapters. So one chapter could be chronological (perhaps charting the evolution of the literature), another could be thematic and yet another comparative in its organisation. The main deciding factor for adopting different structures in this manner is whether they aid clarity and help you explain your points. If you are using two literatures that did not evolve side by side, for example, it could be confusing to adopt a chronological structure unless you split the chapter according to the different literatures.

Redrafting

Redrafting is the final, and most neglected, stage of writing an essay or extended piece of work. It involves exploring and assessing what you have written, considering it from different angles and correcting mistakes that have slipped in during writing. Often at this stage it's useful to print out a copy, sit down and read it through and make annotations. That way any changes to the text get considered twice – first on paper and then when transferring it to the computer. Redrafting can be a long and sometimes painful process, particularly if you realise you need to restructure. Below is a (non-exhaustive) checklist of points to consider when redrafting.

> The first draft of anything is shit.
> Ernest Hemingway

Argument:
- Have I answered the question?
- Is my argument clear throughout?
- Are all points fully developed? If not, are the points integral to the argument?
- Do my examples support my points well?

Writing:
- Are certain words and phrases repeated? Can these be rephrased?
- Do my paragraphs separate my points?
- Will my audience understand what I've written?

Structure:
- Would a different ordering of points make more sense?
- Is every paragraph relevant to the question?
- Does each section (introduction, body and conclusion) do what it is meant to?

Presentation:
- Do all my citations have references?
- Are the pages numbered?
- Is all the formatting the same (font, alignment, typeface)?

Conclusion

Creating good assessed work is a multi-stage process that involves many revisions over time. Often, students spend greater time on the writing stage in the belief that the first draft should be near perfect. Instead of such an approach this chapter has promoted spending more time on the planning and redrafting stages. Spending more time on these stages allows the writing period to be much shorter and more straightforward; having a better idea of what you will write before you write, and not worrying too much about getting the text perfect first time, speed up the process of writing.

This chapter has also sought to highlight the problems that assessed work often contains, in order to help students avoid these problems in their own work. Finally, this chapter has highlighted important key terms used in assessed work. The terms in the textboxes are crucial for decoding a lot of advice about assessed work and should be carefully considered when writing assessed work. They represent the crucial organisational and thinking skills that degree programmes try to improve.

Further Reading

Bryman, A. 2008. *Social Research Methods*. Oxford: Oxford University Press

Burnham, P., Grant, W., Lutz, K. G. & Layton-Henry, Z. 2008. *Research Methods in Politics*. Basingstoke: Palgrave Macmillan.

Cresswell, J. W. 2003. *Research Design: Qualitative, Quantitative, and Mixed Methods Approaches*. Thousand Oaks, California: SAGE.

Halperrin, S. and Heath, O. 2012. *Political Research: Methods and Practical Skills*. Oxford: Oxford University Press.

Moses, J. & Knutsen, T. 2007. *Ways of Knowing: Competing Methodologies in Social and Political Research*. Basingstoke: Palgrave Macmillan.

Yin, R. 2009. *Case Study Research: Design and Methods*. London: SAGE.

Resource 2

Conducting Field Research on Terrorism

ADAM DOLNIK

In the last ten years arguably no other discpline in the social sciences has witnessed as great an increase in academic output as terrorism studies. This has resulted in greatly enhanced understanding of specific contemporary topics such as al-Qaeda, radical Islam, the radicalization process, terrorist uses of the internet, suicide terrorism, terrorist financing, home-grown terrorism, de-radicalization and disengagement from terrorism, and the challenges non-state actors face in acquiring and weaponizing chemical and biological agents. But while this exponential increase in terrorism literature has led to a welcome broadening of the scope of perspectives and approaches to studying the phenomenon, comparatively little attention has been devoted to attempts to systematically develop the quality of the terrorism-studies discipline itself. For instance, while a new book on terrorism comes out roughly every six hours, only three books evaluating the state of the field and its future directions have been published in the last ten years (Silke, 2004; Ranstorp, 2007; Schmid, 2011). All three of these books, as well as many recent panels of terrorism-studies specialists tasked with evaluating the state of the discipline, have unequivocally called for more historical comparative research across different contexts, increased effort to incrementally build on past research conducted by other authors (Cronin, 2006: 10) and, above all, the need for more first-hand research (Alterman, 1999: 15).

The need for field research

The field of terrorism studies has received considerable criticism for: being overly event-driven and essentially descriptive in nature; relying on weak research methods (Silke, 2004: 11); focusing in isolation on individual groups (especially those that dominate the policy and media discourse at the time); and displaying very limited efforts to build on past research conducted by other authors (Cronin, 2006: 10). In addition, considerable self-reflective criticism within the field has focused on the fact that much of the terrorism-studies literature does not incorporate field research. According to Silke, 'very few published attempts have been made to systematically study terrorists outside of a prison setting' (Silke, 2004: 9), confirming Crenshaw's observation that 'the study of terrorism still lacks the foundation of extensive primary data based on interviews and life histories of individuals engaged in terrorism' (Crenshaw, 2000: 410). Silke concludes: 'For a dramatic phenomenon of such intense interest to the media and wider world, such gaping holes in the literature are nothing short of stunning' (Silke, 2004: 9). This point has also become a lynchpin for the somewhat dubious discipline of critical terrorism studies, the proponents of which have also argued that 'terrorism analysts rarely bother to interview or engage with those involved in "terrorist activity" or spend any time on the ground in the areas most affected by conflict' (Jones and Smith, 2009). But the fact is that the relative lack of field research has long been recognized within terrorism studies itself, and many terrorism analysts have in recent years made a significant effort to rectify this problem.

Needless to say, while terrorism research does not easily lend itself to reliable, valid and systematic exploration in the field (Horgan, 2004: 30), there are many ways in which field research on terrorism can contribute to our understanding of the causes, dynamics, and manifestations of terrorism and political violence. Firstly, given the highly emotional and subjective nature of the terrorism phenomenon, available data tends to be strongly politically manipulated by all sides, requiring a higher standard of verification to ensure the reliability and accuracy of findings. This is especially true for historical campaigns that took place in environments where the government possessed a virtual monopoly on the dissemination of information. Field research becomes absolutely essential in such cases. It is also essential because of the historical tendency of researchers to rely heavily on citing each other's work, which has led to the creation of a highly unreliable, closed and circular research system, functioning in a constantly reinforcing feedback loop (Ranstorp, 2007: 6). This has led to the common acceptance of various unsupported myths, which serve as foundations of 'knowledge' in the field until proven otherwise (Reid, 1993: 17). The end product is the exponential proliferation and tacit validation of mistakes made by researchers, their assistants, interpreters etc., including the recording of inaccurate names, places, casualty figures, and even the creation of terrorist plots and cases which never happened (for examples see Tucker, 2000). Today's terrorism research requires fieldwork in order to break this debilitating cycle.

Secondly, much of the current research relies on the government perspective, which brings its own biases. For instance, while effective governmental countermeasures are consistently cited as one of the key historical reasons leading to the decline of terrorist groups, effective tools for measuring success in counterterrorism remain largely non-existent, and contemporary research tends to be further skewed by factors such as comparatively easier access to government data and the one-sided nature of research funding (Cronin, 2006). In this respect, terrorism research is sometimes reminiscent of lung-cancer research funded by a tobacco company. Unsurprisingly, this situation leads researchers to stress the role of government policies as the decisive factor in the decline of terrorist violence (Crenshaw, 1991: 73), even though such a claim rarely takes the form of a testable proposition. As observed by A. K. Cronin, the extent to which terrorist campaigns transform independently of government countermeasures remains on a long list of questions to which we currently lack reliable answers (Cronin, 2006). Field research and interviews with perpetrators and organizers of terrorist violence are crucial in providing at least some counterbalance to this inherent and largely unavoidable bias.

Thirdly, secondary-source data is frequently incorrect on crucial details. This is especially true with respect to historical cases prior to the age of electronic media in countries where access to any reliable and independent sources was practically non-existent. For instance, in my research on terrorist innovation (Dolnik, 2007: 220) I have relied on the meticulous chronological work of Mickolus and his colleagues, who have filled thousands of pages with detailed information on all terrorist incidents recorded since 1968 (Mickolus, 1980). Having had the chance to interview dozens of perpetrators, witnesses, victims and investigators of many of the historical attacks recorded in those chronologies, I found that many of the details were simply incorrect. Sometimes the dates were wrong; in most cases the casualty figures were uncertain or disputed; there would be at least three interpretations of who was behind any given attack and why (including multiple conspiracy theories); there would be multiple claims of responsibility; and the details of the specific modus operandi were frequently subject to the guessing and imagination of the reporter. My overall impression and understanding of practically any historical attack changed dramatically after researching it in the field. This is not to take anything away from the very helpful work of Mickolus and his colleagues; it simply highlights the fact that because of the inherent deficiencies in access to historical data it is important to engage in more rigorous field research to cross-check the facts of specific cases.

There is a cultural element that is crucial in determining the level of trust with which one approaches government data. While during interviews with investigators of the 7/7 bombings in the UK, say, the researcher can have a high level of confidence in the accuracy of the details provided; it would be a mistake to extend the same level of trust to highly controversial cases such as the 1979 hostage takeover of the Grand Mosque in Mecca or the 2004 Beslan school siege, where existing versions are strongly politically manipulated by all sides. In investigating such cases, field research is simply unavoidable if the researcher is to have any confidence in his or her ability to describe what actually transpired. And since much of our analysis of terrorists' intentions, tactics, strategy, and possible countermeasures depends on the ability to accurately reconstruct specific events, the fact is that in most cases this cannot be done from open sources alone.

Fourthly, although there is a considerable amount of data available 'from the horse's mouth' through interviews with terrorists published in mainstream electronic and print media, the fact is that many of the questions asked in such media interviews are designed to trigger a 'soundbite' response as opposed to seeking deeper and more complex insights. In addition, when terrorists speak to the media they have a clear goal of spreading a particular type of message, depending on the target audience. Needless to say, if given the chance, terrorism researchers would frequently ask different questions, in a different setting and in a different way, very likely triggering different responses. This, of course, depends on a researcher's rapport and level of trust with the interviewee, but the point is that deeper access to terrorists via in-depth interviews has a great deal to offer over the selective 'plugging in' of quotes from media interviews that we, as analysts, frequently engage in. This does not mean that in interviews conducted by researchers such problems do not exist; at the same time, conducting the interview personally allows the researcher to ask follow-up questions that help test the validity and reliability of the answers.

Finally, field research is about so much more than data collection. In fact, it could be argued that it is the process itself that plays the more crucial role in educating the researcher and deepening his or her knowledge about the context and everyday realities in which the perpetrators, supporters, and victims of terrorism operate. This exposure to reality alone can rapidly change the researcher's perceptions on many different fronts. Quite simply, one can read all available books and sources on a particular terrorist campaign, but without field visits and exposure to the environment, there is much tacit knowledge the researcher simply will not be aware of. In many ways it is the 'just-looking factor' (Rawlinson, 2007: 304) of field research that by itself justifies its benefits.

Making contact

Making contact with terrorists is not as difficult as most people imagine. In practically any country it is possible to find people (usually journalists) who have studied the respective conflict for many years, speak the language and have had extensive prior dealings with the militant groups; they also often possess all the necessary phone numbers and contacts (Horgan, 2012). These journalists never get the credit in the Western world they deserve for their expertise. The fact is that they are frequently extremely knowledgeable and helpful, taking serious risks in the field without any protection, insurance coverage, or reasonable remuneration. Many get kidnapped or killed in the line of duty (92 per cent of all journalists killed on duty are local journalists) without coming even close to the recognition granted to their Western colleagues.

While many journalists may not be rushing to share such details with people that might be deemed as potential competition, being a researcher (as opposed to member of the press) eases the situation, and many local journalists are genuinely happy to assist without asking for anything in return. In other cases, cooperation can be incentivized, especially when the journalists realize that the researcher's expertise and network of contacts in other places around the world can be very useful to them as well. Similarly, agreeing to be interviewed for their articles or talk shows can constitute a useful quid pro quo gesture. Local journalists can benefit from arranging an interview with high-level officials themselves, as these figures can sometimes be persuaded to talk to a Western professor at a time when they would be reluctant to find the time to meet a local journalist. And, finally, many local correspondents in conflict areas also make a living as fixers for their Western colleagues; their services can be hired for a payment. Such an option can be attractive at many levels, as it is time-efficient, fair, and can help the researcher maintain a professional distance and reduce feelings of obligation, which in turn can help the researcher be more assertive in asking for what he or she wants.

The interview

Effective interviewing is a skill, which needs to be developed and practiced. Unfortunately, this skill is taught at universities only superficially (if at all), and there is a prevailing assumption that interviewing is something all academics know how to do. However, effective interviewing is not just about asking questions from a list; the manner in which the questions are asked and the reactions of the interviewer to the answers both directly influence how much relevant data he or she will get.

The key principle in effective interviewing is the use of active listening, a loose system of style, manner and technique that demonstrates the listener's caring, concern, and attentiveness (Slatkin, 2005: 19). Useful communication techniques in this regard include paraphrasing, reflection, asking clarifying questions, open-ended probing, interpretation, and self-disclosure (Slatkin, 2005: 20). The purpose is to make the subject feel 'heard', satisfying one of the core needs we all have as people. Not only does the interviewer's attentive style encourage a greater sharing of information, it can also have a positive rapport-building effect, especially with people who see themselves as self-defending victims who frame their involvement in terrorism as the only way to be heard. An essential part of this effort is to maintain the mindset in which the interviewer is not talking to a terrorist, but rather to a rational human being who, for some set of reasons, has chosen – or felt forced into – an extreme, violent course of action (Dolnik and Fitzgerald, 2008: 162). Militants rarely dispute the observation that their actions are extreme; they do, however, see them as justified. This acknowledged extremity of terrorism is one of the possible reasons why militants have a tendency to passionately explain and rationalize their actions, especially when speaking to a Westerner whom they perceive (at least initially) as someone who is judging them and who does not understand the true drivers and root causes of their actions. This is where actively listening to their grievances and validating some of their frustrations help contradict many of the terrorists' demonized perceptions of Westerners and make it harder for them to label the researcher as unreasonable, creating chances to build rapport and increase trust.

Most interviews in the terrorism-studies field are unstructured, using open-ended questions in order to allow for a greater breadth of data. Whereas structured interviewing seeks to collect precise data that can be coded and interpreted through a set of prescribed categories, unstructured interviewing seeks to gain insights about the complex behavior of the subject without pre-imposing limitations on the interpretation of the information (Fontana and Frey, 2000: 652). This also means, however, that unstructured interviews leave a wide-open playing field for subsequent interpretation of the data, which can be subject to many biases and interferences. These can be based on multiple internal and external factors as well as underlying assumptions. This section focuses on the biases and traps involved in interpreting data collected via interviews in the field.

Given the elusive nature of terrorists and their activities, most of the interviews are highly opportunistic, which raises the issue of the data's limited representativeness. It is important to recognize that the findings of any study based on interviews with terrorists only apply to the population of terrorists who are willing to speak to a Western researcher, which, by itself, may be a minority. Similarly, when interviewing terrorists it is important to distinguish between the different roles that people play within terrorist organizations. Most interviews will be conducted with leaders, spokespersons, and ideologues of the group, i.e. with people who do not necessarily participate in actual killing. These people frequently come across as intelligent, worldly, and educated, which is a characteristic that may not be representative of the rank-and-file fighters (who typically form the majority of the group). Moreover, if the purpose of these interviews is to determine the characteristics of people who become terrorists then such a study might give too much credit to variables such as education and intelligence, while simultaneously missing the importance of the capacity-to-inflict-violence variable, simply because of the limited representativeness of the data. The final example comes from the realm of the popular area of studies of suicide terrorism, where many of the insights about this phenomenon are based on interviews with suicide bombers. The problem in this case is similar, as the people interviewed represent only failed suicide terrorists, who may be quite different in thinking and personal characteristics from their 'successful' colleagues, who, for obvious reasons, can no longer be interviewed. Some of these limitations in empirical research are inherent, but openly acknowledging them as qualifiers for one's findings is an important part of the research process.

The second bias lies in the process of the interview itself, which tends to be influenced by a combination of different factors. Some of these include liking, rapport, language ability and the environment in which the interview takes place. In other words, it is not only the researcher's questions but also the manner and sequence in which they are asked that determine what the answers will be. In fact, different researchers could be posing exactly the same questions to the same respondent but receive significantly different answers depending on the level of rapport and trust that exists between them and the interviewee, and the conditions in which the interview takes place. Timing of the interview as well as the exact wording of each question are, of course, crucial as well (Horgan, 2012).

The third critical issue, as observed by Goodhand, is that conflict creates an information economy in which the political situation privileges some voices while suppressing others, thus enabling powerful actors to manipulate the content of information and control its dissemination (Norman, 2009). Field research then involves choices about which voices are heard and whose knowledge counts (Thompson, 2009: 112). The fact is that such decisions are not always the sole product of the researcher's methodological choice as these are heavily influenced by the environment. For instance, factors such as greater ease of access, sense of familiarity, comfort and security often lead researchers to privilege information coming from capital cities at the expense of information coming from rural areas. And since capital cities are also more tightly controlled by governments this may inadvertently privilege government narratives (Zahar, 2009: 194). Perhaps this is most apparent in terrorism research where state narratives are often by default given much more credibility and attention than those of the terrorists.

A closely related danger in field research is the problem of so-called seduction, or a situation in which the researcher's objectivity is impacted by favors granted by a party to the conflict, such as providing exclusive access to data or sources, allowing the researcher to embed him- or herself with a combat unit, or simply by being friendly and hospitable. The fact is that even if such acts of seduction (whether deliberate or unintentional) are fairly obvious, as human beings we are programmed to find it difficult not to feel indebted, and have a tendency to repay favors (Coleman, 2006: 5). Whether researchers admit it or not, the principle of reciprocity does affect their views, and consequently the level of critique of government policies in the author's conclusions will at least partially reflect the way the researcher was treated by the government while spending time in the country. This situation can also exist in reverse. Researchers who spend time among militants on their territory and could easily become kidnap victims find themselves subject to a variation of the Stockholm Syndrome, or the mutually positive relationship between captives and their captors that frequently occurs in hostage situations (Poland and McCrystle, 2000: 24). The researcher's awareness of his or her own vulnerability can result in feelings of gratitude toward the militants for not exploiting the situation, which can cause the researcher to view the militants more favorably than he or she might have if presented with exactly the same data in a more detached setting. And, as observed by Zahar, in 'giving voice to the voiceless we could fall for another bias: either accepting the "counter-hegemonic" discourse of the non-state actors at face value or imposing upon them our own interpretation of the situation and romanticizing their reality' (Zahar, 2009: 204)

On a final note, researchers should be aware of the principle of scarcity, or the natural human tendency to assign more value to that which is difficult to attain (Cialdini, 2009: 210). In other words, researchers subconsciously tend to assign greater meaning to data that was difficult for them to acquire, or data to which they have exclusive access. In reality, the information gained from an interview in the process of which the researcher was nearly killed, or a classified document that the researcher spent months trying to get access to, could be less meaningful than information available in open secondary sources more easily accessible over the internet. But the human tendency to assign greater value to the former two can easily skew the researcher's conclusions, frequently without him or her even being aware of it. Although the value of researching terrorism in the field is clear, it is important to remember that the fact that a certain piece of information comes from an interview with a terrorist does not necessarily make it the Holy Grail.

Conclusion

Greater emphasis on field research is the clear next step in taking the discipline of terrorism studies to another level. Field research is useful in helping researchers navigate with greater certainty through multiple contradictory versions of events available in open sources. It contributes to counterbalancing some of the key research biases that inherently exist. It also enhances the reliability and accuracy of findings; and, above all, the process itself can be highly beneficial in educating the researcher by allowing him or her to acquire tacit knowledge of the context. But while many researchers have answered the call and have ventured into the field, there is still an acute absence of attempts to share the know-how on the intricacies of the step-by-step process of conducting such research. This is needed in order to enable other researchers to build on the experiences of their colleagues and to learn from their insights and mistakes.

References

Alterman, J. B. (1999) 'How Terrorism Ends'. United States Institute of Peace Special Report, No. 48 (25 May). Available at: http://www.usip.org/pubs/specialreports/sr990525.html (accessed on 11.5.2007).

Cialdini, R. B. (2009) *Influence: Science and Practice*, 5th edn. Boston, MA: Pearson Education.

Coleman, D. (2006) *Social Intelligence*. New York: Bantam Books.

Crenshaw, M. (1991) 'How Terrorism Declines'. *Terrorism and Political Violence*, Vol. 3, No. 1: 69–87.

Crenshaw, M. (2000) 'The Psychology of Terrorism: An Agenda for the 21st Century'. *Political Psychology*, Vol. 21, No. 2: 405–420.

Cronin, A. K. (2006) 'How al Qaeda Ends'. *International Security*, Vol. 31, No. 1: 7–48.

Dolnik, A. (2007) *Understanding Terrorist Innovation: Technology, Tactics and Global Trends*. Routledge: London.

Dolnik, A. and Fitzgerald. K. M. (2008) *Negotiating Hostage Crises with the New Terrorists*. Westport, CT: Praeger Security International.

Fontana, A. and Frey, J. H. (2000) 'The Interview: From Structured to Negotiated Text'. In: Gubrium, J. and Holstein, J. (eds.) *Handbook of Interview Research*, 2nd ed. London: Sage Publications, pp. 645–672.

Horgan, J. (2004) The Case for Firsthand Research. Silke, Andrew, *Research on Terrorism*. London: Frank Cass, pp. 30–56.

Horgan, J. (2012) 'Interviewing the Terrorists: Reflections on Fieldwork and Implications for Psychological Research'. *Political Psychology Special Issue: Where Do We Go from Here?*, Vol. 4, No. 3: 195–211.

Jones, D. M. and Smith, M. L. R. (2009) 'We're All Terrorists Now: Critical – or Hypocritical–Studies "on" Terrorism?', *Studies in Conflict and Terrorism*, Vol. 32: 292–302.

Mickolus, E. F. (1980) *Transnational Terrorism: A Chronology of Events, 1968–1979*. Westport, CT: Greenwood Press.

Norman, J. M. (2009) 'Got Trust? The Challenge of Gaining Access in Conflict Zones'. In: Sriram, C. L., King, J. C., Mertus, J. A., Martin-Ortega, O. and Herman, J. (eds.) *Surviving Field Research: Working in Violent and Difficult Situations*. London and New York: Routledge, pp. 71–90.

Poland, J. and McCrystle, M. (2000) *Practical, Tactical and Legal Perspectives of Terrorism and Hostage Taking*. Lewiston, NY: Edwin Mellen Press.

Ranstorp, M. (2007) *Mapping Terrorism Research: State of the Art, Gaps and Future Directions*. London: Routledge.

Rawlinson, P. (2007) 'Mission Impossible? Researching Organized Crime'. In: King, R. and Wincup, E. (eds.) *Doing Research on Crime and Justice*, 2nd edn. Oxford: Oxford University Press, pp. 291–314.

Reid, E. (1993) 'Terrorism Research and the Diffusion of Ideas'. *Knowledge and Policy*, Vol. 6, No. 1: 17–37.

Schmid, A. P. (2011) *The Routledge Handbook of Terrorism Research*. London and New York: Routledge.

Silke, A. (2004) *Research on Terrorism*. London: Frank Cass.

Slatkin, A. A. (2005) *Communications in Crisis and Hostage Negotiations*. Springfield, IL: Charles C Thomas Publishers.

Thompson, S.M. (2009) That is not what we authorized you to do...': Access and government interference in highly politicized research environments. In: Sriram, C.L., King, J.C., Mertus, J. A. and Martin-Ortega, O. (eds.) *Surviving Field Research: Working in Violent and Difficult Situations*. London and New York: Routledge.

Tucker, J. B. (2000) *Toxic Terror: Assessing Terrorist Use of Chemical and Biological Weapons*. Cambridge, MA: MIT Press.

Zahar, M. J. (2009) 'Fieldwork, Objectivity, and the Academic Enterprise'. In: Sriram, C. L., King, J. C., Mertus, J. A. and Martin-Ortega, O. (eds.) *Surviving Field Research: Working in Violent and Difficult Situations*. London and New York: Routledge, pp. 191–212.

CONCLUSION

On 21 September 2001 US President George W. Bush declared a war on terror. In a joint address to Congress and the American people he stated that 'Our war on terror begins with al-Qaeda, but it does not end there. It will not end until every terrorist group of global reach has been found, stopped and defeated.' This was not the first time that a US president had sought to crush terrorism; it followed a 1901 declaration by Theodore Roosevelt. Both quests to end terrorist activity have seemingly failed for numerous reasons that have been explored throughout this book. It is clear to see that terrorism and political violence are phenomena that will evolve and persist and so it is imperative to find new ways to understand and engage with these acts.

The study of terrorism and political violence has received much criticism in recent years. Sensationalist accounts, coupled with the severity of debate between traditional and critical approaches to studying these areas, have left the discipline in disarray. Yet despite this, the future is not bleak. Research is gradually becoming more interdisciplinary and many scholars have engaged with acts of terrorism and political violence by drawing on material from other disciplines and by focusing upon different levels of analysis. One of the main goals in writing this book was to pay credence to these different approaches and to link them together. To this end, for example, the first chapter located terrorism studies within the broader canon of security studies, strategic studies and international relations, while the second chapter explored philosophical issues surrounding terrorism and political violence. This multi-disciplinary approach to the study of terrorism and political violence can also be found throughout the rest of the book.

Terrorism and Political Violence has introduced readers to the key analytical and empirical debates in the subject, providing an introduction point to wider discussion. One of the key debates is 'traditional versus critical'. While many suggest that these positions are mutually exclusive, this book has taken the position that they are not, and has treated the analysis of terrorism as separate from our role in constructing the social discourse of terrorism. Insights associated with the critical school can inform our analysis of terrorism – for example, understanding whose interests are served by the use of the term terrorism, in emphasising the role of norms, and questioning how the legitimacy of violence is constructed. Indeed, our ability to analyse and understand terrorism as an academic subject is shaped by our own experiences, resulting in implicit cultural and ideological assumptions. Therefore, it is important to be critical of and reflect on these influences. This should not detract from the focus of analysing terrorism as a subject, and neither should it stop researchers, should we wish, from taking a normative stance with regard to countering terrorism, whether from a state or society perspective.

The importance of norms and contested legitimacy can be seen in the 'definition debate', with the influence of constructivism beginning to take hold. The definition of terrorism is something that will always be debated – that is its role as an 'essentially contested concept' – but it is the analysis of this contestation which is far more interesting. While exploring how the term is used, several questions emerge: When does violence become illegitimate? How did a society become convinced violence was terrorism? How effective is labelling a group as terrorists as a counterterrorism strategy?

There has been a noticeable sociological turn in recent work in terrorism studies, with social-movement theories being applied in order to help place terrorism within a broader context, basing it on real social relations rather than reified ideologies. While the Waves of Terrorism theory has been a durable feature of terrorism studies, the continuing existence of the Religious Wave beyond one generation emphasizes the need to study jihadism as a social movement rather than assuming that its ideology is the glue that holds it together. The discussion on de-radicalization also questions the overemphasis on ideology as an entity that causes people to act in certain ways. The shift towards analysing social relations and influences can show the nuance behind ideology, and even Waves of Terrorism.

What is clear is that more research needs to be undertaken, building on numerous approaches employed by many of the authors involved in this book. We hope that, in time, you too will contribute to the debates involved in studying terrorism and political violence.

INDEX

Page references to Figures or Tables are in *italics*, while references to Notes are followed by the letter 'n'